Michael Bloch

Born in 1953, Michael Bloch read law at St John's College, Cambridge, and was called to the bar by the Inner Temple. He worked for Maître Suzanne Blum, the Parisian lawyer of the Duke and Duchess of Windsor, and wrote six books about the couple. His other subjects include Hitler's foreign minister Ribbentrop, F. M. Alexander (founder of the Alexander Technique) and the politician Jeremy Thorpe. He met James Lees-Milne in 1979, became his literary executor on his death in 1997, edited the last five original volumes of his diary and has written his biography.

The Diaries of James Lees-Milne were originally published as follows

Ancestral Voices, 1942–3 (Chatto & Windus, 1975)
Prophesying Peace, 1944–5 (Chatto & Windus, 1977)
Caves of Ice, 1946–7 (Chatto & Windus, 1983)
Midway on the Waves, 1948–9 (Faber & Faber, 1985)
A Mingled Measure, 1953–72 (John Murray, 1994)
Ancient as the Hills, 1973–4 (John Murray, 1997)
Through Wood and Dale, 1975–8 (John Murray, 1998)
Deep Romantic Chasm, 1979–81 (John Murray, 2000)
Holy Dread, 1982–4 (John Murray, 2001)
Beneath a Waning Moon, 1985–7 (John Murray, 2003)
Ceaseless Turmoil, 1988–92 (John Murray, 2004)
The Milk of Paradise, 1993–7 (John Murray, 2005)

Also by James Lees-Milne

The National Trust (ed.), 1945
The Age of Adam, 1947
The National Trust Guide, 1948
Tudor Renaissance, 1951
The Age of Inigo Jones, 1953
Roman Mornings, 1956 (Heinemann Award)
Baroque in Italy, 1959
Baroque in Spain and Portugal, 1960
Earls of Creation, 1962
The Shell Guide to Worcestershire, 1964
St Peter's, 1967
Baroque English Country Houses, 1970
Another Self, 1970
Heretics in Love, 1973
William Beckford, 1976
Round the Clock, 1978
Harold Nicolson, 1980–1 (Heinemann Award)
Images of Bath, 1982
The Country House: An Anthology, 1982
The Last Stuarts, 1983
The Enigmatic Edwardian, 1986
Some Cotswold Country Houses, 1987
Venetian Evenings, 1988
The Fool of Love, 1990
The Bachelor Duke, 1991
People and Places, 1992
Fourteen Friends, 1996

Diaries, 1984–1997

Abridged and Introduced
by Michael Bloch

JAMES LEES-MILNE

JOHN MURRAY

First published in Great Britain in 2008 by John Murray (Publishers)
An Hachette UK Company

First published in paperback in 2009

1

A CIP catalogue record for this title is available from the British Library

ISBN 978-0-7195-6839-8

Typeset in Monotype Bembo by Servis Filmsetting Ltd, Stockport, Cheshire

Printed and bound by Clays Ltd, St Ives plc

John Murray policy is to use papers that are natural, renewable and recyclable products and made from wood grown in sustainable forests. The logging and manufacturing processes are expected to conform to the environmental regulations of the country of origin.

John Murray (Publishers)
338 Euston Road
London NW1 3BH

www.johnmurray.co.uk

Contents

Introduction

This volume of James Lees-Milne's diaries – the third and last in the present series – is a chronicle of old age. It begins in 1984 when he was seventy-five years old. He was, to be sure, unusually energetic for his years – during 1982 and 1983 he had published no fewer than four books, and thought nothing of walking ten miles in an afternoon. However, just after this volume opens, Jim (as he was known) was diagnosed as suffering from prostate cancer; and although he recovered to live for another fourteen years, he was thenceforth permanently conscious of the process of decline. During the 1980s he was cared for by his formidable wife Alvilde, who was a year younger than himself; but in 1990 her own health began to break down, so that their roles were reversed and he was largely sacrificed to looking after her until her death in 1994, following which he lived on his own for the remaining four years of his life.

During these fourteen years, despite the constant struggle against deterioration and depression, Jim continued to lead a surprisingly active life. He kept up with numerous friends, old and new; he travelled extensively at home and abroad; and notwithstanding failing eyesight, he read voraciously. He also remained prolific as a writer: apart from a steady stream of journalism, he completed eleven books, all praised by the critics. These included two biographies, *The Enigmatic Edwardian* (1986) and *The Bachelor Duke* (1991); two architectural works, *Some Cotswold Country Houses* (1987) and *Venetian Evenings* (1988); a novel, *The Fool of Love* (1990); two volumes of memoirs, *People and Places* (1992) and *Fourteen Friends* (1996); and four volumes of diaries, one covering the years 1948–9, three the 1970s.

However, undoubtedly Jim's greatest literary achievement was the inspired continuation of his diary right up to the month before his death, its final years being hailed by the critics as a masterpiece of the genre. Its varied subjects include country life, a writer's lot, visits to country houses, meetings with friends (and reminiscences of them when they die), books read, works of art seen, moral and spiritual questions, the spirit of the times and memories of the past. His observations are always sharp; he is candid not just about others but about himself; his tone varies between the witty and the poignant. In a sense, it was Jim's diary which kept him going during these struggling years. It was both a safety-valve, which enabled him to release his feelings about the matters which exercised him (though we are spared too many details about his health and melancholia), and a spur to leading an active life – even at moments when he least felt like attending a party, visiting a house, or having an encounter with royalty, the prospect of obtaining 'copy' for his journal helped him overcome his inertia.

As Jim spent much of his last years recalling the past and revisiting the scenes of his youth, a quick survey of his early life may be in order. He was born on 6 August 1908 at Wickhamford Manor, Worcestershire, where he rarely went in the twenty years following his mother's death in 1962 but which he delighted in revisiting during his later years. He had difficult relationships with his parents, though he remembered them fondly towards the end of his life. He had an older sister and a younger brother, both of whom predeceased him (their deaths provoking much reminiscence). He was educated at Eton and Magdalen, to which he nostalgically returned in the 1990s. For thirty years, from 1936 to 1966, he was on the staff of the National Trust and played a leading role in its acquisition and arrangement of country houses, afterwards serving on its committees and regarding with some dismay its transformation from an easy-going association of gentlemanly idealists into a bureaucratic, populist institution. In later years, he revisited many of the houses he had 'saved for the nation', especially during 1991 and 1992 when he was working on his National Trust memoirs *People and Places*. From the 1940s to the 1960s, Jim also established a reputation as a writer of works of architectural history, which continued to be the subject of compliments (and occasional reprints) in the 1980s. A bachelor until his forties who had enjoyed many affairs with both men and women (all of which left lingering memories), in 1951 he married Alvilde Chaplin, an event recalled at the time of their ruby wedding in 1991.

Jim kept a diary during the 1940s which has been acclaimed as one of the great chronicles of the time and which forms the basis of the first volume in the present series. After 1949, however, he did not keep one again for any significant length of time until 1971 (and much of the sporadic diary he did keep during the intervening years he later destroyed). The main reason for this was his reluctance to record frankly the details of his marriage. Alvilde was a handsome and gifted woman who shared many of his interests and looked after him wonderfully; but she was exceedingly bossy and possessive. The fact that they were both predominantly homosexual, and conducted separate emotional lives alongside their marriage, did not always make for harmony. Jim's feelings towards her were highly ambivalent, oscillating between deep devotion and extreme exasperation. The marriage went through a particularly dark passage between the late 1950s and mid 1960s, when they might have separated but for the fact that they found (in 1961) a house to live in which they both adored, Alderley Grange in the Cotswolds.

By the early 1970s they had achieved a satisfactory *modus vivendi*, and in the light of this, and also of the fact that he was now contemplating the publication of his 1940s journal, Jim recommenced his diary. The second volume in this series covers the years 1971 to 1983. Though living contentedly at Alderley, Jim and Alvilde were worried about the economic and social turmoil of the 1970s and feared that Britain might be engulfed by revolution. In 1974 these fears led them to leave Alderley. (This was another place associated with his past which, after an interval of two decades, Jim enjoyed revisiting during his last years.) At first they moved to a maisonette in Lansdown Crescent, Bath, where Jim lovingly restored a library which had been created by his hero William Beckford in the 1830s. But they found the premises too cramped for their needs, and the pocket-handkerchief garden gave little scope to Alvilde's horticultural talents. At the end of 1975 they moved again, to Essex House (known to some of their friends as 'Bisex House'), a delightful Queen Anne cottage on the Duke of Beaufort's Badminton estate, Jim retaining the Bath library for his work.

By the time this volume begins, they had been living at Badminton for eight years. Though Jim frequently grumbled about life there, it was in fact an ideal environment for them. They made the house very comfortable and pretty, and Alvilde won some renown with her acre of garden. The Badminton estate was rather beautiful, very private, and run along splendidly old-fashioned lines. Many sympathetic people (including old friends) lived round about. The 'goings-on' in the village, the antics of their landlord, the hunting-obsessed 10th Duke of Beaufort ('Master'), and the frequent visits of the Royal Family (the Queen being a first cousin once removed of the sweet but 'vague' Duchess), provided excellent material for Jim's diary. One problem for them was that their relations with 'Master' were somewhat frosty, owing to their lack of interest in blood sports and the fact that their two whippets had been known to commit the ultimate sin of chasing foxes. However, in February 1984, just after this volume begins, 'Master' died, and David and Lady Caroline Somerset, friends of Jim and Alvilde who had encouraged their move to Badminton, became the new Duke and Duchess, a development which added a new dimension to the Lees-Milnes' Badminton life.

Jim continued to 'commute' daily to his library in Bath, which gave him tranquillity for his writing and 'space' in his marriage. As 1984 began, he was involved in three substantial literary projects. (During the spring of that year, when he mistakenly believed himself to be dying, he had to think carefully about their priority in what he imagined to be his limited remaining time.) The most absorbing was a biography of Reginald ('Regy'), 2nd Viscount Esher (1852–1930), the *éminence grise* who had exercised immense influence behind the scenes of Edwardian England while refusing all public positions and leading a secret homosexual life. Having been invited to write this by Regy's grandson (whose father had once been Jim's boss at the National Trust), he had already been working on it for two years and it would keep him busy for another two. Secondly, he was revising a novel he had been writing since 1980, about an aristocratic German prisoner-of-war in 1917 who seduces both an English schoolboy and the boy's mother; he had difficulty finding a publisher for this and it would finally appear in 1990 under the publishing imprint of his great-nephew Nick Robinson. Thirdly, he still had to complete the publication of his 1940s diaries: this called for much thought as it included the year (1949) during which he had fallen in love with and undertaken to marry Alvilde. (In the event, the volume published in 1985 was sanitised by the removal of passages in which he expressed well-founded doubts about the marriage, though most of the excised material has been restored in the first volume of the present series.)

On the whole, Jim's marriage to Alvilde was happy and fulfilling during the 1970s, but underwent some revival of tension during the early 1980s. For this I may have been inadvertently responsible; for I met Jim in 1979, when he was seventy and I twenty-five, and we became close friends for several years. Although the relationship was platonic, it made Alvilde intensely jealous, which in turn exasperated Jim. However, by 1984 the first rapture had passed, and as Jim faced the ordeal of cancer he drew close to his wife, a closeness which endured for the remaining ten years of their mutual lives. (Alvilde, who had written me poison-pen letters in the early 1980s, had become quite friendly by the end of the decade, contacting me on one occasion to say she was seriously worried that Jim had no subject for his next book and imploring me to help him find one.)

I did not see much of Jim in his last years and was slightly surprised when, on his death in December 1997 at the age of eighty-nine, I found that he had bequeathed to me (with certain exceptions) his papers and copyrights. By this time he had edited seven volumes of his diary for publication, taking his life up to 1979, the year we met, leaving me the unpublished remainder. This put me in a somewhat unusual position; but I duly edited the remainder in five further volumes which were published by John Murray between 2000 and 2005. The present volume draws from the last four of these, originally published under titles derived (in accordance with the tradition established by Jim) from 'Kubla Khan' – *Holy Dread* (2001), *Beneath a Waning Moon* (2003), *Ceaseless Turmoil* (2004) and *The Milk of Paradise* (2005). (The previous eight original volumes have all been reissued as Clocktower Paperbacks by Michael Russell, who is currently contemplating the republication of *Holy Dread*.) The present volume represents a second effort on my part of refining and cutting down, but I hope I have distilled the essence of this remarkable diary and covered all the main areas of Jim's activity, interests and human relationships (except that I have removed all but a few of his accounts of foreign journeys). I have updated the footnotes and in a small number of cases restored passages or identifications which it was not possible to publish a few years ago.

The people who have helped me during the eight years which I have spent working on Jim's diaries are too numerous to mention, but I must give special thanks here to Patric Dickinson, Sue Fox, Bruce Hunter, Jonathan Kooperstein, R. B. McDowell, Grant McIntyre, the late Hugh Massingberd, Roland Philipps, Gail Pirkis, Liz Robinson, Nick Robinson, Tony Scotland, Moray Watson and Caroline Westmore.

Michael Bloch
mab@jamesleesmilne.com
November 2007

For further information about James Lees-Milne's life and work, visit the Official James Lees-Milne Website at www.jamesleesmilne.com

1984

1984

The past two nights I have been experimenting with a new sleeping pill for which Pat Trevor-Roper[*] gave me a prescription. No use whatever. Just as nasty and ineffectual as the others which Dr King[†] has given me in recent years. Half-sleep, restlessness, semi-headache, the mind floating like jetsam in whirlpools of horror, no shore, no outstretched arm, inability to sleep or wake, an in-between existence of non-reality. This past night during in-between periods of wakefulness I thought I was dying. Was sure that never would I be able to do anything again, never write, never think sanely; that I would be a hulk until death, which was not far off. Now the strange thing is that while in bed, when relaxing, one feels one's worst, utterly feeble, done for. On the contrary one should be feeling re-charged. Talked to Tony Powell[‡] about this at luncheon. He said he experienced exactly the same symptoms at night. Now I understand why most people die in their beds. This is the dangerous time when the body is most vulnerable, not when it is struggling to move itself about, is exerting every muscle and limb, on the move. It is stillness, relaxation that is the killer.

I find myself in curious sympathy with those awful women at Greenham Common.[§] I can't bear them of course – their methods and

---

[*] Patrick Trevor-Roper (1916–2004); ophthalmologist; co-tenant with Desmond Shawe-Taylor of Long Crichel, Dorset.
[†] The Lees-Milnes' GP.
[‡] Anthony Powell (1905–2000); novelist; m. 1934 Lady Violet Pakenham (1912–2002).
[§] A group of feminists were mounting a permanent protest against nuclear weapons outside the US Air Force base at Greenham Common, Berkshire.

manners revolt me – yet I believe it is a great mistake our having American nuclear weapon sites on our soil. I think Britain should renounce nuclear weapons because they cost enormous sums of money and are absolutely useless. They cannot be used and their presence unused is a danger. On the other hand I believe we should arm with conventional weapons to the hilt. If another world war breaks out it will not begin with nuclear weapons. The only hope for preventing war is for a united West to have a preponderance of conventional weapons.

Wednesday, 11th January

Burnet [Pavitt]* and Derek [Hill]† dined with me at Brooks's. Excellent food and claret for a change. Burnet said he was K. Clark's‡ best man at his second wedding, in a Catholic church. At the altar the priest handed him a silver plate on which to put the ring. B. fumbled to get the ring out of its little leather case, and put it on the dish. Both priest and K. looked at it. Then K. could contain himself no longer. He said, 'Have you ever seen a more beautiful object? It is Coptic.' 'No, never,' replied the priest, 'and if you are interested in such things, what about the chasuble I am wearing? It is Puginesque.' K. duly admired. All the while the bride was waiting with outstretched finger.

Saturday, 28th January

Spent last evening with John Harris§ who had come to the American Museum to inspect Ian [McCallum]'s¶ proposals for a new gallery. Took him back to Landsdown Crescent and we dined in Bath. I told

---

* Amateur musician and sometime Trustee of Royal Opera House (1908–2002); friend of J.L.-M. since 1948.
† Landscape and portrait artist (1916–2000).
‡ Sir Kenneth Clark (1903–83); art historian; cr. life peer as Baron Clark of Saltwood, 1969.
§ Writer on architectural subjects (b. 1931); curator of British Architectural Library's Drawings Collection and Heinz Gallery, 1960–83; he and J.L.-M. had lived in the same house in South Kensington in the 1950s; m. 1960 Eileen Spiegel (b. 1932).
¶ Curator of American Museum at Claverton near Bath (1919–87).

him he was a remarkable boy. 'Boy?' he said. 'I am 53.' He disclosed that he had a vast library of books about the First World War, having been close to an uncle who came through it, a sawyer by profession who became a shepherd on the Wiltshire Downs. John comes from Uxbridge, and returns there every year to give a lecture on architecture. Says there are still unspoilt villages on the edge of Heathrow Airport whose inhabitants' lives are made intolerable by planes passing every minute over their ancient roofs. John is tracing his ancestry in parish registers and has got back to 1830. Descended from a line of craftsmen, bookbinders, upholsterers, joiners; yet he himself is no craftsman, except in words. Some of his forebears came from Henley. Is intrigued by the portrait of Lord Malmesbury in one of Reynolds' Dilettante Society groups now at Brooks's. This Lord M. exactly resembles himself, and John thinks there may be a connection *de la main gauche*, for the Malmesburys went to live at Park Place, Henley after the death of Marshal Conway, Horace Walpole's friend. Curious how every historically-minded man wants to investigate his lineage and connect up with a figure or family that played a part in history, the more patrician the better. I like John and am glad to have had him alone again. His interests are wide. Sees no hope for the country house. Asked me what I thought. I said I had given up long ago. There was absolutely no future.

Wednesday, 1st February

To London for the night, staying with Eardley.[*] Spent Wednesday in British Museum archives reading Esher[†] papers. Not very exciting. In evening went to see John Betj[eman][‡] at Radnor Walk. Worse than ever. Very tragic. Sitting in his chair like a sack, his head lolling to one side. Feeble[§] went up, kissed him and said she would set him straight.

---

[*] Painter, formerly on staff of National Trust (1902–91); friend of J.L.-M. since 1941.
[†] Reginald ('Regy') Brett, 2nd Viscount Esher (1852–1930); bisexual Edwardian *éminence grise* on whose biography J.L.-M. had been engaged since 1982.
[‡] Sir John Betjeman (1906–84); poet, broadcaster and writer on architecture; Poet Laureate since 1972; m. 1933 Hon. Penelope Chetwode (1910–86).
[§] Lady Elizabeth ('Feeble') Cavendish (b. 1926); dau. of 10th Duke of Devonshire; Lady-in-Waiting to Princess Margaret; long-standing friend of Sir John Betjeman.

Promptly the head fell to the other side. Did not recognise me. I left feeling very sad.

Sunday, 5th February

On return from lunching at Claverton, and walking the dogs in Park Piece, I was hailed by a shabby old man in a shabby car. It was Bill Llewellyn.[*] I asked what he was doing here. He said, 'I have been talking to Tom Gibson[†] at the Vicarage. You know Master[‡] died today at twelve o'clock?' Sally [Westminster][§] told A[lvilde] last night that she had had to bring him back from following hounds in the afternoon as he felt giddy. He had a very bad heart attack, suffering much pain until given morphia or equivalent. Bill had tried four times to convey to Mary [the Duchess] that Master was dead. All she said the fourth time was, 'Do tell my father' (who has been dead these fifty years), 'I am sure he will be most interested.' Last Sunday Master told the Vicar that when walking his dogs at dawn that morning he saw three foxes sitting on the graves of his father and grandfather. He had never seen any foxes so close to the church before. He has left directions that he is to be buried beside these two graves. The Dukes are always buried in this patch by the church, but I believe the Duchesses are buried separately at Little Badminton. So in death are the exalted divided.

Tuesday, 7th February

Curious what an effect *the* death has caused in this village. A muted silence in the streets these two days past. Much publicity in the local

---

[*] Rt Revd William Llewellyn (1907–2001); Vicar of Badminton, 1937–49; Bishop of Lynn, 1961–72; Assistant Curate of Tetbury since 1977; Eton contemporary of J.L.-M.

[†] Revd Thomas Gibson (b. 1923); Vicar of Badminton, 1974–93.

[‡] Henry Somerset, 10th Duke of Beaufort (1900–84); owner of Badminton estate and the L.-Ms' landlord; leading figure of the hunting world, known as 'Master' from the age of nine; m. 1923 Lady Mary Cambridge (1897–1987), dau. of 1st Marquess of Cambridge and niece of Queen Mary.

[§] Sally Perry (1911–91); widow of Gerald Grosvenor, 4th Duke of Westminster (d. 1967); mistress of 10th Duke of Beaufort.

papers and on television. Cottage tenants expressing loyal appreciation – great gentlemen, etc. They could hardly do otherwise. Yet one did say there were occasions when His Grace could be extremely angry, and they were fearsome. Vicar told A. that on Monday he arranged for the coffin to be taken into the church at a time when Mary was walking in the park with her dogs, accompanied by her nice old friend Tuppie, who is thought to have more influence over her than anyone else. On their return Mary must have sensed that something was happening, for she made for the church and walked in, Tuppie trying to stop her in vain. She went straight up to the coffin and demanded that the lid be opened. This was done. She bent over the face and gently kissed it. Turned away and walked straight out of the church without a word. But went into the kitchen and said to the cook, 'I shall only want luncheon for Miss Tuppie and myself today. His Grace will be out.' So no one yet knows whether she understands or not. Poor Caroline* has been sent for. Discovered in Bangkok, half-way through her tour of Burma and Siam. She had a presentiment, and insisted on being called back if Master died. The Queen is coming to the service, which is very unusual. The Royals looked upon the old man as an uncle figure, like Mountbatten.†

Wednesday, 8th February

Second very stormy night. Did not sleep well. Honey‡ was restless at the bottom of my bed because, I think, the hounds kept baying all night, and our dogs hate the hounds. Normally they never keep up continuous 'singing' (as it is called here) but sing for five minutes or so and then stop. Sally [Westminster] says that when she left Master on Saturday she walked her dog in Swangrove, and heard an owl hoot three times. Owls never hoot in the daytime. Another omen.

---

* Lady Caroline Thynne (1928–95), dau. of 6th Marquess of Bath; m. 1950 David Somerset (b. 1928), art dealer, cousin and heir of 10th Duke of Beaufort.
† Louis, 1st Earl Mountbatten of Burma (1900–79); brilliant careerist, whose many roles included last Viceroy of India (1947) and first Chief of Combined Defence Staff (1965); the Queen's second cousin once removed and Prince Philip's uncle; assassinated by the IRA.
‡ Folly and Honey were the L.-Ms' whippets.

A. returned from London in time for luncheon. By two o'clock so many cars and people on foot were passing our gate for the church that we set out, although service not due to begin before three. Even so there was no room for us in the church. Were ushered into a large marquee on the lawn with an amplifier connected to the church. Marquee likewise jammed with people; everyone from the estate, the hunt, the county had turned up. The old Hornbys* grumbling that they had not been let into the church. Nicole sent messages to the ushers that she was a close relation, and she and Michael (aet. 87) were given a pew. Charlie left behind told us that his mother was no relation at all, but always got her way. The service, hymns, prayers relayed to us in the marquee. Then, when the Committal about to begin, someone undid the flaps of the marquee, so we, sitting in the front row, had a good view of the cortège. Huge coffin trundled on wheels from the church door, draped with the Beaufort standard, fleur de lys, etc., very Plantagenet and medieval. Poor David [the heir], looking miserable, stood alone with Mary, tiny and bewildered in black. Did she realise what was happening? When coffin lowered into the grave they advanced, looked down, and he piloted her away. Followed by the Queen; Queen Mother, splendid in mink tippet down to the ground; Prince and Princess of Wales, he in black morning coat; Princess Anne and Phillips, Prince and Princess Michael, Princess Alexandra. The bearers of the coffin from its wheeled contraption to the graveside included our Peggy's husband, Gerald,† the chauffeur, gardeners. Leslie the butler carrying huge sheaf of irises, flunkeys and dailies following him. The three huntsmen in white breeches, blue and buff liveries, long, brightly polished riding boots, velvet caps, very impressive and handsome. Last Post played by bugler of the Gloucestershire Hussars. Caroline had difficulty keeping her floppy brown hat from blowing off. Icy cold wind. Flag over the house hanging at half-mast. Robust looking coffin – when family flag removed – of grey oak, cut from a tree on the estate sixty years ago for this very purpose, and kept in an attic of the house all these years. What makes people do this sort of thing? It will never be seen again and must rot and be eaten by worms.

---

* Michael and Nicole Hornby of Pusey House, Faringdon, Oxfordshire.
† Gerald Bird, husband of the L.-Ms' daily help, Peggy.

Received very funny bad-taste postcard through the letter-box from Selina Hastings* this afternoon: 'I couldn't help thinking of Honey and Folly when I read the paper yesterday. They must be very happy little dogs. Will they be having a party to celebrate? And will pheasant pâté or fox pie feature on the menu?'† And Derry [Moore]‡ who is staying two nights says the late Duke's mistresses ought to have been parked, like nuns behind a grille, in the gallery of the church during the funeral – the Dowager Duchess of Norfolk,§ Sally Duchess of Westminster, Lady Glanusk,¶ Lady Hindlip,** Lady Cottesloe,†† et al., in order of precedence. How they would have hated each other.

Friday, 10th February

Daphne Moore‡‡ jumped off her old bicycle in the village street to say, 'Have you heard? The public have stolen all the wreath cards of the Royal Family, written in their own hands.' Pretty ghoulish, I admit.

Went this evening to Dr King about my prostate. He examined and said it was swollen but he could not tell if worse than when he last examined. At all events I am to take a 'specimen' to the Royal United on Monday and have an X-ray. I have so many symptoms that I know

---

* Lady Selina Hastings (b. 1945); dau. of 15th Earl of Huntingdon; writer and journalist; sometime literary editor of *Harpers & Queen*.

† A reference to an incident recorded in the diary five years earlier (21 May 1979) when the L.-Ms' whippets chased a vixen, and the Duke, 'beside himself with rage', threatened to have them shot.

‡ Dermot, Viscount Moore (b. 1937); o.s. and heir of 11th Earl of Drogheda (whom he succeeded as 12th Earl, 1989); m. (2nd) 1978 Alexandra Henderson; photographer.

§ Hon. Lavinia Strutt (1916–95), o.d. of 3rd Baron Belper; m. 1937 16th Duke of Norfolk (1908–1975).

¶ Margaret ('Peggy') Shoubridge; m. 1st (as his 2nd wife) Wilfred ('Bill') Bailey, 3rd Baron Glanusk (d. 1948; a cousin of J.L.-M.), 2nd 1966 (as his 2nd wife) 1st Viscount De L'Isle.

** Cecily Borwick; m. 1939 Henry Allsopp, 5th Baron Hindlip (1912–93).

†† Gloria Dunn; m. 1959 (as his 2nd wife) John Fremantle, 4th Baron Cottesloe (1900–94).

‡‡ Gloucestershire hunting personality (1910–2004); friend of Mary, Duchess of Beaufort.

it is worse than formerly. E[ardley] is having similar trouble, and if he is operated on may not be able to come with me to Ravello. Now it is possible I may not be able to go myself.

Friday, 24th February

Eardley's operation went well. Small growth in early stages removed. Prospects are bright, so Mattei* says.

Sunday, 4th March

Having motored A. to Heathrow to fly to France – Jagger's† garden again – I called for Ros[amond Lehmann]‡ and took her to luncheon at the Garrick Club. Indifferent expensive meal, almost £20 for the two of us without wine. Ros says she is pleased with the film of *The Weather in the Streets*, which is generally considered not to do her novel justice. Then, having taken her home, went to Eardley in hospital. Was very shocked by his appearance. He was out of bed, in a chair, back to the window. A very old man, hollow-eyed, waxen white face, become small overnight, his teeth correspondingly too big for him, skeleton thin, not having eaten for a week, large hands tightly gripping the chair arms. Barely a smile elicited, and no interest in anything I had to impart. I felt most inadequate and believe my visit gave no pleasure, and possibly displeasure.

Wednesday, 7th March

Had a bit of a shock this afternoon. Was rung up yesterday by surgery telling me to see a specialist named Charlton in Bath. When I called on Dr King last night for the X-ray photographs of my bladder, etc., he murmured what I took to be, 'The prostate is normal.' I wondered

---

* Mattei Radev (b. 1927); Bulgarian-born picture-framer and gilder; friend of Eardley Knollys.
† Michael Philip 'Mick' Jagger (b. 1943); singer and songwriter, co-founder of Rolling Stones, 1962; m. (2nd) 1990 Jerry Hall; A.L.-M. had been designing his garden at Amboise in Touraine.
‡ Novelist (1901–90); friend of J.L.-M. since 1950s.

what Charlton could tell me. A nice man, talking sensibly and candidly, or what seemed to be candidly. Examined prostate, then said Dress and let us have a talk. Then said, 'Your prostate is abnormal', which I suppose is what Dr King said to me last night. Charlton told me I must have an operation soon. I told him that I was booked to go to Ravello on 5 April, having on the strength of the report that my urine was negative bought an air ticket and booked a room at lovely Palumbo Hotel. He said it would be unwise to go, especially alone, as the prostate might blow up and the bladder refuse to pee, which would be awful. As I left I said casually, 'I presume there is no growth, since you speak of an obstruction.' He replied, 'I don't know. We shall have to see when we examine the tissues.' Not a very nice piece of intelligence. My father died of cancer of the bladder at the age of 69. And, if all goes well, I shall not be able to work for four weeks at least. Damn!

What are my feelings? Of course dreading the worst. But not so shaken as I would have been twenty years ago, for I am approaching the natural term of my life. I don't want poor darling A. to be worried and unhappy. I don't want to leave her. But apart from abandoning her to wrestle alone, without very intimate friends and with that irresponsible and demanding Luke family,* there is no one else but M[ichael Bloch]† I regret leaving. And he being so young cannot miss me for long. One thing I dread, and that is recovering from this operation to be told I have got cancer, and dragging on, operation after operation, drug after drug, being a perfect nuisance to others and an abject misery to myself. In that event I would prefer to die under the anaesthetic. But I would like to finish Regy [Esher], my novel,‡ and tidy up my remaining diaries. I have no other ambitions.

---

* Hon. Clarissa Chaplin (b. 1934); J.L.-M's stepdaughter, o.c. of Alvilde by her 1st marriage to 3rd Viscount Chaplin; m. 1958 Michael Luke (1925–2005); their children Chloë (b. 1959), Oenone (b. 1960), Cressida (b. 1961) and Igor (b. 1965).
† Barrister and historian (b. 1953); friend of J.L.-M. since 1979; then working in Paris as assistant to the Duchess of Windsor's lawyer Maître Suzanne Blum.
‡ The novel described on p.x of the Introduction was eventually published in 1990 as *The Fool of Love*.

Saturday, 10th March

For some reason I am now feeling cheerful and resigned. Is it because my operation has been deferred for a week? And will the dread return? One's reactions under a cloud are strange. Now if I were under a cloud of imminent disgrace, say about to appear in court for some discreditable misdemeanour which would bring distress to A., it would be far worse. After all, I am not disgraced by having a prostate operation. Am not telling friends because I don't want sympathy or attention. Even so, I have told Eardley, because we are in the same boat, so to speak; Alex Moulton,* as he has been clamouring for me to go motoring with him, and I could find no other excuse; and M., who telephoned from Paris yesterday asking the result of my X-rays. I have no secrets from him. But I don't want even him to visit me in hospital; and I want no attentions except from A.

Sunday, 18th March

It is Sunday. I have taken the dogs for two long walks. I have lunched with the Loewensteins† alone, because poor A. feeling unwell. I feel as well as I have felt for ages, better in fact, and yet this time tomorrow I shall be in the operating theatre preparing to meet my fate or Maker. I shall be ill for a month even if the operation goes as it should, without complications. I have written several loving letters to friends without mentioning impending op. Meanwhile I am very worried about Dick's‡ illness. Simon§ told me last night that they are waiting for him to recover from the move to hospital [in Cyprus] before scanning his liver to ascertain how deteriorated it is. I don't like it.

---

* Dr Alexander Moulton (b. 1920) of The Hall, Bradford-on-Avon; engineer and inventor, friend of J.L.-M. since 1940s.

† Prince Rupert zu Loewenstein-Wertheim-Freudenberg (b. 1930) of Biddestone Manor, Gloucestershire; financial consultant, manager of Rolling Stones; m. 1957 Josephine Lowry-Corry.

‡ J.L.-M's younger brother Richard Lees-Milne (1910–84); m. 1938 (as her 2nd husband) Elaine *née* Brigstocke (1911–96).

§ J.L.-M's nephew (b. 1939), o.c. of Richard and Elaine; m. (2nd) 1976 Patricia ('Tricia') Derrick.

Well, here I am, home again, being looked after angelically by A., and feeling fine. Strange experience. Woke up in intensive care, ministered to by succession of sweet nurses. Indeed I have never met with such an agglomeration of sheer goodness and kindness. Every nurse and sister was an angel to me, and I grew to love my surgeon Mr Charlton, a most sympathetic, intelligent and humane man. We had long talks when he visited me in my room. He wants to write the History of the Catheter. I advised him not to make it too surgical, and to search through diaries, such as Parson Woodforde's,* for references. He told me that a hundred years ago country doctors carried catheters in their hats and inserted them into their patients with a minimum of cleaning. In fact excessive sterilisation has lowered our resistance to diseases. He says bacteria take their revenge by being more cunning and persistent than formerly. That is why so many patients develop urinary infections after operations. The bacteria rush in hordes upon the victim, seeking the most unguarded approaches to the bastions from which the sterilisers have sought to exclude them. Charlton told me he did at least thirty operations per week and sometimes forty. Amazing. He cuts out the prostate with an inserted instrument which has a torch and microscope attached, so he can see what he is doing.

On Thursday morning, three days after operation, had my catheter removed. This was agony. Slept very little the previous night. At 6 the nurse did the work. I screamed. She sent for the sister who comforted me like a mother. When it was over I burst into tears. At 8 o'clock a clergyman in full canonicals entered the room. I had forgotten that the previous evening I had said I would like to take Communion. Was convinced he had come to give me extreme unction, and was highly alarmed. I said to this soulless stick of a man, 'I have just been disembowelled and flayed. Will you read the lesson for St Barnabas Day?' He looked astonished and said, 'You can't have been disembowelled. Just hold this prayer book and follow me. I won't be long.' Indeed he wasn't, but I wept throughout, incapable of answering the responses.

---

* James Woodforde (1740–1803), whose diary, kept for almost forty-five years, mostly covers his tenure as a Norfolk parson from 1773.

I thanked him and he asked if I was prepared to offer something. 'Take £5 from my trouser pocket and be gone!' I managed to say through my tears.

Wednesday, 28th March

Simon telephoned with grave news of poor Dick's condition in Nicosia Hospital. The tests reveal that he has cancer secondaries on liver, and primaries on chest and throat. His case is hopeless, and one must hope that his future is as short and painless as possible. I feel sad, sad. Have tried to write poem about Dick, but cannot make progress. Poetry is evanescent and fugitive, will not be cajoled.

Friday, 30th March

Dined with the Somersets* at the Cottage. Caroline told us that Hilda Murrell, A's friend the old rose grower from Shrewsbury, had been murdered. Apparently she witnessed some young people burgling a neighbour's house, so they grabbed her, stabbed her and dumped her in a ditch. There she was found two days later, having, so the doctors affirmed, died just a few hours before. So this old lady of 79 lay bleeding to death in a ditch for 48 hours. There is no limit to the enormities committed today. I believe civil war is not far distant, what with hooligans in London uniting to smash up the City and the miners inciting violence all over the country.†

David spoke to me about the library at Badminton. Asked if I considered it would be wrong to take away a length of morocco-bound books to allow them to put their modern library on the shelves. I said I thought it would be a sad mistake to scrap what is a complete and very beautiful library of calf-bound books. Advised that they should be treated like wallpaper. Rich portraits could be hung on

---

* The L.-Ms' friends David and Lady Caroline Somerset of The Cottage, Badminton, now Duke and Duchess of Beaufort and about to move into and refurbish Badminton House.

† The year-long strike of the National Union of Mineworkers had begun on 12 March.

silken cords and tassels over the books. The room needed deep, warm colours. Could not a modern library be made in a similar room upstairs? I think D. is worried about the responsibilities that have fallen on his shoulders. He has noticeably aged recently, though as handsome as ever. I shall do what I should have done long ago – read up and familiarise myself with the history of the Beaufort family and the architectural development of the house.

Tuesday, 10th April

[J.L.-M's sister-in-law] Elaine telephoned from Cyprus just as we were going to look at a film on the telly. Poor thing, she was probably a little drunk and repeated herself. Said that Dick is no longer in pain, and talking cheerfully. He never refers to his condition. This so often the case with the dying, who do not care to face up to the inevitable, and believe that by some miracle they may recover. Towards the end of the talk she let fall that the doctors give him about ten days. I felt extremely sad and wrote him a difficult letter. What can one say? One cannot express a hope that he will be better soon, yet must not alarm. And jokes seem inopportune.

Sunday, 15th April

This morning Sybil Cholmondeley* telephoned me from Houghton [Hall, Norfolk] to say she had found all Regy [Esher]'s letters to her brother Philip Sassoon.† Says there are so many she cannot read through them, and is posting them all to me. I may do what I like with them, and she will trust me not to publish anything that contains indiscretions. Wondering what she meant by this, I asked her to be more particular. She said Esher was an incorrigible gossip and encouraged her brother to be another. After all, she said, Philip was private secretary to Douglas Haig and Lloyd George, and she would not like to have published any criticisms he may have put on paper about these chiefs, or Winston Churchill or Kitchener. I tried to convey to her

---

* Sybil Sassoon (1894–1989); m. 1913 5th Marquess of Cholmondeley (d. 1968).
† Sir Philip Sassoon, 3rd Bt (1888–1939); politician and aesthete.

that these people are now historical figures. She, being over 90, sees them as friends of hers who have recently died. I begged her to tell me frankly what it was about Esher she disliked, thinking she might imply, if not state categorically, that it was his homosexual tendencies. She explained, 'He was such a busybody, such a gossip, such an intriguer. These things made him a sinister man.'

Tuesday, 17th April

To London yesterday, working in London Library. This morning I went to [the British Newspaper Library at] Colindale to consult old newspapers, rushing back to give Kenneth Rose* luncheon at Brooks's. Emerging from Piccadilly Circus station found St James's Square cordoned off. At Brooks's was told that the so-called diplomats in the Libyan People's Bureau had opened fire on a harmless anti-Gaddafi† demonstration, killing a poor little policewoman and injuring about ten others. All streets in area cleared of traffic and armed police on watch. Kenneth three-quarters of an hour late, having come on foot from Fleet Street. He talked too loudly and boastfully of his social and literary success. Was spiky about Rupert Hart-Davis,‡ whose last vol. of Lyttelton letters I was carrying, because Rupert had written to say it would be absurd for him and his fellow judges to award the W. H. Smith Prize to Kenneth for his *George V* [1983] which had already been awarded three other prizes. Kenneth looking over my shoulder at more interesting eaters. While I was paying the bill, he ganged up with Nico Henderson,§ and Lords Jellicoe¶ and Shackleton,** and brought them to

---

* Historian and journalist (b. 1924); gossip columnist of *Sunday Telegraph*.

† Muammar al-Gaddafi (b. 1942); ruler of Libya since 1969.

‡ Sir Rupert Hart-Davis (1907–99); publisher, editor, writer and Eton friend of J.L.-M.; his correspondence with his Eton housemaster George Lyttelton (1883–1962) had been published in six volumes by John Murray, 1978–84.

§ Sir Nicholas Henderson (b. 1919); diplomatist, HM Ambassador to Paris, 1975–9 and Washington, 1979–82; m. 1951 Mary Barber; their dau. Alexandra was married to the L.-Ms' friend 'Derry' Moore.

¶ 2nd Earl Jellicoe (1918–2007); war hero and Conservative politician; Leader of the House of Lords, 1970–73 (resigning over the 'call girl affair').

** Edward Shackleton (1911–94), mountaineer and Labour politician; cr. life peer, 1958; Leader of the House of Lords, 1968–70.

drink coffee. I didn't mind beyond disappointment at having little opportunity to talk to K. He and Henderson and I walked towards London Library, I meaning to collect sack of books I left there yesterday. Police told us no one could enter St James's Square. Tiresome because I need these books. It is horrifying that these savages should rake the streets with bullets from their embassy window, in our London. Bloody people. When they come out, I hope the assassins will be caught and tried, and the rest packed off. But Gaddafi has the effrontery to announce to the world that England has insulted his embassy officials and that our police did the shooting. Is it likely? The *fiancé* of the little policewoman killed is one of them.

Saturday, 21st April

This morning I went by appointment to see Mr Charlton, my specialist. I told him that my trouble was little better than before my operation; in one respect worse, in that there were times when I was suddenly taken short. He then said, 'I am going to do another small operation on you. I am going to remove your testicles, because they are so nearly connected with your prostate. Your prostate was diseased, you know.' So I, who have always averred that I never wanted to know, said without hesitation, 'By which you mean that I had cancer of the prostate?' 'Yes,' he said. To be told this, which I have always dreaded, was not the tremendous shock I expected. Charlton was wonderfully soothing and encouraging, assuring me that there was an 80 per cent chance of my living another five years or even more.* The removal of my balls was precautionary, an alternative to treatment with female hormones. So brother Dick and I have both got cancer. How odd it seems. This draws me closer to Dick than ever. Unfortunately I cannot get in touch with them by telephone, and they have not rung me for a week.

When I got home darling A. greeted me. 'Well, how did you get on?' 'He told me everything,' I said. 'I now know what I suppose you were told all along.' 'Yes,' she said, 'I knew after your operation. I rang Charlton up this morning and he told me you were to have another operation. So I asked him what he would say if you asked him

---

* He was to survive for another fourteen years and publish ten more books.

outright. He replied that he would tell you the truth.' My one over-powering desire now is to be with A.

Monday, 23rd April

Two nights ago in bed, it being Good Friday, I read the last few chapters of St John's Gospel. Was amazed by the number of references to himself as 'the disciple whom Jesus loved', who during the Last Supper 'lay with his head on Jesus's breast'. And by his depreciation of St Peter, whose exploits on the water he seems to deride and whose slowness in running to the sepulchre is remarked upon. Should Jesus have had a favourite, if indeed he did and St John was not romancing? And do these chapters give credence to the Gay Brigade's assertion that Jesus was homosexual?

Then I read the ultimate chapters of St Luke. Was deeply moved by the story of the two malefactors crucified on either side of Christ, one abusing him, the other rebuking the first one, saying they were both wicked men while Christ was a good man, and turning to Jesus and asking him to remember him, and Christ saying, 'You will be with me this time next day in Paradise.' Such compassion and humanity are rare in the Testaments. And as for St Peter and the denial of Christ before the cock crowed thrice, ending with the words, 'He wept', well, this always makes me weep.

Then read St Matthew's account. Not so vivid as St Luke and St John. Much emphasis on events taking place 'according to the prophets', almost as if the Evangelists were determined to shape events to suit those maddening Old Testament prophecies. Jesus himself emphasises these coincidences. How conservative the Jews were.

Tuesday, 24th April

Tricia rang from Cyprus. Dick is sinking fast. She said he was not unconscious and was struggling to live. A strange circumstance is that Dick asked to see an Anglican priest; has done so twice, and derived much comfort from him. Dick, who never went to church and was, I imagined, thoroughly agnostic. How often this happens to the dying. K. Clark whom his agnostic friends scoffed at for being received by a

Roman priest at the end. I believe it is the teaching of extreme youth, implanted into the infant mind, resurging in second childhood. Dick must have been thinking of the church services at Wickhamford [Manor, Worcestershire, their childhood home], at which he always fainted, we never knew whether genuinely or merely in order to be removed by the nurse. He was able to take in my last letter to him, and laughed at my description of walking round the corridors of the Bath Clinic with my tube and bottle concealed in a shopping bag. I find myself thinking of him most of the day, and feel part of me is draining away with him, as though we were twins. Yet we drifted apart in life, without a jot of mutual dislike, just through sheer difference of environment and interests, coupled with the fact that Elaine never let us have a moment together.

Thursday, 26th April

Last weekend was, apart from our worries, one of the nicest I can remember. Burnet [Pavitt] and Selina Hastings to stay. Selina enchanting. Went for a long walk with her talking about her book and the Mitfords.* She is quick, amusing, a brilliant conversationalist, understanding, with all the virtues I so loved in Vita [Sackville-West].† Yet she, like me, feels ill at ease among the high-brows, whose every sentence has a cerebral import, and who, she feels, are weighing every word one utters. Because I had on Saturday morning learnt about my cancer, I confided in Burnet, who is such an old friend and such a sympathetic one. He counselled me not to confide in anyone else. If I do, he or she will confide in his or her best friend, and so it will circulate. Besides, he says, compassionate though people may seem, the idea of a friend losing his balls is a subject for hilarity.

---

* Selina Hastings was writing a biography of the novelist Hon. Nancy Mitford (1904–73; m. 1933 Hon. Peter Rodd), eldest of the six Mitford sisters, all of whom J.L.-M. had known well since childhood, his closest friend at Eton having been their brother Tom (1909–45).
† Hon. Victoria Sackville-West (1892–1962); novelist, poet and gardener; m. 1913 Hon. (Sir) Harold Nicolson (1886–1968), diplomatist, writer, journalist and politician.

Friday, 27th April

After dining alone with Sally [Westminster] I reached home last night at 10.30. The telephone was ringing as I unlocked the door. Rebuffing the dogs who were giving me their usual ecstatic welcome I picked up the receiver. Tricia from Cyprus to announce that Dick had died at 10 o'clock their time, just as I was going in to dinner with Sally. For a time I was more concerned with the loss of the latch keys to my Bath flat. During my bath and in bed the true sadness dawned.

Saturday, 28th April

Motoring into town yesterday I found myself behind a small car in the back window of which was a printed label, 'Flash your lights if you find me sexy'. I could only see the driver's head. It did not make a sensational appeal. Now ten years ago I would have flashed for the fun of the adventure. Alas, I thought, I have a mere three days left in which I remain a man, and even so, the experience is out of the question.

M[ichael Bloch] came down at midday and spent the night with me here. A great joy to have him. A marvellous guest, and wanted to go for walks. We ambled, sat in the garden, and talked. Perfect spring weather. M. gave me admirable advice – to leave Regy for six months, once I have finished researches at the end of June. For remaining six months of year to concentrate on editing my diaries,* by which writings I am now best known. He could never edit them; I alone can and must do this. It is just possible that within the six months period I may be able to continue my novel. All this if I am spared.

Monday, 30th April

At one o'clock went to the Bath Clinic again, exactly six weeks since my last operation. I was more fearful on this occasion. By the time I was given the pre-med prick in the behind, was in a silly state

---

* That is, the last of his diaries for the 1940s, published the following year as *Midway on the Waves*.

of nerves. Humiliating little ceremony in bathroom with sister shaving my pudenda. Experience of waking up in intensive care not agreeable. Brightly lit, bustling with people in white, much laughter and jokes, and other patients calling out. When one comes to, one wants calm and peace. This was hellish. 'Nurse, nurse!' I found myself calling, just for recognition, reassurance that I was alive, wanting a drink badly. Wanting to be away, wanting calm. Soon wheeled to my own room. Thank God.

Sunday, 13th May

Yesterday we lunched with Billy Henderson[*] and Frank Tait.[†] The latter called me out into the garden and asked me about my condition. He was very reassuring and agreed that my nice specialist Charlton was quite right to have done what he did rather than give me female hormones. Frank said they were given to Cecil Beaton,[‡] who in consequence developed breasts of enormous size and was extremely unhappy. Cecil refused to have his testicles removed, telling Frank he might want to have children one day, a desire his friends had never noticed before. In fact he had a horror of mutilation, of being physically incomplete. Don't we all? I think the psychological pain is worse than the physical in this particular matter. Frank is a heavenly human being – superb cook, splendid doctor with reassuring manner, excellent raconteur, and abounding in understanding and sympathy.

A. and I walked with the dogs along the verge of the Fonthill lake. Most beautiful sunny afternoon, although bitter wind still. Two pairs of swans, lifting themselves out of the water, flying a few yards, beating the quiet surface with harsh strokes. Moorhens cackling. Ancient beeches with their feet in the water. Beckford[§] may have planted

---

[*] Painter (1903–93); wartime aide to viceroys of India.
[†] Australian child psychiatrist (b. 1923).
[‡] Sir Cecil Beaton (1904–80); photographer, artist and stage designer.
[§] William Beckford (1759–1844); writer, traveller and collector, a biography of whom J.L.-M. had published in 1976; builder of the fantastic, neo-Gothic Fonthill Abbey, Wiltshire, which he sold in the 1820s (shortly before its collapse) to live in Lansdown Crescent, Bath, where his property included what was now J.L.-M's library.

them. Then out through the Palladian arch and past the giant ferns. What a beautiful, haunted place.

Wednesday, 16th May

On Monday A. drove me to the Bath Clinic. I was mightily depressed all morning, dreading the operation and 'coming round' process. Put on white smock shroud and lay on bier-bed, the lamb for slaughter. Charlton came with anaesthetist. Examined my poor person. He said there is no discharge, the whole thing is healing, and decided after all not to operate. I felt like the young Isaac snatched from the knife of Abraham. Fortunately no poor lamb took my sacrificial place.

None the less my bleeding still persists. Can it be that the wound just hasn't healed after more than a fortnight, as Charlton maintains? Or is it haemorrhage which is associated with cancer? Am I being deceived? I cannot trust anyone, and don't know that I want to be undeceived. At moments I have awful forebodings that my life expectation is a matter of months, and I ought to drop Regy entirely to concentrate on tidying diaries.

Wednesday, 23rd May

John Betj[eman] died in his sleep at the end of last week. Funeral Tuesday at midday. I telephoned Feeble in Cornwall, where J. died, and she said she would like me to attend. So I went by train on Monday and stayed with the dear Trinicks* at Lanhydrock. Marvellous day of early summer, the spring freshness just gone. The stretch of riviera coast after Exeter and Powderham is exceptionally beautiful. Train chugs through short tunnels. On the right high honeycombed cliffs of soft sandstone, weird lunar shapes, but warm, apricot colour. Wild flowers powdering the slopes of the grassy intervals, the moving train making the focus muzzy.

But the funeral yesterday was in driving rain. Hired a taxi to Trebetherick. Arrived about 11.20, meaning to call on Elizabeth and

---

* Michael Trinick (1924–94); N.T. Historic Buildings Representative for Cornwall, 1953–84; m. 1950 Elizabeth Lyon.

leave my suitcase at the cottage, but we met them on the road. I offered to give them a lift. But E. said you can't drive, only walk. So I dismissed taxi, got out and carried suitcase. Mercifully had put on galoshes in the car, and had my flimsy plastic mac. Even so, after ¾ mile walk across open field to little St Enodoch Church, with low spire, got soaked. Had to shut umbrella which threatened to blow inside out. Plunged into tiny church, dark as pitch save for a few oil lamps and candles. Was put into a two-seater pew next to Jock Murray,* who whispered throughout. In front of us Penelope [Betjeman] and Billa [Harrod].† Church by no means full. Reserved for family, a few intimate friends and some neighbours. The battery of wind and rain somewhat distracted concentration, yet added to the drama. Paul Betjeman read the lesson. He could barely see and had to take the Bible to the only non-stained window pane for light. We stood in the porch while John's coffin was carried by bearers across the field and lowered into grave beside the lych-gate. Struggled back across field with Anne Tree‡ to Elizabeth's and John's cottage where a fire burning. Given toast with cottage cheese and a glass of whisky. The others went to a neighbouring house for luncheon with Penelope whom I did not see to talk to, only embraced silently after the cortège had followed the coffin to the graveyard, to *Nunc Dimittis*.

Horrid journey back in uncomfortable old-fashioned carriage, changing at Bristol. Darling A. arrived back from the Chelsea Flower Show and gave me dinner. Anyway I paid my respects to the best man who ever lived and the most lovable. Have written to the two widows – difficult. The poignancy of sitting on John's little death bed with Archie the teddy bear and Jumbo the elephant propped against the pillow.

Saturday, 26th May

On Wednesday Alex Moulton called for me in his beautiful brown Rolls-Royce and whisked me off to Liverpool. I was tired by my

---

* John Murray VI (1909–93); Betjeman's publisher; Eton contemporary of J.L.-M.
† Wilhelmine ('Billa') Cresswell (1911–2005); m. 1938 Sir Roy Harrod, economist; Norfolk personality, who had briefly been engaged to Betjeman in 1933.
‡ Lady Anne Cavendish, sister of Betjeman's friend Lady Elizabeth ('Feeble'); m. 1949 Michael Tree, painter (1921–2000).

excursion to Cornwall, and this expedition has also tired me. We stayed at the Adelphi, great hotel of Edwardian era, splendour and riches of Liverpool, White Star and Cunard glories. Liverpool now terribly down-at-heel. Rubbish litters the streets, old Georgian terraces being pulled or just falling down, walls disfigured by subversive words. We dined with Larry Rathbone and wife,* nice, tall, straight, grey-haired lady whom he snubs aggressively. Largish uneven house with many good pictures bought for Larry by Eardley, taste non-existent otherwise. Alex very successful, talking to Larry about Liverpool conditions, which are hopeless at present, the city being bankrupt. They warned us that no one ever walked the streets after dark. Indeed Larry summoned a taxi which, we later learned, had arrived and driven away because the driver had not dared leave the cab to look for and pull the bell.

I spent next morning at the University Library looking through some 160 letters to Regy. Found nothing much of interest except several photographs of correspondents attached to letters. Visited the R.C. Cathedral which I think little of. Gimmicky. Of concrete, which has of course weathered atrociously, iron rust streaks. The prominent lantern with too-flimsy skimpy finials. Inside cheerless in spite of large circular nave and high lantern and splodges of ugly glass. On the other hand the Anglican Cathedral by Giles Gilbert Scott really is a masterpiece. Quite traditional of course, foundation stone laid in 1904 by Edward VII, 50 years or more construction, but all of a piece. Alex much moved, as was I.

Stayed that night at Southport, charming Edwardian resort for the proletariat, in Prince of Wales Hotel, cosy and old-fashioned. Next day we visited Walker Art Gallery and Lady Lever Gallery, filled with first-rate furniture and many pictures known since childhood, such as *The Scapegoat* by Holman Hunt. Greatly impressed by Port Sunlight village layout. Houses carefully grouped round grass lawns. Cottages of half-timber, with parget-work dated 1892, pebble-dash, oriels, bow windows, arts and craftsy wood carving and barge-boards,

---

* Senior partner (b. 1913) of Rathbone Bros & Co., J.L.-M's investment managers, and brother of J.L.-M's friend 'Jack' Rathbone (1909–95), Secretary of National Trust, 1949–68.

tile-hanging, casement windows – a museum of pre-1914 style and quality.

Sunday, 27th May

The Nicholas Ridleys* lunched. She, the second wife (the first, Clayre, is a pearl but was driven away by N's infidelities), is a chirpy little trout, very agreeable. Nicholas was, when he first joined the Executive Committee of the N.T., the most beautiful young man imaginable. I remember how on his entry to the board room for the first time all heads swivelled in his direction, and Gerry Wellington[†] nearly fainted. Now he is a middle-aged parliamentarian and Minister of Transport. (We should have known, but had to ask.) He has little charm. I had a short abortive conversation with him after luncheon on the sofa. I asked if he was worried by the Gulf troubles. He said in that airy stiff-upper-lip manner, 'Not at all. We have our own North Sea Oil.' But, I said, we are told that is our chief export, that we keep none for ourselves. He said we get enough to supply our needs. On the subject of conservation he deprecated the scare-mongers, meaning me. I remarked that these days there were no frogs, no butterflies. He said he had many in his garden. Yes, I laughed ironically, but you are too young to remember that fifty years ago the country swarmed with them. Besides, butterflies come in the late summer and are all poisoned by pesticides, like birds. He retorted that many birds throve on pesticides. The falcon has increased in numbers. Yes, said I, but this year no one in these parts has heard a single cuckoo. But there are more buntings, he said. I gave up.

Thursday, 14th June

A. and I drive to London. Appalling traffic jams, London awash with tourists and congestion. To buffet luncheon given by Faber & Faber

---

* Hon. Nicholas Ridley (1929–93), yr s. of 3rd Viscount Ridley; Conservative cabinet minister of forthright views who later resigned from the Government after an unguarded interview (see 14 July 1990); cr. life peer 1992; m. 1st 1950–74 Hon. Clayre Campbell, 2nd 1979 Judy Kendall.

† Gerald Wellesley (1885–1972), 7th Duke of Wellington; architect and conservationist.

for this autumn's paperback authors of which I am one, my three diary volumes and *Another Self** being published in August. I take minimum interest in such an event, but am pleased with the jacket designs. I think Faber's a charming old-fashioned publisher, as Chatto's used to be and Murray's still is.

Joined M. at his new flat in Strathearn Place. He has done it charmingly, with beautifully made double bookcases of mahogany, looking glasses under central pediments, completely covering facing walls of sitting room. He has bought from junk auctioneers a splendid writing table of immense size, *c.* 1900. Sumptuous little bathroom in mahogany and brass. All very cosy and autumnal. I am very impressed that M. who has little visual sense is making such an attractive bachelor nest. He gave me a painting on hardboard dated 1913 of a whippet sitting in a wicker chair. Enchanting. Said it reminded him of Folly, which it does. We dined happily. All is well with him, his second book finished, thank God.

Monday, 18th June

A. and I went to supper with Penelope [Betjeman] at Blacklands [Wiltshire], Candida and Rupert Lycett Green† being away. Lovely midsummer eve. Plunged off horrid main road on the edge of Calne into drive. A tunnel of lush trees, opening into a park of long corn and hay in process of mowing, with vast, spreading chestnut trees like tea cosies. Smell of amber hay strong and sweet. Long shadows. The large Georgian block serene in evening light, front door open with view onto garden side beyond. Wide river softly flowing just below house to a cascade. Garden a dream. Penelope is a stalwart character. Less nonsense about her than anyone I have known in a long life. Cares nothing about clothes or appearances. Like a wizened old apple. Only thing that worried me was her sunken eyes. She talked much

---

* J.L.-M's much acclaimed (and somewhat fanciful) autobiographical work published in 1970.

† Candida Betjeman (b.1942), o.d. of Sir John Betjeman and Hon. Penelope; m. 1963 Rupert Lycett Green, founder of Blades, fashionable tailors; writer on architectural and horticultural subjects and editor of her father's letters in two volumes.

about John and their life together in the old days. Said that I was the first person to mention John's existence to her, when I told her that I had met a real poet. She later met him through sending an article for publication to the *Architectural Review*. Strange that he should have a memorial service in Westminster Abbey, when one thought of her parents' disapproval of her marriage to 'that middle-class Dutchman'. She has made a *démarche* to Elizabeth [Cavendish] who has replied that she cannot bring herself to meet P. for at least a year. Sounds so unlike dear Feeble. We ate in a summer-house, one granddaughter present. P. recalled her 'wedding' to Johnnie Churchill* in the Wytham Woods.† I was to be the priest, but they could not find me. P. believes that, had I been found and 'married' them – I was with Desmond [Parsons]‡ and John Sutro§ – it would have been valid, for the sacrament of marriage is sealed by the consent of the parties. Said that John had been a Quaker before going to Oxford, and became an Anglo-Catholic with Billy Clonmore.¶ Would never reconcile himself to the Romans, which was the principal undoing of their marriage.** A. and I sipped white wine, P. water, while the shadows lengthened, the swans roused themselves on the water and the blackbirds raised their voices. Across the water the Downs and the White Horse. Two steel pylons on the summit actually enhance the view. A nice untidy house full of children. P. told us that she plans to retire to a hotel at Llandrindod Wells, run by nuns.

---

* J. G. Spencer Churchill (1909–94); artist, nephew of Sir Winston, who had been J.L.-M's best friend at Oxford.

† This episode took place in the autumn of 1930, Wytham Abbey near Oxford then belonging to Johnnie Churchill's grandmother Lady Abingdon: Penelope's parents disapproved of Churchill's suit and took her to spend the next year in India.

‡ Hon. Desmond Parsons (1910–37), whom J.L.-M. loved at Eton.

§ Aesthete, *bon vivant*, and film producer; founder of Oxford Railway Club (1904–85).

¶ William Forward-Howard (1902–78), known as Lord Clonmore before succeeding father as 8th Earl of Wicklow, 1946; Oxford friend of Betjeman who later scandalised his family by converting to Roman Catholicism.

** Penelope had become a Roman Catholic in 1948.

Saturday, 30th June

I had a bad scare staying at Brooks's on the 26th. Thought I was having a haemorrhage. Was up four or five times in the night, and nearly chucked N.T. Arts Panel tour next day. It passed. Two days at Belton [House, Lincolnshire] and Calke Abbey [Derbyshire]. Too many staff present, about 30 to 6 of Panel. Stayed one night in hotel in Southwell, and visited the Minster. Very large, purest Romanesque, impressive. Myles Hildyard* showed me the house on the edge of the town where Byron lived before he inherited, the little lame boy with his mother. Nice, unspoilt late Georgian house.

Attended John Betjeman's memorial service in Westminster Abbey. We were given best possible seats, 2 stalls in choir, though A. alas unable to come owing to sprained wrist. I sat next to Michael Tree. I think he wept, and I certainly did at times. Before service opened we listened to John's favourite tunes, *In a Monastery Garden*, other Elgar, and school songs he loved. Immensely long procession of 25 to 30 clergymen I would guess, dear old Gerard Irvine† prancing among them, followed by Archbishop of Canterbury‡ in white mitre. Feeble to whom I blew a kiss was lunching with him afterwards. Billa shocked that he should entertain, as she put it, 'not the widow but the concubine'. The Prince of Wales read the first lesson beautifully, strong, good voice, slowly, pausing in the right places. Jock Murray read the second, equally well until the last sentence when he was so moved that he could barely get out the words. Apposite somehow, and touching. I congratulated him when we left, and he said, 'By Jove, I barely made it.' I thought how amazed J.B. would have been, when I first knew him fifty years ago, at this national hero's apotheosis. Harry Williamson's§ tribute was excellent and paid oblique tribute to Feeble's thirty years of friendship and nursing. The Abbey packed with close friends and unknown admirers. Special prayers written for John.

---

* Squire of Flintham Hall, Nottinghamshire (1914–2005); war hero, local historian, and sometime honorary representative of N.T.

† Anglo-Catholic priest (b. 1921).

‡ Rt Revd Robert Runcie (1921–2000); Archbishop of Canterbury, 1980–91.

§ Anglo-Catholic monk, formerly Dean of Trinity College, Cambridge.

Much emphasis on the love he inspired. Moving and magnificent ceremony.

When I got to Badminton, there was Rupert Loewenstein with Mick Jagger. A nice little man, unassuming. He had been looking at schools for his daughter. Dressed very soberly, as a parent should. He is tiny. Fresh, youthful face. Figure not good. Too thin and chest hollow. Proffers the fingers to shake hand. No firm grip.

Thursday, 5th July

A miracle has happened. My discharge has ended. I really seem to be better, and feel renewed in strength. I wrote to M. in Paris, where he is editing the Duchess of Windsor's letters, that I feel I am walking on the edge of a precipice, but intend to look inland rather than out to sea and hope for the best. I have put Regy temporarily aside, having finished the research and returned the papers to Churchill College. In the fear that I had not long to live, I started editing my diaries for 1948–9 in the last week of June. They are a mess, but I can make something of them. The fact that the thoughts and events of those days are recorded at all is what matters. I have already got to July 1949. To type them up will take several weeks. And I still want to finish my 'German' novel. Meanwhile I have agreed to write two reviews, each of three books, for *Country Life*. Foolish in view of the amount of work I have in hand, but good practice which will keep the hand and eye in tune.

Sunday, 8th July

We are enjoying a heat wave, tempered with usual anxieties about shortage of water. A's garden *embaumé* with roses and honey-suckle, arbutus, clematis, lilies. Never so full and luscious as now. There is a wild convolvulus out at the moment, with a snow white trumpet as virginal and almost as large as that of the arum lily, and yet we take it for granted and scarcely observe it. Yellow stonecrop makes a wonderful curry-coloured cushion along the tops of the remaining stone walls. The lime tree flowers smelling more strongly than usual, due to this exceptionally sunny summer. My divine blue *Geranium praetense* along the verges, which the brutes have scythed before they have seeded. Will there be any next year?

To Communion this morning at the big church. Eight women and three men, all middle class. Never the proletariat, who presumably know a thing or two and are not going to be bothered with all this nonsense. And do the middle classes go to church for prestigious reasons? I don't think so. It is because they speculate, wonder, want something beyond the mundane. Also because they are patriotic, traditionalist, law abiding, decent.

Monday, 9th July

Today I motored to Wellington College to see the Master, David Newsome.[*] Such a nice man. We were at once on Christian name terms. Even so, I find it shy-making to be with a headmaster, although he must be twenty years my junior. He generously gave me extracts from A. C. Benson's journals referring to Esher. Benson clearly did not much like Esher, but his comments are interesting, coming from a contemporary. We lunched at a pub near the College, for it was the end of term. Talked about romantic friendships between Victorian boys. He told me that the 'mores' of the boys changed with each generation. Whereas twenty-five years ago Wellington boys thought it chic to be queer, and boasted of their prowess, true or untrue, today it was an unmentionable subject. Any boy suspected of being so was the victim of taunts. We agreed that we both disliked Oscar Browning who was lecherous, and liked William Cory who was romantic.[†]

---

[*] Dr David Newsome (b. 1929); Master of Wellington College, 1980–89; his book *On the Edge of Paradise* (John Murray, 1980), based on the diaries of A. C. Benson (1862–1925) and dealing with platonic romances between dons and undergraduates, had fascinated J.L.-M.

[†] Oscar Browning (1837–1923) and William Cory (1823–92); renowned Eton housemasters, both of whom were obliged to resign their positions owing to suspicions of improper behaviour with boys in their care.

Friday, 13th July

Walking my dogs on Bath golf course I came upon a man with six whippets on leads. He told me he was retired and determined not to become a crock. He said, 'I have two doctors, my left leg and my right. I walk every day for miles.'

Sunday, 22nd July

Staying at Chatsworth [Derbyshire]. An enjoyable weekend, as nearly always here. At one of our meals, A. said to Andrew [Devonshire],* 'It must be a huge satisfaction to know what you have done for Chatsworth and see the huge numbers of visitors to whom you have given pleasure', pointing to the public outside the window. 'Yes,' he replied with a sigh, 'I love to see them here, but wish it could be for free.' At any rate he is not ashamed to express his delight in getting £20 million for a few drawings at Christie's. At church this morning the vicar gave an admirable sermon. His argument was that it is not merely through words that we reach God, but also through the senses, touch, feeling, smell, taste. In the graveyard Debo took us to look at the Cavendish tombs. She said in her most casual manner, 'Here are two gravestones of my babies. There ought to be a third, I wonder where it can be.' No one else would refer to such things in this way, even if she realised her guests had already noticed them.

Thursday, 2nd August

Real gardeners, like A., don't need to see plants and flowers in bloom in order to appreciate the quality of a strange garden. They are like real musicians who don't need to hear a symphony, but can judge it by the score. I don't mean that a gardener does not prefer to see a garden in bloom, or a musical person to hear a symphony performed; but they can do without. Now to me, such a thing is inconceivable.

---

* Andrew Cavendish, 11th Duke of Devonshire (1920–2004); m. 1941 Hon. Deborah ('Debo') Mitford (b. 1920).

Saturday, 4th August

A. and I drove to Northamptonshire to stay one night with Gervase Jackson-Stops.* Met Gervase with Sachie [Sitwell]† at Weston at midday. Sachie surprisingly well and cheerful. Only his memory is bad. Full of chaff and enjoyed being told stories and telling his own. The same adorable chortle and screwing up of his dear face. Francis‡ and his charming wife now live in part of the house, an admirable arrangement. We three went on to Canons Ashby to see what the N.T. and Gervase in particular have done. It is a miracle of restoration. Three years ago the house was nearly ruinous and empty of furniture. Of course the garden is still bare and new, but the romantic house I knew in the 1930s is there to emerge with the years. A wonderful achievement.

The other great achievement is G's Menagerie at Horton, which I first saw with Robert Byron§ who would have bought and restored it had he survived the war. But poor Robert would not have done such a splendid job as G., whose knowledge and taste are without parallel. The great room a marvel, re-stuccoed out of nothing, for more than half had been destroyed by vandals and cattle.

Wednesday, 29th August

Today being my mother's 100th birthday, were she alive, I decided to do something to celebrate the occasion. So I wrote to the Vicar of Badsey and Wickhamford asking if he would give me Communion in the Church. He replied charmingly that he would be delighted to do so. This was arranged a month ago. So I duly motored over and arrived before 11.30. Walked down the familiar steps into the dear church. The Vicar already there. As charming as his letter had been. He said, 'I expect you would prefer the 1661 version.' 'I would indeed.' 'Where would you feel most at home?' Pointing to our old pew, I said, 'I

---

* Architectural historian and adviser to National Trust (1947–95).
† Sir Sacheverell Sitwell, 6th Bt (1897–1988); writer and poet.
‡ Yr s. (1935–2004) of Sir Sacheverell; m. 1966 Susanna Cross.
§ Travel writer and architectural campaigner (1905–41); pre-war mentor and lover of J.L.-M.

would feel most at home here but as the congregation consists of me only, perhaps I had better be in the Chancel.' Indeed, from the box pew I could not have seen him. Very uncomfortably I perched on a tall upright oak chair in the Chancel, and kneeling on a hassock had nothing to lean against. Got very hot and exhausted from the effort. But it was a lovely experience kneeling before those divine Sandys tombs. I brought with me Mama's silver and tortoiseshell prayer book, which belonged to her grandmother, the print of which was so small and the wording of the liturgy, in spite of it being 1661, different in many respects. It must be over fifty years since I last took Communion at these rails, an extraordinary thought.* Mama would have smiled, did she know that I was doing this in remembrance of her.† After the little service the charming Vicar told me that a great discovery had been made. The Charles II arms under the Doom turn out not to be Charles II in spite of the date, added later, but James II. In view of that monarch's short reign and being a papist, this is very rare. There are only five others known in the whole country. The whole thing is to be restored and, I suspect, touched up. I gave Vicar a cheque for £100 for the church, my favourite church in this wide world.

Then the Vicar took me to the Manor for he had forewarned the present owners, a pleasant young couple called Ryan-Bell.‡ House well cared-for and less gloomy than when I last visited. Garden much deteriorated. Pond choked.

Friday 14th September

M. breakfasted with me at Brooks's. He gave me his typescript of the Duchess of Windsor's letters to read and I gave him typescript of my 1948–9 diaries. Then to the National Trust to talk to half a dozen charming young people who are acting in a play for teenagers on the acquisition of Blickling [Norfolk] by the N.T. in 1941. I am apparently

---

* J.L.-M. was a practising Roman Catholic from 1934 until the late 1960s.
† *In Another Self*, J.L.-M. described his mother's attitude towards religion as 'at first indifferent, and in her middle and old age positively hostile. God, she would declare before the last war, was no better than a nuisance; and during the war indistinguishable from Hitler.'
‡ Jeremy and June Ryan-Bell; owners of Wickhamford Manor since 1979.

the only person left who remembers Lord Lothian,[*] Matheson[†] and the place in pre-war days. I was struck by their profound naivety and ignorance. But they were charming and thanked me profusely when I left them to lunch at the Travellers with Hugh Montgomery-Massingberd.[‡] I like Hugh very much. Such a nice, gentle, harassed, hesitant man. Has two wives and two children to support, and little money. Adores Gunby [Lincolnshire],[§] longs to live there in retirement if he can afford it. Hugh's lack of self-assertiveness may explain the occasional aggressiveness in his writing. We agreed that in writing the devil gets into one at times.

Wednesday, 26th September

To London for the day. A lovely day of golden sun. I walked to M's flat and drank coffee with him. We discussed whether to remove certain passages in my diaries which may embarrass my friends. His view is that I have already caused so much offence in the first three volumes that I might as well continue in the fourth. Walked to Heraldry Today in Beauchamp Place to collect *Ruvigny's European Peerage*, which costs £40 and weighs a ton. Then to Brooks's where Eardley was waiting for me. We lunched upstairs and although we both expressed pleasure at seeing one another our meeting was not a success. I suppose old friends get bored with one another if they do not meet often. Then I walked to Westminster Hospital to see Norah

---

[*] Philip Kerr, 11th Marquess of Lothian (1882–1940); Liberal statesman, whose speech to the Annual Meeting of the National Trust in 1934 inspired the setting-up of the Country Houses Scheme of which J.L.-M. became Secretary, and who bequeathed Blickling, his Jacobean house in Norfolk, to the N.T. on his premature death (at which time he was serving as British Ambassador to the United States).

[†] Donald MacLeod Matheson; the dedicated but eccentric Secretary of the N.T., 1932–45.

[‡] Hugh Montgomery-Massingberd (1946–2007); writer, journalist, publisher, genealogist and author (2002) of a play – *Ancestral Voices* – based on the diaries of J.L.-M.

[§] House and estate in Lincolnshire donated to N.T. during Second World War by Hugh Montgomery-Massingberd's great-uncle and great-aunt, Field Marshal Sir Archibald and Lady M.-M. – an episode of which J.L.-M., who loved both the house and its owners, wrote nostalgically in *People and Places* (John Murray, 1992).

Smallwood* in her ward. Very distressing. She lay with her eyes closed, mind wandering, holding my hand throughout visit. Is maddened by the noise of the ward, lies awake at night in great torment and misery. I left her feeling wretched.

Tuesday, 16th October

Stayed last night with J[ohn] K[enworthy]-B[rowne]† in Hollywood Road. We dined agreeably alone at Brooks's. He is a faithful, affectionate friend. This morning to Archie Aberdeen's‡ memorial service at St Margaret's, Westminster. A beautiful service. Church quite full. Service of Thanksgiving is a new term which I don't much like. It is a euphemism, a cowardly term, a not-facing-up to grief. We must all be cheery instead. I don't feel cheerful when my old friends like Archie are dead. Indeed, in an excellent address given, somewhat to my surprise, by Lord Hailsham,§ he said one should never be ashamed of shedding tears. And he quoted the shortest sentence in the Gospels: 'Jesus wept.' He said he was some sort of relation and remembered Archie as a child some seven years younger than himself, for Archie was younger than me. Archie's brother, the new Marquess, read one of the lessons, and his sister, Lady Jessamine Harmsworth, sang a most moving anthem to the words of S. S. Wesley, 'Lead me Lord in thy righteousness. Make thy ways plain.' She has a fine contralto voice and did it well. Both she and the brother are plain and resemble Archie, the brother's voice exactly like Archie's without the affectation.

---

* The dragon-like former Chairman of Chatto & Windus (1909–84), who had been J.L.-M's publisher from 1973 to 1983.
† Expert on neo-classical sculpture and former historic buildings representative of N.T. (b. 1931); close friend of J.L.-M. since 1958.
‡ Lord Archibald Gordon (1913–84); s. brother 1974 as 5th Marquess of Aberdeen; a friend of J.L.-M. since the 1930s when he worked for CPRE; on staff of BBC Radio, 1946–72.
§ Quintin Hogg (1907–2001); Conservative politician; succeeded father as 2nd Viscount Hailsham 1950, disclaimed viscountcy 1963, cr. life peer (as Baron Hailsham of St Marylebone) 1970; Lord Chancellor, 1970–4 and 1979–87.

Wednesday, 24th October

We went to London for Christina Foyle's[*] dinner to celebrate 80th anniversary of the firm's foundation by her father. I changed into black tie at the Berkeleys'[†] where A. was staying. Although she had ordered a car it did not turn up. In panic we hailed a cab and drove to the Dorchester. Pelting rain and Mitterand's[‡] visit combined to cause terrible traffic jams. We arrived half an hour late. Found Miss Foyle waiting by herself in ante-room, the hundred or so guests already seated at tables in the Orchid Room. I was dishevelled and fussed, the sort of anxiety that takes years off my life. We were both seated at Table 1, and to my intense surprise I found myself placed on Christina's right. Felt honoured but perplexed, for at our table were Lord Balogh,[§] Sir Arthur Bryant,[¶] wife of Harold Wilson.[**] Witty speech by broadcasting man, forget name. Christina Foyle replied fearlessly in a rather sweet little baby voice, but running her words into each other. No punctuation. She is very sweet to talk to. Can't converse, but talks agreeably. She has that milky royal complexion and very good teeth. A nice woman. I like her. At the conclusion she gave everyone a present of her commonplace book, which I see is for sale at £10. A. loved Sir Arthur. I spoke to him for a minute after dinner and he remembers Regy. Told me he was a man whom one could not much like. But he had humility, and great wisdom. His influence upon Edward VII immense and beneficial. He said we must pay him a visit, which we propose to do. The reverberating noise of voices made hearing impossible.

---

[*] Bookseller (1911–99); founder of Foyle's Literary Luncheons, 1930.
[†] Sir Lennox Berkeley, composer (1903–89); m. 1946 Freda Bernstein (b. 1923); A.L.-M. often stayed at their house in Little Venice.
[‡] François Mitterand, President of France 1981–95.
[§] Thomas Balogh (1905–85), Hungarian-born Oxford economist and adviser to Labour governments.
[¶] Sir Arthur Bryant (1899–85), author; m. (2nd) 1941 Anne Brooke of Sarawak (whose brother married a daughter of Reginald, Viscount Esher).
[**] Mary Baldwin (b. 1918); poet; m. 1940 Harold Wilson (1916–95; Labour Prime Minister, 1964–70, 1974–6; cr. life peer, 1979).

The French visit has made London very jittery. Police cars with screaming klaxons force their way through traffic. Papers full of idiotic behaviour of Mitterand's French bodyguard planting unfused explosives in the French Embassy to test English security precautions. Our sniffer dogs of course detected them and we are furious at the impertinence of the French. The press considers it insulting after the Brighton incident, the horror waves of which have not yet died down.*

The Berkeleys gave us dinner before we went to Embassy in their car driven by the dotty French chauffeur George. Ghastly party as I feared. A wooden aircraft hanger erected in garden approached by fabricated passages dotted with Calor gas stoves. We did not even enter Embassy building. From 10.10 to 11.45 we stood in this stark hut, hung with two tapestries it is true, but no seats. Champagne which I hate, served with *petits fours*. First on one leg, then the other. Noise excruciating like waves of the sea or continuous clapping of hands. Hardly a soul we knew. Lost A. at one time and set off on a tour round the room. Decided this was a foretaste of hell, looking for Alvilde and never finding her. Then on leaving we could not find George or the Berkeleys' car. Wandered in the cold (mercifully no rain) up Millionaire's Row, lined with police and detectives.

Today Mitterand visited the office where Clarissa [Luke] works, which was once the headquarters of General de Gaulle. One of his French bodyguard hearing her speak French offered her an invitation to tonight's party. C. did not use it but might have been a terrorist. I told A. she ought to write to the Margeries about this extraordinary incident.

Queen came down the steps of the Embassy into the garden hanger, wearing the most beautiful tiara ever seen. At night she looks her splendid best. Was wearing orange sash, some Frog decoration I suppose. She said to A., 'You live in Badminton, don't you?'

---

* The IRA had detonated a bomb at the Grand Hotel at Brighton during the Conservative Party Conference the previous month, several politicians and their wives sustaining injuries and Mrs Thatcher narrowly escaping death.

Arthur Bryant said to A. that, in his writing, his rule was to cut out every unnecessary word ruthlessly, and go over and over what he has written. An octogenarian, he says he writes today for the semi-educated young. I don't. I write for people like myself, middlebrows and literates.

Wednesday, 31st October

At the end of June I returned to Churchill College the papers they lent me, kept in the back room at Bath. I put aside Reginald, Viscount Esher, intending the break to last until the end of the year. Whereupon I edited for publication, either by me or by M. after my demise, my diaries for 1948–9, and also wrote the third part of my novel begun over two years ago and left unfinished. Whether either book will be published remains to be seen, but I am taking them to Bruce Hunter* in London on 7 November. I have also written an article of 1,200 words for the American *Architectural Digest* for which I am being paid a fee of $1,500. So I am two months in advance, and shall begin writing my biography of Regy tomorrow, All Saints' Day. May it be a propitious festival. The task daunts me, and I wonder if I shall remain well enough for long enough to complete it, and *compos mentis*.

Sunday, 11th November

In the afternoon, A. and I drove to Salisbury to have tea with Sir Arthur Bryant. This delightful old man lives in Miles House, the large early Georgian house in the Close which we looked at years ago. Beautiful but too large; yet ideal otherwise, for one front has outstanding view of Cathedral, and the other a long, narrow garden leading to the river. Fine steep staircase. Lovely library of tunnel shape, like mine, but more beautiful being circa 1720. Lovely furniture and pictures. Delicious tea provided by housekeeper, with chocolate cake, scones, etc. We talked of links with the past. He pointed to a portrait of a young man in Oxford mortarboard, as it might be by Reynolds, name Shakerly, date of birth on label 1767.

---

* Canadian-born literary agent (b. 1941) who had acted for J.L.-M. since 1979.

Sir Arthur told us this was an ancestor of his wife and that, when he first married, he met an old man on the Shakerly estate who actually remembered this man.

Sir A. has a profound belief in the ultimate recovery of the British people. Indolence is their besetting sin. I said that I doubted if the sterling British virtues could survive, given the percentage of people who were of recent immigrant stock. He said the only way to preserve these virtues was by encouraging miscegenation. They were not inherited but transmitted. The do-gooders were doing much evil in not making coloured people integrate but providing them instead with their own schools, housing estates, etc. They should not be kept in ghettos.

He asked us pointedly if we read his books. A. admitted that she hadn't, and naughtily turned to me to ask if I had. I said hesitantly, I fear not convincingly, that I had read his trilogy on Pepys, which I have in fact only skimmed. He gave us a copy of *Set in a Silver Sea*. Agreeable interlude. Charming and wise old man. He spoke again of Regy Esher, but said he had never met him personally. Asked if he had been homosexual, but did not pursue the matter.

When we left, the Cathedral was floodlit, and seen sideways was the most beautiful spectacle ever beheld.

Tuesday, 13th November

M. telephoned this morning that Charles Orwin[*] has been offered a job in Singapore, which he (Charles) regards as a hell-on-earth but where he wants to join his Chinese friend. When dining with me last Wednesday, Charles spoke to me of this friend. I cautioned him that passion generally endures for seven years, and thereafter attachment is dependent on mutual interests. He quite rightly paid no attention. I am sorry for M. and indeed for myself for Charles is a delightful young man. I wish him well, but wonder if I shall live to see him returned home, desperately seeking another job in his late thirties.

---

[*] Publisher (b. 1951); the move to Singapore was a success and brought him contentment and fortune.

Thursday, 22nd November

Hugh Massingberd has written such a vitriolic review of Peter Coats'* admittedly rather ghastly new book that I am wondering whether I ought to stop Bruce Hunter submitting my diaries to a publisher. It would kill me to receive such a review.

Tuesday, 27th November

David and Caroline dined alone here. When telling us of the progress of the works in the big house and mentioning the lift he is putting in, David went out of his way to stress that he was making no structural alterations. He seems to think I am critical of what he does or doesn't do conservation-wise, but I try not to criticise, and don't really care that much anyway. I did however venture to show him a photograph in Green's book on Grinling Gibbons† of the 1st Duke's monument, and pointed out two attendant classical figures which Master removed, asking him why Master had done this. He said because it was not safe, not because Master didn't like them, as he noticed nothing. He agreed he ought to put them back but was fairly indifferent himself.

David told us that his solicitor had come upon files of papers concerning Mary [Duchess of Beaufort]'s having set detectives on Master's tracks when he was in love with [Lavinia] Duchess of Norfolk. On one occasion the detective hid in a cupboard in the very room where they went to bed. All evidence carefully documented. The solicitor said to David, 'Of course I destroyed them all, as you would have wanted me to do.' In fact David would have wanted nothing of the kind. Would have been interested to look through them. But what a devilish thing on the part of the old Duchess [of Beaufort]. She now in her dottiness has turned against Master and tells those she sees that he has left her and run away with the Duchess of Norfolk. That was the affair which touched her most deeply.

---

* Peter Coats (1910–90); distant cousin of J.L.-M. who had inherited a Scottish cotton fortune; friend of the politician and diarist Sir Henry 'Chips' Channon (d. 1958); garden designer and horticultural writer, who had just produced a snobbish book of memoirs, *Of Kings and Cabbages*.
† Wood carver (1648–1721).

Saturday, 1st December

My impotence has altered my character. It has made me judge all human motives and actions objectively. Is it a virtue, I ask myself? Or does virtue lie in potency with restraint? Wilde said virtue was the absence of temptation. Certainly the total absence of lust enables one to love without ulterior motives. But alas, the revelation of how few people one does love under such circumstances is rather a shock.

Sunday, 9th December

On Saturday I motored A. to Northamptonshire for a signing of her book.* Complete waste of time. Who benefits? The local shop in Oundle. We lunched with Molly Buccleuch† at Boughton. Arrived half an hour late, self-invited too, but Molly unresentful and sweet. She has changed and become rather pathetic. Very deaf, teeth giving trouble. The spark gone, and we didn't feel we were a great success. She has a new young Scotch couple whom she adores and finds perfect. They have been with her three months. Nothing too much trouble, love her dog, love her, would die for her, etc. I have witnessed this so often. Within a year they will be gone. Disgusting luncheon, unrecognisable pheasant, watery vegetables. The lovely food we used to get at Boughton. Does she no longer mind? Molly was a moth, and now no candles. The great *châtelaine* of five houses, with her power and excellent taste, now reduced to a dark corner. No silver, no pearls.

Saturday, 15th December

I motored to Tredegar Park [Monmouthshire], where I was received and given luncheon by charming young David Freeman.‡ A touching character, extremely delicate. He told me that, aged 23, he had a

---

* Alvilde had edited *The Englishwoman's House*, published by Collins that September with photographs by Derry Moore.
† Mary Lascelles (1900–93); m. 1921 Walter Montagu-Douglas-Scott (d. 1973) who s. 1935 as 8th Duke of Buccleuch and 10th Duke of Queensberry.
‡ Curator of Tredegar Park, 1979–97 (b. 1956).

growth removed from his stomach. Has recurrent operations and suffers terribly. Is now 28 and looks extremely frail. I can't make out his origins, but he is very sensitive and has excellent taste. Is curator of the house for Newport Borough Council, awful philistines who have already ruined the surroundings with hideous new buildings. He is bringing the house back to life, but says it is a constant battle, as they do not appreciate what he does and treat him vilely. It was totally emptied of Morgan contents save for half a dozen indifferent portraits of the late lords, including my friend, the ineffable John.* Tredegar is interesting architecturally. Good mellow brickwork, with those extraordinary heraldic beasts over the pediments of the windows, can't make out whether original or nineteenth-century additions. Dining room, gilt room very splendid; also cedar closet. But dreadful things have happened since John sold. Nuns and a comprehensive school. Ceilings fell down, dry-rot set in, walls disfigured. David is faced with collecting suitable contents and has done extremely well. I was touched by this young person, so lonely, ill and sensitive. Gave him a copy of my *Beckford*.

Thursday, 27th December

We spent three nights at Parkside [near Windsor] with the Droghedas.† Joan's situation extremely sad. Conversation out of the question, but one makes little remarks of affection. She has become a pretty, touching, sweetly-smiling little doll. All that brightness, fun and quick intelligence, that sharp appreciation of literature, those pertinent comments – gone. Very affectionate, never grumbles and accepts whatever she is told to do. Garrett is too fussy with her, never leaves her alone. She gave me one of those amused eye-lifts as she used to do when Garrett was being particularly tiresome. Derry and Alexandra [Moore] came with the baby for the night on Boxing Day. Burnet [Pavitt] was to have come but ill with influenza.

---

* John Morgan (1908–62); s. father 1954 as 6th and last Baron Tredegar.
† Garrett Moore, 11th Earl of Drogheda (1910–89); businessman, patron of the arts, Knight of the Garter, Eton contemporary of J.L.-M. and longstanding friend of A.L.-M.; m. 1935 Joan Carr (d. 1989).

Went to St George's Chapel on Christmas morning. A. and I were given seats in the front row of the nave, at the corner of the central aisle. So when the royals left by the West Door I had to *reculer* so as not to be in their way, and was so busy bowing that I saw little. A. says she can curtsey and look at the same time.

Much excitement on return to Badminton about the body-snatchers having dug up Master's grave to within four inches of the coffin. They were disturbed by Mary Duchess in the middle of the night turning on the lights in her room, declaring to the nurse that she wanted to open her Christmas presents. Vicar thinks this scared them off. They threatened to sever his head and deliver it to Princess Anne. Charming. The village people extremely shocked, old Staines, who never to my knowledge goes to church, saying it was an offence against God.

Caroline said to A. that she thought Master would rather have liked the idea of his body being thrown to hounds at a meet.

1985

1985

Bruce Hunter writes that Faber's have turned down my novel.* I had guessed this, as Charles Orwin never rang me after reading it over Xmas. I am furious, for even if it is not good, I know it is not bad, and better than many novels which are published – and certainly better than the latest volume of my diary which they have lapped up, outbidding Chatto's. I thought I had Faber's in the palm of my hand. I am now out for revenge, and may not let them have my diaries after all, which will infuriate them, as they rang me last Thursday saying they wanted to publish in October and needed my final corrections immediately. I shall show them. Or shall I?

To London to deliver the revised typescript of *Midway on the Waves* [1948–9 diaries] to Faber's, my resolution to 'down' them having evaporated with my indignation. With A[lvilde]'s help I cut out all the lovey-dovey stuff of our courtship, having previously cut what I had written about our differences and my grave doubts about the whole affair. The runt of the diary for 1949 is a poor thing. Bought socks and shirts at Harvie & Hudson sale, then to lunch with Ros[amond Lehmann]. Ros as alert as ever but wracked with arthritis. She finds Virginia Woolf unreadable – woolly stuff, the characters hazy and unconvincing – but Anita Brookner,† who dedicated her novel *Hôtel du Lac* to Ros, inspired. Ros is critical of contemporary novelists for neglecting form. That is why she so

---

* See Introduction p.x and notes to 7 March 1984.
† Novelist (b. 1928), whose *Hôtel du Lac* won the Booker Prize in 1984.

admires Brookner, who is an old-fashioned novelist – like me, I thought to myself, Faber's no doubt having rejected me on that score. Ros said to me, 'You are going to get an honour. I am seeing to it. You only missed it this time because there were too many candidates.' I assured her that I didn't want an honour – and I don't. Besides, it would only be an OBE, and what would that mean to me?*

Wednesday, 6th February

David and Caroline Beaufort dined alone with us last night. I enjoy taking to David, who is a sensitive man underneath. Like John Evelyn,† he has days when he skulks along the streets hoping to be unobserved. He had an awful experience hunting last Saturday. The 'antis' were out in full strength. He had to protect Princess Anne who was out. 'They' made the most disgusting remarks about her, which David could not repeat even to us. He tried to reason with some of the less objectionable 'antis'. One of them said to him, 'You ought not to be riding that horse, it ought to go free.' D. explained that the horse was comfortably stabled, fed twice a day, groomed, and enjoyed hunting even more than he did; that if 'let free', it would be dead in a week. He says that if this concerted group obstruction persists he will have to close down the hunt altogether. They trample the wheat, which the hunters carefully avoid.

Went to London today, staying at Brooks's, so cosy, comfortable and central. Igor,‡ who is off to Australia, came to tea with me, and was much impressed by the old-fashionedness of the club. The boy is as dotty as ever but has become the squarest of the squares. I fear he will not like Australia and will be back in four months.

---

* J.L.-M. later refused a CBE – see 18 November 1992.
† Government official and diarist (1620–1706).
‡ J.L.-M's step-grandson Igor Luke (b. 1965); o.s. of A.L.-M's dau. Clarissa.

Thursday, 7th February

Robert Rhodes James,* Rosebery's† biographer, lunched with me at Brooks's, after I had been trying to get hold of him for a year. Dry and uncommunicative. I couldn't get to grips with him, apart from the fact that he was difficult to hear with his low, soft voice. Unwilling to talk about Rosebery's homosexuality, and his relations with Drumlanrig who committed suicide.‡ I did glean a few things – notably that Sir Robin Mackworth-Young§ was perfectly maddening, kept R.J. waiting for months reading Rosebery and then objecting to the most trivial things. R.J. said Rosebery was disdainful of Esher for snobbish reasons. Barnbougle, the castellated building next to Dalmeny to which Rosebery finally retreated, is crammed with indescribable treasures. Save for a few such as R.J., no one is admitted, for the family don't want it known what they possess. Rosebery was extremely religious. His recently discovered letters to his wife show his devotion to her, and his private diaries are full of religious perplexities while ignoring sex problems. The Eton Boating Song was played on his deathbed – a scratchy recording, I imagine, on an old phonograph. What Eton did to these men.

R.J. mentioned two other things. How he loathed James Pope-Hennessy.¶ I said, 'You would not have loathed him had you known him in his twenties. You would have been bewitched.' And that Philip Ziegler's** life of Mountbatten is a diatribe; hasn't a good word to say

---

* (Sir) Robert Rhodes James (1933–99); politician and writer, Conservative MP for Cambridge, 1976–87; his *Rosebery* (1963) was one of several books he wrote about bisexual men which barely mentioned this aspect of their lives, other subjects being 'Bob' Boothby, 'Chips' Channon and Anthony Eden.

† Archibald Primrose, 5th Earl of Rosebery (1847–1929); Liberal Prime Minister, 1894–5.

‡ Francis Douglas, Viscount Drumlanrig (1868–94), Rosebery's private secretary and heir to 9th Marquess of Queensberry, died in a mysterious shooting accident on 18 October 1894, which gave rise to rumours that he had taken his own life in the shadow of a suppressed homosexual scandal in which Rosebery was also implicated.

§ Sir Robert ('Robin') Mackworth-Young (1920–2000); Royal Librarian at Windsor Castle and Assistant Keeper of Queen's Archives, 1958–85.

¶ Writer (1916–74); intimate friend of J.L.-M. before and during the Second World War; done to death by 'rough trade' (see 16 October 1989).

** Philip Ziegler (b. 1929); publisher and writer.

of the subject and R.J. wonders what the family will make of it. M. confirms this; says Z. makes Mountbatten out to have been a fraud, a bad sailor, bad Viceroy, a muddle-head, and everything bad except a homosexual.

Sunday, 10th February

Few spectacles are more 'how'* than the upturned soles of communicants kneeling at the altar rails. Somehow the soles have a plaintive air, a mournful aspect. Down-at-heel, worn at the toes, they are sad, rather piteous objects not meant to be revealed in this way to the communicant waiting his turn and having a full view. It is taking an unfair advantage over one's neighbour, like seeing him in his bath through a window.

I am reading a first-rate biography of Edmund Gosse.[†] This is the book I wanted to write, until dissuaded by Rupert H[art]-D[avis], who said a very clever lady was already engaged. Certainly it is a work of scholarship. I could never have done it as well. She quotes from J.A. Symonds'[‡] memoirs: 'The great crime of my life was my marriage.' I felt this remark suited me. Alas, alas. But we are so deeply fond of one another now. Yet I can never make amends. I shall always be haunted by this.

Thursday, 21st February

A. reminded me that all her possessions were destroyed in the war, stored in a warehouse which was totally burnt out. She lost everything she inherited from both her parents[§] – furniture, pictures, papers,

---

* A word from the private language of Harold Nicolson and Vita Sackville-West, meaning pathetic.
† Sir Edmund Gosse (1849–1928); poet, critic and essayist. The biography was Ann Thwaite's *Edmund Gosse: A Literary Landscape* (Secker & Warburg, 1984).
‡ John Addington Symonds (1840–93); poet, classical scholar, and pioneer writer on homosexuality.
§ A.L.-M's father, Lieut-Gen. Sir Tom Bridges, had died in 1939, her mother, Janet *née* Menzies, in 1937.

letters, the lot. What she has now came from Princess Winnie* or was bought by herself. She has not got a single letter from her father or mother. This must be an unusual state of affairs and is indeed sad.

She also told me that Caroline [Beaufort] has changed since becoming a duchess, becoming sharper, too conscious of her dignity, and less intimate with A. One might expect this from a new duchess not born a lady, but from C. it is odd. I am not sure that the whole business of dukes and lords ought not to be abolished. Why, for instance, should C. be made President of the Bath Preservation Trust,† of whose existence she knew nothing before receiving this invitation, whereas others – J.L.-M. is one – who have spent their working lives conserving, are overlooked?

Wednesday, 27th February

Looking at fellow passengers in the train to London yesterday, it occurred to me that most people are caricatures – of themselves, I suppose. If I were Osbert Lancaster‡ I could make a caricature of everyone I passed. The young man with the smooth, unwrinkled face, pot belly, furled umbrella, waddling when we reached Paddington. Foxy woman, looking over her shoulder, in fear of the husband who wasn't there.

Lunched with Charles Monteith§ of Faber's at Garrick. Nice learned man, Fellow of All Souls. Charles Orwin invited too. All his colleagues at Faber's lament his departure for Singapore – even Miss Goad, who asked if I knew his Chinese friend and hoped he would

---

* Winaretta Singer (1865–1943), heiress to sewing machine fortune; m. (2nd) Prince Edmond de Polignac; leading member of Paris society and patroness of artists, writers and composers; A.L.-M., then married to the aspiring composer Anthony Chaplin, was her devoted companion during the last six years of her life, and inherited part of her fortune.

† Vigorous architectural conservation society founded in 1934, on whose committee J.L.-M. had served since 1971.

‡ Sir Osbert Lancaster (1908–86); cartoonist, humorist, writer and dandy, friend of J.L.-M. since their Oxford days; m. 1967 (as her 2nd husband) Anne Scott-James (b. 1913), gardening expert.

§ Publisher and Fellow of All Souls (1921–95); retired as Chairman of Faber & Faber in 1981, but remained as 'editorial consultant'.

be good to Charles. She said he would always get a job if he decided to return for he was extremely well-qualified. At Faber's offices went through typescript of *Midway on the Waves* to deal with libel queries – but all those libelled, poor souls, are dead. Charles Monteith chuckled as he read out descriptions. Which reassures me that the text is perhaps not quite so dull and idiotic as I feared.

To Renoir exhibition at the dreadful Hayward Gallery. All Renoir's women look like sensual variations of his wife, with her sweet, peasant, pudding face and red cheeks. His children most touching, with beseeching, questing eyes. After walking back across Charing Cross Bridge I descended to the Embankment. Although it was only 5.30, down-and-outs were already spreading themselves out for the night on filthy mattresses, shabby coats and rugs. A shocking sight to see in a western capital. Is it necessary?

Stayed the night at Brooks's and gave dinner to M., Richard Shone,[*] charmer of all time, and Kenneth Rose. Kenneth was a little drunk. Said three times to us, 'Were the Messels Jews? Not that I mean it in a derogatory sense.' I replied, 'I should think not indeed.' M. gave me an amused look. Kenneth was very depreciatory of Harold [Nicolson]'s *King George V*.[†] But he told me (did he invent it?) that Mr Patten,[‡] Minister of Health, whom he had met at the cocktail party he had just been to, called me 'the best diarist of the century'.

As I came downstairs from my bedroom at Brooks's this morning, an old boy very slowly descended in front of me, small and fragile, his braces showing through the thin jacket of his bent back. I am always revolted by the decrepitude of the old and thought, Oh God, I suppose he is my age. Sat next to him at breakfast. Discovered he was Sir James Marshall-Cornwall, *aet.* 98.[§] Sidney, the nice breakfast waiter, very sweet and kind to him, kept asking if he was all right. I tackled him about Regy Esher. Rather deaf, but on being addressed his puckered face became wreathed in smiles. So polite. No, he only

---

[*] Art historian (b. 1949); associate editor of *Burlington Magazine* from 1979.
[†] Kenneth Rose's own biography of the King had appeared in 1983.
[‡] John Patten MP (b. 1945); Undersecretary for Health and Social Security, 1983–5; cr. life peer, 1997; a traditionalist on right of Conservative Party.
[§] General and military historian (1887–1985).

met him once. 'An amiable man. Sort of *éminence grise*, you know.' One never gets more than this sort of observation. But what a dear old boy. And nice to meet someone still alive who could be *my* father.

Sunday, 10th March

Derek Hill, painting the Prince of Wales, rings to tell me that the P. feels the mantle of John Betjeman has fallen on his shoulders, and that he must now protest against the demolition of worthy landmarks. D. very full of this 'commission', which Pat Trevor-Roper tells A. is nothing of the kind. D. got to hear that a portrait he did years ago was not liked by Prince Charles, and kept badgering him to let him try and improve it. The P. also lamented to D. that he had not been able to become proficient at one of the arts, music or painting. Poor young man, how could he? D. makes a mistake being so touchy about what people say about or do with his paintings. Would I ask Roddy Thesiger what he has done with D's portrait of his brother Wilfred,* etc., etc.?

Wednesday, 13th March

Alvilde being away in Amboise, 'doing' Mick Jagger's garden, I dined on Sunday with the Beauforts in the big house. They have not properly moved in and I was their first guest. David kept asking how I liked what they had done, which is indeed in the best possible taste. He is rather hypochondriacal, always fearing cancer. I refrained from telling them what they may already know, that I had cancer last year, for fear of alarming them. Merely said that I am an authority on the prostate and when in doubt they should consult me. They are concerned about their son Eddie,† who does not work, and whose child is permanently dumped on them, which they rather love. I asked what Eddie's interests were. They said, being seen dining in expensive

---

* Explorer and travel writer (1910–2003); Eton contemporary of J.L.-M.
† Lord Edward Somerset (b. 1958), yr s. of 11th Duke of Beaufort; m. 1982 Hon. Caroline Davidson.

restaurants, like an Evelyn Waugh character. While we were dining, the man from Chubb came through on the telephone, and David greeted him with his usual excellent manners. Amused me by saying there was nothing to steal (I thought of the Canalettos and a few other treasures), but he did not want to be spied on through the windows, etc.

Sunday, 24th March

Today we lunched with Woman* at Caudle Green to meet Diana [Mosley],† she looking much better, and beautiful again, and cheerful. We talked of M[ichael Bloch]'s books. She said she liked M. immensely, but thought his *Operation Willi*‡ much too long and detailed. I disagreed, saying I thought it a masterly exposition. She asked what he would be tackling after the Windsors. I said a biography of Ribbentrop.§ She greatly disapproved of this, and thought she might even write to the widow and sons advising them not to see M. or give him access to papers. This is an example of her ruthless side. She said that when she and O[swald] M[osley] were living in Ireland after the war they had Ribbentrop's young sons to stay, wanting to learn English. They were charming, and suffered dreadfully from the treatment of their father. It was wicked to hang Ribbentrop, who had never been a criminal. The man who deserved hanging was Harold Macmillan¶ for sentencing to death all those Poles and Russians who were sent back after the war.

---

* Hon. Pamela Mitford, 2nd of Mitford sisters (1907-94); m. 1936 (as 2nd of his 6 wives) Professor Derek Jackson (d. 1982).
† Hon. Diana Mitford (1910-2003), with whom J.L.-M., a schoolfriend of her brother, had been in love aged eighteen; m. 1st 1929 Hon. Bryan Guinness (later 2nd Baron Moyne [1905-92]), 2nd 1936 Sir Oswald Mosley, 6th Bt (1896-1980); lived near Orsay, France.
‡ *Operation Willi: The Plot to Kidnap the Duke of Windsor, July 1940* (Weidenfeld & Nicolson, 1984).
§ Joachim 'von' Ribbentrop (1893-1946); German importer of wines and spirits; Ambassador to London, 1936-8, and Foreign Minister, 1938-45; hanged at Nuremberg. Michael Bloch's biography was published by Bantam Press in 1992 and reissued by Abacus in 2003.
¶ Conservative politician (1894-1986); Prime Minister, 1957-63; cr. Earl of Stockton, 1984.

Diana's granddaughter Catherine and husband, the Neidpaths, were lunching.* Charming and clever young couple. He wears an Alfredo-style floppy tie in a bow with falling ends, very idiosyncratic. Another young man staying with Pam, Justin something,† whom I met with her a year ago, one of the handsomest boys I have ever seen. Fair, blue eyes, wonderful brow and eyebrows, straight nose and chin, an Adonis. Darling Woman beaming and providing delicious Lady Redesdale food.

Wednesday, 27th March

Walking back to the car from shopping, I was stopped in the Circus by a lady with a dog on a long lead. She asked, 'Can you tell me where there is a doctor?' I said I really didn't know. Was it a particular doctor in these parts she wanted, or any doctor? Was it urgent? 'Oh, do come here,' she shouted at the dog, pulling at the lead, adding, 'I don't know what is the matter with her today, I really don't.' 'Is it a vet you are wanting, Madam?' I asked politely. 'What's a vet?' she asked. 'A dog's doctor,' I answered. 'No, of course not,' she said. 'A doctor, mind.' I hesitated, then had a bright idea. 'I would ask, if I were you, at that door with the large sign if they know of a doctor. They are sure to. It's a nursing home.' 'A home? I don't want a home,' she said, looking rather angry. 'Are you suggesting, my man, that I ought to go into a home? Ha! I suppose you think I ought to go into a mental home. Well, you can take that back. None of your cheek.' 'I was only trying to help,' I said plaintively. 'Do you, or do you not, know where there is a doctor?' she said again. 'I am very sorry, Madam, I don't.' 'You wouldn't,' she said, and stumped off.

---

* James Charteris, Lord Neidpath (b. 1948); eldest son and heir of 12th Earl of Wemyss; owner of Stanway, Gloucestershire (see 23 May 1987); m. 1st 1983–7 Catherine, dau. of Hon. Jonathan Guinness (later 3rd Baron Moyne), 2nd 1995 Amanda Feilding.

† This was a distant family connection of the Mitford sisters, whose uncle Rupert Mitford had married Justin's widowed grandmother; Pamela was devoted to him as 'the son she never had'.

Wednesday, 3rd April

Derry [Moore] came to Bath and wasted my whole day photograph-ing the Library. I fear I was not very nice to him. Not his fault. I don't consider that photographers today can be called artists. He took about fifty snaps of me reading at my writing table, one of which may be passable. This is not art. Cecil Beaton used to take one studied photograph with an old Brownie.

Thursday, 4th April

Eardley [Knollys] lunched. Says he is all but cured. Asked how I felt. I said eternally tired. He said he did not feel tired at all.

Wednesday, 10th April

Watched an hour-long television programme about Mick Jagger last night. I could not look at the flashbacks of his performances, the deafening row, obscenity of gesture and grimace. But when inter-viewed he was fascinating. He has beautiful hands with long expres-sive fingers. His face extremely mobile, eyes and eyebrows speaking as much as that ugly mouth. Most attractive profile. Was wearing a yellow sleeveless pullover, showing off bare, snake-like arms. I can understand the teenage adoration. He was modest about his achieve-ments, but refused to give his views on life and politics. I think he is a sort of genius, difficult to define. The vivacity, lack of self, projec-tion of self into any part. When reciting Shakespeare he was excellent. He could have immense power for good, but I suppose *The Times* is right in saying that he is 'insufficiently conscious of his social respon-sibilities'.

I heard from Bruce [Hunter] today that Sidgwick & Jackson* have turned down my novel, damn them. The third rejection, after Chatto's and Faber's. He is now going to try Weidenfeld. I do not think it is a bad book, and am furious with the three refusers. I shall never do anything to oblige them, if requested, which is unlikely.

---

* Publishers of J.L.-M's forthcoming biography of 2nd Viscount Esher.

Tuesday, 16th April

Caroline is in a dreadful state of anxiety about the Queen's lunching at the House on Sunday. Can't sleep for worrying. Princess Michael* not invited, as the Queen does not like her, and was asked instead to the Saturday stand-up luncheon. Princess M. accepted and said, 'No doubt you are expecting me to the luncheon on Sunday too?' 'Oh yes, of course,' said C. When she told David he was furious. He refuses to have her on his left, the Queen being on his right. Is praying that Mary Beaufort will decide to lunch so he can have her on his left, but Mary is unpredictable.

The cheap press is full of the wicked discovery that Princess Michael's father was a Nazi.† This is unfair, for she was only a child when the war was over, and her mother left her father because of his Nazism. And had Hitler taken control of this country, would not 90 per cent of the population have been Nazis? The recent behaviour of the miners,‡ their violence and brutality against those who did not join their strike, convinces me that the English are no better than the Germans, only more hypocritical.

Tuesday, 7th May

Got back from Ravello [Calabria] on Saturday, parting with Eardley at Victoria. I think he enjoyed it in spite of beastly weather. I think we renewed our old friendship. It has never been broken, or even bruised; but of late has declined. Although we got on very well, something was lacking. Some spark. He is so immersed in his love for Mattei that I feel he has little room for others. And I must confess that I too am more indifferent to those of my old friends who survive. I also sense in E. a slight disapproval, even mockery of me. When he

---

* Baroness Marie-Christine von Reibnitz (b. 1945), m. (2nd) 1978 HRH Prince Michael of Kent (b. 1942).

† The press had revealed that Princess Michael's father, Gunther von Reibnitz, who had died in Mozambique in 1983 aged eighty-nine, had served in the SS: it was said that he had been responsible for 'liquidating undesirables' in a region of wartime Czechoslovakia.

‡ The year-long official strike of the National Union of Mineworkers had collapsed in March 1985.

says, 'Who would have thought that *you* would be remembered for your books whereas poor Raymond,* that brilliant and erudite critic, will be forgotten', I am not taken in.

Monday, 13th May

The field in front of Lansdown Crescent now golden with buttercups against fresh, emerald grass. A scattering of fat brown sheep. Only one cuckoo heard this spring, singing in distant Allen Grove. It is depressing that we should practically have eliminated this magical bird.

Tuesday, 21st May

Had a strange dream last night. Met Desmond [Parsons] wearing a dressing-gown loosely around the body, walking along a beach. He looking his most beautiful, but sombre, not teasing. 'Come to bed,' he said, putting his arm around me while we strolled. 'No, I can't,' I replied, and burst into tears. A similar dream to one I had about Tom [Mitford].† Something to do with my castration? Signifying absence of love, inability to consummate, or what?

Sunday, 16th June

A high-spirited luncheon here, with the Nico Hendersons and Patricia Hambleden and David Herbert.‡ Nico a curiously ungainly and untidy man, always with shirt collar too big and overlapping his jacket, but extremely quick and clever. Treated me as an equal, rather nice of him. She a whimsy semi-Bohemian, wearing frilly high shirt collar, scooped grey hair; likewise plain, with long, ungainly knitted dress, but bright. They talked amusingly of Garrett [Drogheda], but both get him wrong. They say he is arrogant, selfish and difficult.

---

* Raymond Mortimer (1895–1980); literary reviewer and sometime lover of Harold Nicolson.

† Tom Mitford and Desmond Parsons were J.L.-M.'s two great Eton loves.

‡ Lady Patricia Herbert (d. 1994), dau. of 15th Earl of Pembroke, m. 1928 3rd Viscount Hambleden; her brother Hon. David Herbert (1908–95), Eton contemporary of J.L.-M. now living in Tangier.

He is difficult, but they do not understand he n... ...
to be teased back. His cheekiness is part of his cha...
ted that the Queen Mother was not pleased the othe...
elbow raised by G. with the request that she should 'gi...
wave'. You can't take the slightest liberty with royals, w...
their presence a bore and a blight at social gatherings. They h...
forgotten or forgiven G's farewell address from the stage of ... ent
Garden – we were present in the audience – when he told the Royal
Family in their Box that he had put on the lightest music for their
benefit and hoped in future they might patronise serious music rather
more. Yet the Q.M. says she is frightened of Garrett, fearing his
tongue, no doubt. Nico has invented a portmanteau word which
applies to people like Garrett and Derek Hill, who are keenly sensitive
about their own feelings while treading on the toes of others. It is
'mimophant'. The mimosa is reputed to curl up when touched; the
elephant – well!

Monday, 15th July

Ian [McCallum] believes Rory [Cameron]* is dying of Aids. This has
been denied; but there is no reason, alas, why it should not be so. M.
says many more people than one would suspect have died of this
ghastly thing, or will die within the next twelve months. I hope I am
immune. But at night, while tucked up in bed, I sometimes feel I
am dying from sheer weakness. Always at night, when relaxed, not in
the daytime.

At 4.30 today I listened to the first instalment of *Another Self* on
Radio 4, with mixed feelings. The reader, Peter Howell, has a good
voice, unbedint,† to which one can take no exception – though he
sometimes puts the emphasis on the wrong word, eliminating irony.
He has edited the passages very well. I was nevertheless surprised by
certain things which I had forgotten. Each reading lasts twenty

---

* Roderick Cameron (1914–85), garden designer and travel writer living in South
of France, old friend of A.L.-M.; both he and Ian McCallum died of Aids.
† 'Bedint' meant 'common' in the private language of Harold Nicolson and Vita
Sackville-West.

...s, quite a long stretch. I dare say the remaining eight will cause me embarrassment.

Tuesday, 16th July

A girl from the BBC, Sandra Jones, came from London to interview me about a new documentary series, *Now the War is Over*. Stayed an hour. Had neither tape recorder nor notebook. Doubt whether she will remember much of our conversation. Wanted to know from me how the landed gentry reacted to Attlee's government. I told her the South Bank exhibition elevated our spirits – the prettiness, the jollity, the lights. We imagined at the time that contemporary architecture would take a turn for the better. I said a bloodless revolution had taken place in my time. The gentry feared they would be ousted by the barbaric proletariat, without taste or a sense of historical continuity. True in some ways, but not in others, for the barbarians have often proved themselves more enlightened than the philistine, sport-loving gentry. But I stressed the worst things to my mind – the spread of Communism throughout Europe (did our defeat of Hitler bring betterment?), and the ruination of the face of the Continent, especially England and Italy, by wires, concrete, bad building development, motorways, etc.

Friday, 19th July

Daphne Moore asked two nights ago if we knew anyone who would take on Mary Beaufort's parrot, now that Mary was bedridden and would never get downstairs again. She said that Mary once told her that her father, Lord Cambridge, owned a parrot which had belonged to King George III, his great-grandfather. So there is someone just alive today who remembers a creature owned by George III.[*]

We are desperately sad about Rory. Daniele Waterpark,[†] who has just returned from Ménèrbes [South of France], rang A. to say there

---

[*] This is quite possible: parrots have been known to live for more than eighty years.
[†] Daniele Girche; m. 1951 Caryll Cavendish, 7th Baron Waterpark (half-brother of Rory Cameron).

is no question he has got Aids, and is dying. Rory, so fastidious, so clean, scented, dandified, so hating squalor, such a health maniac. It is very tragic. Last night we also learnt some other terrible news, a calamity that has befallen one of A's grandchildren, which she has sworn me not to reveal even to my diary. It makes my blood boil that this child should have to submit to such a thing, that such monsters roam the streets.

Sunday, 21st July

The Times consistently refuses to publish my letters, and then months later I see it has published others along the same lines as my rejected ones. For instance, about six months ago, when the public was urged to send money for famine relief in Ethiopia, I wrote suggesting that every package of food should include a packet of The Pill. This was considered in bad taste. Now I read in several papers, including *The Times*, that food packages are a mere drop in the ocean, and that the only solution to the problem is a reduction of the black population in African countries where trees are cut down for firewood, nature is despoiled for food, and deserts are increasing with the increase of people. What fools people are, and what damage left-wing sentimentalists are inflicting upon the world.

Wednesday, 24th July

Delivered to Sheila Birkenhead's* house the little marble bust of Shelley which I bought in 1958 at the Cothelstone House sale of the Esdailes in Somerset, on the death of Will Esdaile, Shelley's great-grandson.† I am rather sorry to get rid of it but promised that it should

---

* Hon. Sheila Berry (1913–92), dau. of 1st Viscount Camrose; m. 1935 Frederick Smith, 2nd Earl of Birkenhead (1907–75); Chairman of Keats–Shelley Association from 1977.

† J.L.-M. had visited Esdaile at Cothelstone in June 1953, when he succeeded in persuading him to allow the copying of a notebook containing unpublished poems by Shelley. He told J.L.-M.: 'You must understand that until the last few years Shelley's name has never been mentioned in my family. He treated my great-grandmother abominably.'

go to Keats' House in Rome. Could it possibly have belonged to Shelley's daughter Ianthe? Or her son, who was a friend of Dowden,[*] S's biographer? Certainly not acquired by Will Esdaile who hated Shelley.

Then to visit poor Rory Cameron in St Mary's Hospital, Paddington. In an extremely bad way. Unable to move hand or foot. Lying on back, propped by pillows, bare, wasted arms over the sheets, pallid white hands. Face razor thin, hollow temples, and that taut, stretched muscle of the neck that betrays a dying man. Eyes staring ahead, expressionless and unnaturally brilliant. Talks in a whisper. Says he likes visitors, but shows no interest or emotion. Dreadful visit for I could not communicate. He does not read, has no radio, just gazes into space. No appetite. I give him about a month. Went on to see M. and talked to him about this appalling scourge.

The librarian of Brooks's, Piers Dixon,[†] nice fellow, said I was the Club's favourite author. My books are borrowed more often than any others taken out by members.

Saturday, 27th July

Motored A. to Heathrow whence she flew to Morocco to stay with David Herbert, for sun and bathing and a holiday from me. I was unable to leave the car, and had such a 'how' little back view of her pulling her heavy suitcase by herself towards the ramp and out of sight. I wondered, as I always do when we part nowadays, whether I would ever see her again, and if I did not, whether this fleeting vision would reduce me to tears for the rest of my days.

A tiresome consequence of my becoming a eunuch last year is that all my trousers have become too short in the leg, owing to my unfortunate obesity. Also the pubic hair under my arms has diminished, which I don't mind. No change in the pitch of my voice that I am aware of. In all other respects a marked improvement. Total disinterest in sex, and enhanced detachment; and where I do love, viz. A. and M., I do so with greater purity of motive and enhanced intensity.

---

[*] Edward Dowden, *The Life of Percy Bysshe Shelley* (1886).
[†] MP (C) for Truro, 1970–4 (b. 1928).

Saturday, 3rd

Colin McMordie* is dead. Am haunted by the thought of that beautiful Adonis, so full of the joys of life, and so exquisite, lying like the figure of Shelley by Onslow in University College, Oxford. Poor Colin.

Lunched today with Angela Yorke† at Forthampton. She lives in a small wing, the Webb part of the house, her son Johnnie‡ and wife now inhabiting the greater part of the Court. An enjoyable gathering, rather to my surprise. Deric Holland-Martin's widow Rosamund,§ charming, and Lady Kleinwort,¶ late of Sezincote, nice old woman who looks frail and seems to be losing her memory. I saw she had difficulty keeping up with her neighbour on the other side, Cecil Gould,** late of National Gallery. He, once so good-looking in the way footmen are handsome, now portly and plain. Very pleased with himself, and full of malice about other museum directors, K. Clark and John Pope-Hennessy.†† The other male, Francis Egerton,‡‡ looks like a blind newt. The moment one thinks one is being a success at a party, one should beware. It usually means that one is being a bore or a show-off, or making a fool of oneself.

Sunday, 4th August

Lunched today with the Lloyd Georges§§ in a posh sort of house which the grandfather would not have liked. Owen L.G. must be

* Expert on early nineteenth-century painting, living in Paris (1948–85); friend of J.L.-M. since 1973, when he was an Oxford postgraduate student.

† Angela Duncan (d. 1988); m. 1937 Gerald Yorke of Forthampton Court, Gloucestershire (1901–83), er bro. of J.L.-M's friend Henry Yorke, who wrote novels as Henry Green (1905–73).

‡ John Yorke (b. 1938); m. 1st 1967 Jean Reynolds, 2nd 1992 Julia Allen.

§ Rosamund Hornby (b. 1914); m. 1951 Admiral Sir Deric Holland-Martin (d. 1977); DBE, 1983.

¶ Elisabeth Forde; m. 1933 Sir Cyril Kleinwort, banker (1905–80).

** Deputy Director of National Gallery, 1973–8 (1918–94).

†† Sir John Pope-Hennessy (1913–94); Chairman of Department of European Painting, Metropolitan Museum of Art, New York, 1977–86; elder brother of James P.-H.

‡‡ Chairman of Mallett & Sons, antique dealers (b. 1917).

§§ Owen, 3rd Earl Lloyd George of Dwyfor (b. 1924); m. (2nd) 1982 Josephine Gordon-Cumming.

...ty, I think. She I hazarded to be bedint until
...d born she was. Friendly woman. When I asked
...aordinary fact of his grandfather sleeping with his
...his premiership and the bloodiest war in history, he
...who knew of it at the time never spoke of it. When
...d Frances Stevenson, someone mentioned that he was
'gla...old man was making an honest woman of her at last'.
Owen, aged 19, didn't have a clue what he meant. He said that,
notwithstanding the liaison, the death of Dame Margaret caused his
break-up.* Huge table, about 15 assembled, including Kenneth Rose,
who served in the Welsh Guards with our host. I liked Owen.
Intelligent, shrewd, unassuming, with a merry eye. My father
would turn in his grave if he knew that his elder son would one day
take a meal from a descendant of L.G., the man most hated by the
squirearchy.

Monday, 5th August

Am reading Hugo Vickers'† life of Cecil Beaton, somewhat hooked.
To begin with I thought Cecil the most lamentable sucker-up and
social climber. He made me feel sick. But underneath that sophistication there is a little boy, bewildered by where his charm has got him.
He was vulnerable as well as tough, gentle as well as vitriolic when his
professional work was assailed.

Saturday, 10th August

A. came to my room this morning while I was writing letters to say
that Mrs Wrightsman‡ (Jayne now to me) had arrived by helicopter
to stay at the big house for the weekend; that this afternoon she was
flying David and Caroline to Cornwall and there was room for one

---

* In 1943 David Lloyd George, later 1st Earl (1863–1945), dismayed his four children
by his 1st wife Dame Margaret (d. 1942) by marrying his long-standing secretary and
mistress Frances Stevenson (d. 1972).
† Writer (b. 1951).
‡ Jayne Larkin; m. as his 2nd wife Charles Wrightsman, President, Standard Oil
(Kansas) 1932–53, art collector, Trustee of Metropolitan Museum, New York.

extra. A. nobly insisted on my going, for last year she joined the party when it flew to Burghley.

We start at 2.15, from the lawn on the east front. A most celestial experience. David sits in front next to the pilot, a smooth-faced young man in his twenties with smart shirt and epaulettes. Caroline, Mrs W. and I in the three seats behind. The cabin is like a sedan chair, or old-fashioned landaulette. The great propellor rotates above, the doors shut like car doors – no safety catches, one could throw oneself out. Little glass sliding windows which open for air. Glass in front down to the pilot's feet. After a little revving we gently rise from the ground. It is The Ascension. One has no feeling of vertigo – just straight, gentle rising. A beautiful day, cloudy and sunny. I just see our house, like a pimple beside the big house. We fly over Lyegrove and Tormarton, leaving Bath on our left. We rise to a thousand feet at most, flying at about 100 m.p.h. Fields swarming with sheep like slugs. Motor-cars like toys, yellow, blue, red, crawling down motorways. Many pylons. I don't always know where we are, but recognise land-marks – the Wellington Monument, Bradleigh Court, Saltram. The country incredibly green after all the rain. Fields show straight paths of the corn-cutting. Many ugly quarries, that at Chipping Sodbury huge and deep like a canyon. Rather noisy and difficult to talk. No feeling of unease or sickness. Gentle swaying. Without the noise it would be like a magic carpet. Within an hour we reach Plymouth, Mount Edgcumbe visible. Distressing how built-up England is, we are never far from a straggling town. Only over Dartmoor is there nothing as far as the eye can see towards the northern horizon. Eerie too. Pilot does not change altitude and we almost graze the hill-tops.

Then Antony comes in sight – on a peninsula two miles from Plymouth. We circle the garden and land in forecourt. David jumps out. I duck the revolving blades. Mrs W. does not get out until they have stopped. Fears for her hair? Sir John Carew-Pole's son Richard[*] now lives in the house. Great charmer. Takes us into house. He and his wife want the mid Victorian portico demolished. I deprecate this

[*] Sir Richard Carew-Pole, 13th Bt (b. 1938); e. s. of Sir John, 12th Bt (1902–93), who donated Antony, where his family had lived for more than 500 years, to N.T.; m. (2nd) 1974 Mary Dawnay.

for it is not bad-looking, and serves a useful purpose in such a draughty place. Look round the beautiful dark house with its portraits of regicides on panelled walls. One of Sir Kenelm Digby before a sunflower, indicating his being a King's man. Good portrait of Charles I at his trial. Sir John, who lives in the grounds, joins us. Charming old man. He and Caroline hug and flirt. Son says, there is someone you know here. Takes me to a pitch dark chamber, where a figure behind an easel with his back to the window turns out to be Edmund Fairfax-Lucy,* painting a series of the rooms. Nice boy with dishevelled hair. We talk of Alice,† who he says is better. We are given tea in the kitchen. I ask Richard C.-P. and Edmund, son and grandson of donors, whether they are pleased that their ancestral homes have been given to the N.T. Richard says it is always nicer to own your own house, but for the house's sake it is a good thing. Should a descendant live at Antony who doesn't like it, he can never break it up. Edmund says that Charlecote would no longer be standing had it not been taken over – or would at best be a hotel for Statford-on-Avon.

We say goodbye, get back into our seats, and within four minutes have crossed the water and landed at Ince Castle (seventeen miles by road). A funny-looking old man in a pyjama suit greets us, with grey hair scooped back and tied in a knot. It is Patsy Boyd.‡ She too gives us tea which we are unable to eat. A nostalgic visit for David, whose father lived at Ince in the Thirties. Attractive four-cornered, turreted house of brick, almost rebuilt inside. Waiting-room taste, Harrod's Hepplewhite furniture. Long passage dominated by large bronze bust of Alan [Lennox-Boyd]. I wonder if Alan took against me after the publication of my first diaries, for I never heard from him again.§

---

* Sir Edmund Fairfax-Lucy, 6th Bt (b. 1945); artist; life tenant of Charlecote Park, Warwickshire, donated by his family to N.T. in 1945; m. 1st 1974 Sylvia Ogden, 2nd 1986 Lady Lucinda Lambton, 3rd 1994 Erica Loane.

† Hon. Alice Buchan (1908–93), dau. of 1st Baron Tweedsmuir (the novelist John Buchan); m. 1933 Brian Cameron-Ramsay-Fairfax-Lucy, later 5th Bt (1898–1974); mother of Sir Edmund.

‡ Lady Patricia Guinness (b. 1918), dau. of 2nd Earl of Iveagh; m. 1938 Alan Lennox-Boyd (1904-83), Conservative politician, cr. Viscount Boyd of Merton, 1960.

§ J.L.-M's diary for 1943 describes the unrequited passion of Lennox-Boyd (then a junior minister in the wartime coalition) for the American soldier Stuart Preston.

More indiscretions about him in forthcoming volume, I fear. We leave after an hour, Caroline saying we must return as her father coming to stay. With the wind behind us we are back by 6.30. Once we see a rainbow ahead. Amazingly, we catch it up. What's more, for several minutes it seems to fly with us, as if we are at the centre of a multi-coloured revolving wheel. Extraordinary experience, during which Caroline writes letters and dozes. How blasé the rich are. Dining with the Beauforts, I ask David how much the jaunt cost Mrs Wrightsman. About £2,000, he thinks. I suppose her journey from London and back costs her the same again. Anyway, I loved my trip.

Wednesday, 21st August

Professor Varma[*] of Canada, an Indian who is an authority on Gothick tales, came to tea, having invited himself months ago. Brought with him a lady whom I made put her name down on paper – Aurelia Duvanel-Hepkema. They wished to 'pay their respects'. A maddening interruption to a difficult passage of my book. They told me two things of interest. In America, people with incurable cancer can have their bodies frozen and kept in deep freezes, to be extracted when a cure for their sort of cancer has been discovered. Then they are to be thawed back into life. Apparently they do not experience the dottiness which is the usual consequence of coma. Next, they told me that Tita, Byron's beloved *gondoliere*,[†] attended Shelley's funeral pyre. Was present at Byron's death, and held the poet in his arms. Then became the servant of Monk Lewis who also died in his arms, of yellow fever while crossing the Atlantic. He then married Disraeli's housemaid, and Dizzy too died in his arms. Tita, who was illiterate despite associating with so many distinguished literary persons, was given a pension by Queen Victoria.[‡] I told them that Tita's grandson, a canon

---

[*] Devendra P. Varma (b. 1923); author of *The Gothic Flame* (1966).

[†] The strapping Tita (Giovanni Batista Falcieri) entered Byron's service in 1818 and remained devoted to him until the poet's death six years later. He was more bodyguard than catamite.

[‡] These details are rather muddled. Lewis (1775–1818) predeceased Byron. It was Dizzy's father who died in Tita's arms, and Tita's widow who received the pension.

of the English Church, sold the ring which Byron gave Tita on his deathbed, which had been given to Byron by his Cambridge boy-love John Edlestone. Jock Murray bought it, and now wears it.

Wednesday, 28th August

Met Eardley at Hungerford, The Bear, at eleven this morning. We walked down the canal to Kintbury where we drank ginger-ale and ate croutons — delicious. Then walked back again. About eight miles in all and I felt weary. Not so Eardley, who was as spry as ever, and would have walked further. From Hungerford we drove to Littlecote, which is to be re-sold next week by the bloody tycoon who bought it lock, stock and barrel from the Wills family last month. It is very dreadful that these mushroom millionaires can speculate in this way with England's heritage. But it is not a nice house, an over-restored rich-man-of-the-Twenties house. Best things are the armour and buff jerkins from Cromwellian times that belonged to the Popham family. Interesting Cromwellian chapel, with pulpit but no altar, and original pews, screen and gallery. Great Hall, with shuffle [-board] table of inordinate length. Pretty library, with nice black Wedgwood plaster-cast busts over the bookcases which I coveted. Long Gallery, with restored ceiling. No, not a satisfactory or an endearing house.

E. is in extremely good form and quite recovered from last year's severe illness. He said he wished someone would write Eddy [Sackville-West]'s* biography. He thinks Eddy's haemophilia gave him a grudge against life, though he persuaded himself that he was iller than he really was. Got on well with women and enjoyed being pampered by them. A good person underneath, though selfish. The pity is that Eddy destroyed his diaries, keeping only a short account of his conversion to Catholicism.

The tranquillity and isolation of canals. We passed along distant stretches of water between a thick drama of trees, poplar, grey willow,

---

* Hon. Edward Sackville-West (1901–65), writer and music critic; Eardley's some-time co-tenant at Long Crichel, Dorset; s. father as 5th Baron Sackville, 1962; a biography by Michael De-la-Noy would shortly be undertaken (published in 1988).

birch. Sometimes a rosy red brick bridge, constructed on a curve, with knapped flint – superb engineering of Regency times. The long tow-path flanked by the brown canal and a hedge of pinkish willow-herb. A world of its own, disturbed by the occasional flight of a moorhen.

Sunday, 1st September

Yesterday was Audrey's* eightieth birthday. How can I reconcile the Audrey I knew and played with at Ribbesford† and Wickhamford with this sweet little octogenarian, with snow-white hair and a pretty face, surrounded by hefty grandchildren? Party at Moorwood,‡ a sort of *Cherry Orchard* occasion, for the house is to be let. Dreary collection of friends and relations – really, the boredom of conversation with such as Alice Witts.§ Are you writing a book now? Well, just finishing something. May I ask what it is about? I fear the subject would mean little to you. Oh do tell, I'm sure it must be most interesting. It's about someone I dare say you've never heard of, few people have. Who? Lord Esher. Who is that? A. says I am foolish to say I am writing at all. So today at the Hollands',¶ if asked, I shall say that, being now senile, I have given up for good.

Tuesday, 3rd September

I am feeling tired and unwell. Yesterday morning, sitting at my table typing out the fair copy of Regy, I had twinges in the bladder, and wondered whether it might be the dreaded return of cancer. As the

---

* J.L.-M's sister Audrey Stevens (1905–90); m. 1st Hon. Matthew Arthur (later 3rd Baron Glenarthur), 2nd Cecil ('Tony') Stevens.

† Ribbesford House near Bewdley, Worcestershire; home of J.L.-M's paternal grandmother, where he and his siblings lived during the First World War.

‡ Moorwood House, Gloucestershire; ancestral seat of Audrey's son-in-law Ted Robinson (widower of her daughter Prudence [d. 1976] and father of her grandsons Henry, Nicholas and Richard) who had died in March that year.

§ Second cousin (*née* Wrigley) of J.L.-M (1902–90) – see note p.460.

¶ Sir Guy Holland, 3rd Bt (1918–2002); farmer and art dealer, who held an annual concert in aid of the National Art Collections Fund; m. 1945 Joan Street.

day wore on, it passed. Indeed, as the day goes on I always feel better. I just hope I may finish Regy. I doubt whether I shall have the energy or enthusiasm to start another book.

Cecil Beaton had a shock looking at himself in the glass to find that his upper lip had become strangely long. This has happened to me. I used to wonder at Aunt Dorothy's* upper lip, and then John Fowler's,† thinking how ugly they were, making them both look like the Ugly [Red] Duchess in Lewis Carroll.

Saturday, 7th September

A lovely, cloudless, golden day. A. went out to a luncheon party and I went for a long walk with Folly down the Gloucester–Sharpness canal, two hours from Slimbridge to Frampton. Dragonflies with brown striped bodies, and peacock butterflies. A wind ruffling the water. A few boats passing when the bridges are wound, not up but round. Talked to a middle-aged couple with largish boat moored. They said you could get to Manchester by canal and the River Severn, and then to Leeds by another canal. Felt pleased with myself, happy that I can still walk six miles.

I wish A. were not so keen on social events. Always inviting people who mean nothing to me and are a great distraction, so that I find it difficult to read or work during weekends at Badminton. I suggested to her this morning that she had no friends and preferred acquaintances. She admitted this was true, that even Freda Berkeley had ceased to be an intimate.

Sunday, 15th September

Death is the end of expectation; that is all. So long as one can look forward one is still living. Total lack of sex, as in my case, does not matter. On the contrary, life is fuller without it.

---

* Dorothy Edwards-Heathcote (d. 1968) m. 1912 J.L.-M's uncle Alec Milne Lees-Milne (d. 1931); as a widow she lived with another woman, grew a moustache and smoked a pipe.
† Interior decorator (1906–77).

Drama in the village. Poor Daphers – Daphne Moore – took 90 sleeping tablets and walked into the pond. But she did it in the morning when there were workmen about. When she was fished out and taken into the House, the butler Leslie said, 'Mind my clean floor.' She has now more or less recovered in hospital, but has told the Vicar she intends to repeat the performance. David Beaufort said he hoped she would be more successful next time. Poor woman, her shame and misery are not assumed.

Wednesday, 18th September

On Sunday afternoon I accompanied A. to Paris by air. There we were met by [David] Mlinaric* and a young colleague – difficult to know whether boy or girl – who dropped me at Temple de la Gloire, Orsay. I had the whole evening and following day alone with Diana [Mosley]. Very rewarding. She is extremely clever and well-read. Sitting with her elegant legs crossed before me, I was reminded of the photograph I took of her at Asthall when she was sixteen. Certainly beautiful, though her skin much creased. We talked of everything – her parents, her sisters, Tom, and of course Nancy. She gave me a proof copy of Selina's biography to read. Too much about early life, much of it silly and shaming. Whenever Nancy ventures upon an opinion it is child-ish, whereas Diana's views are always reasoned. More interesting when N. marries the lamentable Prod [Peter Rodd]. But oh! her love for the pock-marked Colonel† is sad. D. talked to me of Hitler. I said I regarded him as a mountebank, with his Charlie Chaplin moustache and swagger. She said he was not vulgar, but tender and understand-ing. His ability to charm and to lead was superhuman – like that other cad, Napoleon. On the second night we were joined for dinner by Ali and Cha,‡ and A. arrived from Amboise, dog-tired.

---

* Interior decorator (b. 1939), then engaged at Mick Jagger's property at Amboise where A.L.-M. was creating the garden.
† Gaston Palewski (1901–84); principal wartime aide of General de Gaulle and the great (and largely unrequited) love of Nancy Mitford's life.
‡ Alexander Mosley (1938–2005); Paris publisher, er son of Hon. Diana Mitford by her 2nd marriage to Sir Oswald Mosley; m. 1975 Charlotte Marten.

Thursday, 19th September

Last night after dinner David Hicks[*] telephoned to say Rory had died at 7.30. A. pretended she knew already – so odd of her. She adored Rory and cherished the knowledge that she had known him years before David and other grand and rich friends. This morning, poor Gilbert[†] telephoned from Ménèrbes, saying that he had spent the whole night with Rory on his bed, unable to believe he was dead.

Wednesday, 25th September

Yesterday I went to London for the day. Bruce Hunter lunched with me at Brooks's. So nice, gentle and quizzical. Takes knowing. How I now wish I had gone to him with every book. As it is he is going to take over all my books retrospectively, as it were, with paperback reissues in mind. Bruce asked if I would consider doing an 'album' – the fashion these days – on Tony Powell's *Dance to the Music of Time*, describing all the books and paintings mentioned therein. Extraordinary idea. I explained that I liked Tony immensely but his novels left me cold.

Saturday, 28th September

Season of mists and mellow fruitfulness. Beautiful Indian summer. The sun takes hours to force its way through, but it is then very hot, and the dogs pant when I take them blackberrying in Westonbirt. Poor little Honey is in decline, suffering from heart murmur. The other darling unaffected as yet, in fine fettle. Last night A. and I leant out of my bedroom window and heard one owl talking to another, somewhere in the garden of the big house. The moon was full, percolating through the cedar trees. We thought it moving to hear an owl hoot – to such a pass have things come, with the elimination of natural creatures.

---

[*] Interior decorator (1929–1998); m. 1960 Lady Pamela, yr dau. of 1st Earl Mountbatten of Burma.
[†] Rory Cameron's French lover.

Tuesday, 15th October

Lunching at Brooks's today I sat next to Alan Clark.* Couldn't remember his Christian name at first, but mercifully did so in time to insert it into a sentence. He said he was bored to tears with his work. I said he could always chuck being an MP. He said it wasn't quite as easy as all that. I asked whether he was a Minister. He said, 'Yes, I am, and I can't just up-sticks. What I would like is to go to the Foreign Office.' I suggested he ask Mrs Thatcher. He said, 'You don't know her, evidently.' We talked about Philip Sassoon, as I recently read K's description of staying with him at Port Lympne. Alan remembers him well. He was sweet to children. Had a smooth face, looked incredibly young, walked on the tips of his toes and impressed one as being a person of importance. He was adored by Alan's mother Jane, who learnt the social graces from him, having been without them at the time of her marriage. Strange thing for a son to say. On getting home and reading *The Times* I saw Alan was in the news, disagreeing with the latest edict enjoining firms to employ more blacks. Alan quite rightly argues that businesses to flourish must employ the best staff irrespective of ethnic considerations.

Thursday, 21st November

From 30 October to 15 November we were in the USA.† It was not much of an adventure. On reflection I enjoyed it, but while I was there I counted the days till we could return. Too much movement. In Washington we stayed at the Hilton and were entertained at the opening of the Treasures of British Country Houses exhibition,‡ the

---

* Hon. Alan Clark (1931–99), er s. of Baron Clark of Saltwood ('K.' Clark); writer and Conservative politician, then a junior minister at the Department of Employment; he later achieved celebrity as a diarist, declaring J.L.-M. to be his favourite exponent of that art.

† This was J.L.-M's only visit to America.

‡ The exhibition *Treasure Houses of Britain: Five Hundred Years of Private Patronage and Art Collecting* took place at the National Gallery in Washington from November 1985 to March 1986. It was conceived and organised by Gervase Jackson-Stops (who took leave from his job at the N.T.) and the Gallery's Director, J. Carter Brown (1934–2002). It received the patronage of the Prince of Wales, and the financial sponsorship

best loan exhibition I have ever seen. Then a bus tour with some sixty of the lenders to Virginia country houses, Williamsburg, Monticello, etc. Beautiful country, deep, vivid autumn colours. Three nights in Philadelphia with Henry McIlhenny* in his sumptuous triple house crammed with art treasures. Then New York for four days. I liked Washington, a beautiful city, but did not care for NY apart from the 'scrapers. The canyon effect of the streets. Went up the World Trade Center.† Good architecture, of straight perpendicular, close lines and ogival tops to panels. Only lacking a spire to alleviate flat skyline. Became immersed in picture galleries – National Gallery in Washington, Philadelphia (where most exhibits given by Henry), Metropolitan and Frick in New York. Weather pretty bad throughout visit. Social events most tedious. Americans uniformly kind and welcoming, but *gushing*. Oh the gush, wore me out. Dined one night in NY with John Pope-Hennessy, who I hoped had not read *Midway* where I criticise his mother.‡ Stiff occasion. But lovely to see Kay Hallé§ in Georgetown, who is eighty but looks hardly changed. Johnnie [Churchill] staying with her, a silent pudding for she will not let him drink in her house. On leaving I felt a pang for I do not think I shall see either of these beloved old friends again.

We had special VIP treatment on return journey which was not tiring. Nevertheless it took several days to adjust sleep. Came back to find reviews of *Midway* appearing, but could not bring myself to read them. On Tuesday attended poor Rory's memorial service in Grosvenor Chapel at which I read a lesson – chosen for me – from Revelation.

---

of the Ford Motor Company. Some seven hundred objects were lent by some two hundred private owners. The lenders, along with a host of distinguished guests including the J.L.-Ms, were fêted at the glittering opening ceremonies, which included a dinner at the Gallery, official receptions at the White House and Capitol, and a tour of Virginia country houses.

* Henry P. McIlhenny (1910–86); art collector, philanthropist and *bon vivant*; Curator of the Decorative Arts, Philadelphia Museum of Art, 1935–63; owner of Glenveagh Castle, Co. Donegal.

† Destroyed by terrorist action on 11 September 2001.

‡ Dame Una Pope-Hennessy (1876–1949), writer and bluestocking; Jim found her forbidding and commented on her self-centredness.

§ Pre-war American friend of J.L.-M. who wrote books on Churchill family (d. 1992).

Spent some time with dear M., our relations on the happiest plane. We confide in each other entirely. Am concerned about his debauches which divert him from work. The most cheering news is from Bruce Hunter who thinks Anthony Blond* is interested in my novel – possibly thanks to the good offices of Desmond Briggs† to whom I mentioned it. After seven rejections out of hand, this is encouraging. Have told Bruce that, if Blond reject, we had better give up.

Friday, 22nd November

Stayed the night with the Eshers‡ in their Tower [at Watlington Park, Oxfordshire]. Received with open arms. With intervals for tea and dinner, I went through the Regy typescript with Lionel. He was full of praise, but had several minor but helpful corrections, and a few major objections to what he called 'smut' – notably references to Regy's vicarious enjoyment of his son's affairs at Eton.§ I remonstrated, but feebly, that we must be careful not to overlook his homosexuality, for without reference to it readers would find him a stuffed shirt. Finally I gave way. He called up Christian and read the offending passages to her and she (who never contradicts him) agreed. I understand his objections, for Regy was his grandfather, though all the passages he made me remove had already been used by Oliver in his unpublished book.¶ I now have a week's work of rewriting, and long to get rid of Regy.

---

* Bisexual publisher (1928–2008).

† Anthony Blond's former publishing partner (1931–2002); novelist (as Rosamond Fitzroy); a JP for Wiltshire; he and his partner Ian Dixon became great friends of J.L.-M's in later years.

‡ Lionel Brett, 4th Viscount Esher (b. 1913); architect; m. 1935 Christian Pike. It was at his invitation that J.L.-M had undertaken the biography of his grandfather, Reginald, 2nd Viscount (1852–1930). His father, Oliver, 3rd Viscount (1881–1963), had been Chairman of Historic Buildings Committee of N.T., of which J.L.-M. was Secretary in the 1940s.

§ As J.L.-M. was to describe in his biography, Reginald Esher had an incestuous relationship with his younger son Hon. Maurice Brett (1882–1934).

¶ Oliver had been amazed, on inheriting his father's papers, to learn about his secret homosexual life, and had written a monograph on the subject, which Lionel had shown to J.L.-M.

In the morning motored to Oxford. Attended memorial service to Colin McMordie in Oriel Chapel. This beautiful building lit by candlelight was filled with young friends of Colin. John Martin Robinson[*] read an address – very good, what I could hear. We were invited to go to the Common Room afterwards but I sloped off. I didn't want to meet Colin's father and see what the beautiful Colin might have become.

Friday, 6th December

At Euston, joined Dudley Dodd,[†] Bobby Gore[‡] and Brinsley Ford[§] and trained to Bangor, North Wales. They produced delicious pheasant sandwiches and wine, which we consumed at a table for four. Much merriment. They stay at Beaumaris Hotel, I with the Douglas-Pennants.[¶] Talk over tea a strain owing to Lady Janet's extreme shyness. Yet she is a nice woman. We drove to Penrhyn Castle for great dinner given to the Douglas-Pennants to thank for all they have done for the National Trust. It was 1951 when I first stayed with them, and I am flattered that they should have asked for me to be included in the celebration. Penrhyn much improved by hanging of some excellent pictures, notably of superb Rembrandt over fireplace in the breakfast room. I sat between Lady Williams-Bulkeley[**] and Lady Anglesey.[††] Latter fascinating and beautiful. Spoke frankly about the Nicolsons, saying there was never any

---

[*] Architectural historian and genealogist (b. 1948); Librarian to Duke of Norfolk, Fitzalan Pursuivant of Arms (later Maltravers Herald of Arms) Extraordinary, and Vice-Chairman of Georgian Group; a friend of Colin McMordie who had been his fellow research student at Oxford.

[†] Deputy Historic Buildings Secretary of N.T., 1981–2000 (b. 1947).

[‡] Francis St John Gore (b. 1921); adviser on pictures to N.T., 1956–86; Historic Buildings Secretary, 1973–81.

[§] Sir Brinsley Ford (1908–99); sometime Trustee of National Gallery, Chairman of National Art Collections Fund, and Hon. Adviser on Paintings to N.T..

[¶] Donors during the 1950s of the neo-Norman Penrhyn Castle and a large area of Snowdonia to the N.T.

[**] Renée Neave; m. 1938 Sir Richard Williams-Bulkeley, 13th Bt.

[††] Shirley Morgan; m. 1948 Henry Paget, 7th Marquess of Anglesey (b. 1922), military historian.

likelihood of her marrying Nigel.* She thinks he will never write a great book, good writer though he be. He will be remembered for the faultless editor he is. Lord A. came up in a very noisy, jolly manner, laughing too loud for ease, in a subtly patronising way which I don't like. Extreme friendliness amounts to condescension. He was patronising about the Douglas-Pennant boy, yet well informed about his family. Talking and gesticulating with Brinsley, the tiny boy looked to me like a figure in a Thomas Patch conversation piece.

Saturday, 14th December

Today motored to Stourhead to meet Audrey at The Spreadeagle, where we lunched off soup, toasted sandwiches and coffee. Poor A., her last King Charles died yesterday. She was brave and showed no sign of distress, whereas I would have been in tears. On parting I said, so as not to let her suppose that I did not sympathise deeply, how sorry I felt for her. Without a tremor, she replied, 'Yes, when one lives absolutely alone and sometimes sees no one to talk to for a week, one does miss one's constant companion.' She hates her cottage in Penselwood, wishes she had taken a flat in Cirencester to be near other old fogies, and thought she might still take one, though this seems unlikely at eighty. She said she felt fairly well, but had so little to look forward to. Poor little Audrey, she has always wrung my heart-strings.

Tuesday, 17th December

Jamie Fergusson† came to lunch in Bath where he was shopping around old book stalls. He is a clever and civilised young man, more so than any of my family, all of whom, save Nick [Robinson], are utter barbarians and bore me stiff. Then I went to London. Stayed with J[ohn] K[enworthy]-B[rowne] who kindly met me at Paddington,

---

* Soldier, politician, writer and journalist (1917–2004), yr son of Harold Nicolson and Vita Sackville-West, who had invited J.L.-M. to write his father's biography in 1976; lived at Sissinghurst Castle, Kent, which he had donated to the N.T. in 1968.
† Antiquarian bookseller (b. 1953) and founding obituaries editor of the *Independent*, whose father was a second cousin of J.L.-M.

and the following morning motored me to Brooks's. Very sweet and solicitous he was. Still working on Paxton.* I have never heard of any scholar taking so much trouble over detail as he.

Wednesday, 18th December

Carried my Regy typescript to Sidgwick & Jackson, having telephoned last week to forewarn Mr Robert Smith, my new editor. Hateful dealing with new people who know not my ways, probably not my name even. I reached the door on which a notice directed me to another entrance in Museum Street. I suppose I was looking around while walking, for I stumbled on the pavement and fell headlong into the gutter. Lay there a few seconds, assessing situation. Decided I was not badly hurt, and picked myself up. Contents of my pockets were strewn in the gutter, but not so my typescript, which remained in its cardboard box. Arrived shaken, hands cut, clothes torn, face dirty. Surprised lady directed me to lavatory. No concern. When I indicated the typescript, she said coolly, 'Just put it down there, will you.' After four years' intensive labour, the precious thing was accepted as though it might be an unwelcome Christmas card. God knows if it will even reach Mr Smith. How I hate Regy. Fed up with him. And the more I revise, the more corrections I find to make. I hope to spend the next month without hearing of him. But when I do, no doubt it will be to be asked to cut the book down by a third.

I then went, sent by Bruce Hunter, to Waterstone's, a new bookshop and publishing enterprise run by young persons. Very laudable. Was delighted to hear they intend to open a shop in Bath. They asked if I would like to write a biography for them of Robert Byron, Guy Burgess,† Brian Howard‡ or E.F. Benson.§ I said 'No' to all these

---

* Sir Joseph Paxton (1803–65); gardener and architect, known for his design of the Crystal Palace and his work at Chatsworth.

† Diplomatist and traitor (1910–63), with whom J.L.-M. had been at Lockers Park preparatory school; a biography was eventually undertaken by Andrew Lownie.

‡ Aesthete (1905–58), the model for Anthony Blanche in *Brideshead Revisited*, already the subject of an enormous biographical anthology by Marie-Jaqueline Lancaster, *Portrait of a Failure* (1968).

§ Novelist and archaeologist (1867–1940), whose 'Tilling' novels had recently been successfully adapted for television; a biography by Brian Masters appeared in 1991.

people, as I liked none of them except Robert, and him not much. They then asked whom I *would* like to write about. I said a romantic figure such as Byron, Beckford, or Ludwig of Bavaria, on all of whom there are too many books already. Or Gustav III of Sweden, who is insufficiently well-known and would involve me in language difficulties. Then (put up to it by Bruce, no doubt) they talked of reprinting *Roman Mornings* [1956] and getting me to do a sequel, *Venetian Evenings*. Could I write the Venice book in nine months? Impossible, I said, for though I know Venice well, much reading would be necessary. But I promised to think about it. The truth is I feel worn out mentally, without a spark left inside me. Yet I don't wish to have no work to do.

Lunched with Geoffrey Houghton-Brown* in South Kensington. He much aged, lined and grey, and resigned to nothingness. Very sweet, but without purpose. After leaving Geoffrey, went to see Emily and Dolly.† A rude shock. Emily broke her leg ten months ago and is now a bent, lop-sided, tiny old lady leaning heavily on a stick. Pitiable in their horrid little cabin on fifth floor of Sutton Estate. Still waiting for modernised flat on ground floor. I left them with dreadful feelings of guilt and sadness. Called on M. on way to Paddington. Hardly had we begun talking when his father entered. A tall, broad, distinguished man, but with certain vacant look in the eye. Not interested in any subject raised. Something very wrong. M. is worried. On train I felt sad – over the wrecks I had seen today, over my own disintegration in body and mind, and the fact that I am a bore to M. His sweetness never relaxes, but I am a lame dog to him.

Sunday, 29th December

Christmas not yet over. I went to Bath to work on Friday, but all shops shut, and that feeling of emptiness in the city. Until New Year festivities are over things won't be normal.

---

* Antique dealer and dilettante (1903–93), in whose house in Thurloe Square, South Kensington, J.L.-M. had kept a flat from 1946 to 1961.
† The sisters Emily and Dolly Bradford, servants who had looked after J.L.-M. in Thurloe Square.

Coming out of church at Acton Turville this morning, I fell on a sheet of concealed black ice over concrete. Tom [Gibson] full of solicitude and rushed to my assistance. But I was all right, except for some stiffness in right arm; returned home, and took the dogs for a walk on the Slates. I seem unable to keep upright these days, and may soon break a limb.

Clarissa [Luke] stayed with us for Christmas, without husband, whom she has at last discarded, and without children. A dear goose. Could not remember the name of her mother-in-law. On Boxing Day the Henry Robinsons* brought their five-week-old son. I was bidden to admire the little creature, resembling a baby piglet. It was lain on my bed upstairs. After luncheon I held it while we were photographed. The children think it astonishing to have a great-great-uncle and nephew immortalised together. I think it is revolting.

Tuesday, 31st December

It is odd to think that typescripts of two of my books (Regy and novel) are with two different publishers, while the synopsis of another book (Venice) is with a third. I feel drained and incapable of writing anything again. My fall last Sunday has given me much pain in left leg and right arm. I am perpetually tired. Would like to hibernate and not leave my bed until the spring comes.

---

* The Robinson brothers – Henry (b. 1953; m. 1984 Susan Faulkner), Nicholas (b. 1955) and Richard (b. 1957) – were J.L.-M's great-nephews, grandsons of his sister Audrey, and the relations with whom he felt the greatest affinity. Henry was a farmer; Nicholas, a publisher; Richard, a banker. Henry's son, first of the new generation, was Alexander Robinson – see 16 February 1986.

1986

1986

Went to Charlecote [Warwickshire] for wedding party of Edmund Fairfax-Lucy to Lucy Lambton, Harrod that was.[*] She is a very positive and determined girl and I wonder if she won't bulldoze that nice, vague little Edmund, who is a painter first and foremost. About two hundred people there. Never seen such a scrum. I went for old times' sake, A. because she likes any party. A hundred old faces, N.T. and non-N.T. Billa [Harrod] present.[†] Alice F.-L. looking perfectly well, and affirming that she was so in spite of her appalling accident, but wearing a hat and dark glasses. She has always been neurotic, hiding behind protection. Lady Lambton, the bride's mother, tried to dress like Henry VIII and succeeded, for she has a large florid face. Wore a dress that looked like ermine, and a hat such as the monarch wore in the Holbein portrait, pulled down one side of her head, and gloves of dark blue velvet given to her by David Somerset. I said how generous David was. 'Yes, but I too give expensive presents,' she said. She was sitting on a piano stool in the library, and to hear her I had to kneel on the ground. 'Is this a proposal?' she asked. Amusing woman, whom I had not met before; she and John Wilton[‡] were inseparable years ago.

---

[*] Lady Lucinda Lambton (b. 1943); dau. of Antony ('Tony') Lambton (1922–2006; succeeded as 6th Earl of Durham 1970 and disclaimed peerages but continued to use courtesy title of Viscount Lambton; resigned as MP and junior defence minister 1973 after 'call girl affair'; m. 1942 Belinda 'Bindy' Blew-Jones [1921–2003]); photographer, writer and broadcaster; m. 1st 1965 Henry Harrod, 2nd 1986 Sir Edmund Fairfax-Lucy, 6th Bt, 3rd 1991 Sir Peregrine Worsthorne.

[†] She was the bride's former mother-in-law.

[‡] John Egerton, 4th Earl of Wilton (1921–99); intimate of J.L.-M. during 1940s; m. 1962 Diana Galway.

Wednesday, 15th January

I asked Helen Dashwood* to lunch with me at Claridge's yesterday, after Freda Berkeley told me how crippled she was. She was rather pathetic, the old fire subdued. Conversation not easy because she was inattentive, though not gaga. She is very immobile, shuffles with two sticks. Occasional sparks in that she is still beastly to porters and taxi drivers. I had to smile and joke with them to placate. When I took her back to her flat afterwards, she said she had enjoyed herself, kissed me, and said, 'Now we are chums again, aren't we?' Poor, dear Helen. She is convinced that there is an afterlife and she will be reunited with her loved ones. But won't the loved ones take flight, in flocks?

For dinner I had Selina [Hastings] alone at Brooks's. Conversation never flagged. Her *Nancy Mitford* is doing well. Hamish Hamilton have now asked her to write a biography of Evelyn Waugh and offered an advance of £80,000 which she can't refuse, having no money of her own, she says. I thought there were enough books about Evelyn, but she says there is no straightforward biography, only literary assessments and memoirs by Frankie Donaldson† and Christopher Sykes.‡

Saturday, 18th January

Sanjay, that clever and sensitive assistant of Anthony Blond, telephoned, not with the hoped-for news that a paperback publisher had accepted my novel, but to say that he has had an offer of a better job and leaves his present employment on 1 February. I am delighted for him. So strange that I can communicate with this youth, an Indian and fifty-five years younger than myself, as if we are contemporaries. I can't think of anyone else over so wide a gap with whom I can do this.

---

* Widow of Sir John Dashwood, 10th Bt (1896–1966) of West Wycombe Park, Buckinghamshire, wartime headquarters of N.T., whose foibles J.L.-M. had (to her indignation) described in his wartime diaries (she d. 1989).

† Frances ('Frankie') Lonsdale, writer (1907–94); m. 1935 J.G.S. 'Jack' Donaldson (1907–98), Eton contemporary of J.L.-M., cr. life peer 1967; her *Evelyn Waugh: Portrait of a Country Neighbour* appeared in 1967.

‡ Writer, journalist and broadcaster (1907–86); his *Evelyn Waugh: A Biography* appeared in 1975.

Sunday, 26th January

We dined last night at the House. The Somersets have now completed the Yellow Room, happily keeping the Edwardian gilt curtain boxes and curtains chosen by Duchess Louise.* Pictures re-hung, and my suggestion adopted of putting the young 4th Duke with his tutor over the fireplace. Other paintings fetched from upstairs; they have such a lot of lovely things to draw on. Their taste impeccable, and more David's than Caroline's. It is so lucky for Badminton to have David as proprietor between those two philistines, Master and Harry.†

The Woodrow Wyatts‡ staying. She a pretty Hungarian; he much aged with white hair, shuffling, smoking cigars, over-indulging. Very clever. After dinner he talked about Rupert Murdoch,§ who has accomplished a wizard's victory at *The Times* by sacking the printers and keeping only the electricians. It is sucks to the Sogat Union who have caused so much trouble. A fortune will be saved in production costs, for henceforth only one-seventh of the former staff will be needed. He said my *Last Stuarts*, which he favourably reviewed when it came out [1983], was a first-rate book which had not received justice. I sat next to his daughter,¶ aged seventeen and about to go to Worcester College, Oxford to read history, specialising in the eighteenth century. On being told by her father than I was an expert on the period, the child talked *at* me about Dr Johnson and Wilkes, her chosen subject, impressively but too earnestly.

---

* Louise Harford (d. 1945); m. (2nd) 1895 Henry Fitzroy Somerset, 9th Duke of Beaufort (1847–1924).
† Henry Somerset, Marquess of Worcester (b. 1952); e.s. and heir of 11th Duke of Beaufort.
‡ Sir Woodrow Wyatt (1918–98); former Labour MP; Chairman of Horserace Totalisator Board; cr. life peer, 1987; m. (4th) Verushka Racz.
§ Australian media tycoon (b. 1931). He had bought the *Times* group of newspapers in 1981 and in 1985 moved its headquarters from Fleet Street to Wapping. The printing workers went on strike, refusing to accept the new technology there; but after a year-long battle he forced them to capitulate, thus revolutionising an industry where they had long prevented modernisation.
¶ Petronella Wyatt (b. 1969); journalist; dau. of Sir Woodrow by his 4th marriage.

Monday, 27th January

A film on TV of Molly Keane's* *Time after Time* which I read last year. About a terrible Irish family of three sisters and one brother living in a *délabrée* Victorian house. Haunting story of decadence, genteel poverty, meanness, stealthy little squalors, oh so well told. How I hate the Irish. Must write to congratulate John Gielgud,† who played the brother.

Saturday, 1st February

Managed to get to London on Thursday despite deep snow here, with blocked roads, telephone wires down, etc. No snow in London but a bitter east wind. Stayed in a room on top floor of Brooks's, and dined with Eardley and Richard Shone, E. looking well after latest operation and cooking delicious dinner. Much laughter. On Friday I saw Agnew's exhibition of nineteenth-century watercolours, including some Edward Lears; Wildenstein's exhibition of splendid French impressionist paintings from the collection of the foundress of *Reader's Digest*; then Reynolds at Burlington House. Reynolds knew everyone and was full of culture and erudition but is not a good painter. His portrait of the future Duke of Hamilton who married Beckford's daughter Susan was captioned 'Commissioned by William Beckford, millionaire homosexual snob'. Must complain about this to Secretary of Royal Academy.

At 11.30 I went to see Robert Smith of Sidgwick & Jackson, a nice, decent bald-head of forty, lacking enthusiasm or emotion. Said he had enjoyed my typescript, but admitted he had not yet finished it and was worried about its length. I begged Smith to show it to Frank Longford‡ who had got me to write it in the first place. Smith did say however that they were determined to publish it this year. We discussed the

---

* Mary Nesta Skrine (1905–96); playwright and novelist, friend of John Gielgud, who successfully resumed her writing career in 1980s after an interval of more than twenty years; m. 1938 Robert Keane.

† Actor (1904–2000) with whom J.L.-M. had 'a short-lived affair' in 1930.

‡ Francis Pakenham, 7th Earl of Longford (1905–2001); politician, humanitarian campaigner, writer and publisher, who as Chairman of Sidgwick & Jackson in 1981 had originally suggested that J.L.-M. write life of 2nd Viscount Esher; m. 1931 Elizabeth Harman, writer.

title. He does not like *Viscount Esher With Humble Duty* and suggested *The Power behind the Throne*, which made John Saumarez Smith* squirm when I told him.

Sunday, 2nd February

Dined with Sally Westminster to meet Molly Keane, delightful lady of over eighty though looking sixty. Full of humour and diffidence. Said Chatto's had turned down both *Good Behaviour* and *Time after Time*, silly idiots. She had enjoyed the film, though thought the Jewish cousin overplayed her part. The producer barely asked her advice. A nice, sharp, jolly, Irish country lady, not outstandingly intellectual. Feels deeply about Ireland and hates the Ulstermen, holding them and not the English responsible for Ireland's ills during the past century. She has a good-looking, dumpling face like dear Billa [Harrod]. Must have been very pretty, and is great fun.

Saturday, 15th February

Am reading Proust's *Albertine Disparue*, which in Scott-Moncrieff's translation has the absurd title *The Sweet Cheat Gone*, because of the section on Venice. At times I think it the most boring rubbish I have ever read. I must have read it once before, for I read the whole of Proust at a sitting, so to speak, when I was in the Hospital for Infectious Diseases in the 1930s, Harold [Nicolson] having sent me the lot. Found I had then marked with a pencil certain passages I would mark today. I dare say it is the case that Proust meant boys when he wrote of the girls of 'the little band'. The names he chose – Gilberte, Albertine, Andrée – are boys' name adapted to the feminine, just as an English writer might call his loved ones Frances, Alexandra, etc., in disguise for Francis and Alexander.

Richard Wood,† who dined with us last night, told me that he was once present when Master interviewed a gardener. He told the man that his three conditions for engaging him were that he must be a

---

* Managing Director of G. Heywood Hill Ltd, booksellers in Curzon Street (b. 1943).
† Land agent of Badminton estate.

supporter of fox-hunting, a Conservative, and a member of the Church of England.

Sunday, 16th February

A delicious day at Moorwood. The christening of my great-great-nephew Alexander James Winwood Robinson at Bagendon church by Mr Woodhouse, the old parson retired and great friend of the family. Perishing cold day and east wind. Moving little service. We all clustered round the font, a party of young friends of Henry and Susy, and a few oldies like us, Audrey, and old Willy, who is 85 and told us he had known and served five generations of Robinsons. The child behaved perfectly when a mug of ice cold water from the stream (all taps frozen) was poured over him. Never cried or showed any disapproval of this barbaric treatment. Mr Woodhouse said the child must feel he belongs to this place, *his* place, for he would be the next squire. Luncheon at Farm Cottage. Sat next to niece Dale* and new wife of Terry Faulkner, Susy's brother. I brought a pair of silver hair-brushes engraved with initials, which A. thought an unsuitable present for these days; and I left a long letter to be given to Alexander on his twenty-first birthday, telling him what I remember about our upbringing and our forebears – matters which the young are not interested in until they cease to be young and there is no old member of the family left alive to consult. Listening to the gaiety, fun and laughter of this luncheon I thought how lucky Henry and [his younger brother] Nick are to be parentless and well-off, with a nice house and property and all the responsibility which they assume so happily. If only I had had some money and independence when I was in my late twenties.

Monday, 24th February

Dear Nick [Robinson] lunched with me at Brooks's. I noticed in the shaft of pale sun through a window that he already has a few silver

---

* Dale Stevens (b. 1944); o.c. of J.L.-M's sister Audrey by her 2nd marriage to Cecil ('Tony') Stevens; m. 1964 James Sutton (b. 1940), mechanical engineer, yr s. of Sir Robert Sutton, 8th Bt.

hairs in his otherwise raven head. The hair of the old is seldom silver, rather grey or white, but the odd turned hair in a young head is bright, burnished silver. Nick so sympathetic. Has finally given up smoking, and is eating less in order to keep his figure.

Thursday, 27th March

Maundy Thursday, and a day of mourning indeed. I telephoned Riley the vet who suggested I brought Honey at 6.30. What with Easter on our heels, A. agreed I should take her today – better than further delay and the agony of watching her decline. Riley a saintly man, who bore with my bitter tears which I could not control. I sat in the waiting room with Honey, stroking her neck and ears without daring to look at her. For her it was no worse a visit than many previous ones. Riley came in with syringe in hand and instantly gave her a prick which she did not even feel. In five minutes she was asleep, having lain herself on the floor. I apologised for my emotion. He said it was normal and right and he felt the same over his own dogs' demise. When it was clear she was unconscious, he said, 'You may go now. Just give her a pat.' I did so and kissed her little head, and bolted. This was pre-arranged, for then he would despatch her. A. had gone to Communion in my absence; when she returned, we both shamelessly wept. I said the piteous thing about dogs was their innocence. She said it was their implicit trust in us. Whatever it be, they wring the heart. I felt remorseful over my occasional irritation with Honey, who did have some tiresome habits – not coming in when put out last thing, and other sillinesses. Remorseful about the times I was angry with her and smacked her. *Eheu*, I grieve and am miserable. She was good, good, good, devoid of malice and spite. My companion for over a decade who, until she became incontinent, slept on my bed at nights. The hell of it all.

Thursday, 3rd April

Hugh Massingberd lunched at Brooks's. He is worried about his weight, which has increased from twelve to sixteen stone. Always modest and self-deprecating, yet a delightful man, with humour.

Extremely prolific. Writes regular articles on small squires' houses, reviews for every journal, and does pot-boilers, including one on Kingston Lacy which he wanted to talk to me about. I asked after his uncle, Peter Montgomery.* Alas a cabbage now, and does not recognise him. Told me how bigoted the Irish still were about divorce. He stayed three weeks with his friend Mark Bence-Jones,† whose mother, who lives in the house and has known Hugh all his life, would not address a word to him on account of his divorce and remarriage.

Tuesday, 15th April

Am in blackest depression. Confided in A. last night on way to dine with the Thomas Messels‡ who had William Rosse and his charming young son Patrick§ staying. Earlier I had been to Lacock [Abbey, Wiltshire]¶ where William was opening an exhibition of photographs by his great-grandmother Mary Rosse,** she being an early pioneer, somewhere between Fox Talbot and Mrs Cameron. I stayed only half an hour, and was so overwhelmed by claustrophobia and unknown people talking to me that I fled before the ceremony. A. says it is the relentless appalling weather we have been having, and indeed, there is still a scattering of snow on the fields as I drive to Bath. But it is not that. There is no reason for it.

Billa telephoned yesterday to say that Penelope Betjeman had died in India, as she was getting off her pony on the Himalaya foothills. Just as she would have wished – but oh, the sadness. This morning, Max

---

* Captain Peter Montgomery of Blessingbourne, Co. Tyrone (1909–88); musical conductor and former President of Arts Council for Northern Ireland; Eton contemporary of J.L.-M.
† Writer (b. 1930) of Glenville Park, Co. Cork.
‡ Thomas Messel of Bradley Court, Gloucestershire (b. 1951); designer and furniture maker; m. 1981 Penelope Barratt.
§ Thomas Messel's cousin William Brendon Parsons, 7th Earl of Rosse (b. 1936); his son Patrick, Lord Oxmantown (b. 1969).
¶ Lacock had been owned by the photographer William Fox Talbot (1800–77); his granddaughter donated the property (1944) to the N.T., which established a Museum of Photography there.
** Mary Field (d. 1885), photographer; m. 1836 3rd Earl of Rosse (1800–67), inventor.

Hastings,* editor of *Daily Telegraph*, rang to ask if I could write 1,000 words on her by tomorrow. I was filled with dismay, and telephoned Billa for help. She clearly wanted to do it herself so I rang Hastings back and told him so. Thank God I have got out of that task.

Then Freda Berkeley telephoned to say Heywood Hill† had died in his sleep of pneumonia, having become skin and bones. Lord, is there an end to it? Never was there a happier couple than H. and Anne. Both these deaths may be called mercies. Penelope was not happy and hadn't been so for years before John's death. She had just sold her house and was planning to retire to a nunnery, which cannot have been an altogether jolly prospect. And H. suffered cruelly from Parkinson's.

Sunday, 20th April

Everyone says Penelope would have wished it. But would she? I think of the pretty, pouting, determined little face when we met in the woods at Wytham Abbey on a hot June day, all of us naked but for a few bracken branches. That must have been in 1930, when Johnnie [Churchill] had the mouth of a Botticelli angel.

On the 16th, Selina [Hastings] and her mother‡ lunched in Bath. We were called for by a grand hired car and taken to the Huntingdon Chapel,§ where we waited and waited in an overheated room for the Duchess of Kent.¶ When she came and we were presented, she said 'Yes' in a daze of non-recognition. That is all we waited for. When her back was turned I saw how thin she was – anorexia – and when

---

* (Sir) Max Hastings; journalist and military historian (b. 1945).

† Bookseller (1906–86); m. 1938 Lady Anne Gathorne-Hardy (1911–2006), o. dau. of 3rd Earl of Cranbrook, who had been engaged to J.L.-M. in 1935.

‡ Margaret Lane (1907–94); writer; m. (2nd) 1944 as his 2nd wife John Hastings, 15th Earl of Huntingdon (1901–90).

§ In the eighteenth century, Selina, Countess of Huntingdon founded a nonconformist sect known as the Countess of Huntingdon's Connexion, designed to bring religion to the upper classes, and established several chapels, one in Bath. The Bath chapel, long out of use and derelict, had just been restored by the Bath Preservation Trust, and is now the Museum of the Building of Bath.

¶ Katharine Worsley (b. 1933); m. 1961 HRH Prince Edward, Duke of Kent (b. 1935).

she turned round again, how drawn, with *Weltschmerz* in her eyes, an unhappy, tormented woman half in this world and half in her own. She is Isabel Briggs's[*] first cousin, and looks rather like her. Margaret Huntingdon holds Selina on an invisible leash, like a lady her little dog on a pavement – keeps an eye on her and addresses her when she is really speaking to us. Yet Selina is not in awe of her.

On the 17th an utterly charming man came to tea, one David Burnett[†] (stress on *-ett*), like a breeze from the Dorset Downs. Tall, strong, handsome and sensitive. Begs me to write a book for his little publishing company, similar to David Cecil's[‡] last, on *Some Cotswold Country Houses*. He enthused my flagging spirit and I said I would if I could possibly manage it. Told him of my other commitments, namely Venice (certain) and Bankes[§] (as yet uncertain).

Andrew Devonshire came for the night on Friday, very charming and appreciative. We had a dinner party for him, asking the Michael Briggses and Charlie Morrisons.[¶] Andrew held the floor. Towards the middle of dinner the telephone rang. A boy said he was the son of John Poë[**] and was stranded in the park, having lost his wallet and failed to meet up with friends. Wanted a bed, but A. would not hear of it. I felt very guilty and unchristian, advised him to sleep in his car and come to us for breakfast in the morning. This he did, looking scruffy and not very attractive. Anyway he was polite, and I gave him money. Andrew agreed with A. not to let him in during dinner, having an aversion to inarticulate teenagers; but Isabel (a generation younger than the rest of us) would have let him come.

---

[*] Isabel Colegate, novelist; m. 1953 Michael Briggs; they lived at Midford Castle near Bath.

[†] Novelist and publisher, owner of Dovecote Press (b. 1946).

[‡] Lord David Cecil (1902–86); yr son of 4th Marquess of Salisbury; writer, historian and Oxford don.

[§] William John Bankes (1786–1855); art collector, MP, friend of Byron and traveller in the East, who was obliged to live abroad for much of his life owing to homosexual scandal, and whose house and estate at Kingston Lacy, Dorset had recently become the property of the N.T. J.L.-M. toyed for some years with the idea of writing his biography (a task later accomplished by Anne Sebba).

[¶] Hon. Sir Charles Morrison (1932–2005), yr s. of 1st Baron Margadale; MP for Devizes, 1964–92; m. (2nd) 1984 as her 2nd husband Rosalind Lygon (b. 1946).

[**] Army officer who was a second cousin of J.L.-M.

Andrew said he asked Lord Hailsham the other day in what particulars he thought he might achieve immortality. H. replied that it would not be through any of his actions or speeches, nor his diaries or memoirs (as he had written none), but perhaps through one of the half-dozen portraits which had been painted of him. 'Which one is that?' Andrew asked. 'By an artist called Derek Hill. Do you know him?' I have passed this on to Derek.

Tuesday, 22nd April to Thursday, 1st May

In Venice, entirely on my own, staying at Pensione Seguso on the Zattere. Weather disappointing – April is not a safe month in Italy. Little sun, much rain, blustering wind, dull skies. I worked extremely hard, off at 8.30 every morning, returning from churches to snooze on my bed and read guide books. Room full of outdated furniture, heavy, comfortable mid nineteenth-century hanging cupboard and pretty (but bogus) Venetian glass-framed mirrors. Bathroom to myself. All this time I saw hardly a soul to speak to. Lunched and dined alone. Made acquaintance of nice American couple at next table, David and Patricia Cleveland, educated and enthusiastic sight-seers. He works for Voice of America, she economist.

I have now selected my monuments for *Venetian Evenings*, studied them with care and made notes. Yet am I inspired to write a second *Roman Mornings*? No, I am not. My love affair with Venice ended years ago. The terrible scourge in Italy today is the schoolchildren and undisciplined teenagers who swarm like locusts, making shrines disgusting with their litter, their transistors, their rudeness, their mere presence.

The Duchess of Windsor died while I was away. M. attended the funeral service at St George's Chapel, which was eerie. No sign of official mourning, and never once was the name of the deceased uttered. The Queen however was seen to be in tears at the graveside, touched perhaps by the sadness of those wretched lives. Meanwhile the *Daily Mail* is publishing extracts from the Windsors' love letters, which will bring M. as their editor notoriety and I hope some money.*

---

* *Wallis & Edward, Letters 1931–37: The Intimate Correspondence of the Duke and Duchess of Windsor* (Weidenfeld & Nicolson, 1986).

Thursday, 5th June

On Tuesday I motored to Marske-in-Swaledale, 270 miles, to stay two nights with Rupert and June [Hart-Davis]. The usual wonderful welcome, Rupert assuring me we were the last survivors of our Eton group. He has changed since my last visit. Much older, though in splendid form; his legs all over the place, his face longer. Reclined most of the day in a tilted chair, his feet on a gout stool, getting up to go through my galleys at a table, breaking when exhausted. Never takes exercise, of course. ('Never use *of course* in writing', he says.) They have not stayed away or gone further than Richmond for five years. Family come to him. When I remarked that it shocked me now how our parents had addressed their parlourmaids by their surnames, June said gently, 'My mother was a parlourmaid, and her mistress changed our name, which was Bowel, to Bowles because it sounded better.' June is a slave to R., she adores him and he her. Never says a stupid thing; very quiet, good and sweet. R. showed me a first edition of *Zuleika Dobson* which had belonged to Beerbohm* who had scribbled illustrations on the margin of every page. He was given it by Lady Beerbohm's sister for whom he has managed Max's literary estate all these years out of love. He has been offered £10,000 for it. Speaking of his friend J.B. Morton† ('Beachcomber'), R. said his inspiration was prodigious. On the spur of the moment he composed such lines as

> Here lies Albrecht Kartoffelspiel
> Best known as Lord Fitzwarren,
> A corner of an English field
> That is forever foreign.

Conversation and anecdotes were non-stop.

Saturday, 7th June

Dining with the Loewensteins we met Mick Jagger, who had unexpectedly turned up from Germany for the night. Just the five of us.

---

* Sir Max Beerbohm (1872–1956); writer, caricaturist and critic.
† Humorist (1893–1979); took over *Daily Express* 'Beachcomber' column in 1924 and continued it until 1975.

He was wearing a thick open-neck jersey of diamond pattern and thin tweed trousers, tidy but not chic. Hair down to shoulders, tiny body, gesticulating arms, huge hands, large head, pig eyes (not unlike mine), mobile features, pugnacious chin, ugly, expressive mouth. Magnetic personality. Ready to act a part, but by no means a clown. Entertaining and delicious company. He and A. get on well and tease each other.

Friday, 20th June

The Royal Librarian Oliver Everett[*] telephoned this morning to say that I need make no alterations to the extracts of my Regy manuscript which I sent him, apart from his request that in my footnotes I put 'RA' for Royal Archives. However, he did say that the Queen had read them, and was hurt that Lord Esher should have criticised her great-grandfather King Edward VII as a man of limited intelligence and no reading. I explained to Everett that these views were not mine but E's. The Queen was also slightly shocked by E's reference to Edward, Prince of Wales having had his first 'amourette' while in France during the Great War. I replied that most young men had their first woman at some time or other. Thirdly, the Queen was rather shocked by Esher writing in his Journal that he was slightly in love with the Prince himself. At this, I thought it best to warn Everett that there were other revelations concerning E's amorous feelings which might dismay the Queen were she to read the book. He said he had guessed as much from a remark contained in the extracts I sent him, referring to E's incestuous attachment to his son [Maurice]. So I said I would be prepared to cut out, even at this late stage, anything that offended the Queen. No, he said, let it all stand. I do hope the book will not cause further offence in royal circles. It amazes me that the Queen should read these extracts herself. Everett asked me to be sure to write the usual dedication in the copy I am to send her, assuring me that she would much like to have it, and will doubtless put it among her

---

[*] Diplomatist and courtier (b. 1943); Comptroller to Prince and Princess of Wales, 1981–3; Royal Librarian and Assistant Keeper of the Queen's Archives, 1985–2002.

collection of books on the royal family in her private sitting room. He said the publicity following the Duchess of Windsor's death had distressed her.

Sunday, 6th July

We attended a dinner at the Warrenders'* last night for about twenty people. Didn't enjoy it much. Full of lords and ladies, yet A. and I given *places d'honneur*, I suppose being the oldest present. It is good of them not to observe the absurd formal precedence at meals. On my right was Lord Ampthill,† a man in his fifties whom I much liked. I think he must have been the baby in the famous Russell Baby Case,‡ whose mother Christabel became a pen-friend of mine to whom I wrote when she was ill in Ireland (addressing my letters to the Cavalry Hospital until she told me it was Calvary). Geoffrey Ampthill is Deputy Speaker of the House of Lords who sits on the Woolsack when the Lord Chancellor is absent. Says the House is the best club in the world, cherished by all who take their seats there, irrespective of party or whether they arrive by heredity or promotion. He has inaugurated a long table in the dining room at which all peers sit when not entertaining guests. This makes for good feeling, and they all get on well. He said it was wonderful how diplomatically they manage to dispose of mad backwoods peers who tried to thrust themselves forward. Among the younger peers, Lord Melchett§ is

---

* Hon. Robin Warrender (b. 1927), yr s. of 1st Baron Bruntisfield; m. 1951 Gillian Rossiter; underwriting member of Lloyds.

† Geoffrey Russell, 4th Baron Ampthill (b. 1921); chairman of committees and Deputy Speaker of the House of Lords from 1983.

‡ In the sensational divorce case of *Russell* v. *Russell* (1922–4), Hon. John 'Stilts' Russell, future 3rd Baron Ampthill and a transvestite, claimed that the baby Geoffrey Russell was not his but the fruit of the adultery of his wife Christabel (*née* Hart). Despite medical evidence to the effect that Mrs Russell had been a virgin at the time of the baby's conception, his claim was accepted by the High Court and the Court of Appeal. The House of Lords, however, allowed Christabel's appeal by a majority of 3 to 2. After the death of the 3rd Baron in 1974, Geoffrey Russell's claim to succeed him was contested by his younger half-brother, but eventually accepted by the House of Lords after a ruling by its Committee of Privileges.

§ Peter Mond, 4th Baron Melchett (b. 1948); environmental campaigner.

considered rather bumptious, whereas Simon Glenarthur* is regarded as perfection. He said peers are discouraged from dying in the House because the Coroner has no jurisdiction. When the former Labour cabinet minister Gordon-Walker† died in a taxi on the way there, the red-liveried usher failed to persuade the driver to take him to the nearest hospital. As it was a busy moment when he had to attend to the arrival of other peers, he shoved him in a wheelchair into a broom cupboard. Later, Lady Gordon-Walker arrived and asked for her husband, whereupon the usher wheeled the corpse out of the cupboard. Ampthill says there is no need to reform the House of Lords, because the public can see from television‡ that they are harmless.

Monday, 14th July

I now have a car radio and listen to it while driving to and from Bath. The news these days is appalling. Nothing but murders, assassinations and bombings in Ireland, Spain, the Near East, India; and the ostracism of South Africa horrifies me. Those bloody Commonwealth Games in Edinburgh! I wish we had called them off to cock a snook at those African countries boycotting them. Awful that we, a once great country, have to submit to insults from savages. Mrs Thatcher is absolutely right not to give in to pressure for sanctions.§ An article in *The Times* gives abbreviated biographies of all the black rulers clamouring for sanctions, who are all without exception thugs, terrorists and tyrants, motivated by communistic tendencies. At my age I should not read the daily newspapers or listen to the radio, but my curiosity gets the better of me. I can't sit back like an ostrich and bury my head

---

* Simon Arthur, 4th Baron Glenarthur (b. 1944); son of Matthew, 3rd Baron by his 2nd wife Margaret (his 1st wife having been J.L.-M's sister Audrey); Conservative politician, then a Foreign Office minister.
† Patrick Gordon-Walker (1907–80); Oxford historian and Labour politician; cr. life peer, 1974; m. 1934 Audrey Muriel Rudolf.
‡ Proceedings of the House of Lords had been broadcast since 1984. (TV cameras were not allowed into the House of Commons until 1989.)
§ Mrs Thatcher's Government reluctantly imposed limited economic sanctions against the 'apartheid' regime in South Africa in the autumn of 1986.

in the sand. Yet I am appalled by the views of the people I hear on the radio, all soppy socialists who are against the police and what they call 'the Establishment'. Bring back the birch and the rope, I say. Actually, not the rope, which is a degrading form of execution; rather a lethal prick, which raises no revulsion among either public or perpetrators and is no doubt a delicious sensation in the victim.

Thursday, 17th July

A. and I went to Diana Cooper's* memorial service at St Mary's, Paddington Green, at noon. We had an hour to spare beforehand, and went to the Berkeleys'. Freda in despair over Lennox who is quite gaga, recognising no one. Cannot speak except in broken sentences and wanders round the house after Freda. She almost confesses that she wishes him dead. We walked to the church, lovely sunny morning, Freda guiding Lennox while the others walked ahead. One of the most beautiful services I have ever attended. Lasted an hour. Packed with friends. Began with Gloria from Mozart's *Missa Brevis*, sung by choir in gallery. Then stirring hymn, 'For all the Saints'. Lesson read by Henry Anglesey.† Menuhin‡ played Gavotte and Praeludium of Bach, which sounded rather squawky unaccompanied. Edward Fox§ read beautifully from *Intimations of Immortality*. Hymn 'He who would valiant be' (which was Diana's attitude to life). Address by Martin Charteris,¶ another nephew. Told story of Diana in early 1900s giving sixpenny notebook to Eddie Marsh,** who loved her like all his

---

* Lady Diana Manners (1892–1986); ostensibly dau. of 8th Duke of Rutland (though she believed her father to be Harry Cust – see 7 January 1989); m. 1919 Alfred Duff Cooper (1890–1954), cr. Viscount Norwich 1953, diplomatist, politician and writer; mother of writer and broadcaster John Julius Norwich, 2nd Viscount (b. 1929; m. 1st Anne Clifford, 2nd Hon. Mary 'Mollie' Philipps).

† Lord Anglesey's mother, *née* Lady Marjorie Manners, was Lady Diana's sister.

‡ Yehudi Menuhin (1916–99); violinist; cr. life peer, 1993.

§ Actor (b. 1937).

¶ Lord Charteris of Amisfield (1913–99); Private Secretary to HM The Queen, 1972–77; Provost of Eton, 1978–91; m. 1944 Hon. Gay Margesson; his mother, Lady Violet, was Lady Diana's other sister.

** Sir Edward Marsh (1872–1953); civil servant and writer who befriended young literary men, including Rupert Brooke before 1914 and J.L.-M. in the 1930s.

generation. Eddie kept notebook all his life and got 120 famous writers to contribute some piece to it. Martin managed to buy it for Eton College Library for a price rather greater than current equivalent of sixpence. When Diana visited Eton, he showed it to her and she wrote on the last page an affectionate letter to Eddie as if he were alive. Lilian Watson, soprano, then sang Schubert, followed by the choir singing 'God be in my head, and in my understanding'. Finally the congregation gave a rousing rendering of 'Mine eyes have seen the glory of the coming of the Lord'. Most moving ceremony, the sun streaming through the clear windows into this packed and pretty little church. Nigel Ryan[*] added a short appreciation of Diana's help to friends in trouble. All these tributes to Diana made me feel an unworthy person, not so much a worm as like that fragment of broken translucent glass set in the floor.

Friday, 25th July

We dine at the House to meet the Beits[†] who are staying. Sat next to Clem who says that although Alf makes light of the latest robbery of his pictures,[‡] he is very upset and broods. Thinks IRA are involved. If so, they are robbing Ireland of some of the world's best pictures, for they no longer belong to Alfred, who has left them in trust to that stinking nation. He does not believe they have been acquired by 'gloaters' – i.e., eccentric millionaires in South America who seek to acquire world-famous pictures for their secret collections – but that in a year or so a ransom will be demanded. The alarm went off in the middle of the night; curator awakened; police arrived; nothing found disturbed; police left, and curator retired to bed. But meanwhile one of the gang remained hidden in the house and managed to de-activate

---

[*] Journalist, writer, broadcaster and translator (b. 1929).
[†] Sir Alfred Beit, 2nd Bt (1903–94); art collector and sometime Conservative MP; m. 1939 Clementine Mitford (1915–2005), cousin of the Mitford sisters.
[‡] This was the second of a series of audacious art robberies from Russborough House, the Beits' seat in County Wicklow. The Provisional IRA was responsible for the first, in 1974; the second turned out to be the work of a professional criminal, Martin Cahill, who was later murdered by the IRA. Most of the pictures stolen were recovered on each occasion.

the alarm system and admit his accomplices. They cleared out the saloon and were off.

Monday, 28th July

A. being bogged down with great-grandchildren, I went alone to spend weekend with Billy Whitaker* at Pylewell [Hampshire]. Utmost comfort and luxury, tables groaning with silver, butler, old housekeeper and army of unseen housemaids. The first day was one of delicious idling, largely spent in my room where I read or dozed. Loelia Lindsay,† Margaret-Anne Stuart,‡ Tom Parr§ and Tony Pawson¶ staying. At first the upper-crust chatter and gossip was fun. After twenty-four hours I had had quite enough. The others left on Sunday afternoon and I spent the last night alone with Billy and sister Penelope. Both sweet but so devitalised that I found tea and dinner heavy going. Billy showed me a school group taken in 1920 at Lockers Park, in which he and Peter Coats are sitting on the ground in front row next to each other. Other recognisable boys are myself, Tom Mitford, Dick Bailey,** Ava†† and Matthew Arthur.‡‡ *Eheu fugaces!*

Returned to Bad. to find A. exhausted from looking after these children. I hate to see her thus, but she will do it. Chloë§§ looking fat,

---

* William Whitaker (1910–88); bachelor landowner whose ancestors had made their fortune from the importation of Marsala wine from Sicily and had lived at Pylewell for three generations; contemporary of J.L.-M. at preparatory school and Eton.

† Hon. Loelia Ponsonby (1902–93), dau. of 1st Baron Sysonby; m. 1st 1930–47 2nd Duke of Westminster, 2nd 1969 Sir Martin Lindsay of Dowhill, 1st Bt (1905–81).

‡ Margaret-Anne Du Cane; interior decorator; m. 1979 as his 3rd wife 2nd Viscount Stuart of Findhorn.

§ Interior decorator (b. 1930), then Chairman of Colefax & Fowler.

¶ Algernon ('Tony') Pawson (1917–90); former wartime intelligence officer and lover of the rich Chilean collector Arturo Lopez Wilshaw.

** Cousin of the Mitford sisters (1908–69).

†† Basil Blackwood, 4th Marquess of Dufferin and Ava (1909–45); politician and soldier, killed on active service in Burma.

‡‡ Hon. Matthew Arthur (1909–76); s. father as 3rd Baron Glenarthur, 1942; his great-uncle married J.L.-M's great-aunt, and he himself was married to J.L.-M's sister Audrey during 1930s.

§§ A.L.-M's granddaughter Chloë Luke (b. 1959).

in trousers with enormous bottom. Talking rot about organising an exhibition of pictures in Burlington House for Band Aid, the crusade to help the starving Africans who take everything and give nothing, and want weeding out, not encouraging to multiply. The whole thing makes me sick.

Sunday, 3rd August

David and Caroline dined with us in the middle of the week. D. said he could not bear X. because of his dirty clothes, and wondered whether it was wrong to take against people for such trivial reasons. I said that I was apt to judge from first appearances, and although I might subsequently change my opinion, I usually found in the end that my first reaction had been right. Then he asked whether I looked at the faces of the mourners at funerals as they processed out of the church. He does so out of the corner of his eye as it interests him to see which mourners are sad, which mightily relieved, which pleased or displeased by their inheritance, etc. I said I tried not to look as I did not like to see people trying to restrain their tears, and also coffins revolted me for I always wondered what the corpse was looking like within.

The next night, 31st, we dined alone with Charlie and Rosalind Morrison. Charlie spoke critically of Mrs Thatcher, saying that unless she is made to stand down before the next election the Tories stand no chance of returning. Also doubted whether there would be another female PM for a hundred years, for she has demonstrated the worst failing of the female mind – obduracy.

Wednesday, 6th August

My [seventy-eighth] birthday. I went to London for the day and had Hugh Massingberd and M. to lunch at Brooks's, each having expressed a desire to meet the other. A great success. Hugh asked M. to write obituaries for the *Daily Telegraph*. M. saw the point of Hugh, a delightful baby, all harassed and pursued, but brilliant, missing nothing. Noticed his endearing habit of making asides to himself, commenting on what he has just said.

Monday, 11th August

Punctual to the minute, a huge Mercedes drew up to the door at 9.30. A nice youngish driver with excellent manners took me to Kedleston [Derbyshire]. Was glad of this, as it was a filthy day. We got there at 12.30, too late and too early, and went to a pub for lunch. He ate little, and nothing on return journey except a mug of tea. Though he could not have been nicer, conversation was uphill. On passing Worcester, I told him that the tump on the left was where Cromwell stood before the battle of Worcester, while Charles II was in the Cathedral tower. He knew nothing of Cromwell or Charles II. On the way back, I explained that another tump was where the last witch was burned. He asked, 'Was that before the Great War?'

Kedleston is a truly wonderful house, not outside but in. Paine's front is stodgy, Adam's south front unfinished. But the inside unparalleled. The alabaster hall could not be more splendid. The pretty fireplaces seem too elegant for so much Roman robustness; the drawing room likewise superb – the inset frames to pictures, the alabaster door-frames and Venetian window, and the view therefrom, over the delicate railing and Adam gates to the lake and the bridge. The dining room has been painted hideously, also the library – mulberry walls and yellow ceiling. Some Lady Scarsdale had no taste at all. I was last here forty years ago.

Tuesday, 19th August

A. being absent in Tangier, Eardley came to stay for four days. I arranged several entertainments to avoid meals at home. First night we dined at G.D's, where I hadn't been for ages. Charles Monteith and a couple of queens staying. D. too awful for words, got drunk, kept asking E. whether he had had affairs with various people. Charles M. spoke about All Souls, where they cannot stop John Sparrow,* who thinks he is still Warden, dining every evening and boring them all to tears with his drunkenness and senility. On the

---

* Warden of All Souls College, Oxford, 1952–77 (1906–91).

13th E. and I motored to Upton to see the Bearsted pictures. My first visit for over thirty years. What a splendid collection it is. There is something of everything – Rembrandt, Rubens, Reynolds; Dutch, French, English and Italian. Dick Bearsted* was away but we were told he had had a stroke. His father and mother such dear people. Dinner with Alex [Moulton] on the 14th was a success. E. much impressed by enthusiasms of Alex, who showed photographs of his inventions and brought in his latest bicycle. On the 17th we lunched with Janet Stone† in Salisbury. She was very sweet and charming, dressed not in her usual Edwardian get-up but sensible cotton skirt and blouse. Is publishing a book of photographs. Is delighted by two paintings by Jones which K. Clark left her. Folly bit her hand when leaving.

Eardley and I got on well but there was not the rapport of old. Few giggles, not much laughter, some reticence and disapproval on his part, some irritation on mine. For some reason the spectacle of him helping himself to spoonful after spoonful of marmalade at breakfast irritated me profoundly. I am getting more irritable than I used to be.

Thursday, 11th September

We were sitting cosily in front of the fire last night at 7.45 when the doorbell rang noisily, to accompaniment of barking from Folly. A pathetic boy at the door presented an identity card and explained that he and his friends, who were from Nottingham, were travelling round the country selling household goods rather than go on the dole. At once suspicion seized me and I kept him talking while calling for A. Boy produced a large roll bag from which emerged dish cloths, car sponges, dusters. We wanted none of these things, and I was irritated by the infringement of privacy and element of blackmail implied in

---

* Marcus Richard Samuel, 3rd Viscount Bearsted (1909–86), whose father had donated Upton House, Warwickshire with its garden and picture collection to the N.T. in 1946.

† Janet Woods (1912–98); m. 1938 Reynolds Stone (1909–79), designer, wood engraver and artist.

this unsolicited touting. Nevertheless we gave him £10 for an assortment of things he calculated cost £9.50, and wished him good luck. He thanked us politely, adding that it was a good day whereas the day before he had only sold £4 worth of stuff. He smelled dreadfully, the poor youth. For the rest of the evening I was tormented by a mixture of shame at my original suspicion and irritation, distress that this boy has to descend to this sort of livelihood, and admiration that he chooses to work this way rather than live off the state. Youth unemployment has become a national cancer.

Friday, 12th September

A lady with a notebook accosted me as I was coming out of Waterstone's bookshop in Milsom Street, asking if I had two minutes to spare. 'Well, I suppose I might spare half a minute,' I replied grudgingly. She belonged to some research unit, and wanted to know how many books I read a year. When I said about two hundred, she was aghast. 'You don't mean it?' I explained that many of them were library books which I did not buy, nor did I read every book from beginning to end.

Monday, 15th September

On Saturday we lunched with Billy [Henderson] and Frank [Tait]. Michael and Anne Tree present, he full of anecdotes, she very clever and direct with the most upper class accent in the world. Michael said David Beaufort was praying for a socialist government which would stop hunting. He is fed up with it, but cannot of course close down the Beaufort himself. An enjoyable luncheon for there was conversation, rare these days in the circles in which we move.

Wednesday, 17th September

To London for the night. At Sidgwick's I signed copies of Regy. A. keeps telling me not to give away so many copies, at least to the rich. But it is often the only way I can repay their kindnesses. Already I have given fifteen copies, including those to the Queen and Oliver Everett. To the Queen, I put 'Her Majesty the Queen with humble duty from her grateful and loyal subject J.L.-M.'. Am not sure whether this sort of address is too flowery and deferential for these days, but I wanted to get in the 'humble duty' because that is how Regy began all his letters to King Edward.

In the evening, A's publishers, Viking, gave a party in Hardy Amies'* rooms in Savile Row to launch her new book, *The Englishman's Room*, which promises to be a great success. Many old friends. The Enoch Powells† there, she sweet and simple, he difficult and rather deaf. When he asked me on what subject A. was now engaged, I mumbled 'gardens'. He turned to A. and said, 'Your husband tells me you have chosen an interesting new subject – gowns.' She replied that 'gowns' was not a word I would use. Derry told him I was not a businessman. 'That's good,' he replied. 'A useless profession.' I said I thought businessmen were what the country needed, as we produced too little. 'Rubbish,' he said, 'we don't need to produce anything. There are other troubles.' M., whom A. had invited, reported a similar snatch of unsatisfactory conversation. He drew Powell's attention to the unpublished diaries of Sir Ronald Storrs‡ in a Cambridge library, including interesting descriptions of visits to country houses in Powell's Downshire constituency. He replied, 'Diaries are useless, because they are written with an eye to publication.' End of talk. Powell is a small, compact, greyish man. I have long wished to meet him, but on such occasions I cannot click with distinguished strangers.

Rosemary Chaplin§ present, sweet and tiny and rather aged. Seeing her with A. and myself, Junie [Hutchinson]¶ called us 'the incestuous trio'. 'Yes,' I said, 'but we all had such fun, and loved each other.' This shocked some people at the time.**

---

* Dressmaker by Appointment to HM The Queen (1909–2003).

† Writer and politician (1912–98); Ulster Unionist MP for South Down, 1974–92.

‡ Colonial administrator (1881–1955).

§ Hon. Rosemary Lyttelton (1922–2004), dau. of 1st Viscount Chandos; m. 1951 3rd Viscount Chaplin (formerly husband of A.L.-M.).

¶ June Capel; dau. of J.L-M's friend Diana, Countess of Westmorland (d. 1983); m. (2nd) Jeremy Hutchinson QC (cr. life peer, 1978).

** In his latest diaries J.L.-M. had described how he, his future wife Alvilde, her then husband Anthony Chaplin and Chaplin's future wife Rosemary all stayed together at Alvilde's house in France in June 1949.

Friday, 26th September

On Monday I went to stay with Diana [Mosley] at Orsay for two nights. Enjoyed myself enormously. We talked and talked, scarcely stopping to go to bed. She told me all kinds of things without reservation.

Before O[swald] M[osley]'s death she was advised to obtain a copy of their marriage certificate (the original having perished in a fire at their Irish house), since in the event of his predeceasing her she would have to pay massive French death duties unless she could prove she was his widow. This was difficult, as they had married in the garden of Goebbels' house in Hitler's presence. She applied to the West German government who told her she must write to the East German government, as the site was now on the eastern side of the Berlin Wall. Amazingly, such is German efficiency, she obtained it, though house and garden long gone.

I told her about the *Berlin Diaries* of Missy Vassiltchikov[*] which I so much enjoyed. She denied that Hitler watched a film of the slow strangulation by piano wire of those involved in the attempt on his life in 1944. It was not the sort of thing he would do. She said Hitler would never have declared war on England, which he loved even more than the Kaiser did. He wept when Singapore fell to the Japanese. Had we not declared war on him, he would have defeated Russia. She despises Stauffenberg[†] for being a coward, bolting from the scene before his bomb went off. Cowardice is what she most despises in humans, even more than disloyalty.

Hitler, she said, had the most delicate hands and beautiful blue eyes. Everyone he met fell under his charm. I tackled her about the Jews and concentration camps. She admitted that what had happened was dreadful and inexcusable, but wondered whether he was aware of it, for he was not naturally cruel or callous. But she said that we in

[*] Princess Marie ('Missy') Vassiltchikov (1917–78); Russian aristocrat who worked during Second World War as a translator in German Foreign Ministry; her diaries, published 1985, are a fascinating source for both wartime social life in Berlin and the anti-Nazi resistance.

[†] Count Claus Schenk von Stauffenberg (1907–44); would-be assassin of Hitler on 20 July 1944.

England overlooked the fact that the German Jews bled the economy in their own selfish interests, much as the blacks do in Britain today.

At Chatsworth, O.M. met the Prince of Wales, who talked to him with fascination for three-quarters of an hour and asked to see him again. But O.M. begged to be excused a further meeting, as it would not be in the Prince's interest. They talked of the future of the monarchy.

Diana once asked K. Clark what the attitude of King George VI and the Queen Mother towards the Duke and Duchess of Windsor really was. 'Vicious,' he replied.

A. awfully cross when I told her these stories on my return. Thinks me weak for being taken in by Diana's charm. Possibly.

Wednesday, 1st October

Strange occurrence at Lansdown Tower* meeting this evening. After the usual boring agenda – maintenance costs, dry rot, drop in number of visitors during season, etc. – we were shown a portrait of Beckford as a child which the Duke of Hamilton† offers to us for £20,000, along with three oils by Maddox of Beckford treasures, painted for the coloured lithographs in the book of 1844 of which I have a copy. We decided that we could not afford the portrait, but would offer £6,000 for the Maddoxes. Then Graham Cave‡ produced a loose flannel bundle from which fell a cascade of gold spoons which had belonged to Beckford, also the Duke's who wants to get rid of them. With eyes glistening like werewolves, we greedily examined this loot, clawing at teaspoons, sugar tongs and tea-caddy spoons, all with Beckford's crest,

---

* Having sold Fonthill in 1822 and moved to Bath, William Beckford commissioned the architect H.E. Goodridge to build an ornate Tower (completed 1826) on the hill above Lansdown Crescent, where he spent much of his later years, reading and admiring the view. On his death in 1844, he was buried next to it. It later became the property of the local parish church, and deteriorated through neglect. A couple named Hillyard, Bath doctors, bought it in the 1970s, restored it, established a museum there, and set up a trust for its conservation (later incorporated in Bath Preservation Trust).

† Angus Douglas-Hamilton, 15th Duke of Hamilton (b. 1938); connection of William Beckford, whose daughter had married 10th Duke.

‡ Poultry farmer; trustee of Beckford Tower Trust.

pelican with fish in beak or Latimer Cross. We decided that the Trust should buy the pick, some to exhibit, others to keep in the bank as an investment, and that we ourselves might buy any of the remainder which we wanted. I took six tea spoons and a pair of silver-gilt dessert spoons, for which I paid £150, less than they would have fetched at auction. As we left, Sidney Blackmore* said to me, 'How Beckford would have hated that scene.' He would indeed, and may well haunt me at No. 19 for being a participant.

Saturday, 11th October

We dined tonight at the House. In Caroline's absence, I found myself sitting next to David's mistress Miranda Morley,[†] whom I have hitherto avoided for diplomatic reasons. Very sweet and pretty, and unobtrusive. She did not take the head of the table, or welcome guests or seat them. Yet I was assailed with a slight feeling of disloyalty to Caroline, and wondered what the servants thought about her being in the House. On my other side was Liliane Rothschild,[‡] Poppy Price-Jones' sister. A dumpling with snow-white hair, white face and currant eyes. A great friend and patroness of Winckler,[§] the French artist I have to meet in Paris next week. I gathered that neither she nor her husband, Baron Elie, had a high opinion of Alan Pryce-Jones.[¶]

Wednesday, 15th October

Left Brooks's at 7.30 for Heathrow. Arrived Paris 10.30, took taxi to Grand Palais. Filthy day, pouring with rain, whereas London had been

---

* Civil servant and art lecturer; trustee of Beckford Tower Trust, later Secretary of Beckford Society.
† She married 11th Duke of Beaufort in 2000, five years after the death of his 1st wife Caroline.
‡ Liliane Fould-Springer; m. 1941 Baron Elie de Rothschild.
§ Jean-Marc Winckler (b. 1952); French artist; J.L.-M. had been commissioned to write an article comparing his work with that of three other contemporary artists for the *Architectural Digest*.
¶ Writer and journalist (1908–2000); editor *Times Literary Supplement*, 1948–59; Eton contemporary of J.L.-M.; his first wife Poppy, Liliane's sister, had died in 1953.

divine. Spent rest of morning at François Boucher[*] exhibition. I do not like Boucher – ladies with blue ribbons round their necks, tending sheep or goats; even a cook courted by a baker's boy is a Dresden shepherdess being seduced by a swain. In landscapes, the sunlight on broken tree-trunks is a favourite trick. He is a rococo painter, and rococo is only tolerable as architectural decoration. Though it was only a few yards away, I had some difficulty finding the Travellers' Club, as no one could tell me where it was. Lunched there with Stuart [Preston],[†]who showed me around this hideous but interesting Second Empire residence of some renowned odalisque.[‡] Horrid luncheon.

S. accompanied me to the Elie de Rothschilds' extremely posh residence in the rue de Courcelles. Really, these Paris town houses. Concièrge at gate; forecourt; butler at front door; entrance hall with curved staircase and elegant railings. Several grand people in large first-floor drawing room drinking coffee after luncheon. Was introduced to Jean-Marc Winckler, young, merry, plain youth of thirty-four who insisted on kissing my hand. I looked at coloured photographs of his interiors and conversation pieces. Liliane de R., the youth's patroness and impresario, has other works of his hanging upstairs in her bathroom. Pastiche, yet competent and attractive. The four artists whose work I must write about are near-indistinguishable in style, with their revived eighteenth-century miniaturist technique. Liliane is intelligent and social, with excellent taste and lovely possessions. One room full of portraits of and objects which belonged to Marie Antoinette.

Despite Stuart's help, I had much trouble finding a taxi in the rain to take me to the airport. Was glad to get away. Don't feel happy in Paris. Never have. Hope never to go there again.

---

[*] French artist (1703–70).

[†] American bibliophile resident in Paris (1915–2004), with whom J.L.-M. had conducted an intermittent love affair between 1939 and 1945; known as 'the Sarge' since 1942, when he had arrived in London as a sergeant in the US Army 'attached to headquarters'.

[‡] 25 Champs-Elysées, built in the 1860s by the courtesan Thérèse, Marquise de la Païva (born Esther Lachsmann), and prized today as a surviving example of the ostentatious decoration of the period, became the Travellers' clubhouse in 1904.

Sunday, 19th October

Am extremely depressed as Regy has been almost totally ignored by the press. Only two reviews by friends, Kenneth Rose and M. Whole thing a flop after the pains of more than four years. Yesterday received aggrieved letter from Angela Thornton, horrified by revelations of the intimacy between her grandfather Regy and father Maurice. Asked me not to write to her again. The only cheering thing has been a telephone call from that distinguished man Noël Annan,* whom I barely know, to say how good he thought it was. I shall never write another book after the silly little Venetian volume I am now finishing. I am a third-rate failure and must recognise it.

Sunday, 2nd November

While A. and I were kneeling together in Little Badminton Church this morning and reciting the Confessional, it suddenly occurred to me that millions habitually made this act of contrition, yet their names were forgotten on earth, and probably unrecorded in the scrolls of Heaven. I was reciting something which, within five years at most, I shall have ceased to recite, 'I' having vanished forever, and with it all my resolutions. Yet I felt I was not wasting my time, but rather contributing to the contrition of the whole of mankind, of which I was so fragmentary a part as to be of no importance to God. This came almost as a visionary understanding, and not one that was wholly agreeable to me.

Saturday, 15th November

We lunched at the House, about twenty at the long table. Sat between Cosima Fry,† to whom I had little to say, and Claire

---

* Academician and writer (1916–2000); Provost of King's College, Cambridge, 1956–66, and of University College, London, 1966–78; Vice-Chancellor of London University, 1978–81; cr. life peer, 1965.
† Lady Cosima Tempest-Vane-Stewart (b. 1961); ostensibly yr dau. of 9th Marquess of Londonderry (though in 106th edition of *Burke's Peerage* she claims paternity of Robin Douglas-Home); m. 1st 1982–6 Cosmo Fry, 2nd 1990–6 Lord John Somerset, yst s. of 11th Duke of Beaufort.

Ward,* as sweet as once was her mother, who is now out of her mind. Talked afterwards to Tony Lambton, writing yet another biography of Mountbatten, whom he hates and regards as the vainest, stupidest and most scheming of men. Before Prince Philip married, Mountbatten summoned him and said, 'You know where your duty lies. For twenty years you must be absolutely faithful.' Mountbatten was obsessed with the interests of the Hesse family, but may not have been one of them himself, as his father was probably illegitimate. Lambton dark, balding, saturnine.

We dined with Rupert Loewenstein to meet Littman and wife.† He said to be the cleverest lawyer alive, she American and pretty. Littman said that, at a dinner party in the 1930s, the name of Oliver Cromwell was mentioned. A very old lady present said, 'Ah, Oliver Cromwell, my first husband's first wife's first husband knew him well.' I suppose just possible, assuming vast age-gaps between spouses.

Sunday, 30th November

To the Rodin exhibition, a disappointment. His drawings of nude women, lying on their sides and exposing their nude pudenda, I find offensive. Oh how I loathe sex these days. Is this my middle class upbringing? Or resentment? Or my neutrality? Or is it a right and proper attitude, simply revolting from something disgusting? A beautiful head of *La Pensée*, 1886, redeems him by its beauty and purity.

Sunday, 14th December

Elspeth Huxley‡ said that to be made a literary dame or knight you must accept every invitation to lecture or make speeches. They are the only ones which qualify. You can be a Milton or a Dickens, but if you

---

* Claire Baring (b. 1936); m. 1956–74 Hon. Peter Ward, yr s. of 3rd Earl of Dudley; her daughter Tracy Ward (b. 1958) married the Beauforts' heir, Harry, Marquess of Worcester, in 1987.

† Mark Littman QC (b. 1920); m. 1965 Marguerite Lamkin of Louisiana (b. 1932).

‡ Elspeth Grant (1907–94); m. 1931 Gervase Huxley (d. 1971); writer.

do not speak in public, you will not be recognised. She laughed at my question whether she would like to be made a dame herself.

I am reading Alan Pryce-Jones's autobiography* – which is not yet out, but [John] Saumarez [Smith] is always ready to oblige. The book is typical of Alan, reads just like him speaking, is very brilliant and sparkling and one enjoys every word. Yet somehow one does not admire him for it. It is like a highbrow's 'Jennifer's Diary', names dropping like autumn leaves – my aunt Mary Minto, my uncle Hillingdon, my cousin Harewood, all presumably through his Dawnay mother, for the Pryce-Joneses were quite dim, like my family. All the while there are protestations against snobbery, and veils are tightly drawn over his propensities. One is expected to believe that his relationship with Bobbie Pratt Barlow† was totally avuncular and disinterested, that he is a tolerant hetero, amused by the venial peccadilloes of his queer friends. Interesting that, like myself, he feels the Church let him down after he became a Papist. Had he known what John XXIII was going to do he would never have signed up.

Sunday, 21st December

I believe everyone has a secret spark of *Schadenfreude*. So when told that Bruce Chatwin,‡ who is suspected of suffering from Aids, felt better, I experienced a momentary pang of disappointment. This was instinctive rather than rational, for were God to ask me point-blank, I should express an unhesitating wish that Bruce should recover. It is a case of the civilised self banging down the brutish self. They say old people enjoy reading of the deaths of their old friends in *The Times*. I am not sure what my own true feelings are in this respect.

---

* *The Bonus of Laughter* (Hamish Hamilton, 1987).
† In his book, A.P.-J. describes how, from 1931 to 1934, he was supported by this rich and languid bachelor, with whom he travelled all over the world in sumptuous style. 'No doubt this looked strange to some. I was twenty-two – Bobbie was in his forties . . . At no time did his private life impinge on mine.'
‡ Travel writer and novelist (1940–89), whom J.L.-M. had got to know when they had been neighbours in Gloucestershire in the early 1970s.

Wednesday, 31st December

We lunched at Combe [near Newbury] with the Moores and the Hendersons. Roy and Dame Jennifer Jenkins* there too. Though we had met before at Ann Fleming's,† he said to me as we shook hands that he had looked me up in *Who's Who* before setting out. He said Asquith had the best brain of any Prime Minister of our history, but was not creative; Dizzy was an exhibitionist; Gladstone was not clever, but immmensely honourable and religious, tormented by doubts. Praised Regy to me, but told A., next whom he sat, that I had made mistakes in the politics. She said he should tell me so. When he told her he was now writing on Baldwin, she said I had known B.,‡ and Jenkins should ask me about him. He did neither, must be a shy man. Nico Henderson in raptures about Regy, which embarrasses me, coming from someone so much more intelligent than myself. After luncheon I sat in the long window overlooking the wide, totally unspoilt downland landscape, and talked to Dame J. about the National Trust [of which she had become Chairman that year]. She is worried about many things, such as the Kedleston Appeal, which has not even been launched. I praised the way historic houses were shown these days, far better than when I was in charge. But you were starved of money, she said. True, I replied, we did everything on a shoe-string. Nevertheless, men like Martin Drury§ and Gervase [Jackson-Stops] are extremely competent and clever. I cracked them up.

---

* Roy Harris Jenkins (1920–2003); Labour politician; President of European Commission, 1977–81; co-founder and leader of Social Democratic Party, 1981–3; cr. life peer, 1987; m. 1945 Jennifer Morris (b. 1921; DBE 1985; Chairman of National Trust, 1986–90).

† Ann Charteris (1913–81); m. 1st 1932–44 3rd Baron O'Neill, 2nd 1945–52 2nd Viscount Rothermere, 3rd 1952 Ian Fleming, novelist (1908–64).

‡ In Edwardian times, Stanley Baldwin (1867–1947; Prime Minister 1923–4, 1924–9, 1935–7) had been a friend and neighbour of J.L.-M's grandparents in Worcestershire; J.L.-M. had met him at a house party in 1935, during his last premiership (their encounter being described – possibly rather fancifully – in *Another Self*).

§ Historic Buildings Secretary (1981–95), subsequently Director-General, of National Trust (b. 1938).

1987

1987

I wonder if M. is bored with me. His attentiveness and kindness never cease to amaze me. But have they become perfunctory? We never seem to write letters these days, or exchange tokens of affection as we used to. I am still devoted to him, though anxious. He is idle and slothful. Although loyal in his friendships, would he put off doing a friend a service if he was bored by the idea? He keeps bad company, and may end up like Jamesey,* as I keep warning him. I am beginning to wonder whether I have done the right thing in making him my literary executor. What worries me most is whether he will ever be recognised as a writer. He is a procrastinator, and puts off his work to fritter away his time on the tiles.

Thursday, 15th January

The appalling cold persists. Television and newspapers revelling in the deaths of the old from hypothermia, inviting us to blame the Government for not being prepared. But England never is prepared for extreme temperatures, though they arrive annually. I might have got to Bath today, but as we are enjoined not to stir unless our journey is really necessary, I obeyed. But more snow due tonight. M. telephoned on his return from Paris, where conditions are even worse than here. He found himself walking in the streets entirely alone, the severe weather coinciding with a transport strike. Felt like Hitler when the streets were cleared for him. This afternoon, while I was walking

---

* As described by J.L.-M. in his diary, James Pope-Hennessy was done to death in January 1974 by ruffians whom he had invited into his flat in Ladbroke Grove.

with dogs* down the verge and back through the woods, the sky suddenly became the colour of gunmetal. It was very still. No shadows, only pools and walls of darkest green. Nothing stirring except an occasional pheasant's cry and a crackle of snowy ice. On reaching home I noticed that the sky had turned from gunmetal to black ink. The leaves of the privet hedge were a vivid orange rust colour.

Monday, 19th January

Weather still bitter, but thaw on way. A. and I went to London for the night to attend Nigel Nicolson's seventieth birthday dinner at Escargot Restaurant, in private room upstairs. Arranged by Rebecca,† Nigel unaware of it. Was expecting to dine with children alone. Some thirty guests assembled, drinking champagne. At eight lights dimmed, company silenced. Nigel walks in. Shades his eyes to take in crowd before him. His face breaks into smiles, and he utters cries of delight. Great success. George Weidenfeld‡ made a speech in which he paid high tribute to Nigel, his first helper when he started as a penniless refugee, the most loyal friend and collaborator, his beloved best friend, etc. Nigel gave an impromptu reply as only a sometime MP could do. Because of the tremendous din I could hear but little, though I think it was a splendid occasion. I had many compliments for Regy, which I take with a grain. Terence de Vere White§ told me – I wonder how truthfully, for he is Irish to the core – that at a recent meeting at Chatto's, it was said that Paddy L.F.,¶ I and someone else were the three best prose writers today. Baba Metcalfe,**

---

* The L.-Ms' whippets were now Folly and Missy. Missy had been bought in May 1986 to replace Honey; having proved unsatisfactory, she was returned in June 1987 to the kennels whence she had come.

† Yr dau. (b. 1963) of Nigel Nicolson; m. 1988–96 Hon. Guy Philipps.

‡ Austrian-born publisher (b. 1919); co-founder with Nigel Nicolson of Weidenfeld & Nicolson, 1948; cr. life peer, 1976.

§ Solicitor, writer and journalist (1912–94); m. 1982 (as her 2nd husband) Hon. Victoria Glendinning, writer (b. 1937).

¶ (Sir) Patrick Leigh Fermor (b. 1915); writer, living in Greece; m. 1968 Hon. Joan Eyres-Monsell, photographer (1912–2003).

** Lady Alexandra Curzon (1904–95); yst dau. of Marquess Curzon of Kedleston; m. 1925 Major E.D. ('Fruity') Metcalfe (d. 1957).

suddenly shrunk to a small old lady, made a touching speech. Stayed at Brooks's.

Tuesday, 20th January

Went to Rota's in Long Acre to discuss the disposal of my papers. Mr Rota* was at a board meeting, which to my embarrassment he dismissed in order to talk to me. I explained that Misha [Michael Bloch] was to be my literary executor but I didn't want to burden him with sorting and storing my papers. Mr Rota will pay us a visit to look through A's and my papers to assess their worth, and decide which American libraries to approach.

John Julius [Norwich] asked me last night if I researched each chapter individually before writing it. No, I said, I did all the research for the whole book, taking copious notes, and then began writing. But, he asked, do you not find you have forgotten the research for a particular chapter before you have reached it? I admitted this was often the case, and that I had to rely on the completeness and good order of my notes.

Wednesday, 28th January

Put out to receive letter from Mark Girouard† this morning asking if he may quote several extracts from my published diaries in the country houses anthology which he is compiling. Of course I do not mind his quoting, but I do mind that he is doing the very same book that I am pledged to do. It would be wonderful if Mark and I could amalgamate, but I fear unlikely. He has presumably got his own publisher, and being a giant will not want to associate with a pygmy like me. Perhaps it will be a blessed way out of a book my heart is not in. Yet I deplore a whole month's wasted labour.

---

* Anthony Rota (b. 1932); managing director of Bertram Rota Ltd of Long Acre, dealers in books and literary manuscripts; m. Jean Kendall.
† Writer and architectural historian (b. 1931); Slade Professor of Fine Art, Oxford, 1975–6.

Wednesday, 4th February

To London and Pat Trevor-Roper for eye test. He gave me a prescription for reading glasses to help me see the scripts I am typing
without bending too low and developing a dowager's hump. Full of
gossip as usual. He told me that Sheridan Dufferin,* Bruce Chatwin
and Ian McCallum all have Aids; that they might seem to recover
from some mild ailment, only to get another, but when a serious
attack of pneumonia or the like assailed them, they would go under.
Very terrible. Derek Hill, who is rather proprietary of Bruce, naively
denies it in his case, insisting to Pat that Bruce caught a mysterious
disease from bathing in the South Seas too close to a whale, or some
such nonsense.

Friday, 6th February

Bruce Hunter writes that Penguin have turned down my novel. We
must regard it as dead now. He can do no more. Sends me their letter
in which the usual things are trotted out – excellently written, but
characters not sharply enough drawn, etc. Now it may not be brilliant,
but I know parts of it are good, and thousands of worse novels are
published every year. I have thanked Bruce and also told him that
I am joyfully chucking the anthology, which leaves me with the
Cotswold Country Houses only. After that, which should keep me
busy for most of this year, it is the end. I don't want further suggestions
such as the ones I have lately received – travel books in Northern Italy,
picture books with young photographers. I am finished. Debo writes
to A. that Joan Haslip† wants to write about the Devonshire House
set (she is welcome), and Jim had better hurry up with the Bachelor
Duke.‡ But I am not sure. Who has heard of him? And do I wish to

---

* Sheridan Blackwood, 5th and last Marquess of Dufferin and Ava (1938–88); o. s.
of J.L.-M's friend and contemporary Basil, 4th Marquess; m. 1964 Serena Belinda
('Lindy') Guinness.
† English writer living in Florence (1912–94).
‡ William George Spencer Cavendish, 6th Duke of Devonshire (1790–1858); Whig
statesman, art collector, improver of Chatsworth and patron of Sir Joseph Paxton:
Debo Devonshire had for some time been trying to persuade J.L.-M. to undertake
a biography of him.

spend years researching a biography which will sell two thousand copies and get no reviews? No, I don't.

Monday, 9th February

That charmer David Burnett lunched in Bath, and we drew up plans for the Cotswold Country Houses book. The odd thing is that, when he arrived, I did not at first recognise him, though finding him no less attractive than when we met last May. I have now written six letters to owners of those houses we most want to include.

Tuesday, 17th February

To London for the night. In afternoon I went to see Ros[amond Lehmann]. Her eyesight no better. Reading an agony. She is eighty-six, and says she wants to die. Would like to stay away, but what friends can have an immobile guest for a week or ten days? The trouble with Rosamond is that she has been a star, and is now a decayed old lady whom a few friends visit out of kindness. Conversation is not easy. I did a terribly unkind thing. She produced a rather ugly mauve bottle with stopper and children engraved in white on the bowl. She said, 'I am giving things away and was going to give this to you, but now I can't because I find there is a hole in it.' I looked at it and admired it rather coldly because I didn't like it. Put it down and went off without it, not having referred to it again. I think I should have gushed and put it immediately in my coat pocket and taken it with me. Oh dear.

Then dined at Boodle's with Derek Hill, Anne Norwich[*] and the Snowdons.[†] Tony's present wife is not pretty but charming. So easy and relaxed after Princess Margaret. Had a long talk with him after dinner. He had just come from Liverpool, and was appalled by the disintegration, the deserted streets, the empty and decaying terraces, the smashed churches, the hooligans. Thinks it hauntingly awful.

---

[*] Anne Clifford; m. 1958 (diss. 1985) John Julius Cooper, 2nd Viscount Norwich.
[†] Anthony Armstrong-Jones (b. 1930); son of J.L.-M's friend Anne, Countess of Rosse by her 1st marriage; photographer; m. 1st 1960 HRH Princess Margaret, 2nd 1978 Lucy Davies; cr. Earl of Snowdon, 1961.

'Does the Government know? And does it care?' I said I had the same impression when last there, but did not know what could be done about it. He said what he could do was to take photographs and get the popular press to publish them.

Wednesday, 18th February

Nick [Robinson] breakfasted with me at Brooks's. His very presence does me good. He arrived like a breath of fresh Scotch air in a neatly fitted tweed suit. I explained to him the dispositions in my new will, which names him as residuary legatee. He understood, as he understands everything. I asked him when he was going to settle and cease being a gypsy. He said he might marry, but wasn't certain. 'Be very certain,' I said, like any old grandfather.

Saturday, 21st February

Gervase Jackson-Stops stayed two nights with us. He is preparing two articles on the House for *Country Life*. This morning I accompanied him to the House. For the first time I entered the Muniment Room, which is the south-east pavilion on the east front, approached from outside. Very pretty inside with shelves and gallery, copied by Stephen Wright from the Kent pavilions which were adaptations of Gibbs's* designs. Looked at several drawings in a portfolio. They prove beyond dispute that Kent took over from Gibbs, presumably on the death of the 3rd Duke [d. 1746] who was a man of culture as well as a sportsman, probably the last Duke of Beaufort to combine these qualities. One fascinating discovery was an outline drawing – I'm sure a projected design for it is very simple, without adornments – of the Almshouses and our Essex House. It is signed one T. Hayward, and I feel sure is seventeenth-century. Moreover, in pencil, Hayward calls Essex House 'the Parsonage'. He also indicates that the east elevation, now obliterated by the Victorian lodge, was the same as the north elevation. Then G. and I went round the House with Caroline. I learnt much from Gervase who is extremely quick. In the dining room he remarked that

---

* James Gibbs (1682–1754); architect.

the dentils of cornice were all of different flower heads. They must be by the rococo carver Poynton, who is known to have made the door-cases with involuted pediments. A really remarkable craftsman. He also did the panel in the library which David has now scrapped in favour of the fine Lely of 1st Duke [d. 1699] and Duchess. This panel, which David thought Victorian, is dated 1732 from a drawing.

Sunday, 22nd February

To church at Acton Turville at 9.30. Usual smattering of some half a dozen parishioners, and a young woman sitting in front of me whom I did not recognise, wearing a scarf which partly concealed her head. When we left the church she smiled at me, to which I responded. The Vicar told me she was Mrs X.; that she had never been to church before, but this was her third Sunday running, making him wonder if there was something wrong with her. When I told A., she said that X. had recently started a wild affair with another woman, on learning of which Mrs X., in a towering rage, had kicked him in the balls.

I asked Vicar why it mattered so much if the Synod voted for women priests.* He is dead against it because (1) it has been traditional for two thousand years that only men are priests, and (2) it would mean never a getting-together with the Orthodox and Catholic Churches which are fundamentally opposed to the idea. Nevertheless, I support the proposal because women are generally more devout than men, and there is a dearth of theological students. Our own vicar has four parishes instead of one.

We lunched with the Johnstons.† Much talk of poor Rosie. She has no sanitation in her cell, just a pot, which she has to empty out of the

---

* The General Synod voted to ordain women priests in 1992. Almost 500 clergy left the Anglican ministry as a result. The first women were ordained at Bristol Cathedral in 1994.
† Nicholas Johnston (b. 1929); architect; m. 1956 Susanna Chancellor. Their daughter Rosie (b. 1964) had been sentenced at Oxford Crown Court in December 1986 to nine months' imprisonment for supplying heroin the previous June to her friend Olivia Channon (dau. of Rt Hon. Paul Channon MP, Sec. of State for Trade and Industry, 1986–7), who had died of an overdose.

window to avoid beastly encounters at latrines. Owing to the wide publicity of her case, all the inmates know about her. Being girls of the criminal class, they hate her and bully her. During the exercise hour in the prison yard, they cover her with jeers and taunts. 'Does the Queen fart, Rosie? You know, Rosie. Tell us, Rosie!' On one visit, Susanna noticed Rosie had a black eye caused by inmates hitting her. When they do not brutalise her, they make lesbian advances. On hearing of Susanna's concern, Lord Longford, aged eighty-two, by virtue of his privileged access to any prisoner at any time, made an expedition to Essex during the worst weather spell. Stayed with Rosie for an hour and a half, bringing her newspapers and books. He will give a luncheon for her at the House of Lords on her release. Never again will I scoff at him, says Susanna.

Wednesday, 25th February

To Chatsworth by train, changing twice. Was ushered into Debo's little room with the green pleated hangings, and the little spy window overlooking the entrance gate. We were alone the first night. Debo full of excitement at the prospect of my doing the Bachelor Duke. I soon discovered what I had feared, that his handwriting is appalling and gets worse as his life progresses – or as it ebbs, as mine is doing. There are masses of box files of diaries and letters, and a variety of other matter. At the end of the day Michael Pearman, one of the librarians, a gentle, neurotic man being treated for acute depression, gave me a straight talk. He said he dared not say what he was going to tell me in front of Her Grace, to whom the B.D. was hero and god, but he wondered whether he was a sufficiently important subject for a biography. Would it not involve years of hard labour, resulting in a book which might be remaindered after six months? This was wise counsel, and I took it well of him. Debo, when I put these points to her, dismissed them, assuring me that any publisher would jump at the biog. There was sex (which seems to amount to his having kept a mistress at the Rookery for several years, like any other aristocrat, and hardly exciting); there was royalty (true, relations with George IV and William IV may prove interesting); he was one of the greatest collectors of books, pictures, furniture, and, above all, sculpture; and he was a great builder and gardener, with Paxton. Friendship is another quality which Debo emphasises. So I find myself in the predicament of trying to respond to D's immense enthusiasm while having grave doubts – about my ability to read the writing, about my having to spend months here, or near here (for I don't suppose they will let me take the papers away), and about my state of health, for I doubt if I can summon the strength to embark on another long book of this sort. Luckily the Cotswold Houses will give me some months to think it over.

Thursday, 5th March

I have written a long letter to Debo and told her frankly that unless I may be allowed to have the Bachelor Duke's diaries (if no other papers) on loan in Bath, I cannot tackle his biography. Mentioned that Churchill College had allowed me to have all the Esher papers, and Nigel Nicolson the Harold papers, on these terms. That at my age I should not be away from A. for months on end, kind though she was to offer to put me up in the house. I don't know whether I hope the business is off or on.

Tuesday and Wednesday, 10th and 11th March

Two blissful days being motored by David Burnett round Cotswolds, reconnoitring houses for our book. From the outside, we must have seen twenty. It is a long time since I have driven round the counties and looked at houses with a critical eye. I am shocked by the dreadful examples of in-filling in villages, and the appalling invasion of the remote Cotswolds by London weekenders. At Eastington Manor, for example, we saw a humble little house slightly tarted up with a neat, trim garden. David found a farm worker in a barn, of whom he asked the owner's name. 'A Mr Docker from London, who comes down about four times a year' was the reply. 'How dreadful,' said David. 'It be,' was the answer. The village people don't like these fly-by-night, new rich, suburban-minded, totally non-country folk, who bring their middle class friends and cocktail bars for a few days and are of no use to the community. Then so many of the large country houses are being converted into flats. This is a good idea in principle, but seldom are the conversions sympathetic. As for Northwick Park, the spectacle was horrifying. There stands the great house in the middle of the erstwhile park, a mile from Blockley village in an area of outstanding natural beauty. It was unapproachable, for one drive was blocked up, the other so churned by tractors and tree-felling vehicles that we could not get up to it. A long row of hideous garages with blue doors newly erected; pegged strips in the park where new residences will be built. Northwick, where George Churchill* lived surrounded by precious pictures and works of art, can henceforth be erased from the memory. Dowdeswell Manor has been divided into three. The charming Georgian gazebo made into a residence, with ghastly window inserted. Carriage lamps abound. Broadwell Manor under scaffolding, having recently been bought – by whom? Adlestrop Park by Sanderson Miller† now a second-rate preparatory school with flimsy shack annexes like so many public lavatories surrounding it. And so on.

David a perfect companion. Treats me as though I were Dresden porcelain. Always solicitous as to whether I am not too cold, too tired, etc. He leaps from the wheel to ask directions and questions while I sit like Buddha wrapped up in front seat poring over the map. We eat deliciously in pubs, make jokes and laugh. He has the sort of humour that I appreciate.

Only once did we encounter an owner – at Whittington Manor, a prominent Elizabethan house we saw from the road and drove to. Met owner in drive. Nice modest professional from Surrey and sympathetic wife. They showed us round this empty, dilapidated white elephant. The wife left it by friends. Feel it their duty to restore and inhabit, bringing daughter and her children to share. What an enterprise. I suspect they already regret that cosy villa in Chobham.

---

* Captain E.G. Spencer-Churchill (1876–1964), grandson of 6th Duke of Marlborough; inherited Northwick Park from his mother, stepdaughter of last Lord Northwick; High Sheriff of Worcestershire, 1924; a Trustee of National Gallery, 1943–50.

† Gentleman architect in the Gothic style (1717–80); friend of Horace Walpole.

Saturday, 14th March

There on breakfast table is reply from Debo. Make A. read it. Answer is yes, Andrew will allow me to take away papers. So now I am committed, and nothing but a stroke or death can prevent me embarking upon this vast enterprise.

We dine again at the House. I tell A. this is a mistake; we are becoming bores, and have little to say to them. I know David loves A. and Caroline is fond of her; but they tolerate me just. I feel awkward.

Wednesday, 18th March

David Burnett called at ten, having taken his children to school somewhere near Bournemouth, and off we set on our third recce. A fine, bright day but piercingly cold. At first I thought that the first fine careless rapture must have passed, but after an hour's motoring I started enjoying the outing as much as before, recapturing the sympathy, the empathy (a word coined by Gerard Manley Hopkins, I believe, and much used incorrectly today). We saw ten or twelve houses, most of which we instantly dismissed. But the first visited was Alderley Grange [where the L.-Ms had lived from 1961 to 1974], which D. was much taken with and wants included. I must say the Acloques* have filled it with wondrous things, and it looks a charming little country house. Extraordinary experience at Holcombe and Hilles, two houses beyond Painswick once owned by Detmar Blow.† At the first we saw a coal-black negro in the garden. David leapt out of the car to ask him who the owner was. 'I am,' he replied. Thinking he had misheard, David asked again very politely. With exquisite courtesy the blackamoor replied, 'I am the owner and have been these forty years.' Gave his name as Pollock and said we were welcome to see over. However we didn't and went on to Hilles which Blow built. Liked both houses and decided to put the two together under one heading. On getting home,

---

* Guy Acloque; m. 1971 Hon. Camilla, dau. of 9th Baron Howard de Walden. They had purchased Alderley Grange from A.L.-M. in 1974 and maintained the garden she had created there.
† Architect and sometime adviser to 2nd Duke of Westminster (1867–1939).

I rang Simon Blow* to ask to whom at Hilles I should direct myself. He said to Mrs Gopal, the Indian widow of his uncle Jonathan Blow, now remarried to another Indian. Strange squires to find cheek-by-jowl in the deepest Cotswolds.

Tuesday, 24th March

A ghastly morning in Bath. How can I be expected to write books? The plumber who promised to arrive at 10.30 came at 11.30, and then had to go off to get the parts he needed. Then a man came about the gas boiler in the basement, where the tenant is currently without heat or hot water. Man said flue is blocked, and he would report to headquarters and advise me of what needed to be done. I rang the HQ all afternoon to ask when they would repair, without getting through to anyone who knew about the trouble. Terrible interruptions. Then, while talking on the telephone to Prince Michael's secretary, I see Folly retching. Desperately with my leg I manoeuvre her off the Persian carpet onto the linoleum floor, where she is sick. In the evening I tell A. that I want to live in a 'home' where there are no responsiblities. She says, 'You are living in one now, with minimal responsibilities.' The darling.

Wednesday, 8th April

On Sunday last David Burnett motored me to Bourton House, Sezincote and Batsford. The first has changed hands eight times since Miss Bligh lived there when I visited in 1944 or thereabouts. It has suffered much in consequence. Land below the great barn was sold by one owner to a speculator who has built two cheap little houses cheek by jowl. Some very bad things done to the building. The old thick sash bars removed from the south front and thin ones substituted, and four panes for the original three across. Some ghastly

---

* Writer, former racing jockey (b. 1943); yr s. of Purcell Blow (e. s. of Detmar Blow) and Diana Bethell (dau. of Hon. Clare Tennant by her 1st marriage); his publications include works of family history and autobiography including *Broken Blood* (1987) and *No Time to Grow* (1999).

decoration, a sort of velvet paper splashed on the undersides of the staircase. One big room made out of two on the garden side and rococo fireplace substituted for the original William and Mary. Nice bedint couple have now bought it, and love it. Intend to improve it gradually, though what we saw of their taste was pretty poor.

A very different state of affairs at Sezincote, where we lunched. The owner, Mrs Peake, daughter of Cyril Kleinwort,* very distinguished-looking. Charming husband, City man, intelligent too. The house in excellent taste and well kept up. From there we hopped across the road to Batsford. Tony Dulverton† has the same teasing manner as he had when a boy. I pulled the bell and when I did not hear it ring was about to walk off to find another entrance, when he opened the door and said abruptly, 'Aren't you going to say how do you do to your host?' Nice friendly wife, sister of the late Peter Farquhar.‡ We were quite impressed by the hall and the ballroom, but a beast of a house really.

The following day, Monday, we went to Nether Lypiatt [seat of Prince and Princess Michael of Kent] in the morning, losing our way as we tried to cross the deep valley above Stroud. Taken round the outside by gardener-cum-clerk-of-all-works with enormous nose like spout of a teapot. This house likewise spoilt since Mrs Woodhouse§ had it. The fire escape an eyesore. The garden ruined. Hideous rose maze of floribundas within wooden curbs. Lamps down the lime avenue for benefit of guests gazing after dark from drawing-room window. The house also too tarted-up. More and more I admire the taste of Mrs Woodhouse's generation in doing up old houses – Reggie

---

* Susanna Kleinwort (b. 1942); m. 1962 David Peake.

† Anthony Hamilton Wills, 2nd Baron Dulverton (1915–92); m. (2nd) 1962 Ruth, dau. of Sir Walter Farquhar, 5th Bt.

‡ Sir Peter Farquhar, 6th Bt (1904–86).

§ Violet Gwynne (1870–1948); m. 1895 Gordon Woodhouse; harpsichordist and bohemian, who lived in a *ménage à cinq* with four men, as well as having lesbian associations. (See biography by Jessica Douglas-Home, *Violet: The Life and Loves of Violet Gordon Woodhouse* [1996].) The *ménage* moved in 1923 to Nether Lypiatt Manor, where J.L.-M., who greatly admired the house, visited her on several occasions towards the end of her life (as described in his early diaries).

Cooper,[*] Ted Lister,[†] Gerry Wellington and the like. The next house we visited, Ablington Manor, was a disappointment. Again too tarted-up. It has changed hands several times since the war and is now owned by a rich scrap metal merchant whose children won't live there when he is dead. So it goes on. No one stays long. Each owner undoes what the previous one did. No owner leaves well alone. Still, the outside is attractive – alterations of every date, all in the traditional style, of gables and harling, a motley of yellow and orange.

John Lehmann[‡] has died. I telephoned poor Ros who is sad but philosophical. 'It feels odd being the only one of us four[§] left,' she said. She was not pleased with the *Times* obit., saying it did not give him credit for his poetry, and he was a good poet if not a great one. Said he became nicer towards her as he got progressively iller, but always remained hostile to her [spiritualist] religious beliefs. 'Poor old boy,' she said, 'he will be having a strange surprise now.'

Saturday, 2nd May

Have been reading Simon Brett's[¶] anthology of diaries, unable to put it down. His arrangement, running through the calendar and choosing extracts for each day, is a good one. One quickly gets to learn the character of each diarist as his extracts appear, though I don't know that my character emerges very clearly. It becomes obvious that the majority of diarists write for their own glorification and pathetic immortality.

I am appalled by my bad temper. This week I was enraged by our tenant in the basement at Bath, demanding £100 compensation for

---

[*] Lieut-Col. R.A. Cooper (1885–1965); school friend of Harold Nicolson, some-time diplomatist and soldier; garden designer and restorer of country houses, some of whose best work may be seen at Cothay Manor nr Wellington, Somerset, where he lived in 1930s.

[†] Edward Graham Lister (1873–1956) of Westwood Manor, Wiltshire (which he bequeathed to N.T.); diplomatist, furniture restorer, needleworker and harpist; bachelor admirer of J.L.-M.

[‡] Writer, poet, publisher and critic (1907–87); brother of Rosamond.

[§] Their two other siblings had included the actress Beatrix Lehmann (1903–79).

[¶] Novelist and playwright (b. 1945).

having been a fortnight without hot water. I asked why, in my absence, she had not chivvied the gas company to come and fix the boiler. She assured me she had done so. They promptly came and fixed it when I telephoned myself. I told her I want her to leave, whereupon she said it would be difficult for her to find other premises, and I would be hearing from her solicitor. I shall now write to her giving notice and pointing out that the £160 a month which she pays is ridiculously little. Then I lost my temper with poor little Missy* who seems to have collapsed, takes no interest in anything, hates going for walks, and might almost be a stuffed dog for all the notice she takes of A. and myself. When obliged to return to the foot of a steep hill on the golf course I had climbed for her benefit to find her still standing there, I put on her lead and literally dragged her up the hill in a rage. Am overwhelmed by depression as bad as before I went to Majorca [in April], if not worse. Poor Alvilde. Oh the guilt and *Angst*, as bad as ever, even in extreme old age.

Friday, 8th May

I am too conscious of my failing powers. They accelerate week by week. I notice how my knees grow feebler, how I walk shorter distances, get puffed and tired. Always tired. Little things upset me inordinately. My eyes give constant trouble; I find it difficult to focus, to see any print in a dim light. Now I have developed a red patch on the left cheek. I dabbed it with TCP, only to find next morning that it had doubled in size. I fear it may be skin cancer, brought about by the sun-drenching I got in Majorca. I know sunshine does not agree with me, although it was delicious there owing to the air being cool. Nevertheless it was very strong and I was obliged to buy a straw hat which I did not always wear.

Tuesday, 12th May

Rupert and Josephine Loewenstein have just returned from taking Princess Margaret on a tour of her German relations. Rupert very

---

* See note to 15 January 1987.

shocked that she did not know who any of them were. Stranger would come up, kiss her, and say Hello Margaret. Rupert would explain that this was the daughter of Missy or the grandson of Ducky, as she must know. She would reply, 'I don't know and I don't care. Mummy hates the Germans, who killed her brothers and killed Papa.' The last a slight exaggeration surely, George VI having died seven years after the war. He also told me that Peg Hesse,* that charming woman I once met at Ian [McCallum]'s, had refused point-blank to let Tony Lambton see the Hesse papers for his book on Mountbatten; she would not have him poking around, scavenging for scandal. Then she told Rupert an astonishing thing – that her father-in-law, the Grand Duke of Hesse who was the son of Queen Victoria's daughter Alice,† was homosexual, and had been seduced by his uncle, Edward VII. I asked Rupert what earthly proof she had for this astonishing statement. He said he would ask her the next time he saw her.

Wednesday, 13th May

Lunched in London with M. at his new club, the Savile in Brook Street. He is very proud of it, but the food was poor and the company not very distinguished. M. took me upstairs to see the bathroom in which poor Loulou Harcourt‡ took his overdose. Bathroom remosaiced since his time but I thought the tub might be the same, though lacking the mahogany which would have gone with it. Two fixed cupboards against the bedroom walls are clearly Edwardian French, what in this building is termed 'Loulou Quinze'. Then J.K.-B. had tea with me at Brooks's. He was in fine fettle, most affectionate, and forgiving about my having forgotten our lunch at Brooks's

---

* Hon. Margaret Geddes (1913–99), dau. of 1st Baron Geddes; m. 1937 Prince Louis of Hesse (1908–68), who succeeded as head of the Grand Ducal House of Hesse when the plane carrying his elder brother and children to his marriage in London crashed with no survivors.

† Grand Duke Ernst Ludwig (1868–1937); reigned in Darmstadt from 1892 to 1918.

‡ Lewis, 1st Viscount Harcourt (1863–1922); Liberal politician, friend of Reginald, Viscount Esher; committed suicide at 69 Brook Street after 'pouncing' on J.L.-M's Eton contemporary, Edward James.

last week, the day I was to have attended the dinner for Betty Hussey.[*]
He is slightly better off, having paid off the mortgage on his house,
and seems happier generally.

Saturday, 23rd May

I find the general election not only boring but horrifying.[†] Every news
on wireless and television is concentrated on politicians abusing one
another, telling outrageous lies, making promises they will never fulfil.
They are a contemptible race. If we had a Green candidate I might
vote for it, because at least their programme concerns itself with the
fundamental issue of the future of this earth and whether human life
will continue or no – though I sometimes think no the preferable
outcome.

M. told me on the telephone that the retiring British Ambassador
to Paris[‡] invited himself to tea with Maître Blum.[§] The old lady, now
eighty-eight, supposed he and the ambassadress wished to say goodbye
and thank her for all her efforts on behalf of the Duke and Duchess
of Windsor. Not at all. The Ambassador came without wife, but with
a private secretary clutching an important-looking envelope addressed
to the Maître, bearing royal ciphers on the flap. The Ambassador
announced that the Queen had commissioned Mr Philip Ziegler to
write the official life of King Edward VIII, and hoped the Maître
would co-operate to the extent of lending such papers and photographs as she had in her charge, and giving permission to quote
copyright material as executor. She resolutely refused, saying she had
her own official biographer lined up, namely Misha. Having been
given a dusty reception, the Ambassador left, not without giving a nod
to the secretary which apparently conveyed that he was not to deliver

---

[*] Elizabeth Kerr-Smiley (1907–2006); m. 1936 Christopher Hussey, architectural
historian (1899–1970), of Scotney Castle, Kent (later donated with its gardens to the
N.T.).
[†] The election took place on 11 June and returned Mrs Thatcher's Conservative
Government for a third term with a majority of 102.
[‡] Sir John Fretwell (b. 1930); HM Ambassador to France, 1982–7.
[§] Venerable Paris lawyer (1898–1994) who acted as executor of Duke and Duchess
of Windsor, for whom Michael Bloch had been working since 1979.

the clutched envelope, presumed to be some honour from the Queen, only to be conferred if the old lady complied. M. is upset by this news, which means he must now put aside Ribbentrop to finish his book on the reign of Edward VIII, which he was hoping to do later on. He fears Ziegler's book, despite being an official royal biography, is bound to be ungenerous and unsympathetic, for Z. is given to unsympathetic biogs (*vide* his Mountbatten), and generosity is unimaginable with the Queen Mother alive who loathed the Duke. I sympathise with poor M.

The last few days I have been incensed by my bitch of a tenant declining to answer my letter of three weeks ago giving her six months' notice (though I am only obliged to give her three under our signed agreement). I am further enraged by my Bath solicitors, who are cautious and pessimistic, warning me that under current legislation it is not easy for landlords to rid themselves of undesirable tenants. A sense that one is in the right, but apparently unable to do much about it, engenders a sense of frustration and arouses one's most aggressive instincts.

David Burnett and I had an enjoyable day at Stanway on Wednesday the 20th, spending so long there that there was no time to visit Sudley as we had intended. We arrived for luncheon and were surprised to find the drive littered with cars, wondering if we had come on the wrong day. But it was just a gathering of businessmen for the afternoon's clay pigeon shoot. Jamie Neidpath met us and took us round the garden, up to the Belvedere, and ambled so slowly, talking all the while, that we did not get back to the house and luncheon, famished, until three o'clock. Luncheon in the kitchen, very *intime*, with wife Catherine and small boy. I like him immensely. He is extremely bright. Loves Stanway, knows its history, very well informed and clever on every count. Could not have been kinder. Took us over the house, explaining every picture and piece of furniture. Catherine also easy and friendly. She has none of the beauty of her grandmother Diana [Mosley], being plain with a large chin. The so-called Elcho boudoir, with its portraits of Lady [Mary] Elcho and the Souls, includes William Acton's* drawing of Diana, now a Stanway ancestress.

---

* Artist, brother of Sir Harold Acton.

Tuesday, 26th May

These past few days I have been in a rage with the tenant in Bath. It is nearly a month since I wrote telling her she must leave, out of the goodness of my heart giving her six months' notice instead of the agreed three. I have since written her two further letters but heard nothing and last Friday I called to see her to ask why she had not replied, nor thanked me for the cheque I had sent at her request to compensate her for a fortnight without hot water. She said she was writing to me that very day – I told her I required merely a word of acknowledgement – but this morning there is still no reply from this bloody bitch of a girl. So I have asked my Bath solicitors to write to her, but they warn me that I have little chance of getting rid of her if she is determined to stay. It is monstrous that the law prevents a landlord sacking an undesirable tenant. I am determined that, come what may, I shall rid myself of this pestilential female.

Friday, 26th June

Only on Sunday I was showing Feeble [Cavendish] Master's tombstone by Verity.* She thought it rather pretentious, with the coronet on the cushion. I said I admired it very much, but couldn't for the life of me see how Mary [Beaufort] would fit in when her time came, as the coffins have to be concreted down to guard against vandalism. Then, on Wednesday, poor old Mary died. James Fergusson asked me to write an obituary for the *Independent*, which I composed within an hour this morning and dictated down the telephone. Hugh Massingberd, who is writing about her for the *Telegraph*, also asked me for anecdotes; I gave him some, and felt a bit of a cad.

On Wednesday I went to London to collect proofs of *Venetian Evenings*. Had Jamie Fergusson, M. and J.K.-B. to luncheon at Brooks's. Thought it a good way of getting the last two to meet without previously warning either. They seemed to like one another,

---

* Simon Verity (b. 1945); memorial sculptor, commissioned, on J.L.-M's recommendation, to execute memorial to 10th Duke of Beaufort ('Master'); m. 1970 Judith Mills.

and M. much taken by Jamie who has developed a distinction with his tall, upright figure, thick dark hair and whimsical mouth.

Saturday, 11th July

Very hot day. We drove to Oxford to lunch with Leslie Rowse.[*] I told A. that were I younger I would certainly sniff cocaine or take heroin to get me through occasions such as this luncheon, which I presumed would be of intellectuals unknown to me. Like Diana Cooper who had to drink before she could face a party. A. replied that it was a form of conceit, this feeling that I must shine. But I feel it is just a case of sheer nerves, from which I have suffered all my life, and which seem if anything to get worse in old age. Impossible to find a parking space when we got to Oxford, which must be the worst city for parking in the British Isles. We drove round and round until the porter at All Souls took pity on us and let us park in the Warden's drive. I enjoyed the luncheon immensely, sitting between Christina Foyle and Lady Monson.[†] Christina, with her clipped, bedint little voice and inattention, is very sweet. Lady M., a daughter of Anthony Devas whose painting I have always admired, very bright and sympathetic. Henry Thorold[‡] also present, and Leslie's literary agent and wife. Leslie a dear old pussy-cat. He has become rather deaf, but is as voluble as ever and an excellent host. Called us all 'dear', irrespective of age or sex. Afterwards he took us round the College. The Codrington Library has perfect proportions, though the ceiling is not as Hawksmoor intended and could do with some gilding. Unsuitable marble-topped table just given by Simon Codrington[§] which might have belonged to Beckford. Chapel screen fine, early Georgian but Leslie says not by Hawksmoor. He showed us a pair of fine fifteenth-century statues taken down from the towers and put in the crypt for preservation, of Sainted Henry VI and Archbishop Chichele, founder of All Souls. Is

---

[*] A. L. Rowse (1903–97); historian and Fellow of All Souls.

[†] Emma Devas; m. 1955 John, 11th Baron Monson (b. 1932).

[‡] Revd Henry Thorold of Marston Hall, Lincolnshire (1921–2000); clergyman, schoolmaster and architectural historian; author of Shell county guides, and books on cathedrals.

[§] Sir Simon Codrington, 3rd Bt (b. 1923), formerly of Dodington Park near Bath.

it possible that they were done from life? That of the King is very tragic, lean and worn and devout; one senses the hair shirt under the emaciated figure; the crown is broken, whether by accident or design. The Buttery by Hawksmoor splendidly Baroque, small oval tables and kidney-shaped benches to fit. Before we left, Leslie said to A., 'Jim writes for me, and I write for him.'

Sunday, 19th July

After dining last night with the Beauforts at the House, we were taken upstairs to see Mary's bedroom. Rather 'how', with bedside photographs of her plain soldier brother killed in the Great War, and other mementoes untouched. David and Caroline quite without sentiment in deciding what things to remove and what to throw away. Charming watercolours in matching rope frames of Lord Arthur ('Podge') and Lord Henry [Somerset], both rather plain-featured, which Caroline decided to hang in her bedroom. I wonder how much Mary knew about the two delinquent males.*

Thursday, 6th August

My beastly [seventy-ninth] birthday. Several cards from unknown fans, all of which must be answered. Audrey lunched alone with me in Bath. Desultory talk of old times. Sweet she was, yet I could not get going. When she left me a gift of two expensive ties, I felt remorseful, and sent her an affectionate note. As she says, we are the only ones left who can remember Wickhamford and Ribbesford days.

---

* Lord Henry Somerset (1849–1932; Comptroller of Royal Household, 1874–9; m. 1872 Lady Isabelle Somers) and Lord Arthur Somerset (1851–1926; sometime Equerry and Superintendent of Stables to Prince of Wales) – younger sons of 8th Duke of Beaufort – were both obliged to live abroad for most of their lives owing to homosexual scandals. Lord Arthur fled in 1889 after the police raided a male brothel of which he was a client in Cleveland Street, Marylebone; he was helped to avoid arrest through the influence of his friend Regy Brett, future 2nd Viscount Esher. Lord Henry, who settled in Florence where he achieved some distinction as a poet, was great-grandfather of the L.-Ms' friend and landlord David, 11th Duke.

A. organised a little dinner party for me, with the Beauforts and the Moores. Excellent dinner of quails, over which she took much trouble, and enjoyable gossip. But oh, the sadness of everything. And now Joanie Altrincham* dying.

Friday, 14th August

Mr and Mrs Rota turn up in Bath at 11 and stay till 5 looking through my papers, letters and diaries. I tremble at some of the things he may have read, but he can't have spent much time looking at anything in particular. A charming man with exquisite manners, who reminded me of Eddy Sackville before he grew a beard. Mrs Rota also charming, and read her book quietly in the library until her husband summoned her to the back room, where the papers were laid out, to take notes from his dictation.

I left them to attend Joanie Altrincham's funeral at Tormarton. Beautiful little church with truncated tower. Much to my surprise, it was packed, her relations having come in droves from London and elsewhere to say farewell to this recluse of almost ninety. Dear June [Hutchinson] came and sat beside me. As we embraced, our spectacles clashed; as I now wear mine almost permanently, I forget to remove them at such moments. We sang 'All Things Bright and Beautiful' – which makes me want to cry, as A. has decided to have this hymn at her funeral, and I already imagine myself in the role of chief mourner. Was fascinated by seventeenth-century monument opposite me commemorating in verse the virtues of the agent to the Marquess of Somebody. It was horrid outside standing at the committal. I did not like the yellow coffin with its fancy brass cross at the foot end. Church path lined with wreaths. I caught a glimpse of ours as I left – gypsophila and white daisies.

Joanie was a stalwart woman. She grumbled too much (like me), but was very intelligent. Very direct with high standards and

---

* Hon. Joan Dickson-Poynder (1897–1987); o. c. of 1st and last Baron Islington; m. 1923 Sir Edward Grigg MP (1879–1955), cr. Baron Altrincham 1945; mother of John Grigg (1924–2001; m. 1958 Patricia 'Patsy' Campbell), historian and journalist, then obituaries editor of *The Times*; she lived at Tormarton near Badminton.

principles. Not beautiful like her mother Lady Islington,[*] whom I think she rather resented, always refusing to go to concerts at Dyrham which Lady I. had once rented. The *Times* obituary, probably by John [Grigg] himself, was excellent on her work in the Great War, in which she served as a nurse by pretending to be older than she really was. She was not a happy woman and did not get on well with her sons.

When I got back to Bath, the Rotas had finished. He seemed to think my papers worth preserving, and said he would write and make me a proposition. I said I would like them to be kept together, for they form a sort of picture of my life.[†]

Saturday, 15th August

Today I lunched at Nether Lypiatt [with the Michaels of Kent]. In rather a fuss lest I be late. The secretary telephoned yesterday to inform me that luncheon was to be promptly at one and I must be there at 12.30. I asked her, did 12.30 really mean 12.30 with the Princess? Answer yes, tempered by advice to be five minutes late. So armed with map of how to find this elusive house I arrived at 12.40. Entrance is now by north door. Escorted through house to bathing pool where crowd of children in the water. Table with drinks on the edge. Effusive greeting from Princess Marie-Christine. Prince Michael very friendly and less shy, a dear, sensitive, courteous and very stupid little man. He started mixing Pimm's and got in a fix. She soon settled things, with much advice. 'Now darling, you must first give it a stir, and then darling, when you pour you must not let the fruit splosh into the glass.'

A heavenly warm day, blue sky with a ruffle of wind. We did not sit down to eat until 1.45. All this time I stood talking to him, first about Cotswold houses and the problems of living in one, then about Mary Beaufort. The last time he saw her, lunching at Badminton, she took him for a foreign grand duke. Said his favourite relation had been

---

[*] Anne Dundas; m. 1896 Sir John Dickson-Poynder, 6th Bt (1866–1936), Governor of New Zealand 1910–12, cr. Baron Islington 1910.

[†] They eventually found an excellent home in the Beinecke Library at Yale.

Princess Alice of Athlone,* whose memory was clear to the end, and who vividly recalled Queen Victoria's *Golden* Jubilee. His nephew George St Andrews† and fiancée staying. A very nice young man, not the yob or buffoon one is led to suppose by the newspapers. Wears a fuzzy ginger beard, a pity. Intelligent and interested in current affairs. Talked of *Spycatcher*. Little fiancée née Apponyi, Canadian by nationality, Hungarian on father's side, Italian on mother's. A clever and well-informed girl. Princess M. appears to be very fond of them both.

We ate under a large umbrella over a long table out of doors on the east front. I was placed at one end opposite the Prince and on her right, with the fiancée on my right. Hostess kept jumping up a lot which interrupted conversation. Food not good – two very dry cutlets (no wonder at 2 p.m.) and a huge common sausage covered in hickory sauce. Butler a handsome young man of about twenty-three. I thought of Igor and wondered if he could do this job.

The truth is one cannot dislike the Princess. She is extremely friendly, anxious to please, does please, and makes one feel interesting. Also she enjoys conversation and has a poor opinion of the English, calling them the stupidest nation in Europe. She particularly dislikes their false modesty, which she finds hypocritical. They must always deprecate themselves. At that moment, one of the guests, Ian Bond, asked me across the table, 'Which of your books do you think the best?' I at once replied, 'They are all pretty bad.' 'There you go!' said HRH. 'What did I tell you?' She is aggrieved over the reception of her book‡ here. Said she had frankly confessed in her preface that she had done no original research and derived her opinions from other

---

* HRH Princess Alice (1883–1981); o. dau. of HRH Prince Leopold, Duke of Albany, youngest son of Queen Victoria; m. 1904 Prince Alexander of Teck (1874–1957), bro. of Queen Mary, cr. Earl of Athlone, 1917 (Governor-General of South Africa, 1923–31, of Canada, 1940–6); a much-loved figure during her widowhood, when she became Queen Victoria's last surviving grandchild.

† George Windsor, Earl of St Andrews (b. 1962), e. s. of HRH Prince Edward, Duke of Kent. In 1988 he gave up his rights of succession to the throne to marry a Roman Catholic, Sylvana Tomaselli.

‡ *Crowned in a Far Country: Portraits of 8 Royal Brides* (Weidenfeld & Nicolson, 1986).

learned historians whose names she quoted. Neither Weidenfeld's nor Elizabeth Longford who read her text noticed the so-called plagiarisms. 'Anyway,' she said, rubbing her hands, 'all the beastliness has given me much publicity and I have sold 60,000 copies so far, with American sales still to come.' I congratulated her heartily, telling her that no book of mine had sold 6,000. She makes it very clear by innuendo that she dislikes the Royal Family. She mentioned her father in passing, saying that 'he was a sweet man in spite of all *they* say about him'.

Mrs Thatcher lunched here last week. I asked the Princess if she appreciated this gem of a house. Princess thought she did, but without knowing how to express her feelings. Before she came, Princess told her children the Prime Minister was coming, explaining that she was 'the headmistress of the country'. They said they thought 'Cousin Lilibet' was that, but the Princess added, 'No, the Queen is the mother of the country. She sends you to school but it is the headmistress who makes the rules you have to obey.' Not a bad explanation.

We talked of Barbara Cartland,[*] her great friend. I said I used to meet her when I was about eighteen as I knew her young brother Ronnie Cartland[†] when they lived near Tewkesbury. 'Oh,' she said, 'then you must lunch with me in London on Monday. She is coming, along with Queen Geraldine[‡] of Albania who is a Windischgrätz cousin of mine, etc.' Perhaps foolishly, I demurred. As we rose from the table at 3.45 for a walk round the garden, she begged me to think it over. I forgot all about it, and suppose she did too. I forgot to bow to her when we said goodbye, though I did bow deeply to him after he had very courteously insisted on accompanying me to my car. Now I wonder if I should have accepted her invitation. She offered to motor me to London, saying she was a safer driver than her husband. I said that of course I would far rather accompany her than the Prince!

---

[*] Authoress of more than 550 novels (1901–2000); m. 1st 1927 Alexander McCorquodale, 2nd 1936 his cousin Hugh McCorquodale.

[†] A Conservative MP for Birmingham, 1935–40 (1907–40); killed in action.

[‡] Countess Geraldine Apponyi (1915–2002); m. 1938 King Zog of Albania (1895–1961).

It is rather snobbish of me to write at such length about two people who are not out of the ordinary, but then I *am* a snob in that I am interested by people in the public eye. But though interested I don't want to be with them much. I have no wish to be taken up by royalty or move in royal circles.

Monday, 24th August

Today I motored to lunch with Tony Scotland* and Julian Berkeley[†] between Newbury and Basingstoke, running into a huge traffic jam near Hungerford, I can only suppose because of morbid desire of the populace to gloat over scene of last Wednesday's massacre.[‡] What a contrast to last night![§] At this funny little white cottage were gathered six male couples, counting Tony and Julian, I the odd man out. All very discreet, no mention of relationships which were explained to me by Tony aside. One a Chinaman. All conventionally dressed in suits, and well-off I gathered from the makes of their cars and their descriptions of their weekend cottages. We ate out of doors. So intelligent they were, easy and interesting. Talk of art, architecture and crime (the last prompted by Hungerford). Much hilarity and laughter. I enjoyed their company far more than the Badminton party, though it was odd to see quite so many men, wondering who belonged to whom. Perhaps the Aids threat has contributed to the fidelity of which Sophia[¶] spoke last night.

While walking Folly this morning, I ran into Don** who told me that Boris is beside himself because his precious motor-bike was stolen

---

* Writer, broadcaster and journalist; on staff of BBC Radio, 1970–91 (b. 1945).
[†] 2nd son of Sir Lennox Berkeley and Freda *née* Bernstein; musician, founder of Berkeley Guard Automatic Security Systems, and defender (like his father) of the traditional liturgy of the Catholic Church (b. 1950).
[‡] On 19 August Michael Ryan, aged 27, had indiscriminately shot to death sixteen people and wounded fourteen more in the streets of Hungerford, Berkshire, finally killing himself when cornered by the police.
[§] J.L.-M. had attended 'a large party of the young, with wives, concubines and friends' at Badminton House.
[¶] Lady Sophia Vane-Tempest-Stewart, present with her boyfriend, had suggested to J.L.-M. 'that her generation were more faithful than mine because they lived together before marrying'.
** Don Lane, the Beauforts' chauffeur at Badminton; his son Boris.

while he was at work in Bristol last Friday, and he wanted to talk to me about it. I regretted that I was going off for the day. Nevertheless Boris called this evening while I was cooking my supper, and though tired out I hadn't the heart not to ask him in. He told me that he 'worshipped' his bike, that if he ever met the thief he would murder him. Seemed so upset that I thought he would break down. I was able to sympathise with him, for I had similar feelings towards the motor-scooter Uncle Milne* gave me when I was sixteen. A substitute for a girl, I suppose. He told me he sometimes got 120 mph out of her on a deserted stretch of motorway, though the force of the wind could be frightening.

Saturday, 29th August

Birthdays thick and fast. Today we dined at the House for Caroline's. She in high spirits, throwing her arms about, not listening to a word I said to her at dinner. David told us that a group of squatters had arrived in two charabancs at Swangrove. Mervyn [the keeper] was indignant and persuaded D. to confront them. They were polite but filthy. He told them that visitors were always welcome to walk in Swangrove but he could not allow them to camp there. If he did, there would be no end to the numbers who might follow them. They must go within three days. But they pleaded to remain until Friday when they got their dole money, and he allowed this. Later, while out riding, he stopped to see them. The grove was littered with washing and chaos. One matriarchal woman seemed educated. They gave him tea from a dirty mug which he did not like to wipe in front of them. Meanwhile Mervyn tells them menacingly that if they don't bloody well clear out they will be thrown out by the police. Mervyn's language is colourful. When asked how he is, he replies, 'Bugger you, I be well enough, Sir.' Which reminds me that Haines our chauffeur used sometimes to address Dick or myself as 'you bugger you'.

---

* Alec Milne Lees-Milne (1878–1931).

Wednesday, 2nd September

To London in the morning, changing at Paddington for Ealing Broadway. From there by taxi to Old Court Hospital, Montpelier Road. Cosy Victorian suburb where the birds sing. A sort of cottage hospital, half-timber plus modernismus. Given a room overlooking garden, enormous sycamore tree visible from bed. Meet the nurse who is to sit with me throughout the first night, a dear woman from the Isle of Skye, costing me £70. A big beaming sister introduces herself. Then the anaesthetist, a genial man, who examines me and asks the usual questions. Then the accountant, a stout, genteel lady, to whom I give a cheque for £1,000. I am weighed and found to be less than the 12 stone which has been my constant weight for many years. Strange, as my belly is much larger; but I suppose my chest and limbs are wasting. Various orderlies come, one to take my valuables to put in hospital safe, another bearing a cup of tea (I am allowed to eat nothing, and am ravenous), a third to attach a bracelet to my wrist identifying me as belonging (like a dog) to Mr Casey. Finally a Filipina nurse gives me a jab in the bottom, and an enormous black man with a shining smile deftly lifts me onto a hearse and wheels me down corridors to operating theatre. I am still conscious, and greet my anaesthetist rather cheekily with, 'Mr Deacon, I presume?' That is the last I remember. I pass comfortably into total blackness, no dreams, no flicker of the subconscious, no sense of the world beyond. I wake in my room at 3 a.m. with the dear lady from Skye bathing and soothing my head.

Forty-eight hours later Mr Casey rips off the bandages. When I am first able to see with my new eye, which I keep open for only a few seconds, everything is vivid and looks blue like those photographs of the earth from the moon. Mr C. explains how the implant operation came about, when an American soldier got a piece of glass inside his eye and found to his surprise that he saw better than before. He says his profession owes much to Clementine Churchill who left her eyes for ophthalmic research, an example which has been followed by millions.

Each morning I wake from a nightmare. In one of them, I am sightseeing in some foreign capital with John Betjeman and Feeble,

Nancy [Mitford] also being with us. We are all staying at the Embassy, which is about to give a grand banquet to some potentate. I cannot find my evening clothes. Time is running out. There is Nancy dressed in the smartest conceivable dress by Lanvin and covered with jewels, saying gaily, 'I'm going downstairs now.' There am I still in my dressing-gown, searching desperately.

Eardley, M. and J.K.-B. all came to see me. So kind of them to slog all this way. E. talked about the success of his latest exhibition at the Parkin Gallery; J. about his Paxton book, half-way through; while M. read me a chapter of his forthcoming book,[*] based on letters written by Duke of Windsor to his Duchess while he was attending Queen Mary's deathbed in London.

Thursday, 10th September

Back home now, being nursed adorably by A. My new eye will, I feel sure, be a success. Already it sees colours more vividly than the other eye. Yesterday I worked all day, correcting my novel before submitting it to Collins. Foolish of me to make yet another attempt after some ten rejections. And David Burnett came to show me the edited type-script of *Cotswold Houses*. He is an excellent editor, and all his proposed changes are improvements.

E. told me that his millionaire friend Christopher Selmes,[†] who has Aids, is planning to give a huge expensive party at Lyegrove[‡] for all his friends, following which he intends to commit suicide.

Sunday, 13th September

Went to the tedious annual meeting of the local branch of CPRE in the hall at the House. Gerald Harford[§] in the chair, did it well apart

---

[*] *The Secret File of the Duke of Windsor* (Bantam Press, 1988).

[†] City entrepreneur (1946–88); in 1975, then aged twenty-eight, he had been accused of fraudulent practises in a Department of Trade report.

[‡] Country house near Badminton formerly owned by J.L.-M's great friend Diana, Countess of Westmorland (d. 1983).

[§] Of Little Sodbury Manor, Gloucestershire (b. 1948); m. 1985 Camilla, dau. of Alistair Horne.

from too many 'ums'. I sat at the back so I might escape, which I did after ninety minutes. A nice young man from the National Parks Commission gave a talk, but I could hardly hear him. Deaf and blind, what is the use of my attending such occasions? He wore a signet ring on his middle finger, usually a sign of bedintness among men. Looking at the audience, I noticed as usual that they were all of the middle class; none from the lower, and needless to say not one of the Somerset family. One may deride the middle classes, but it is they who really care about country things. Having looked through Simon Blow's book on hunting, I think I hate the upper classes. Their arrogance, their unquestioning superiority is, or until recently was, insufferable.

Thursday, 17th September

A nice young solicitor came yesterday morning to see A. and me about the woman we are trying to evict from our basement flat in Bath. Only last Monday, just after the expiry of the notice period, did we finally get a reply from her solicitors, merely to announce that she had no intention of quitting. Our young man says she will produce as much dirt against us as she can find, and says we should do the same with her. I am accumulating it eagerly.

Tuesday, 13th October

On Saturday, we motored to Chatsworth in an unremitting downpour. The cross-country route recommended by Pam not a success. Poor A. had to do most of the driving, owing to my eyes. Return by motorways much easier and less exhausting. Enjoyable visit. Party consisted of Lord and Lady Gowrie,[*] Jacob Rothschilds,[†] Tatton Sykes,[‡] Sophie

---

[*] Alexander Ruthven, 2nd Earl of Gowrie (b. 1939); Minister for the Arts, 1983–5; Chairman of Sotheby's, 1985–93; m. (2nd) 1974 Adelheid, Gräfin von der Schulenburg.

[†] Hon. N.C.J. Rothschild (b. 1936); s. father as 4th Baron Rothschild, 1990; m. 1961 Serena, er dau. of Sir Philip Dunn, 2nd Bt, and Lady Mary, dau. of 5th Earl of Rosslyn.

[‡] Sir Tatton Sykes, 8th Bt (b. 1943), of Sledmere, Yorkshire.

Cavendish.* Curious company for us, as all the males (including of course Andrew Devonshire) are multi-millionaires. I liked pretty Lady Gowrie, born Schulenburg. Told me her father, a friend and ally of Stauffenberg, was killed by the Nazis after the failed attempt of July 1944. She was only a baby, but her family and their friends had to lie very low until the end of the war. Jacob R. very friendly, better looking than I remembered; she, Serena, daughter of Mary Erskine, has little of her mother's charm, but has inherited the looks of her grandmother, old Lady Rosslyn. Sophie still very pretty but has become highbrow in a self-conscious way, and rather embarrassed me with her intellectual jargon. Tatton, charming dilettante bachelor landowner, is beautiful, with lovely eyes.

Andrew complained to Gowrie that the present Poet Laureate[†] was no good, and wanted to know who had chosen him. 'I did,' retorted Gowrie cheerfully. When asked why, he explained that it was for political reasons. He claims to be a great authority on contemporary painters and intellectuals.

I have come away with four boxes of the 6th Duke's diaries. His writing still strikes me as appalling. Before I left, I had a further word with the nice librarian Michael Pearman, who reiterated that a biography of the Bachelor Duke would never be a successful book, though it is heresy to say such a thing here where one walks daily in his footsteps. I promised I would not let him down by betraying his feelings to the Devonshires, and explained that, in my eightieth year, it mattered little to me if my book was remaindered in six months, so long as the work was interesting and I was able to do it well. I realised it was not a subject for an aspiring young biographer.

Saturday, 17th October

Anne Hill stayed with us for two nights. Unchanged mentally, but physically she has become an old woman, hobbling on two sticks. We enjoyed her visit, though she has a habit of not finishing

---

* Yr dau. (b. 1957) of 11th Duke of Devonshire; m. 1st 1979–87 Anthony Murphy, 2nd 1988 Alastair Morrison, 3rd William Topley.
† Ted Hughes (1930–1998); succeeded Sir John Betjeman as Poet Laureate, 1984.

sentences, and an alarming aptitude to make jokes about the deaths and misfortunes of her friends and relations. Our betrothal has never been forgotten by her; talking of some incident which took place in the 1930s, she said, 'It must have been around the time I was engaged to Jim . . .'*

Sheridan and Lindy Dufferin called on us this morning before lunching at the House. Everyone says he has Aids, and makes no bones about it. I looked at him closely while talking. He certainly looks drawn, and there are some spots on the neck. Nice man, gentle and sweet. She is very different. Greets one with a gush of kissing. Her mouth is like that of her mother,† or Madame Cyn the Streatham brothel keeper.‡

Thursday, 29th October

This morning A. heard from John Keffer,§ Chairman of American Museum, that Ian McCallum died at 4 a.m. It was double pneumonia that killed him, brought on by Aids. He wants no funeral and no memorial of any sort. What a fearful death, the second from Aids of an intimate friend of ours. A. will be more upset than I. He was a superb curator of the Museum, and made it what it is. I suppose he had a good life until last year, when he began to come down with one serious illness after another. He was probably infected by his young lover, the sinister-looking Gerry,¶ who was nevertheless good to him and looked after him. Ian was one of the handsomest young men

---

* The engagement was announced in May 1935 and broken off by J.L.-M. in January 1936.

† Lady Isabel Manners; m. 1936 as his 2nd wife Loel Guinness, MP (C) for Bath 1931–45.

‡ Cynthia Payne (b. 1932), boisterous owner of a house in Ambleside Avenue, Streatham, was charged in 1986 with running a brothel (an offence of which she had already been convicted in 1980). After a hilarious court case occupying the early weeks of 1987, she was acquitted. A film, *Personal Services*, was later made about her and her establishment; she stood for Parliament to draw attention to the absurdity of the law relating to prostitutes, and became a television personality.

§ American engineer and lawyer (b. 1923), working in London as general counsel to oil companies; Chairman of Trustees of American Museum from 1982.

¶ Gerald Theaker; manager of kitchen equipment store, Sloane Square.

when I met him with John Fowler during the war. He was then a pacifist who had been in jail for his beliefs. I respected him for that, but always found him cold, calculating, and filled with social ambitions which sat uneasily with his left-wing views, hostile to authority and the police. He was a good entertainer and loved giving parties to the élite. We were frequent guests at Claverton where the meals were delicious, but I never much enjoyed the company, seedy duchesses and blue-rinse American millionairesses. He was a marvel at milking them of their money for his museum which he adored. A pity he never trained anyone to take his place.

Eardley, to whom I foolishly wrote that I was selling my papers, has written back furiously to say that unless I withdraw all his letters to me, this will be the last I receive from him. But it is too late. I am committed. I have replied that he need have no fear, as none of my papers will be seen until I am safely dead, by which time he ought to be too. And that the alternative would be to destroy them all now.

Friday, 30th October

Punctually at ten, Mr and Mrs Rota arrive with cardboard boxes. In three-quarters of an hour they have swept away all my papers, leaving dusty, empty drawers. It is a relief, like a satisfactory evacuation, yet leaves me slightly shaken and wondering. Shall I miss them? Shall I regret allowing them to be preserved in some American university library, for all to rifle through and deride? The alternative was mass destruction, which I could not bring myself to perpetrate.

Saturday, 31st October

Roxane the great-grandchild [of Alvilde] has been staying the week. A. has enjoyed it, while I have been bored to death. Today another child, aged five, came to tea with her. On arrival, the visiting child said, 'Is it just you? I thought I was coming to a party.' Over tea, R., aged seven, snapped at the other, 'Don't shout! You are giving me a headache.'

Friday, 6th November

We dine at the House. David, just back from New York, says the latest snobbery is to boast of how many millions of dollars one has lost in the recent stock market crash.* All are anxious about Reagan,† who is now senile. After dinner, D. told me that he and Rupert Loewenstein often amuse themselves by imagining the caustic remarks I write about them in my diary.

Friday, 13th November

I have now read two of the four boxes of diaries of the Bachelor Duke. On the whole I am disappointed. He knew everyone in London and cosmopolitan society, and had hundreds of guests to stay at Chatsworth and Devonshire House, where he entertained more lavishly and exclusively than any other nobleman. Yet seldom does he give any description of these endless acquaintances and his meetings with them. I am seizing upon any straw to suggest that he is an interesting character, but so far I don't think he is one who will appeal to the readers of today, who are not interested in dukes merely because they are dukes and have left lists of encounters with their peers. He had his mistress; but what duke did and does not? That is of no interest unless scandals and domestic complications ensue, and being a bachelor he had no wife to take exception. He was highly neurotic, writes of his health on every page, was always gripped by some cold or fever, and always tired. I suspect he suffered from depression, and drank. I dare not tell Debo that I don't really think he is the material for a biography; nor do I wish to concentrate on his great works at Chatsworth and Bolton and Hardwick, about which too much has been written already. Oh dear! Meanwhile my *Cotswold Houses* comes out next week, which will have local rather than national appeal.

---

* Amid scenes of panic, the New York Stock Exchange had lost almost one-quarter of its value on 19 October 1987 – 'Black Monday'.
† Ronald Reagan; President of USA, 1981–9.

Saturday, 14th November

A Mrs Bishop,* late curator of the Holburne of Menstrie Museum, a mild little woman, came to tea to ask me about William Beckford about whom she is writing for *Bath History*. She asked several questions to which I answered, 'I must consult my notes', only to remember they were gone to Rota. This I foresee is going to be awkward in future.

Sunday, 15th November

A most enjoyable evening with the Charlie Morrisons. Charlie told me that, a few days ago, Mrs Thatcher sat next to him in the House of Commons dining room and candidly confessed that she saw no solution to the Irish problem, no glimmer of light – the first time he had heard her admit defeat on any issue. Rosalind as beautiful as ever. She told me that, to her utter surprise, she had received a letter from the Madresfield Trustees offering her the house and estate on the death of Lady Beauchamp,† now aged ninety-two. She had previously understood it was all going to Lady B's Danish grandchildren. But Rosalind is, after all, the last of the Lygons, who would have succeeded to the Earldom had she been a man.‡ She and Charlie are delighted, in spite of just having completed the conversion and decoration of their present house fashioned out of three cottages, which is indeed very charming and I expect she will keep for her dowagerdom. Rosalind also told me that Robert

* Philippa Downes (b. 1929); m. 1963 Michael Bishop; Curator, 1961–5 and 1977–85, of Holburne of Menstrie Museum, Bath (founded 1882 to house art collection of Sir William Holburne of Menstrie, 5th Bt [1793–1874]). She was writing an article on 'Beckford in Bath' for the periodical *Bath History* (Vol. 2, 1988).
† Else 'Mona' Schiwe (1895–1989); m. 1st C.P. Doronville de la Cour of Copenhagen (d. 1924), 2nd 1936 Viscount Elmley, MP, of Madresfield Court, Malvern, Worcestershire, who s. father 1938 as 8th and last Earl Beauchamp (1903–79); her only child was a daughter by 1st marriage.
‡ She and her sister were the only grandchildren of the 7th Earl (1872–1938), who had devoted himself to Madresfield until being forced into exile in 1931 – see 23 December 1990 and 23 December 1994.

Heber-Percy* left instructions for the pigeons at Faringdon to be dyed purple and black for his funeral, which they were. The other guests the Duff Hart-Davises.† A. finds him difficult, but I like him. He is uncompromising and highly intelligent. She, Phyllida, is clever too, and delightful. Dinner consisted of smoked salmon and smoked eel, the latter with a delicious strong-scented taste; then mutton, rather cold; and a pudding made of blackberries. Two kinds of white wine, and claret. I drank too much.

Saturday, 21st November

Gabriel Dru‡ has an obituary in the *Telegraph*, and quite rightly too. Of the Herberts of Pixton [Park, Somerset]§ with whom I so often stayed, only Bridget is left. There was a time in the mid Thirties when I thought I was in love with Gabriel, and she seemed a little in love with me. She was plain, and her fingers were unkempt, but she was a dear. Had the spirit of her mother Mary, without Mary's magnificent charm. Was very gallant, and during the Spanish Civil War drove ambulances for Franco. She used to return to England full of adventure stories, which bored me rather. I should have paid attention, for she was a daredevil. In truth, I preferred her company when the rest of her family were present. She was a pious and devoted papist, as we all were then. After she married Alick Dru, some sort

---

* The great love (1912–87) of Gerald Tyrwhitt-Wilson, 14th Baron Berners (1883–1950), composer, writer and aesthete, who bequeathed to him his fortune and Faringdon House, Oxfordshire; m. 1st 1942–7 Jennifer Fry, 2nd 1985 Lady Dorothy ('Coote') Lygon.

† Duff Hart-Davis (b. 1936); writer and journalist, son of J.L.-M's old friend Sir Rupert; m. 1961 Phyllida Barstow.

‡ Gabriel Herbert (1911–87); m. 1943 Major Alexander Dru.

§ Gabriel's siblings Bridget (1914–2005; m. 1935 Captain 'Eddie' Grant), Laura (1916–73; m. 1937 Evelyn Waugh) and Auberon (1922–74): children of Hon. Aubrey Herbert (1880–1923) m. 1910 Hon. Mary Vesey (1889–1970). J.L.-M. knew the family through his beloved Eton friend Desmond Parsons, whose mother had married Mary Herbert's brother, 5th Viscount de Vesci, as her 2nd husband; the widowed Mary and her four children were ardent Roman Catholics who applauded Jim's conversion to their faith in 1934 and often welcomed him at Pixton.

of professor, I hardly saw her. We faded out of each other's lives, as so often happens to great friends when one of them marries. She took to farming and was seldom off a tractor, wet or fine. Auberon, that big, burly, ugly, clumsy idealist, was the one with the greatest charm.

Thursday, 26th November

Collins have today sent me the first copy of *Venetian Evenings*, rather too soon on the heels of *Cotswold Houses*, and a reviewer has telephoned for a photograph of myself. I said I would not be photographed now but would send an old one if I could find it. The jacket looks pretty, but the photographs are rather muzzy, and the distressing thing is that, in my *dédicace* to Alvilde, they have spelt her name wrong, leaving out the second 'l'. Maddening. Moreoever, A. is not pleased with my dedicatory remark that she is 'always in a hurry' – which exactly describes her sightseeing, and this is a sightseeing book. How one always gets into trouble. Thank goodness I changed my mind about dedicating *Cotswold Houses* to the Somersets. I will try to get A's page cut out, if it is not too late. Just goes to show that one should never try to be, not exactly funny in this case, but too bright I suppose, and facetious.

Friday, 27th November

At midday I installed myself in Waterstone's shop in Milsom Street at a round table piled high with *Cotswold Houses* and some of my other books, mostly paperbacks, for a signing session. A total flop. In two hours about eight women turned up, chatted, and got me to sign. Mercifully the staff were nice. Peter French, the young manager, was most friendly and gave me a book on minor classical architects brought out some years ago by their short-lived publishing firm. To show good feeling, I bought in turn the new edition of Ruskin's *Modern Painters*, which I have been trying to find for years. Finally David Burnett turned up, and we lunched around the corner. How sad I am that my association with this adorable man is coming to an end.

Tuesday, 1st December

The dailies and weeklies are already publishing their 'books of the year' (I have not been invited to contribute any), and Bruce Chatwin's *Songlines* seems to be top of the poll. I suppose I shall read it, and probably be irritated. I saw him last week when he came up to me in the London Library. Somewhat changed. Those fallen angel looks have withered. Poor complexion, rather spotty, though he is active and upright again after his severe illness. I said to him, 'You are having a swimgloat.' He had never heard of the expression, nor of its author, Logan Pearsall Smith.[*]

Sunday, 6th December

A very dark day. We lunched with Nicky and Susanna Johnston, large party. Little Rosie came in after our arrival, and begged to talk to me alone. She dragged me into the hall, where a woman was suckling her young, so we sat on the stairs, where she described her nine months in prison. She went to three, the first, Holloway, the worst. The wardresses peddled drugs to the prisoners and were mostly lesbian. If you did not respond to their advances – and R. did not – they took it out on you. R. made up her mind early on to write a book about her experiences. It was this which kept her going. The worse the experiences, the better copy for the book. That is how she consoled herself.

Saturday, 12th December

This was an event. When Peter Scott[†] thanked me for my congratulations on his CH (oh coveted honour!), he invited us to visit him one

---

[*] American writer and bibliophile (1865–1946), whom J.L.-M. knew in London in his last years; a coiner of words and expressions.

[†] Sir Peter Scott (1909–89); o. c. of J.L.-M's friend Kathleen Kennet (*née* Bruce; 1878–1947) by her 1st marriage to Captain Robert Scott 'of the Antarctic' (d. 1912; she married 2nd Sir Edward Hilton Young, cr. Baron Kennet, 1935); sportsman, artist, naval officer, naturalist and writer; Chairman of World Wildlife Fund, 1961–89; m. 1st 1942–51 Elizabeth Jane Howard, 2nd 1951 Philippa Talbot-Ponsonby. In *Fourteen Friends* (published seven years after Scott's death in 1989), J.L.-M. wrote: 'He was always jolly with me, while knowing full well that I was not

day at Slimbridge. So I let four months elapse and wrote again, goaded by A. He replied asking us to come this morning 'for a sherry'. His little house what one would expect, modern, modest, commonplace, without taste good or bad. Received at door by wife, no-nonsense woman in jeans. Peter bustled forward to greet us, a little gnome, bent and small, white face, dewlaps. Never an Adonis, he was once attractive, sturdy and vivacious. Now an elder of great distinction. Very welcoming, hands outstretched, how delightful to see you at last, etc. Affability itself. Led us to their large studio room, walls of books, unfinished paintings of birds on easels. Untidy and cosy, the working man's den. The entire west wall is a huge picture window looking out onto a large pond, on which are swarms of birds, some of great rarity, two mud islands covered with squatting ducks, geese, swans. An astonishing and wonderful sight. Then a 'huroch' – and a flotilla of Bewick swans descend like aeroplanes. Indeed some geese have to take off from a sort of airstrip, and descend like Concorde. At times the sky almost black with birds.

Peter produced the actual telescope which had belonged to Thomas Bewick,[*] through which we looked at the Bewick swans. Or rather, A. managed to – the vision was too narrow for me to see much, but it was nevertheless an experience. He says Slimbridge costs £3 million a year to run, largely owing to the huge quantities of grain needed for feeding. While we watched, a boy appeared with a barrow, slinging a shower of grain. Those birds which knew their turn had not arrived waited, while others surged forward. What a wonderful and praise-worthy enterprise. Each migratory bird is ringed. Most are known individually and given nicknames, Big Brother, the Little One, etc. One of the girls who keeps the records in the office visited Russia, where in a bay on the Baltic she instantly recognised Big Brother and wife, paddling on the shore.

A fascinating hour and Peter most affable. He got on splendidly with A., a fellow ornithologist, and asked her what I did. I asked Peter

---

his sort. Nor was he mine . . . There was nothing cosy about his extraverted ward-room bonhomie . . . He was a high-minded, conventional, successful leader of men; and as a conservationist of wild life, without an equal. But he was a self-centred philistine without a glimmer of humour, and with a heart as cold as stone.'

[*] Ornithologist and wood engraver (1753–1828), illustrator of *A History of British Birds*.

if the swans had been affected by the Chernobyl fall-out.[*] He said no, not at all; it was a coincidence that the disaster occurred just at the time they were moulting.

Thursday, 17th December

I thought I should tell Dr King about the swelling on the right side of my face. He took it seriously and said he would find a specialist to look at it. After consulting Charlton, the surgeon who cured me of prostate cancer three years ago, he is sending me to a Mr Young in the Circus [Bath]. Odd thing is that I feel no pain and am not conscious of any growth inside the cheek, though Dr K. seems to have detected one.

Selina Hastings came here yesterday after calling on Daphne Fielding[†] to talk about Evelyn Waugh. She was so exhausted, having just returned from France, where she had seen Diana [Mosley] in Paris and Graham Greene[‡] in the South, that A. put her to bed in the afternoon. By the time I returned from Bath she was up, and as bright as the proverbial button. As A. says, the little kitten face is an illusion. She told us that Caroline Blackwood[§] had written a strange sort of book about Maître Blum[¶] and submitted it to *Harper's* for serialisation. It is vicious, not only about the Maître but also poor M., and in S's view unpublishable. Blackwood is not just a demon but a fantasist. She

---

[*] The world's worst nuclear accident had occurred on 25/6 April 1986 when a reactor exploded at the Chernobyl nuclear plant in the Ukraine. It was later believed that the accident had affected the physical environment of the whole northern hemisphere for some three years.

[†] Hon. Daphne Vivian (1904–97); novelist, mother of Caroline, Duchess of Beaufort; m. 1st 1926 Henry Thynne, later 6th Marquess of Bath, 2nd 1953 Xan Fielding, war hero and writer.

[‡] Novelist (1904–91).

[§] Lady Caroline Blackwood (1931–96); novelist; dau. of 4th Marquess of Dufferin and Ava.

[¶] Lady Caroline's book *The Last of the Duchess* – effectively a novel in which she omitted to change the names of the real people upon whom her story was loosely based – only appeared in 1995, soon after Maître Blum's death and not long before her own.

was recently sent by *Harper's* to interview Mrs Kinnock,[*] and was so drunk that she passed out on arrival. When she came to, Mrs K. could only talk to her for a few minutes before her next appointment. Next day B. delivered a brilliantly written piece, which was duly submitted to Mrs K., a condition of the interview. It transpired that Mrs K. had uttered not a single word which had been attributed to her, and B. had simply made the whole thing up. I must warn M.

Christmas Day – Friday, 25th December

We have Burnet [Pavitt] staying, a perfect guest. He is happy doing anything or nothing, and full of chat and entertainment. A. overwhelmed me with presents. I wish she would not give me quite so many things that I do not need, like a small wireless set. The more such gadgets one has, the more they have to be replenished. In addition she gave me a large red pullover, a pair of woolly-lined gloves, two pairs of pyjamas, and an ivory-backed hairbrush to replace the one I lost in a train. How good and kind she is; yet I feel sick at heart. We lunched at the House – more exchange of little gifts. Ate in the big dining room, David at head of table, double doors left open so he could look straight through the lesser dining room and the windows into the park and east avenue. David looking bored, that look that freezes me up. I sat next to Caroline, great fun, and that loony girl Tracy [Worcester], talking of Friends of the Earth. Eddie [Somerset] in another world. Beautiful table, long white cloth covered in shining silver, some twenty seated. Marvellous banquet, turkey melting in mouth, best plum pudding ever. A sauceboat of flaming brandy was brought in, terrifying the girl who carried and also me as I ladled it onto my plate. Crackers, and paper hats. I managed to acquit myself with reasonable cheer. Burnet enchanted by the beauty and lavishness of the scene, wondering that it did not engender revolutionary feelings. It is certainly civilised living – or is it? Such empty heads, the children.

---

[*] Glenys Roberts (b. 1944); m. 1967 Neil Kinnock (b. 1942), Leader of Labour Party 1983–92, European Commissioner, 1995–2004, cr. life peer 2005.

Wednesday, 30th December

To Bath Clinic this morning for my biopsy.* A. insisted on accompanying me, the greatest solace having her there. I felt nothing. There was no interval between local anaesthetic and operation, which took about twenty minutes. I await the verdict next Tuesday. If it is malignancy, I dare say I shall be upset. Yet I am reaching a condition of resignation owing to my advanced age, brought home to me when I am shown a photograph of my red, haggard face. After all, my life is almost done, cancer or no cancer, and my working life finishing. I wish, oh how I wish it had been more successful.

---

* A procedure recommended by Mr Young, the specialist J.L.-M. had consulted on 22 December about 'the swelling on the right side of my face'.

1988

1988

My total, abysmal muffishness shames me. I used to think it did not matter that I could not mend a fuse, or even put a light bulb into a socket. Now I think it is despicable. How I have got through life I don't know. Such elementary tasks ought to be taught in schools like Eton. Perhaps they are today. Working-class children learn them naturally at father's knee, almost imbibe them with mother's milk.

To see my specialist Mr Young for result of my biopsy. Hoped desperately it would be all right, but from head-shaking of my GP and dentist, feared the worst. Entered No.20, The Circus. Shown into consulting room by girl in white coat, so bloody bright and cheery. Mr Young proffered a limp hand. I am always reluctant to shake hands with doctors because it means they must wash them immediately. Instead I grasped his finger-tips. He dropped his eyes and looked furtive, so I knew. 'Well,' he began. I interrupted with, 'I presume it is malignant?' 'Yes,' he said. If I hadn't asked him, would he have told me directly, or left it to Dr King? He said I would need treatment from a radiologist. I told him I would rather not, for the sooner I died the better, having had cancer once already. But he remonstrated gently, pointing out that, if I did nothing, the cheek would suppurate and I would be unable to wear my dentures. That decided me. Alvilde and I had a long discussion and decided that it would be absurd to make a mystery of it because my face would in due course reveal all. So I am telling any friend who is interested. But I don't want commiseration, or to discuss with strangers.

Wednesday, 6th January

I told M. my news this morning. He was very upset and told me how much I mattered to him. I wanted to reciprocate and tell him what he knows already, but could not get the words out, so just hung up. When I managed to compose myself I rang him back, to his relief, as he feared he must have said something to displease. As if he could. I also rang up dear Clive Charlton and told him the verdict. He was encouraging and cheering, telling me to keep my pecker up. Of course they all have to make light, even my darling A., who is so wise and caring.

Thursday, 7th January

I sit awaiting my appointment with the radiologist, like Patience on a Monument. Meanwhile I continue pegging away at the Bachelor Duke's boring diaries, because otherwise I would go mad.

Saturday, 9th January

Selina comes to stay the night, always a welcome guest. We dine with the Loewensteins. Selina very entertaining and sharp. A. calls her 'the acid drop'. I am pleased by a review of my little *Venetian Evenings* [about to be published by Collins] in *Books*, admittedly a slight mag, but any kind of recognition is pleasing.

Sunday, 10th January

Spent morning talking to Selina, who had been told about my impending treatment by Andrew [Devonshire]. Was very sane and sparing of compassion, while expressing interest in my symptoms and wanting to know how I felt when I awoke in the night. She told me she might be able to get me a fatal dose which a doctor once prescribed for her mother in Africa when she was frightened of being captured and tortured by natives. Said it was important not to take too little or frightful consequences would ensue, which did not reassure. But her offer may come in handy if my illness becomes terminal – though I can't decide whether it is sinful to take one's life or not.

Selina believes that Ros[amond Lehmann] can still see to read a little. She notices that whenever Ros asks her to read out to her the pile of letters by her bed, they are always from fans, never the tax inspector or the telephone company.

Tuesday, 12th January

A. accompanied me to Bath Clinic, where we were interviewed by Dr Rees, radiologist. Charming, clever and direct young man, absolutely frank. Told me I would have to undergo treatment on cheek daily in Bristol for four weeks. Would suffer loss of taste and much soreness but no loss of hair, etc. He took some preliminary tests. If these are satisfactory, I start treatment next week.

Wednesday, 13th January

Radio Four had a 'phone-in' about homosexuality. I don't know what annoys me more, the biblical abhorrence of pious Christians or the exhibitionism and proselytising of the Gay Brigade. There should of course be no prejudice, harassment or loss of rights – but equally no flaunting of sexual deviancy. It is nobody else's business what a person does in private, provided no violence or cruelty is involved. As for the Church, no candidate for ordination should be questioned about his inclinations, and no objection taken if he is living with a person of his own sex, provided all is done discreetly; but no promiscuity should be tolerated among the clergy, whether homo or hetero. Is this illogical of me?

Thursday, 14th January

Mr Rees telephones me to confirm that my treatment will begin next week. At night when depressed I imagine 'the thing' gnawing away at me, undermining me. I have finished the Bachelor Duke's diaries and rung up Debo to arrange their return.

Saturday, 16th January

Derry and Alexandra [Moore] came for luncheon, I think to be kind to me. Very sweet of them; but although I have decided to make no mystery of my complaint, I find it a bore talking about it to all and sundry. D. rather haggard, the result of too much dashing about the world in Concorde.

Thursday, 21st January

Darling A. accompanied me to Bristol Hospital and waited while they made a sort of death-mask of me, needed for the treatment. Her devotion to me is beyond any recognition. She is efficient and fearless, takes up the telephone and gets straight to the fountain-head, refusing to be fobbed off by secretaries, whereas I am forever hesitant and fearful of being a nuisance or causing offence. After much thought, we decided that I should be a private patient, though the treatment would be the same were I 'on the Health'. But being private means I can ring up Dr Rees to discuss progress whenever I feel inclined; and he is very candid.

Friday, 22nd January

We dined at the House, wondering how Caroline feels about the house on the edge of the park in which David is installing his mistress [Miranda]. Yet in talking to David alone on a sofa afterwards I fell completely under his spell. He is worried about the future of Badminton; unless Harry or Eddie produces a male heir, the dukedom will pass to a distant cousin in Australia. Cannot decide whether to declare any of his works of art national heirlooms, for if he does so, future generations will be unable to sell. After much delay, Simon Verity has written a grovelling letter and will come to put an inscription on the 'slab', as David calls it, of Master and Mary.

Monday, 25th January

To Bristol for my first treatment. The death-mask fills with a delicious smell of the sandalwood with which I douche my face each morning. Dr Rees declared himself confident of destroying 'the thing' and hoped he might do so by the middle of next week; if he did, I would only need five more treatments to be on the safe side.

Tuesday, 2nd February

Just before I left Bath for my treatment in Bristol, the telephone rang. It was Miss X., the frightful basement tenant we are trying to get rid of, to say her bedroom had been flooded. I suggested she either contact my solicitors or call a plumber. Five minutes later the doorbell rang, and I was confronted with an unknown middle-aged woman. 'I am Miss X's mother,' she said. 'You must come down and do something about the water.' I declined. 'But this is my daughter's home and she is not well,' she continued. This raised my ire. 'Your daughter is a squatter in my house,' I retorted. 'It is not her flat at all. She is remaining there in flagrant breach of our agreement.' Woman then turned very nasty. 'She has every right to remain,' she hissed, 'as you will find out when the case comes up.' I then told her that her daughter had no sense of honour, adding, 'And she is a little bitch.' That was a mistake. I rang Alvilde to tell her of the encounter, and drove off to Bristol.

Saturday, 6th February

Billa [Harrod] has come all the way from Norfolk to stay the weekend, an act of true friendship before I depart to another sphere. Overjoyed to see her, but after ten treatments my mouth is so sore I can hardly speak, and eating is a torment. She told me an extraordinary tale about the two Hesketh brothers, Roger[*] and Peter.[†] (Peter died two years ago, Roger last Christmas.) They adored each other, but there was a shadow between them. An uncle who died in 1938 left many family treasures, Wrights of Derby, silver, etc., then valued at £100,000 and now worth millions. As the elder brother, Roger assumed they were left to him, and kept them all. Peter never raised the matter during his lifetime, and Roger used them for his loving recreation of Meols Hall, which he rebuilt in the Palladian style and made the chief interest of his later life. Now Peter's daughter is claiming her father's share of the treasures from Roger's widow and son. What distresses Billa, who is

---

[*] Roger Fleetwood Fleetwood-Hesketh (1902–88) of Meols Hall nr Southport, Lancashire; Mayor of Southport, 1950.

[†] Peter Fleetwood Fleetwood-Hesketh (1905–85) of The Manor House, Hale, Liverpool; architect, writer, illustrator and sometime Hon. Representative of N.T.

devoted to Roger's memory (he having been in love with her all his life), is that, in the course of this wrangle, documents have come to light suggesting that Roger deliberately cheated Peter of his share. An eerie country house saga.

Wednesday, 10th February

My thirteenth treatment at Bristol today. The usual machine being serviced so they use an old one, a board to which I am tied like Gulliver in Lilliput, forced to listen to rubbish on Radio One. I wondered how I would feel if I were trapped like this after an earthquake or bombing, unable to budge or cry out. Would the droning radio be a comfort or irritant? I'm sure I would rather be killed outright than have to wait interminably for a possible rescue, unable to shift, stir or cry. My doctor is back from his skiing holiday and says 'the thing' has already diminished by two-thirds.

Wednesday, 17th February

Truly, I don't remember ever suffering such agony as I am now undergoing. Mercifully this may be my last week of treatment. Meanwhile we endure endless harassment from the bitch tenant, who has demanded we repair the damage caused by the recent flooding, which in the builder's view was caused by her letting either the bathwater or lavatory cistern overflow. Surely the responsibility for this sort of damage should be the tenant's? We thought up a wheeze, getting David Beaufort to instruct his agent Richard Wood to send us a notice to quit Essex House, leaving the Bath flat as our sole remaining residence. This I joyfully forwarded to our solicitor, who promptly telephoned Richard to ascertain whether his letter was a forgery.

Friday, 19th February

Had my last treatment this afternoon. Saw the doctor afterwards who is confident 'the thing' has been destroyed. Warns that I may suffer discomfort for another fortnight, but in fact the pain is already much reduced. A blessed relief.

Saturday, 20th February

A. and I drove to Penselwood to see Audrey, my first outing for a month and one which depressed me to extremes. Audrey's cottage is an absolute beast, so low-ceilinged that I could not stand upright in the downstairs room. When not frozen by howling draughts, one is blinded by smoke from the log fire. Whole place stinks of cats. Surely something can be done for this little old lady who lives in this hovel year in year out, never going away? The poor thing complaining she has no friends. It is not really surprising. When away from her I love her deeply. When with her, am exasperated beyond endurance. O vile beast me.

Saturday, 27th February

I never learn. I wrote a long letter to *The Times* expressing my horror at the Pope's encyclical of last week enjoining the clergy to sell treasures from their churches for the benefit of the Third World.* Particularly mentioned by him are gold and silver (so bang goes the Pala d'Oro in St Mark's for a start), and paintings, i.e., altar pieces by Tintoretto, Tiepolo, anyone you care to mention. I am amazed that no newspaper has criticised this proposed vandalism, and no museum directors have written to protest in the press.

Sunday, 28th February

The Times having as usual ignored my letter about the Pope's encyclical, I sent a line to kind Hugh Massingberd at the *Daily Telegraph*. He asked me to dictate it down the telephone, and published it. Hugh told me his uncle Peter Montgomery had died. Peter was a gentle, kind, humorous man, good-looking without being handsome, a squire with a sense of duty. I had not seen him for years, perhaps not since the night we spent together in the basement of the Piccadilly Hotel, both in uniform, cowering from the bombs raining down on us.† The bedroom

---

* J.L.-M. is presumably referring to the encyclical *Sollicitudo rei socialis* of 30 December 1987, a long and diffuse document offering 'guidelines' to priests in social policy.
† As depicted (though Montgomery insisted that the portrait of himself was fanciful) in the last chapter of *Another Self* (1970).

we had been obliged to take when the raid started was destroyed after we descended. We were nearly drowned in the flood caused by smashed drains and tanks in the basement. In the morning, after the All Clear, we wandered around Mayfair and St James's lamenting the damage done, wondering if the whole area would have to be rebuilt. In the dawn, the skies were red with fires from the East End. Peter's quirk was gerontophilia. He told me he used to sleep with a great-uncle to whom he was devoted. I wonder if Hugh is aware of this.

Friday, 4th March

A dotty Beckford enthusiast called on me in Bath without warning. I was displeased, but let him in. Rather a smelly youth. Wants to buy a plot of land in the Mendips and build his own tower. Has the money, being guitarist in a pop group. Claims to be haunted by presence of Beckford, which he 'felt' very strongly in my library. How Beckford attracts the loonies.

Saturday, 26th March

Anne Somerset's* wedding at Badminton, for which Margaret-Anne Stuart and Derek Hill stayed with us. They arrived for luncheon, to which we had also asked the Martin Charterises, who turned up late owing to breakdown on motorway. I accompanied them all to church, but did not go to reception or ball. A. and I given 'family' seats, on balcony where Queen Mary† used to sit. We had a fine view of the packed church, decorated like a floral hall. Air of spirituality non-existent. Smart guests dressed as for Ascot. Laura Marlborough‡ wearing hat like enormous toadstool. Daphne [Fielding] standing on her seat, waving and screaming at friends. Bride and groom looking very pretty, Anne in white satin dress. Photographers flashing from

---

* Lady Anne Somerset (b. 1955); o. d. of 11th Duke of Beaufort; m. 1988 Matthew Carr, artist.

† Queen Mary, Mary Duchess of Beaufort's aunt, had lived at Badminton during the Second World War, and remained a legend in the locality.

‡ Laura Charteris (1915-1990); m. Jan. 1972 as her 4th husband John Spencer-Churchill, 10th Duke of Marlborough (d. March 1972).

behind altar. Derek said to me, 'I have come only to see you,' which was obviously absurd – he came to see the show and the smart folk. So did Stuart Preston, whom I collected at Chippenham; he was delighted to have been invited (as who would not be?) to a grand wedding in a ducal country house. A. and our guests dressed up and went to the ball, but were back within an hour.

Sunday, 27th March

A. much opposed to my motoring self to Chatsworth [Derbyshire], but I did it quite easily in four hours. Enormously enjoyed my five nights. Only Debo and Andrew, both sweet to me. We met at meals. Otherwise I worked in the old housekeeper's room, where the nice librarian Michael Pearman brought me thirty-three box files to wade through. He advised me to concentrate on letters actually written by the Bachelor Duke, reading the exchange only when it had a significant bearing on his story. I followed his advice and managed to get through half of the B.D's letters.

Every day I had tea with Andrew. For the first time I feel I have broken the barrier with him, and I find him extremely sympathetic as well as kind, clever and friendly. Before dinner, I walked around the garden, about a mile and a half – my long walking days are over. Delicious weather, sun and deep purple clouds. Never have I seen Chatsworth more beautiful. In the evenings we sat in Debo's little room at the NW corner, with tiny window overlooking the entrances. They let me go to bed early. I am never happier than when engaged in research, and the conditions here are perfect – *tout confort, grand luxe*, and independence. Am feeling extremely well, apart from a lingering metallic taste in my mouth.

While I was working, the clock man came to wind the clock above my head. I asked how many clocks he wound. Answer – sixty-three in the house. It takes him four hours every Wednesday morning. There are seven gamekeepers, three river-keepers, one weather chart man, two telephonists, and so on. Debo showed me two chapters of her new book on the Chatsworth estate. It will not have the huge sales of her book on the House. The first chapter about cows and sheep, their problems and ailments. She was amused when I said it was far above my head. Second about sport and what the public owes to sportsmen – coverts, copses, etc. I could understand all this.

On way home stopped at the old church at Strensham,* near the M5. A perfect Worcestershire church, as lovely and unspoilt as I remember. My heart turned over, remembering ancient visits with Harry Batsford.† The dear village lady busily cutting churchyard grass with shears. Church unlocked. Floor of nave old dusty bricks and mediaeval tiles. Gothic pew ends. West and gallery panels filled with primitive paintings of saints. Walls still plastered. Decent electrified wall sconces. Three-decker pulpit. In dark chancel three fine monuments, Jacobean on right, Georgian on left. All Russells of Strensham. A stone on the floor announced that a Miss Hoare of Stourhead married one of these Russells. Strange to think of her coming from that great Palladian house and garden in Wiltshire all this way to live in [Strensham Court] a small, half-timbered house like Wickhamford. What delight and nostalgia I derived from this place, just far enough away from the hurly-burly of the motorway. O Worcestershire of my childhood, so precious and infinitely remote.

Sunday, 3rd April

Today we lunched with Jessica Douglas-Home‡ at the Mill, Quenington. She intrigues me vastly – mysterious, wheedling, attractive, gipsy,

---

* The manor of Strensham, Worcestershire dates from 972 and came into the possession of the Russell family around 1283. The Taylor family, button manufacturers, bought the estate in 1824 and owned Strensham Court until its destruction by fire in 1970. The church, situated between the M5 and the River Avon, features a Norman tub font, a late 15th-century gallery formed out of the painted rood screen, 16th-century pews and famous early 18th-century bells. The care of these treasures became too much for the parish and the church was vested in the Churches Conservation Trust in 1991.

† Publisher, bookseller and author, specialising in books on architecture (1880–1951); his visit to Strensham with J.L.-M. (whose publisher he then was) took place on 3 March 1945 (as described in *Prophesying Peace*).

‡ Jessica Gwynn; artist, stage designer, and author of a biography of her grandmother, Violet Woodhouse; m. 1966 Charles Douglas-Home (1937–85), editor of *The Times*, 1983–5.

clever, earnest. I gave her a Chatsworth tray as an Easter present. A rare sunny day, and we ate on the grass at the front of the house. Uncomfortable, as picnics always are. She wanted to hear about my cancer, being hooked on the subject because of poor Charlie. She talked of her campaign to stop the wholesale destruction of old buildings and monuments in Romania. In Bucharest, they have wiped out not only the churches, but all palaces and houses which provide any reminder of the 'bourgeois' past. She is trying to get UNESCO to intervene before the whole country suffers the same fate.

Gerda Barlow* brought Peter Coats to see us. He is the most self-centred man, who never stops telling stories aimed at his own glorification. Pathetically lonely, and will stay with anyone who will have him. Kept repeating that I was his oldest friend, older even than Billy Whitaker. True perhaps in that we all attended prep school together – but oh dear, not in endurance. I am sure he has never forgiven me for what I wrote about his beloved Chips [Channon] in my first diaries. Peter looks like a ghost, with transparent skin and sunken eyes. Freda [Berkeley] is sure he has Aids, poor old thing.

Thursday, 7th April

I have always considered lawyers the enemies of the human race, having seen during my days at the National Trust how their pedantic follies lost us several splendid properties. This afternoon at two o'clock, A. and I attended the hearing of our 'case' at Bath Guildhall v. that beastly girl who refuses to leave our downstairs flat. We were kept waiting an hour before finally being ushered into the presence of Judge Davies. For the next two hours, our counsel and hers argued some pettifogging point about whether the notice to quit served by our solicitors should be held to expire on Lady Day or some other day. All muttered in low voices so that we could hardly hear a word. Reference made to nineteenth-century cases and famous lawyers of the past; huge tomes containing relevant writings handed up to judge. Neither we nor the bitch were called as witnesses. Finally we were dismissed for the day, another date being fixed to suit the convenience

---

* Widow of Basil Barlow of Stancombe Court, Gloucestershire.

of her, not us – though we are paying our costs while she (whose mother is selling her house behind Lansdown Crescent for £750,000) gets legal aid. The law is not just an ass – it is a fiend. A. and I return to our car, fuming.

Saturday, 9th April

I can never remember a spring more glittering with wild flowers. Primroses in abundance. Amelanchier almost out, a fortnight ahead of time. Saw an unusual phenomenon in Vicarage Field, near the Orangery. On an ancient and not very large chestnut tree, suspended from a long twig (too slender to be called a branch), hangs a great wen of encrusted, scoriated bark, the size of a football, covered with opening chestnut buds. Folly and I very interested. Told A. I would like her to see it. Where, she asked. I said, close to the square stone on a slight mound where I would like my ashes to lie. Oh, she said, you would talk like that just on my return from France.

Thursday, 14th April

We dined alone with the Beauforts, the four of us waited on by Steven the butler and Bronwyn the parlourmaid. On leaving the table, David said in apparent seriousness, 'I can never believe that anyone I invite really wants to come here.' 'What nonsense,' I replied, wondering who would refuse who had the opportunity. Can David, with his superb good looks, charm, rank (in the Victorian sense), and his marvellous house, famed far and wide, really mean it when he talks like this? A. asked David, rather rashly I thought, 'Who decides which trees on this estate should be cut down and where others should be replanted?' 'I do,' replied D., a trifle peevishly. 'I have planted twelve thousand trees since Master's death. Why, is anything wrong?' 'No, everything's wonderful.' The truth is that D. is not much of a conservationist, and unconcerned about hedgerows, brambles, elders and bird life.

Jane, our nice gardener girl, said to A. this morning, 'Isn't it wonderful hearing the birds singing so loudly?' Alas, A. and I now hear nothing at all. This is one of the sadnesses of age. No more dawn choruses. No more blackbirds' songs – there are many blackbirds about now. No more thrushes.

Friday, 15th April

Driving to Bath, I listened to Arthur Scargill* on *Desert Island Discs*. This man, whom I and thousands like me detest as a public fiend for his wicked iconoclasm and Marxist views, has a beautiful soft speaking voice. He spoke of his passionate beliefs, instancing how Tolpuddle martyrs, suffragettes, general strikers of 1926, etc. suffered defeats at the time in their efforts to promote freedoms which are now accepted. Similarly feels that World Socialism is bound to come (he may be right) in spite of present reverses. His choice of music included the Prisoners' Chorus from *Leonora* and the Slaves' Chorus from *Nabucco* – political choices, yet who would suppose such a barbarian would be familiar with Beethoven and Verdi? His choice of book *Huckleberry Finn*, and his luxury item, of all things, the Mona Lisa.

Saturday, 30th April

Vicar wonders why the Royal Family no longer stay at the House. I say it is surely because neither the Queen nor David was minded to continue the tradition after old Master died. He thinks it is because the police protecting the Queen would bring their sniffer dogs which might detect the drugs the young people take.

Monday, 9th May

This morning Roy Strong† came to see me in Bath with BBC Radio Three to talk about the National Trust for a series to be called 'Pillars of Society'. Don't know that I was any good. Roy is charming, gentle

---

* President of National Union of Mineworkers since 1981, who had led its disastrous strike of 1984–5; former Communist, and founder during 1990s of Socialist Labour Party (b. 1938).

† Sir Roy Strong (b. 1935); Director, Victoria & Albert Museum, 1974–87; writer and broadcaster.

and modest. Brought four copies of my diaries to sign; said my *Tudor Renaissance* [1951] first inspired his interest in Tudor art. I am bewildered at times when clever people tell me what I have done for the cause. He asked me if I thought that I had had insufficient recognition. Of course I deprecated that notion. I asked if he was relieved to be free of the V&A. He replied that he was, and that I was the first person to ask him such a question. It had been a nightmare constantly having to haggle with the Treasury over money, and having nearly every scheme and proposition thwarted for lack of funds.

Tuesday, 10th May

Selina [Hastings] stayed last night with us, on the way to see Lady Sibell Rowley* in her Evelyn Waugh quest. She said that Auberon Waugh[†] held all the cards and played one biographer off against another. She thinks he hated his father and will do anything to discredit him. Selina praised my novel, which she returned. Said I must not give it up. I said that since it had been turned down by at least half a dozen publishers I didn't see how I could send it to another. S. said that Anthony Blond was starting up again as a publisher. Would I mind if she told him how much she liked it and urged him to take it? Would I?

Wednesday, 11th May

This evening Folly and I drove down to Swangrove. No nightingales ever heard up here. Little life; no more rabbits; few birds this beautiful evening. Lakes of bluebells, and primroses still. At the rond-point a covey of cowslips. I picked one, trying to catch that nostalgic gentle scent; but I couldn't. Sense of smell almost gone since my cancer treatment.

---

* Lady Sibell Lygon (1907–2005), 2nd dau. of 7th Earl Beauchamp (on whose family situation Waugh based the Flytes in *Brideshead Revisited*); m. 1939 Richard Rowley (he d. 1952).
† Evelyn Waugh's eldest son, the leading satirical journalist of his time (1939–2001); m. 1961 Lady Teresa Onslow.

Monday, 16th May

The solicitor telephoned saying he could get no answer from the bitch's solicitor in reply to our letter offering her £1,000 to settle the case which is due to be heard next week. Thinks she is playing us like a fish, keeping us guessing until the last minute. I asked whether this would not annoy the judge, who might find a whole day of his time wasted if she accepted our offer at final moment. He did not seem to think so. 'You can do nothing,' he said. When I reported this to A. in the evening, she said we should send an ultimatum to the bitch's solicitor saying that unless she accepts our offer within forty-eight hours, the case is on. A. is far brighter than I am.

Sunday, 22nd May

We had a luncheon party – the Guy Hollands, Rory Young and wife.* We much liked the Youngs. Both craftsmen – she expert marbler and restorer of furniture, he a specialist in building construction, plasterer according to old-established fashion, no cement used by him. I took them into the church here. He was very informative about the marble used for the monuments, nearly all from Italy. The large Rysbrack sarcophagus must weigh a ton. How did they get it here? By sea from Leghorn to Bristol, then by wagon to Badminton? He knew at a glance how thick was the veneer of marble, how it was dowelled, how and where joined. Splendid young man. How I admire and feel small beside people, especially dedicated young people, who work with their hands and have knowledge, love and taste for their crafts. How boring Guy and pretentious Joan seem by comparison.

Tuesday, 24th May

Today two BBC men came down and took me to lunch at the Lansdown Grove Hotel, to vet me for a film about architectural

---

* Rory Young (b. 1954); m. 1987–92 Jane Rickards.

conservation and the National Trust. Nice they were. One Julian Henriques, dusky, gold earring, smiling, delightful. He is the producer. The other Patrick Wright, who will compère. I think I was all right, but I find these interviews a strain nowadays, keeping my end up, trying not to be slow and muddle-headed, trying to remember. They left at 2.45 and I hurried home to meet Simon Verity in the church at Badminton. He had gone, but to my inexpressible joy the 'Angels', as the Vicar will call them – Justice and Prudence, in fact – are up where they belong on the Grinling Gibbons monument.* They look splendid, and have transformed the monument, which is more noble, less stiff, pointful. I always said to A. that I hoped to live to see them put back. Now I have.

Thursday, 26th May

David and Caroline dine with us alone. A. always provides a delicious dinner for these two, whom she dearly loves, as do I. After dinner I mentioned the reinstatement of the 'Angels'. They showed indifference, neither having even been to see them yet in their restored glory. C. said to me rather sharply, 'You were one of those who made such a fuss over their removal.' I have to be careful.

Friday, 27th May

On my return from Bath, I persuaded A. to come and look at Jus and Pru in the church. She was delighted and vastly impressed. We found the two Veritys working at them, Simon before our eyes assembling Jus's gold-tipped scales and sword. He disputed Pru's title; indeed, why should Prudence be gazing at herself in a glass, with a snake twisted around one arm? I can't get over the splendour of this monument. Simon said that surely there was no other parish church in England with a finer display of monuments. Both Veritys in working clothes, he wearing thick once-white sweater grey with dust, his hair covered with plaster. A splendid pair.

---

* See 27 November 1984.

Then Folly and I walked in Vicarage Fields round the big house. Overjoyed to hear cuckoo singing its head off. On and on it went. I wept with pleasure. A marvellous, clear, brilliant evening light on the north front, all the pilasters, cornices and sharp angles shadowed by the slanting sun.

Sunday, 29th May

We lunched with the [John] Griggs at Tormarton. They are obliged to sell the house because Joanie [Altrincham] foolishly left it jointly to her two sons, and the other insists on selling. John is sentimental about the place and would like to buy or build a smaller house in the village. Iris Murdoch and John Bayley[*] lunching. I sat next to her. Very amiable she was, quiet, diffident and dowdy. He looks like a large tadpole turning into a frog, ugly and bald but jolly. Very forward in manner and anxious to please. They told me that nice things are said of me in Bevis Hillier's[†] first volume of John Betjeman's biography. She talked to me about the young's method of writing on computers, which she thinks must have an adverse affect on their style, as they no longer correct their own syntax but leave it to the machine. She writes all her books in longhand, then has them typed up in the old-fashioned way. Patsy [Grigg]'s charming brother and wife staying from Northern Ireland. They railed against the Anglo-Irish Agreement,[‡] saying it was infuriating that a foreign state should have a say in the government of their country. They live two miles from Clandeboye. I told him that Basil Dufferin had been my friend from private school days; that I knew Sheridan but little, but so much liked what I did know of him.

---

[*] Dame Iris Murdoch (1919–99), Oxford philosophy don and novelist; m.1956 John Bayley (b. 1925), Professor of English at Oxford.
[†] Writer, journalist and critic (b. 1940); the first volume of his life of Betjeman was about to be published by John Murray.
[‡] Agreement signed by Margaret Thatcher and Irish premier Garret FitzGerald in November 1985, under which the Irish Government agreed that Northern Ireland should remain part of the United Kingdom so long as her people wished it, and the British Government agreed to allow the Irish Government a consultative role in the formulation of policy with regard to the Province.

Monday, 30th May

Opened the *Daily Telegraph* at breakfast, and lo, an obituary of Sheridan Dufferin. This clouded my day. He was only forty-nine – and I was older than his father. Basil and I shared a dormitory with Tom Mitford in our last year at Locker's Park. Both Tom and Basil long gone – and now Basil's son. This is the end of the Dufferins – and of Clandeboye too, I suppose. Sheridan was a gentle, sweet-natured, art-loving man, attractive without being good-looking. I wish I had known him better. The *Daily Mail* has the headline, 'Marquess dies of Aids'. The brutes.

Wednesday, 1st June

To Knole [Kent] with Julian Henriques and Patrick Wright. A sunny day but Arctic cold. Was distressed on entering park to see appalling tree devastation.* Camera crew arrived in van. P. Wright and I were made to walk from the screens passage into the Stone Court and walk down the colonnade, talking. This we did some four times, first attempts interrupted by aeroplanes flying over, etc. It is difficult to be natural on the fourth repetition. Then for two hours we continued our talk sitting on a bench in the park with our backs to the wicket entrance. The cold was intense, but because we had worn no great-coats in the sheltered Stone Court, we could not wear them in the park. Can't remember much about what said, but it was all rather drivellish – I recalling my first visits to Knole in the mid 1930s as Eddy [Sackville-West]'s guest, and later interviews with his father Lord Sackville.† Before we left, Lionel Sackville‡ called us into his part of the house to have a glance at Graham Sutherland's§ portrait of Eddy hanging there.

---

* Following the great gale of October 1987.
† Major-General Sir Charles Sackville-West (1870–1962); s. brother as 4th Baron Sackville, 1928.
‡ Lionel Sackville-West (b. 1913); s. cousin as 6th Baron Sackville, 1965; m. 1st Jacobine Hichens, 2nd Arlie de Guingand, 3rd Jean Imbert-Terry.
§ Artist (1903–80).

Wednesday, 8th June

I lunched in London with N.T. publicity man Warren Davis[*] to meet Patrick Garland,[†] who told me that Paul Eddington,[‡] the actor in *Yes, Minister*, proposed to do a one-man show based on my diaries. P. E. regards the project as a sort of rest cure, his doctor having warned him against overstraining his heart. P. G. will write the script and suggests a trial at Aldeburgh, Bath or some N.T. country house. He thinks it may take off and get to the West End. That would certainly be very gratifying for me.

I knew I would like Patrick Garland because I remember how wonderfully he looked after John Betjeman during the Laureate's later broadcasts. Indeed he is surprisingly like a member of John's old circle, though not yet fifty. Full of witticisms and anecdotes at everyone's expense. He said that his father knew John when they were children, both P. G's grandmother and John's mother having come from Australia, which I never knew. P. G's father remembers how worried John's mother was when John got into what she regarded as a fast and immoral set at Oxford. But Garland Senior reassured her that the Warden of Wadham was protecting him. This of course was Maurice Bowra.[§] Little did she know. Garland Senior remembers how John as a small boy at preparatory school noticed and criticised buildings. John taught him to look upwards when walking the streets. The two boys were sent by their respective parents to Paris and told to visit a brothel. John told P. G. that he hated the experience, while Garland *père* enjoyed himself. P. G. did not know Bevis Hillier's volume about to come out. Hillier had not been in touch with him.

P. G. said Paul Eddington is a very serious actor who makes a prodigious effort to identify himself with the characters he interprets on

---

[*] On staff of N.T., 1967–2002 (b. 1937); cousin of J.L.-M's late friend the architectural historian Terence Davis (1924–83), author of *The Gothic Taste*. The idea of a one-man show based on J.L.-M's diaries arose out of a suggestion by Davis that he give a public reading from them at an N.T. house; J.L.-M. was unwilling, but suggested that an actor be found to do the reading.

[†] Writer, broadcaster and theatre director (b. 1935).

[‡] Actor (1927–95), famous for his portrayal of the vacuous politician James Hacker in the immensely popular 1980s television series *Yes, Minister*.

[§] Sir Maurice Bowra (1898–1971); Warden of Wadham College, Oxford, 1938–70.

stage. P. E. is going to Australia this autumn, but might be ready next spring or summer for this task. All rather exciting. It staggers me how intellectual folk believe my embarrassing and mediocre diaries to have substance. P. G. spoke of them almost with reverence.

Thursday, 9th June

I listen to myself on Radio Three. I was on for about two minutes – whereas I remember having an interesting conversation with Roy Strong of about three-quarters of an hour. I shall not agree to these broadcasts in future because it is a waste of time, and disjointed snippets taken at random do nothing to enhance one's reputation.

Friday, 10th June

We dined with Caroline tonight, who said she needed help with entertaining Grace Dudley* in David's absence. On arrival we found some twenty people, including children and spouses. I sat next to Lady Christopher Thynne,† a tough and temperamental woman whom I don't like. Don't much care for her husband either, with his aggressive drivel. What a lot they all are, redolent of the worst aspects of the Edwardian age. A crowd of fatuous, arrogant drones, waited on by a regiment of servants. It is so archaic as to be barely true. I only cared for Caroline tonight, who has the sweetness of a wild deer.

Saturday, 11th June

I fetched Misha from Chippenham station to stay the night. We had the Humphrey Stones‡ and Mary Keen§ to luncheon. No greater contrast to last night's dinner party could be conjured up. Mary such

---

* Grace Kolin (born Dubrovnik, Yugoslavia); m. 1st Prince Stanislas Radziwill, 2nd 1961 (as his 3rd wife) 3rd Earl of Dudley (1894–1969).

† Antonia Palmer; m. 1968 Lord Christopher Thynne (b. 1934), brother of Caroline, Duchess of Beaufort.

‡ Humphrey Stone (b. 1942); typographical designer; m. 1968 Solveig Atcheson.

§ Lady Mary Curzon (b. 1940), dau. of 6th Earl Howe; garden writer; m. 1962 Charles Keen (b. 1936), director of Barclay's Bank.

a dear and beautiful woman – M. adored her sparkling grey-blue eyes, grey hair, simplicity, naturalness and knowledge. Humphrey and Solveig are perfection, dedicated to arts and crafts, the quiet life, the country. It was Humphrey's birthday and A. produced a chocolate cake with little candles which when you blow them out relight themselves and set fire to the sideboard. I gave him a copy of *Venetian Evenings*, by which he seemed pleased. M. is so strange. Sits speechless at meals until roused. Worked at proofs all afternoon after guests gone, apart from joining me on a short walk with Folly in Vicarage Fields. 'Why come to the country?' asks A. No domestic graces. Yet I am devoted.

Wednesday, 22nd June

Gary Conklin,[*] American who came with daughter to film me in Bath a year ago, telephoned from Eton at 2 p.m. to ask if they might come forthwith to film again and ask some more questions. I had just finished reading Lady Greville's letters, so said they might. They kept me until six, asking me to elaborate on some tales I told them last year – but I wonder how they will get over the fact that I was presumably wearing different clothes today, and must look older.[†] This film seems to be along the same lines as Henriques' – social and literary life before, during and after the last war. A mania for this period. Conklin had just come from interviewing Leslie Rowse and Peter Quennell,[‡] but was turned away from Eton when he arrived there without warning.

Friday, 24th June

M's Duke of Windsor book[§] is being serialised in the *Daily Mail*. The newspaper has typically confined itself to publishing some sensational

---

[*] American film-maker based in San Diego (b. 1932). His *A Question of Class: English Literary Life between 1918 and 1945* was released in 1992.
[†] J.L.-M. was indeed changed from the year before (as can be seen from clips of Conklin's film on the James Lees-Milne website – www.jamesleesmilne.com).
[‡] Sir Peter Quennell (1905–94); writer, editor and journalist.
[§] *The Secret File of the Duke of Windsor* (Bantam Press).

letters of the Duke which only come at the end of the book, which is otherwise sober and serious. Ali Forbes,* whom I ran into in St James's Square, told me that he knew for a fact that the Windsors had not wanted these letters published. But he is wrong, for M. has shown me a copy of the Duchess's letter to Maître Blum authorising her to publish them. Ali was extremely offensive, referring to 'Bloch whom you love', and saying that it had been 'a good wheeze' of me and Alvilde to get married.†

Saturday, 2nd July

On Thursday Tony Mitchell‡ motored me to Kedleston [Derbyshire] to join the N.T. Arts Panel. A delicious day. Lovely to be with the Trust chaps, all so charming and clever. A most scholarly report had been prepared by Professor Leslie Harris of Derby, who knows everything about Kedleston; gives history of every room's redecoration, when and how. It bears out my theory that even the greatest country houses, built all of a piece at one period of history, can never be kept as first decorated. Harris shows that Kedleston was repainted internally at least once every thirty years, different colours each time. Martin Drury warned me that Patrick Wright who interviewed me at Knole is a Marxist of the most mischievous sort. Martin knew that I had taken him to see Lionel Sackville, who had complained about having to admit the public one day a week into his wing – a statement which could be used to make trouble.

Greatly enjoyed this visit which somehow rejuvenated me, renewing my interest in architectural problems and invigorating my spirit. Nevertheless I have today written to Dudley Dodd tending my resignation from the Arts Panel. I am sure I am right. One must go when old. Besides, dear old Brinsley Ford has resigned. This severs my connection of fifty-two years with the National Trust. *Eheu!*

---

* Alastair Forbes (1918–2005); American-born and English-educated journalist resident in Switzerland, famous for his social knowledge and his long and eccentric book reviews.

† Forbes had been known to refer to Essex House as 'Bisex House'.

‡ Anthony Mitchell (b. 1931); N.T. Historic Buildings Representative 1965–96 (for Wessex Region, 1981–96); m. 1972 Brigitte de Soye.

Friday, 15th July

Derek [Hill] telephoned at breakfast to say he had seen Bruce Chatwin yesterday, whose appearance is quite horrifying. Cannot stand and is wheeled in a chair. Is becoming a member of the Greek Orthodox Church next week, and has got the monasteries at Mount Athos to pray for him. I am amazed that he has succeeded in being accepted by that Church. I tried once and was rebuffed.

Saturday, 16th July

Met Hugh Massingberd at Chippenham by an early train and took him to Badminton to meet A. Both A. and I were shocked by his fat and puffy appearance. But what an amiable man and good companion. Splendid old-fashioned manners. We spent a delightful day together. Motored first to Dyrham [Park, Gloucestershire], where Tony [Mitchell] conducted us round, informative and intelligent. A nice young female photographer arrived from London and took pictures of me in soppy attitudes, beside a peacock, against a piano, next to Neptune on the hill. We lunched at The Crown, where Hugh spoke intimately. Told me his prep school headmaster had caught him kissing a boy whom he liked. Young H. hadn't a clue why it was wrong to do so. Was expelled, his parents not told why. His father, still alive and younger than me, knows nothing to this day. Father a puritan of deepest dye, appalled by recent disclosures of his late brother Peter's relations with Anthony Blunt.* Hugh says the result of his childhood experiences is that he is deeply shy and awkward in company. This I witnessed today. It may also explain the subversive element in his writing.

We continued to Flaxley Abbey.† Mr Watkins now eighty-eight, dry and intensely boring, but welcoming. Min the old companion scurrying for the tea trolley. The house is now a macabre shrine to Oliver

---

* Art historian (Surveyor of the Royal Pictures, 1945–72), officially disgraced in 1979 when it was revealed that he was a former Soviet agent (1907–83).
† For the unusual recent history of this mediaeval property in Gloucestershire's Forest of Dean, see 6 November 1988.

Messel.* Nothing since his time altered, but time has wrought decay. No windows opened since Oliver's day. Smell of stuffiness. H. to be polite offered to buy a guide book he saw lying about. It cost him £12, I hope refunded by *Telegraph*. To his dismay, H. found that it only gave history of the house up to the Reformation. Written by Mr W., who insisted on autographing it.† Hugh fascinated by whole set-up, Oliver hovering overhead in every room. There is no house and no family in England that Hugh does not know about, if not know.

Wednesday, 27th July

M. is having much publicity over his book. Today's *Times* has a long article about him, entitled 'Bounder or Biographer?' A rather nice photograph of him lying on his sofa like an oriental odalisque. When asked by the interviewer whether it was right to publish a letter in which the Duke of Windsor describes his female relations as 'a bunch of seedy, worn-out hags', M. suggested that this showed a poetic touch. I deprecate this remark and have warned M. that he makes a great mistake in mocking the Royal Family. It will always tell against him – *vide* John Grigg.‡ M. seems insensitive to the fact that the spectacle of himself and Maître Blum, with their Jewish backgrounds, attacking the Royal Family will make a disagreeable impression on some people. He asks if I have been embarrassed by his dedication of his book to me. Nothing can hurt me now, but much can hurt him. I feel protective of him and jealous of his reputation.

---

* Theatrical producer, designer and artist (1904–78); brother of Anne, Countess of Rosse.

† Hugh Massingberd writes of this episode in his memoirs *Daydream Believer: Confessions of a Hero-Worshipper* (2001): '. . . the owner, a ponderous retired businessman, manoeuvred me into forking out some vast sum for an immensely dreary tome he had produced on the exhaustive history of the old Abbey going back to its Cistercian foundation in the twelfth century. "You fell right into the crasher's trap, didn't you?" chortled the impish Jim as I beggared myself.'

‡ In 1957, Grigg, then 2nd Baron Altrincham, provoked reactions which today seem astonishing when he published an article in the *National Review* (which he owned and edited) mildly criticising the monarchy for being out of touch. He was assaulted in the street, excluded from the radio programme *Any Questions*, and found a promising career as a Conservative politician in ruins.

Sunday, 31st July

Oenone* for the weekend bringing lover, one Guy Lubbock,† a gent for a nice change, very easy, charming and good-looking. Knows lots of our friends' children and speaks our language. They slept together in one room, in one bed. How lucky they are, for we could never have done this in our grandparents' houses. We asked the Henry Robinsons for dinner to meet them. A successful evening. Susy told me that their son Alexander, after attending his sister's christening, was taken to see his grandparents' grave in the churchyard. 'Dig them up!' he said.

Thursday, 4th August

A. and I and Folly set forth by road to stay three nights with Billa [Harrod] at Holt [Norfolk]. Perfect old-fashioned weather for a change. Immensely enjoyed visit. Object to get away from [eightieth birthday] celebrations and sticky little gifts from greats, great-greats and steps, with their kind intentions. Even so, before departure this morning receive present from Peggy with two fat embraces, and a case for my watch from Oenone's nice friend Guy Lubbock.

Friday, 5th August

We lunch with Sybil Cholmondeley at Houghton, not open to public today. She is rising ninety-four and frail, yet robust mentally, full of anecdotes and fun. Took us round the house after, through all the state rooms. Lavinia Cholmondeley staying with her son David Rocksavage,‡ charming and sensitive young man, immensely handsome. Told me that he hates shooting, and the neighbours think him wet in consequence. The Houghton shoot adjoining Sandringham will be an embarrassment to him, for he is to inherit Houghton

---

* A. L.-M's granddaughter Oenone Luke (b. 1960), 2nd dau. of Hon. Clarissa Luke; m. 1992 Richard Gladstone.
† Old Etonian charmer (b. 1957).
‡ Earl of Rocksavage (b. 1960), o. s. and heir of 6th Marquess of Cholmondeley (whom he succeeded as 7th Marquess and Joint Hereditary Lord Great Chamberlain of England, 1990).

from his grandmother. (His parents live at Cholmondeley [Castle, Cheshire].) Billa told us he was queer, on account of which he spent some years living in Paris. (Surely that can't have been the reason? Tax, more likely.) I hope nevertheless that he eventually marries and produces an heir. Before departure we visited the harness room, beautiful bridles with silver crests on eye blinkers, all polished and shining. A cousin of Billa's came to dinner, Robert ffolkes,* baronet. Middle-aged and unmarried. The aristocracy seems doomed to extinction. I like the double ffs, deriving from George IV's reign and Sir Walter Scott, I suppose.

Saturday, 6th August

I am eighty. Have been so since 1.30 this morning. A beautiful day dawns, misty sunlight. Folly and I join A., who hugs me and gives me *Who's Who* for 1988, a smart cotton pullover, and Bevis Hillier's *Young Betjeman*. We buy the *Daily Telegraph* in Holt. On front page of literary section an article about me by sweet Hugh Massingberd, which gives me enormous pleasure. Too eulogistic, but most welcome. We visit the Lasts'† curious garden at Corpusty, greatly expanded and now something splendid. A mill house on the noisy village street. Then we visit Felbrigg [Hall near Cromer] and lunch there very well. Kind ladies in the house come up and ask to shake my hand. I feel like John Betj. In the evening, Billa motors us to Burnham Market for a concert in church organised by Margaret Douglas-Home.‡ Violin and piano. In the interval we talk to Silvia Combe§ who reminds me that I stayed with her on my fiftieth birthday. She says I was in tears on that occasion.

---

* Sir Robert ffolkes, 7th Bt (b. 1943).

† Two brothers, one of them a poet, whose garden, 'profuse in plants and flowing with water', and featuring 'grottos, follies and busts', the L.-Ms had first visited in August 1980.

‡ Lady Margaret Spencer (1906–96), yr dau. of 6th Earl Spencer; m. 1931 (diss. 1947) Hon. Henry Douglas-Home (1907–80), yr s. of 13th Earl of Home.

§ Lady Silvia Coke (b. 1909), dau. of 4th Earl of Leicester; m. 1932 Simon Combe (J.L.-M's company commander in Irish Guards, 1940; he d. 1965); she lived at Burnham Thorpe near King's Lynn.

Tuesday, 9th August

On return to Badminton last night found an avalanche of cards and letters congratulating me on being so disgustingly old. Also another article about me, by John Martin Robinson in *Spectator*, excellent and less embarrassing than Hugh's eulogy. Photograph of me in *Telegraph* has aroused favourable comment. Aristocratic, says M.; sexy, writes Myles Hildyard.

Saturday, 20th August

I lunch with the Michaels of Kent at Nether Lypiatt. Sign visitors' book in hall and see Caroline's name above mine. We would have come together had we known. A long wait till nearly two before we eat. Two couples, one called Sherwood I think, he the owner of the Orient Express and Cipriani's in Venice, a great beefy man with a bland smile; she, Shirley, dressed in Reckitt's Blue,* with black hair and intelligent face, who tells me she was a scientist 'before we became so rich'. I am put on the right of the Princess, who is very friendly. Takes me by the hand and leads me to the seat. I like her exuberance, intelligence, sharpness, quickness. She gets me to sign four copies of my little Cotswold book, which she then hands out to the other guests. She talks too much, perhaps. I watch her. Still a handsome woman, in a simple, pretty blue and white frock with a minimum of jewelry. He at far end of long table wearing check shirt open at sun-burned neck with gold chain and cross suspended, a blazer with bright gold buttons, blue trousers and black shoes.

Marie-Christine says to me that the Prince is reading a book dedicated to me. 'He is deeply shocked', she begins, and I fear the worst, 'by . . . the dreadful way they treated the Duke of Windsor. He used to see the Duke in Paris and was very fond of him, not so much of her.' The Princess told me to talk to the Prince about the book after luncheon, which I did. He remarked how well-balanced and clearly written it was. That showed some intelligence. He is a dear little man

---

* Bright blue clothes-washing substance popular during first half of twentieth century, manufactured by Reckitt & Sons Ltd of Hull.

and no longer shy with me, makes little jokes and is rather simpatico. Was charitable about Nicholas Ridley's dilemma in having to build more houses in the Cotswolds, though is dismayed by the new village recently built to the east of the house. Even this remote, secluded place is now surrounded. She aired her grievances against the Family. Said that because she and her husband received nothing from either the Queen or the Civil List, they could do more or less as they pleased, but in consequence came in for much criticism. That the Queen was enormously rich but did not have much to spend her money on, the upkeep of her palaces and children all paid for by the state. That the real demons were the Household, who ruled the roost. That she hated the press, who never gave her credit for the good things she did – 'though occasionally', she added a trifle archly, 'I do something naughty'.

Did not get away until five. Alone with her would have been more fun. She calls me James – which I like, just as I like being kissed on both cheeks. And I enjoy hearing indiscretions. She said that, before she married, the Queen told her that unless she joined the Anglican Church her children would be cut out of the succession. She replied that, though a bad Catholic, nothing would induce her to renounce her faith, unless Michael asked her to do so. He of course deferred to her. I don't know what the status of the children now is.[*]

Friday, 26th August

The bitch tenant has finally vacated the flat, but D-Day has come and gone without any word from her about our settlement offer of £1,000. I have at last finished answering letters of congratulation for being eighty. I would guess I received about that number. One lady writes, 'I have been re-reading *Midway on the Waves* and have "felt" your father close at hand.[†] He wants me to let you know how happy he is that you have drifted back to the Church of England.' Now

---

[*] Unlike their father, they remain in line of succession to the throne.

[†] J.L.-M's diary for 1949 recorded the death of his father George Lees-Milne (1880–1949).

would my dear parent have minded that much? True, he was cross when I went Papist [in 1934].

Saturday, 3rd September

Arrived home last night, worn out after driving in the rain from Castle Howard. My state of near-collapse not mitigated by the discovery that one of the 'greats' was staying. It took me until this afternoon to recover from the strain of this long journey, reading signs and following the road. Spent two days at Castle Howard during this second visit, hardly worthwhile as the Bachelor's letters I saw there of little interest. Paid £20 for the privilege, and £100 for two nights in The Worsley Arms. Fighting my way to the cafeteria through the Castle's vaulted basement, I pondered on the tricks of time. There I was aged eighty, old and venerable, struggling to get a bun and Nescafé, eating cheek-by-jowl with 'bedints' off a flooded plastic tray. Whereas thirty years ago I stayed in the state bedroom and dined with George and Cecilia* in the state dining room. Such contrasts are the spice of life.

Monday, 5th September

I drove to Wickhamford today, A. unable to come because she was returning the great-grandchild to London, thank God. Anyway she would not have understood my pious pilgrimage, for Wickhamford means nothing to her. I would have liked to have my sister Audrey with me, but even she would not have appreciated the Holy Communion which the very nice Vicar of Badsey gave me at eleven o'clock, eighty years to the hour since my christening in 1908. Sat in the chancel; I would have liked to be in our old pew in the nave, but that would have been inconvenient for the Vicar. So I perched on one of those two tall oak Puginesque chairs facing the Sandys monuments. A wonderful experience taking the sacrament in the same beloved

---

* George Howard of Castle Howard, York (1920–84); sometime N.T. Honorary Representative for Yorkshire; Chairman of BBC, 1980–3; cr. life peer as Lord Howard of Henderskelfe, 1983; m. Lady Cecilia FitzRoy (d. 1974), dau. of 8th Duke of Grafton.

church where I first did so eighty years ago. The church is beautifully kept, the brass hinges to the pew doors brightly polished. I regret the strip lighting my father put in just before his death, to replace the old hanging oil lamps. I talked to the Vicar afterwards. The people in the Manor, whom he likes, do not attend, but are generous in a crisis. I gave him £100 towards the upkeep and shall haunt him ever after if the PCC spends it on converting the heathen.

When the Vicar left I took Folly for a short walk across the funny old bridge, with its narrow 'V' stile at either end, across the brook into Badsey Field, full of thistles and nettles and unkempt. Looked into the Manor garden through the trees. Then walked a little way up the lane past the Donkey Patch. There were apples tumbling off a few orchard trees close to the large sycamore. Apart from the field, and the clumps of trees which give a park-like effect, the country around is very bare and built upon. Then I returned to the churchyard and read the head-stones with their familiar village names – Taylor, Mason, Colley. One to Mrs Hartwell, whom I have written about in *Another Self*,* and who lived in the row of red brick cottages on the site of that horrid fake my father built, Hodys. Her husband died the year I was born; she lived from 1852 to 1935.

I re-entered the church. The old stone-flagged floor with ventilator flue now covered with a genteel grey carpet. Deep red carpet in chancel, not quite the thing. Tombs in splendid condition and the thumbs of Sir Samuel Sandys, which my father seized from an American woman visitor who broke them off as a souvenir, are still in place, showing the marks of the breaks. The funny neo-Gothick font, which Papa and I fetched from Ombersley (where old Lord Sandys gave me a box of cigars for some favour now forgotten), still in the chancel. How low the ceiling where Mrs Hartwell got tangled up with the bell-rope, just above the oak cupboard where the Vicar keeps his copes. The panelling came from Ribbesford and is early sixteenth-century, rather rare, associated with the Acton family who owned Ribbesford in Henry VII's reign. I doubt whether anyone in the

---

* She appears in the book as a benevolent but bizarre widow who was the mainstay of the village church, and once while bell-ringing got carried into the air and ducked in the font.

village now knows what it is or by whom it was given. I inherited it from Uncle Milne and brought it from Scotland.

Perhaps foolishly, I decided not to call at the Manor to ask to walk in the garden. I think the present owners are the people who asked me to come over and talk of the past and I refused, saying it was too painful. Instead I drove round to the field where asparagus was grown in the Great War, now full of sheep, and walked down to the brook which separates the field from the garden. Splendid view of the house all spread out. Instead of being black and white it is now black and yellowish, which I don't much like. Church visible on extreme right, pine trees planted by Papa now higher than the church tower. Much activity – someone up a ladder attending to the window of Mama's bedroom, woman pushing a wheelbarrow into the yard. Two dogs noticing me started to bark, people stared at me, suspecting me no doubt of evil intent, and I turned and walked slowly back to the car.

Saturday, 8th October

Sally [Westminster] most kindly motored me to Sachie [Sitwell]'s funeral. Took place in the little village of Moreton Lois [Northamptonshire], a mile from Weston. Pretty church with mural tablets which I could not read from where we sat. We had reserved seats in the front. Church packed with friends from London, and locals. Peter Quennell gave a short, too-short address about his old friendship with Sachie, describing him as the greatest genius of the three Sitwells. Peter had cut his forehead, across which he wore an old bandage, exuding blood. He looked extremely old and emaciated, wife supporting him up altar steps. Moira Shearer and Ludovic Kennedy* recited four of Sachie's poems. Sally found them childish, but I was moved by them. We returned to Weston where Francis and wife had laid on excellent stand-up luncheon for almost whole congregation. Gertrude [the housekeeper] there looking surprisingly young. Grasped my hand with tears and told me of Sachie's peaceful end in his sleep. 'To think that I have looked after this wonderful genius for sixty years.'

---

* Ludovic Kennedy (b. 1919; ktd. 1994); broadcaster, politician and humanitarian campaigner; m. 1950 Moira Shearer (1926–2006), ballerina.

I too was on the verge of tears, though I think few others were, because of Sachie's great age and readiness to die. Reresby* a great bore, telling long-winded stories with a hint of loucheness. Before leaving, seeing Reresby at the door of Sachie's little writing room, I asked whether I might have a look at it for the last time. He let me and Sally in, saying, 'This may be my last time too. My brother [Francis] and I are not friends.' 'In which case,' I replied, 'this is the moment to become friends again.' Baba Metcalfe embraced me and said she would be coming down to Bath to see her mother's dresses and would like to lunch with me. Sally a surprisingly good companion, her sweetness outweighing her silliness.

Sunday, 16th October

We motor to Wilton [near Salisbury, Wiltshire] for David Herbert's eightieth birthday. As we drive, the mist rises and a beautiful autumnal day emerges. David greeting friends with embraces and darlings. Our host Lord Pembroke,† tall, slim, handsome man with aquiline features, advances to meet us, saying 'I am Henry'. Some forty of us sit at separate tables in the library. I am seated next to Candida Lycett Green and Moyra Lubbock, charming mother of Oenone's nice friend Guy. (A. sits next to the father, equally charming.)‡ She too is longing for the pair of them to marry, but agrees there is nothing one can do to bring it about.

Candida told me that her birthday present to David was a Victorian book of illuminations which I had once given her father, and inscribed. Strange that only two days ago I was wondering what had become of that book, which I hadn't thought about for twenty years. She also said how much she resented 'the little man's criticisms of my dad' – i.e., Bevis Hillier's very occasional unfavourable remarks about John Betjeman. As an example, she mentioned his emphasis on her

---

* Sir Reresby Sitwell, 7th Bt (b. 1927); er s. and heir of Sir Sacheverell; m. 1952 Penelope Forbes.
† Henry Herbert, 17th Earl of Pembroke (1939–2003); nephew of David Herbert.
‡ Lieut-Commander Roger Lubbock (b. 1922); m. 1955 Moyra Fraser, actress (formerly married to Douglas Sutherland, author of *The English Gentleman*).

Chetwode grandparents'* disapproval of the marriage. Yet John himself deliberately emphasised Lady Chetwode's objections because he found them funny, always hooting with laughter at her 'middle class Dutchman' jibe. And to be fair, Lady C. did object a good deal – as she had also done with her daughter's previous suitor, dear Johnnie Churchill, whom she described as 'a parlour trick man'.

David made a nice little speech of thanks to us for coming, and to his nephew Henry for giving the luncheon. We were all nearly in tears, as was he. It is always moving to see how one's contemporaries are held in affection by the younger generation.

Friday, 28th October

Gervase [Jackson-Stops] stayed the night with us. He is a dear little good egg, so full of life and enthusiasm. He made us do what we have never yet done – motor into the park after dinner to look at the House illuminated by the anti-burglar searchlights. A hazy moon to the east, just on the wane; stags roaring in the background. He and I then sat up watching the Prince of Wales talking about modern architecture. I agreed with every word, as did Gervase. He spoke well and confidently, never tripping up. Very outspoken on how during the Sixties the landscape was blighted by tower blocks etc. The next morning the papers already full of headlines nagging at the poor Prince; but the majority of his audience will be behind him. The modernist architects build for themselves without considering either the public at large or the wretched victims obliged to live in their terrible cages of torture.

Sunday, 30th October

In the evening, we watched Patrick Wright's television film in which I feature, called 'Brideshead and the Tower Blocks'. I saw with horror a very frail-looking old man, with scrawny neck and puff of white hair at rear of head, advancing into the Stone Court at Knole beside tall, upright P.W. This was a shock, for although I often feel ghastly and

---

* Field Marshal Lord Chetwode (1869–1950); Commander-in-Chief of the Army in India, 1930–5; m. 1899 Hester Stapleton-Cotton.

tired, I still think of myself as a middle-aged man. One catches up slowly with the stark facts only too apparent to others. As I sat in front of the wicket, in a bitter wind but wearing only a summer suit, the cold gave me a pinched look. My voice seemed deeper than usual, and my utterance was slow. I fancy I looked just as dear Lord Sackville looked when I visited him in his eighties – rather dandified, neat, red-faced, meticulous and slow. P.W. introduced a political note by contrasting Knole with St John's Institute, Hackney, the one aristocratic and lavishly maintained, the other plebeian and neglected.

All Saints' Day, Tuesday, 1st November

To Eton for the night, to stay with the Charterises. I found driving in the failing light a strain, and needed a stiff whisky on arrival. How nostalgic Eton in November, mists rising through setting sun. Martin Charteris in bed with pneumonia, so Gay received us. A dinner for thirty, given jointly by Provost and Headmaster. We knew none of the guests, most of them clever academics. Bit of a strain keeping up. Headmaster Anderson and wife[*] both delightful. She teaches English. Vice-Provost an economist. We ate in College hall, more restored than I remember; after pudding we saw the kitchen, fifteenth-century and likewise over-restored, claimed to be the oldest still in use; then through the glorious library to the Election Room where we had dessert at a long table with silver candles and tankards, having brought our napkins. At dinner I sat beside Mrs Anderson, who reminded me of K[athleen] Kennet, with her grey hair close-cropped like a boy, and her enthusiasms. She told me that Eton was flourishing, having gone through a bad patch under Chenevix-Trench[†] when it sank to a low level of dissipation. The boys now eager and happy. Buildings too in apple-pie order (we looked out of our window in the morning to see roofs and walls restored). Lupton's Tower clock striking

---

[*] Eric Anderson (b. 1936); Headmaster of Eton, 1980–94 (Provost from 2000); m. 1960 Poppy Mason.

[†] Anthony Chenevix-Trench (1919–79); Headmaster of Eton, 1964–70, notorious for his readiness to administer corporal punishment; he was also over-fond of alcohol, and went on to become Headmaster of Fettes, where his charges included the future Prime Minister Tony Blair.

the quarters, on the hour the highest note, brought back melancholy memories.

Several masters expressed their liking for *Another Self*. Indeed I get tired of this book being praised, just as Harold grew to regret *Some People*.* Mrs Anderson quizzed me about several of the stories, but I would not be put upon. She has read it to her class of boys who, instead of being amused like the adults, were appalled by the predicaments I got into.

Sunday, 6th November

We dined with the Thomas Messels at Wotton-under-Edge. Large party, including Sally [Westminster] and the Snowdons. Sat next to Lucy Snowdon, who is charming and clever. Looks plain at a distance and handsome close to, unusual. Talked to her and Tony afterwards about Anne Rosse,† now a great trial. Lucy fags for her ceaselessly which Anne takes for granted. I gather half the trouble is the bottle, poor thing. Tony extremely friendly with me as always, embracing me on both cheeks. Said he missed his Uncle Oliver [Messel] more than anyone. We agreed the story of Flaxley Abbey would make a splendid film. Mr Watkins, as a poor boy living in the neighbourhood, looks wistfully across park at large house. Eventually buys it from Crawley-Boevey family. Mrs Watkins goes to a play designed by Oliver Messel. Writes to him. Oliver's mother dies and he is miserable. Regards Mrs W. as a substitute. She falls head-over-heels in love with O. At first Mr W. resents it, but seeing no harm can possibly result, acquiesces and himself falls for O. Oliver sells much of his inherited furniture to the Ws, and arranges it in the house. The Ws will not touch an item in the house unless it is arranged by O., unarranged rooms remaining under dust-sheets. O. dies. Mrs W. dies. Mr W. still living there with Min . . . When we left, Tony said he would like to

---

* J.L.-M. had to some extent modelled his *Another Self* (1970) on Harold Nicolson's *Some People* (1927): both works are autobiographical novels written in the first person, describing how their authors were 'tested' by being faced, at various moments of their youth, by hilarious embarrassing situations.

† Anne Messel (1902–92); m. 1st Ronald Armstrong-Jones, 2nd 1935 Michael Parsons, 6th Earl of Rosse (1906–79); Lord Snowdon's mother.

photograph me, and was quite pressing. A. said I should agree, it is such a compliment. But I don't want to be photographed.

Thursday, 10th November

Dining with us, David [Beaufort] spoke about Lucian Freud,* with whom he lunches once a week. Freud brings his mistress of the moment, currently Y., who is expected to remain silent. Freud himself sometimes goes into a brown study and does not talk, strange for D. who was brought up, as we all were, not to allow silences. Freud is totally dedicated to his painting, at which he works all day long, and with which he is never satisfied. He hates praise of his work by reviewers who fail to see its failings. He longs to produce one flawless masterpiece. Is obsessed with sex and often has to have it on the spur of the moment – while walking round a garden, in the bath, between courses. Apparently he has no trouble getting women to oblige him in these unromantic urges. I asked, rather absurdly, whether he was a nice character. D. said yes, he is fundamentally generous and kind. I would not have guessed so.

Monday, 14th November

Towards the end of his sad, degraded life, Bonnie Prince Charlie wrote to his brother the Cardinal† that he was 'bothered in the head'. This is my experience now – nightmares day and night, awake or asleep, or rather half-asleep which I am most of the night. Not a headache exactly, no violent pain, just a bother in the head, like the grinding of a coffee machine. Days when I am completely free of these 'bothers' are rare. I then feel wonderfully well and begin to suppose I am as good as I was.

---

* Artist (b. 1922; CH, 1983).
† Princes Charles Edward Stuart, 'the Young Pretender' (1720–88) and Henry Stuart, Cardinal Duke of York (1725–1807); sons of Prince James Stuart, 'the Old Pretender' (1688–1766), who in the Jacobite canon were his sucessors to the throne as Charles III and Henry IX.

Sunday, 27th November

This morning my article in the *Telegraph* about Nicholas Ridley's frightful speech saying the old families should clear out of their houses if they cannot afford to keep them up to make way for the *nouveaux riches*, and about the Mappa Mundi. Printed exactly as I sent it in for a change. A. thinks I went too far in saying that the Dean and Chapter of Hereford should be boiled in oil.*

Tuesday, 29th November

I began Chapter 1 of the Bachelor this morning, writing a page and a half. At this rate it will take me ten years to finish. Had to leave Bath at 3.45 as it was becoming dark and foggy. These short days retard me greatly.

Thursday, 8th December

As a sort of echo of times past, a wave of pleasure passes over me when A. goes off to London for the night. I am now free to take my own time, do silly fuss-pot things, get on with letter-writing without being called on to do things I don't want to do. But when she has been away for twenty-four hours, I long to have her back, and begin to worry about her. Folly and I are quite happy; I sleep with her cosily in A's bed, relishing her little grunts in the night, and the way she rests her muzzle on my feet.

Friday, 9th December

Yesterday before leaving Bath at 4.30 I rang up Audrey, about whom I have been worried lately. Was surprised to receive no answer, for I could not suppose she was in her garden at that hour. This morning Dale [Sutton] telephoned to say Audrey had had a stroke while cutting up meat for her cat. Managed to crawl to telephone and ring up Dale.

---

* The Mappa Mundi, compiled *circa* 1290, was 'saved' for Hereford Cathedral and became the centrepiece of a museum opened there in 1996.

She and James sent for doctor and whipped her off to Yeovil Hospital. She cannot speak, not a good prospect for her eighty-three years. Poor darling. Waves of sadness and remorse assail me.

Sunday, 18th December

A. and I motored to Yeovil to see Audrey in hospital there. A dark, foggy morning. Found it difficult to read signposts. Reached hideous hospital at 12.30. Few nurses about. Saw little Audrey sitting in a ward of eight trying to eat an ice cream with her left hand. Think she recognised us. She looks dreadfully ill, the right side of her poor face still blotched with marks of the fall she had. She cannot speak and was pitiful yet contented-seeming. Occasionally smiled and even laughed a little. Don't know that she understood what we said. We gave her presents which meant nothing to her, I a scented head pillow, A. a beautiful white shawl which she put around her. All the while the other seven lay silent as corpses, while the television blared nonsense like a snowstorm. O the poignancy of it all.

1989

1989

I have had a Christmas card from Patrick Garland mentioning that the dramatisation of my diaries is going ahead, the first performance booked for August under the title *James at War.** I hope it will not be on the weekend of the 13th when we celebrate A's eightieth birthday here. I am also slightly sensitive about the title, as some reviewers of the diaries criticised my 'war', unaware that I had served in the army, admittedly for a short period before that bomb in Hyde Park Square.†

Wednesday, 4th January

Caroline asked me to enquire of my new friend Rouge Dragon‡ (whom I have yet to meet) by what title they should call Harry [Worcester]'s child if he is born a boy later this month. He has sent me a long reply dismissing my suggestion of Earl of Glamorgan on the grounds that the grant of this title was never confirmed by Charles I, who seems to have changed his mind after promising it to the then

---

* The play was not finally produced, owing to Paul Eddington's declining health. Hugh Massingberd's dramatisation *Ancestral Voices*, starring Moray Watson, opened at the Jermyn Street Theatre in November 2002 and ran for five years as a touring production.

† J.L.-M. spent a few months in an Irish Guards training battalion before being caught in a London blomb blast in October 1940. This triggered off a nervous disorder eventually diagnosed as Jacksonian epilepsy. After a year's convalescence, he was discharged from the army and allowed to return to his old job at the N.T.

‡ Patric Dickinson (b. 1950); Rouge Dragon Pursuivant, 1978–89; Richmond Herald of Arms from 1989. He had been put in touch with J.L.-M. by Freda Berkeley.

Marquess of Worcester. For reasons hard for a layman to understand, he suggests instead Earl of Somerset, even though this is not a title enjoyed by David. He sent me reams of fascinating papers on the subject, which I have dropped at the House and are now being studied.

Saturday, 7th January

John Julius [Norwich] and Mollie lunched. They have bought a derelict mill house near Castle Combe, at the head of a pretty valley. He is full of enthusiasms, a great worker, successful television showman, but not a man of sensibility like K. Clark. A good writer but no scholar. Has a quick eye for the humorous, yet lacks a sense of humour. Too pleased with himself to be lovable; mulled wine in a cold decanter. Mollie, his adoring slave, is an attractive, clever woman. We talked of Mrs Thatcher. J.J. told how, soon after she became Prime Minister, he as chairman of some opera thing had to take her to *Tosca*. To his amazement, she knew everything about the history of past performances, when and where and who sang in them. When the performance was over, he asked whether she had not thought it a splendid one. 'Yes,' she replied, 'but her *fichu* should not have been scarlet but cerise.' That tells much about her. He said it was quite possible that Mrs T's grandmother, a housemaid at Belton, was seduced by Harry Cust,* who was the real father of Diana [Cooper], and notorious for his attentions towards girls in service. Diana always referred to Mrs T. as her niece.

Thursday, 19th January

To Somerset House to search for the will of the Bachelor's mistress Eliza Warwick. To my surprise there were numerous Eliza and Elizabeth Warwicks. I looked up four, but don't think any of them was my lady. A beautiful sunny winter's morning, mist rising from

---

* Henry John Cockayne Cust (1861–1917); editor, *Pall Mall Gazette*, 1892–6; MP (C) Grantham, 1895–1900; heir presumptive to cousin 4th Baron Brownlow (1844–1921) of Belton, Lincolnshire.

river. Wandered to Law Courts to admire Gothic hall, then crossed to Temple. How lovely those ranges of seventeenth-century chambers, so well restored since war. Had nostalgic feelings at 4 King's Bench Walk. Harold [Nicolson]'s old rooms* no longer seem to be residential, glass door at entrance. Felt inspired to write a book of reminiscences mingled with philosophising, based on places which have coloured my life – Ribbesford (done in a sense),† Eton, Magdalen, Park Lane,‡ Portman Square,§ K.B.W., Buckingham Palace Gardens,¶ and so on. Curiously enough M., when I called on him for tea, suggested something similar. He also reminded me that we met ten years ago next month.

Rouge Dragon lunched at Brooks's. I liked him. Very intelligent, well-informed and correct; in looks a handsome Sebastian Walker,** which does not mean handsome. Talked non-stop. I found him difficult to hear, and had to guess much. To Heywood Hill, where Joan Haslip praised my *Esher*; then to Sotheby's exhibition of pictures from Monet to Freud. Too fast – yet how else can one?

Bruce Chatwin is dead. A grievous loss to literature, the papers say. For one so comparatively young and recently acknowledged the obituaries are amazingly long and eulogistic. You would suppose Lord Byron had died. Does he deserve it? I think of Bruce with fascination and a certain repulsion. He had a very original mind, and was one of the most physically attractive mortals. I used to tell him that he looked like a fallen angel. He, Charles Tomlinson†† and I were a sort of trio, all living within a mile of each other,‡‡ yet not on letting-down-hair terms, quite. I was stimulated by him when we went for long,

---

* Where J.L.-M. was a 'paying guest' from 1934 to 1937.

† Ribbesford (once spelled Wribbesford), J.L.-M's grandmother's house near Bewdley, was the model for 'Wribbenhall', the setting for J.L.-M's first novel, *Heretics in Love* (1973).

‡ Off which J.L.-M. lodged in Norfolk Street during the early 1930s.

§ Where the proconsul and politician George, 1st Baron Lloyd (1879–1941), for whom J.L.-M. worked as private secretary from 1932 to 1935, had his London house and office.

¶ Site of the N.T's pre-war headquarters.

** Children's publisher (1942–91).

†† Poet and don (b. 1927); m. 1948 Brenda Raybould.

‡‡ In Gloucestershire's Ozleworth Valley, where the L.-Ms lived from 1961 to 1974.

rapid-striding walks around Alderley. Once we walked from Badminton to his house at Ozleworth, down Worcester Drive, past Oldfield, till we crossed the Bath–Stroud road by Tresham, he never halting in stride or talk. But I was irritated by his false cackle. He was a great self-pusher and publicity-seeker, and a terrible show-off. I recall one evening Bruce and I dined alone at Alderley. He and I sat before the fire, drinking and talking late into the night. I wondered whether to ask him to stay the night, and decided not. Just as well, perhaps. He was very beguiling, stretched on the rug in a cock-teasing attitude. He was, with all his intense vanity, discreet. Yet on this occasion he admitted that he would never decline to sleep with any male or female if pressed, but only once. Nonce with me.

Wednesday, 8th February

This morning Nick [Robinson] breakfasted, looking pale but distinguished. I can talk to him openly now about my will and my wishes. Spent morning at Public Record Office, Chancery Lane – shades of dear Noel Blakiston* – looking through lists of will-makers between 1837 and 1858 in vain hope of finding elusive Eliza Warwick. Then lunched at Garrick with Mark Amory† who is writing biography of Gerald Berners.‡ A nice, smiling man, tall, sallow, balding. He spoke very fast like a Cecil, and I had difficulty keeping up. I warned him that I did not know Gerald intimately. He asked what I thought about the relationship with the Mad Boy.§ Well, I said, of course Gerald must have been in love with him from the start, and possibly throughout; but he must have reconciled himself to no return, and kept the love of a paternal sort. Amory suggested my writing a book of memoirs of friends. I said I might, if spared by the Bachelor.¶

---

* Sometime Assistant Keeper of Public Records (1905–84); m. 1929 Georgiana Russell (1903–95).
† Writer and journalist (b. 1941); literary editor of *Spectator*.
‡ Amory's biography of Berners, *The Last Eccentric*, appeared in 1998.
§ The handsome but unstable Robert Heber-Percy (1912–87).
¶ It was published by John Murray in 1996 as *Fourteen Friends*.

Saturday, 25th February

Richard Robinson motored me to see Audrey in his grand Mercedes full of gadgets. Loudspeaker system playing Haydn; telephone on which he rang up his wife telling her not to put on the vegetables for another half-hour. A. is put off by this tycoon yuppie boy and thinks he wants shaking. But he is a sweet, gentle character, clever and sensitive. Poor Audrey gets very muddled in speaking, switching from one subject to another. At one moment she was talking about her sad situation when Matthew [Arthur] left her in the 1930s; this turned into a dog she had had getting run over by a bus. Richard touchingly gentle and sweet with her. I was surprised that he had never heard of Stourhead [Wiltshire], for he is interested in architecture. Is also chairman of the Knightsbridge Environmental Committee and has been asked to stand for Westminster Council.

Monday, 6th March

Caroline dined with us last night. She told us that, after many hesitations and contradictions, Glamorgan has finally been accepted by the College of Arms as the grandson's title. I may have been responsible for this, and feel absurdly pleased. I am amazed by the rich. Caroline wanted to visit Botswana. When the bill for the expedition came, she read it as £9,000. She thought this rather a lot, but David said after all, they had but one life, etc. It then transpired that the 9,000 were not £ but whatever the local currency is, equivalent of £1,000.

Friday, 17th March

We dined alone with David, sitting cosily at a table in the library before a roaring fire. Much as I like him and enjoy his company, I don't love him or ever feel intimate. Yet he is the kindest man alive (perhaps also the cruellest). When A. mentioned I might have to quit my library, he at once offered to find a room for me in the House. After dinner he took us round the west wing, to a room over the *porte cochère* in a passage hung with washed linen. I did not fancy this. Then to the upstairs of north wing. Didn't fancy the larger room here either, and wondered if I could bear to be parted from Bath. During dinner, he said he would be quite unable to live here were he not earning a great income from his gallery,* and wondered whether the Worcesters, when the time came, would either want to live in the House or be able to afford to. We said that in any case they would be spared the capital outlay he had so lavishly provided.

Wednesday, 22nd March

We motored to Osterley [Middlesex] and back, two hundred miles, for luncheon given to Graham Thomas,† N.T. garden adviser, on his eightieth birthday. Several old N.T. friends. Lunched in breakfast room at separate tables, buffet style. Went round the house with Martin Drury afterwards. He feels as I do about the horrible redecorations of library and upstairs bedrooms by the V&A. Incredible to us that these academic pedants have such bad taste. But Martin tells me the V&A are handing both Osterley and Ham over to the Trust with endowment of £10 million – which is little enough, but will enable N.T. to scrap what the museum have done. They have certainly made a museum of this house, a country house no longer.

Saturday, 1st April

Staying with Eardley alone at The Slade. I used to think it rather a horrid little red-brick Edwardian box. True, it has no architecture outside; but inside it is almost ideal for a single person, or in the case of E. and Mattei, two who are seldom here together. Of course made charming by E's paintings and Regency furniture. There is a distinct period and sub-Bloomsbury feel. Reminds me of Raymond [Mortimer]'s and Paul [Hyslop]'s house in London, very art-twentyish, a taste I find sympathetic. Every reference and art book to hand. Cosy deep sofas. Then the situation almost ideal, unspoilt landscape, fields with cows sloping across a small valley to woods. E. in benign mood, and wonderful for his age. He is utterly independent,

---

* Marlborough Gallery in Albemarle Street, founded in 1946.
† Graham Stuart Thomas (1909–2003); adviser on gardens to N.T., 1954–74.

drives, cooks, does housework, paints as though twenty years younger than eighty-six. Only a little deaf. Most reprehensible of me to be irritated by deafness in another. I suppose it is because we talk incessantly. E. walked off after breakfast and worked. I read and wrote letters and walked. Gorgeous weather, like May. Bluebells on verges.

Tuesday, 18th April

Got back last night from Ireland, where I swore never to go again, and had not been for twenty years at least.* Stayed at Lismore Castle [Co. Waterford] with the Devonshires. Travelled there Thursday; came back Monday. A stupendous pile and the most picturesque site imaginable. Sheer above the Blackwater river, with a thin slip between castle and water of pouffy trees and yews, like cushions onto which one is almost tempted to jump, expecting to be bounced back. To left and right, east and west stretches the river, wide and fast-flowing, its long line broken only by tributaries. My bedroom in Flag Tower facing north overlooking the water-meadow, tops of Knockmealdown Mountains in distance. Vast castle round central courtyard. Agent lives on one floor of east wing; family and staff in north wing; offices in part of south wing; the rest empty. A wonderful place, but melancholy, like everything Irish. One merely has to live in this strange, remote, isolated world to become eccentric, casual and forthright.

I got there to find Debo, Kitty Mersey† and latter's charming daughter-in-law Anthea Bigham.‡ Andrew joined us on the Saturday. This is the Devonshires' annual visit, and he will have spent two nights, she a week. Neither of them may step outside the house, not even into the garden, without two policemen, guns at the ready, following at a discreet distance. I think the embarrassment of this and the trouble it gives explain why they come so seldom. Enjoyable visit and profitable

---

* He had in fact visited Donegal in August 1971 to stay with Derek Hill and Northern Ireland in August 1977 to do research for his biography of Harold Nicolson.

† Lady Katherine Petty-Fitzmaurice (1912–95), dau. of 6th Marquess of Lansdowne; m. 1933 Hon. Edward Bigham, later 3rd Viscount Mersey (d. 1979); s. bro. to Lordship of Nairne, 1944.

‡ Anthea Seymour; m. 1965 Hon. David Bigham (b. 1938).

Bachelor-wise. Hideous Pugin* furniture which inspires amazement if not admiration. 'Do you feel His presence here?' asks Andrew.

I consider Debo the most remarkable woman I know. Because she is a Duchess? Largely yes, because this status has brought out her astonishing Mitford qualities. I feel that, in any crisis, she would come out top, organise, keep her head, show her innate courage and self-assurance. As it is, her charm, her 'unbending' (for she does have to unbend from her olympian height), and her dignity never fail to captivate.

Sunday, 21st May

We lunched at Lasborough Manor [Gloucestershire] with Jonathan Scott and wife,† unknown to us but friends of Mary Keen. They have bought back the house which previously belonged to his grandmother. I remember it as a romantic, down-at-heel Cotswold manor. Now absurdly over-restored with yuppie-style Versailles garden laid out in the valley. Long drawing room upstairs with swagger Tudor fireplace, so high that it thrusts itself through ceiling. He is a tight-lipped, clever merchant banker, chairman of Export of Works of Art Committee to which I once briefly belonged. Said to me after luncheon, 'I have long meant to tell you that your book on Italian Baroque [1959] inspired me to become addicted to that style.' I fear he has been taken in, for in those days there were few books of that sort.

Thursday, 1st June

Was telephoned in Bath this morning by youngish academic at Lincoln College, Oxford called Edward Chaney‡ who had written

---

* A.W.N. Pugin (1812–52); architect and designer with a passion for the Gothic.
† Ian Jonathan Scott (b. 1940); Director of Barclay's Bank, 1980–92; Chairman of Reviewing Committee on Export of Works of Art, 1985–95; m. 1965 Annabella Loudon.
‡ Art historian (b. 1951), expert on 'the Grand Tour'; lived in Florence, 1978–85; Fellow in Architectural History at Lincoln College, Oxford, 1985–90, subsequently Professor of Fine and Decorative Arts at Southampton Institute.

to me about his biography of Inigo Jones.[*] I warned him I knew little now. He nevertheless begged to meet me, and see Beckford's library. I dare say that were it not for Beckford I would meet no one new. He came for tea. Tall and bearded with the bluest eyes, like the Son of God. Refreshingly right-wing in his views. Told me he had lunched last week in Florence with Harold Acton[†] and John Pope-Hennessy, the latter frailer than the former and no longer fierce. Chaney was very flattering, praising my article in *Modern Painters*, treating me with a deference I don't deserve. A delightful man.

Saturday, 3rd June

Why I continue with this diary God knows. Pedestrian and costive, like my life now. M. will doubtless destroy. Yet there is Mr Rota, hovering. This courteous man writes me sensitive letters explaining why no antiquarian bookseller would buy my library in my lifetime and let me hold on to it until death.

Thursday, 8th June

John K.-B. lunched with me in London. Affectionate as always, but he notices that I am becoming vague and inattentive. Keeps saying things like, 'You aren't losing your balance, Jim?' with an apprehensive look. He told me two dreadful things. First, Lord Tavistock[‡] is selling Canova's *Three Graces*, for which he has been offered £7 million by Getty Museum. John has testified to Export of Works of Art Committee on importance of this group, for which the Woburn sculpture gallery was more or less built. He says this is but one

---

[*] Architect (1573–1652) who introduced Palladian style to England; Surveyor of the King's Works, 1615–35; J.L.-M's book about him was published by Batsford in 1953.

[†] Sir Harold Acton (1904–94); writer and aesthete; owner of Villa La Pietra, Florence.

[‡] Henry Russell, Earl of Tavistock (1940–2003); e. s. of 13th Duke of Bedford (from whom he received Woburn Abbey in 1970s, and whom he briefly succeeded, 2002).

example of country house owners rushing to sell their treasures to America, a phenomenon he attributes to the Washington exhibition of four years ago. Secondly, he says the National Trust want to build a hotel on the land they own at Stonehenge. I find this hard to credit.

Saturday, 24th June

I finished the Bachelor yesterday – that is, got down his tale from birth to death. Am as amazed by my quickness as I am aware of its badness. Just the dull facts about a not very interesting man, who only achieved what he did because he happened to be extremely rich. I still have much to do – revision, addition, omission, etc.

Sunday, 25th June

Last night we attended ceremony to celebrate two centuries of Lansdown Cresent. The Colonel, who is chairman of the Lansdown Crescent Association, asked us to dine. We arrived at 6.30. Crescent barred to traffic by police. Bands played, Mayor made speech, residents dressed in bonnets and other unbecoming togs which they presume were worn then. I turned up my shirt collar and wore a white scarf like a stock into which I put a pin with the Thomson crest, never worn by me since inheriting it. Colonel introduced me to Chris Patten[*] the Bath MP, who asked to see my library. Stayed a time talking. Nice man, ring on centre finger, yellowing teeth, stocky, Catholic and friend of Rees-Mogg[†] who is godfather to his children. Affable and well-informed like most Tory MPs today. Told me he prayed to God for personal things, a fine day, a good dinner, etc. 'How can you waste his time?' I asked.

---

[*] Conservative politician (b. 1944); MP for Bath, 1979–92; Sec. of State for the Environment, 1989–90; Chairman of Conservative Party, 1990–2; Governor of Hong Kong, 1992–7; European Commissioner, 1999–2004; elected Chancellor of Oxford University, 2003.

[†] William Rees-Mogg (b. 1928); editor of *The Times*, 1967–81; cr. life peer, 1988.

Saturday to Monday, 1st to 3rd July

We go off for the weekend. First motor to Send to stay a night with Loelia [Lindsay]. A sad experience. This dear little spruce house is no longer spruce but very faded and down-at-heel. One pleasant Australian girl, without a clue of course. Garden a wilderness. Silver and furniture unpolished, rooms unswept. Loelia has quite given up. Can one wonder? Is haunted by poverty, and showed us two love letters written to her by Ian Fleming which she is thinking of selling. Her mind is all right, except that she cannot remember any name. Who was the man during the war who smoked a cigar? Yes, Winston. In the morning remained in bed. We said goodbye to her in her bedroom.

On the way to Send we lunched at Parkside. An equally sad experience. Garrett [Drogheda] bent and white as a sheet. Took me up to Joan's bedroom to see her. Joan lying screwed up on a daybed, fully dressed, fast asleep, snoring, tongue hanging out. I said to Garrett, perhaps we had better return after luncheon when she is awake. What's the point, he said, she won't know you. Doesn't know him.

From Send to Sissinghurst. Very different experience, highly enjoyable visit. Never have I seen the garden more beautiful. Party consisted of Lady Rupert Nevill,* Sue Baring,† Philip Ziegler and dear Richard Shone. Lady R. does not charm me. One front tooth badly cemented in, like an over-pointed brick. Ziegler improves as visit goes on. At first faintly furtive and gauche, doubtless shy. But clever and agreeable. Believes Maître Blum a bad woman who has done harm. Is lunching with her and M. in Paris on Monday – think of it. A. and I given the cottage to sleep in, she in Vita's old room, I in Harold's, sleeping in the bed in which he died in 1968. They would not have been pleased by the hideously vulgar way the rooms have been decorated by the tenant, American literary agent.

---

* Lady Camilla Wallop (b. 1925), er dau. of 9th Earl of Portsmouth; m. 1944 Lord Rupert Nevill (1923–82), yr s. of 4th Marquess of Abergavenny, friend and aide of HRH The Duke of Edinburgh.
† Hon. Susan Renwick (b. 1930), dau. of 1st Baron Renwick; m. 1955 (diss. 1984) Hon. Sir John Baring (b. 1928; s. 1991 as 7th Baron Ashburton).

Nigel told story of how he was the officer responsible for deporting some Cossacks in 1945, on the orders of Harold Macmillan. At the time he thought it a dreadful thing. The victims were told they were being sent to Italy, and so went unprotesting. He sent in a memorandum criticising the order, and was severely rebuked. Wishes he had had the guts to disobey and face court martial, like William Douglas-Home.* I was fascinated and horrified. Nigel is to be a leading witness for the defence in case to be brought next October by Lord Aldington against Count Tolstoy.† He has invited Tolstoy to live at Sissinghurst if he loses the action and is ruined.

Saturday, 8th July

Vicar told us the following story. While Master was alive, it was traditional for an annual meet to take place in his honour on his birthday. One year the birthday fell on Good Friday, and the Vicar told him he could not possibly have a meet that day. Whereupon the Duke took up the telephone and put through a call to Buckingham Palace. He asked for the Queen, who came on the line. 'Our Vicar tells me . . .', he began, and told the story. Then a long pause, and the Vicar heard him say, 'Well, if you really think so, Ma'am. That's what the Vicar advises. Seems incredible to me.' He put the receiver down, and said not a word. There was no further question of it.

---

* Playwright (1912–92), court-martialled when he disobeyed orders on moral grounds.
† The historian Count Nikolai Tolstoy (b. 1935), whom J.L.-M. had met on 4 November 1981, had published a pamphlet accusing the former Brigadier Toby Low (1914–2000; cr. Baron Aldington, 1962) of personal responsibility in deporting of prisoners of war to their deaths in the Soviet Union in 1945. Aldington sued for libel and was awarded damages of £1.5 million. Tolstoy has since attempted to challenge this verdict, and the European Court of Human Rights has ruled the award to be excessive. Nicolson gave evidence for Tolstoy, but was critical of his later assertion that he had failed to receive a fair trial.

Monday, 17th July

Last night Selina stayed, in order to take us to Hardy [Amies]'s eightieth birthday dinner. I had been dreading it, what with the heat wave and all. Given by the Faringdons* at Buscot Park. About forty. Extremely posh surroundings and gold plate. I was given a place at the top table, between Debo on Hardy's left, and Loelia on my left. On Hardy's right as guest of honour Princess Peg [Margaret of Hesse], that dear and charming old bundle with large white tombstone teeth like a cook's. Also at our table Henry Bathurst† and Lord Briggs.‡ Loelia talked whole time but I could not hear a word. At one point I took my napkin and wiped food off her chin. Enjoyable on the whole – but oh dear, the horror of my old contemporaries! Peter Coats a white skeleton. Hardy looking drained, skin taut and shiny, wearing large black-rimmed spectacles like a tycoon's. Made speech which was well-delivered but embarrassing. Stressed his humble, corrected to humdrum origins; then thanked the Countess of Somebody, grandmother of our hostess, who had given him patronage fifty years ago; went on to thank Devonshires for welcoming him into bosom of Chatsworth, etc. Call me snobbish, but I thought all this rather ill-bred. A pity, for he is a dear man who deserves his swimgloat. Is to be knighted this week.

Sunday, 6th August

As a birthday treat, the dear Mitchells motored us to Highclere [Hampshire], not seen by me before. Another grilling day. We arrived long before opening time and picnicked in the park, against a wire fence, squatting on hard-baked earth, persecuted by wasps. How anyone can honestly enjoy a picnic beats me. Nevertheless we quite enjoyed ourselves. House better in photographs than actuality, though a noble picturesque pile in Tudoresque rather than Gothick style.

---

* Charles Henderson, 3rd Baron Faringdon (b. 1937); of Buscot Park, Oxfordshire (donated by uncle to N.T.), and Barnsley House, Gloucestershire; m. 1959 Sarah Askew.

† Henry Bathurst, 8th Earl (b. 1927), of Cirencester Park, Gloucestershire; m. (2nd) 1978 Gloria Robinson.

‡ Asa Briggs, historian (b. 1921); Provost, Worcester College, Oxford, 1976–91; cr. life peer, 1976.

Crowds of visitors. The 1870s Gothick vestibule a noble thing, with Early English pointed roof and colonnettes of red and blue. Little furniture or contents worth looking at. Napoleon's desk and chair used at Longwood. Dreary 1930s decoration on bedroom floor. Nothing can be said for the taste of that deplorable decade. A female guide nearly died with excitement when I casually remarked that I knew Tilly Losch,* whose name is not mentioned by the present Carnarvons,† but of whom there was a photograph behind a rope. Of course I didn't know her the least well. Tom [Mitford] had an affair with her. She was a real bitch I imagine.

Tuesday, 8th August

To London. Collected Harold [Acton]'s medal from British Academy. Was received by Sec. and Deputy-Sec. Handed medal. What to do with it, and how to get it to Florence? Went to Julian Barrow's‡ studio in Tite Street at height of afternoon heat. Was so fagged I barely made sense, and did not know how to give praise. Must now write introduction to his exhibition catalogue. Kindly motored me to Paddington, where dear M. had tea with me at station hotel. Brought me enormous book on French Revolution as a present. Said he was now keeping a diary, which he wrote up daily before going to bed, i.e., at 4 a.m. Said he considered himself slow-witted. It is true that he does not have quick responses, but ponders and ruminates. I told him this was his strength as a writer.

Saturday, 12th August

The dreaded eightieth birthday party for Alvilde was a triumphant success, as all the guests assured us. A. herself delighted, which was

---

* Ottilie Ethel ('Tilly') Losch, Austrian actress and dancer (1907–75); m. 1st 1931–5 Edward James (art patron and Eton contemporary of J.L.-M.), 2nd 1939–47 (as his 2nd wife) Henry Herbert, 6th Earl of Carnarvon (1898–1987).

† Henry Herbert, 7th Earl of Carnarvon (1924–2001), s. of 6th Earl by 1st marriage and sometime stepson of Tilly Losch; m. 1956 Jean Wallop.

‡ Painter (b. 1939), who had recently completed a portrait of J.L.-M. in his Bath library; m. Serena Harington.

the main thing. We were lucky with the weather, the long spell of relentless sun, accompanied by drought, having at last come to an end. Yet sunshine on the day, accompanied by strong wind and scurrying clouds. We received the guests on the porch at Sheldon* – a difficult climb for the halt, Loelia and Woman having to be escorted on both sides. Champagne for sixty, wandering in the house and sitting on benches on the terrace. Then a painful procession to the stables where we ate at nine tables. A. had Andrew [Devonshire] and Garrett [Drogheda] next to her, I, Patricia Hambleden and Rachel Bridges†. Piano playing by young BBC man found by Freda, Paul Ginnery. A's grandchildren dressed as toreadors, looking hideous. Andrew gave us both a toast in a few words to which A. tossed off a cursory yet rather charming reply as she wrestled with the huge birthday cake. Instead of 'Happy Birthday to You', which she hates, Ginnery struck up with 'Rule! Britannia', very jolly. He played the accompaniment for a song which little Kane, aged six, was supposed to sing; but he lost his nerve, so A. took him and waltzed with him. A pretty sight.

I can't say I enjoyed this extremely expensive party, though delighted by its success. Thank God it is behind me – it kept me awake at nights. On reflection, it worked because we were not too ambitious. Unlike Hardy we did not stage a lavish banquet in a rarefied setting. We chose a simple but genuine manorial setting for a squire-archical feast. What with the Gibbs family portraits, antlers, saddles, brick paving of loose boxes, iron posts topped with balls and decorated with trailing ivy and periwinkle, we contrived a rustic, almost a Breughel scene, and an air of jollity which suffused ancient and infant alike.

Wednesday, 16th August

David Beaufort is a fascinating subject for study. We lunched with him today, Daphne [Fielding] the only other guest. Why does he

---

* Sheldon Manor, Wiltshire, seat of Major Martin Gibbs.
† Rachel Bunbury; m. 1953 Thomas, 2nd Baron Bridges (b. 1927), second cousin of A.L.-M., HM Ambassador in Rome, 1983–7.

suddenly ask us? He telephoned last night, infinitely polite, so glad, looking forward so much; and then when we arrive today, so pleased, which he can't be particularly. Never refers to the hostile press articles. One last week in the *Mail* stating that he has £100 million, owns 50,000 acres, is investing £14 million in BAT,* leads a separate life to his wife (not quite true), has a son with a drink problem (true). He must be totally indifferent, as he is to comment about Miranda moving into a house he has had converted for her on the edge of the park. Talks of so-and-so being frightfully rich, while *he* must be ten times richer. Casually remarks that the lovely old Turkey carpet in the library, torn to shreds by the young with their heels and stilettos, cost him £10,000 four years ago, and that a similar one to replace it will now probably cost him twice as much. He is ruthless yet charming, apparently highly sensitive to one's feelings, yet would probably not care tuppence if one dropped down dead at his feet.

When we left, he pointed out the two cupolae which he has repaired, releaded and repainted, and said he was very irritated with the Heritage people. He wants the House exempted from death duties, for whereas ten years ago a large house was assessed as of little value, today, owing to sheikhs, etc., it is valued at millions. Although he does not open it to the general public, yet every year thousands came to Badminton for dinners, meetings, etc., and the great crowds attending the Horse Trials and other shows benefit from the House, even if they do not enter it. I agree with him – a historic house ought to be exempt just like a painting or tapestry.

Friday, 18th August

This morning at 9.30 I answer the telephone and am surprised to hear Jock Murray's voice. Asks how Bachelor Duke getting on. He wants to publish it very much. This is nice to know, and flattering. He has returned the first two chapters with comments.

---

* British American Tobacco.

Friday, 1st September

A very tragic event reported today. Uppark* burnt down. By a blow-lamp, Midi [Gascoigne]† tells me, informed by her great friend Jean Meade-Fetherstonhaugh, Meg's daughter. When I think of Meg and the Admiral sacrificing themselves and everything to the preservation of that magical house, I ask myself – does God care? Is He a philistine too? Furniture apparently all but saved, chandeliers of course all gone and those wonderful mulberry curtains which Meg restored so painfully with her saponaria on which the V&A experts poured such scorn. O the cruelty.

Sunday, 3rd September

In church at Little Badminton today, the replacement Vicar (Tom [Gibson] still being away) gave a sermon about the last war. All the papers are writing about its outbreak fifty years ago. It is glorious weather, as it was then; and oddly, the days of the week are the same. So far away. I think I was at Cheyne Walk, but can't remember quite. A. and I listened to the repeat of Chamberlain's broadcast at 11.15. I certainly heard the original delivered. Moving and well-done, coming from a disillusioned and disappointed man, with none of Churchill's histrionics. I remember my intense unhappiness and wondering what the future held for me. Vicar today said our declaration of war was absolutely justified. I suppose he is right.

Thursday, 7th September

David Beaufort at dinner said Derek Hill was undoubtedly an influence on the Prince of Wales, and responsible for the Prince sticking those thin pilasters onto the front of Highgrove. We were surprised when he introduced two subjects close to home. First, drugs. He wondered if it might not be better to allow them, so that they might

---

* William and Mary house in South Downs, donated to N.T. by Meade-Fetherstonhaugh family in 1954 – see 19 October 1995.
† Hon. Mary ('Midi') O'Neill (1905–91); m. 1934 Frederick ('Derick') Gascoigne (d. 1974); friend of J.L.-M. since 1920s.

'find their own price on the market'. The second was mistresses, he telling us that Alfred Beit wanted one but could not afford one. He asked us whether Alf was really rich at all. As if we would know. D. had just returned from playing golf with the Duke of Marlborough[*] in Scotland. I'm not sure how much they really like each other, but I suppose dukes find one another cosy company, and talk ducal 'shop'. Caroline looking extremely handsome and dignified, stout but upright. We sat in the little yellow room. Delicious dinner of crab, obtained by Mervyn the Keeper.

The Keats–Shelley Bulletin says Keats suffered from something called cyclothymia – a quick alternation of depression and comparative elation, similar to manic depression but faster in cycle and not as devastating. Of course it is what I have suffered from all my life. Why did I not recognise this before? Because I have never heard the word until today.

Thursday, 28th September

I feel smug when I have accomplished all I meant to do on a day's jaunt to London, and disgustingly so when I have entertained the humble and visited the sick. Bought at Austin Reed the waterproof which Eardley wore in Scotland and I much admired. It is pale brown like a pre-war dust coat of the sort which used to be worn in open touring cars, made in Japan, very long, and folds up into a pocket handkerchief so as to be put in a bag the size of a pin-cushion. Had A's umbrella mended at Briggs. Then Igor [Luke] to luncheon at Brooks's. Have decided this boy is a hopeless case, and I can no more be sharp with him than with a dog. Is now humbly employed in a travel agency, doing odd jobs in back regions, not in front issuing tickets. Complained to me about his inability to get on with girls. He blamed his looks and his voice, but I told him that the fault lay in his manner rather than his appearance. Then I went to see Ros [Lehmann], who has fallen in love, aged eighty-eight, with a beautiful youth, a distant cousin aged twenty-eight.[†] Waits for him to telephone. Thinks only of him. He is

---

[*] John Spencer-Churchill, 11th Duke of Marlborough (b. 1926).

[†] Alexander Norman.

writing a life of the Dalai Lama.* Is being encouraged by Ros in his
pursuit of the spiritual. Ros seemed dreadfully flushed. Did she in her
blindness paste her poor face with rouge, unseeing? She recalled how
we had first met in France. I don't believe that I so fell for her that I
exclaimed, 'Too late, too late!', having just married A. Can't be true.

Tuesday, 3rd October

A vicious article by that nasty little man [David] Pryce-Jones† about
Diana Mosley. I telephoned Debo who had not seen it, and thought
she might get Frank Longford who loves her to write in protest. Debo
is going to America to lecture. On what, I asked? Oh, the dump of
course. You are the Queen of Dumps, I said. I told her that A. was in
France and going to do the garden of Giscard d'Estaing.‡ 'Isn't it
strange how we are all wanted in our old age?' said Debo. Too late, I
replied.

Thursday, 5th October

Went to London just to attend John Murray's party at No. 50
Albemarle Street. What a civilised house – dear old staircase; first floor
room hung with early nineteenth-century portraits; on stairs K.
Clark, Osbert [Lancaster], John Betj[eman] – and Paddy [Leigh
Fermor], survivor among eminent contemporary authors. Peter
Quennell, very old, murmuring that this was like the last party in
Proust. Conversation with him not easy, as one senses he expects more
than one can give. Diana Menuhin§ said she and I had known each

---

* Lhamo Dhondrub (b. 1935); recognised aged two as reincarnation of 13th Dalai
Lama; assumed religious and political authority in Tibet, 1950, but forced into exile
by Chinese invasion, 1959; awarded Nobel Prize for Peace, 1989. His book *Ethics for
the New Millennium*, written 'with Alexander Norman', appeared in 1999.

† Journalist; son of Alan Pryce-Jones and his 1st wife Poppy Fould-Springer; he had
fallen out with the Mitford sisters (except for Jessica) over his book *Unity Mitford: A
Quest* (1976).

‡ Valéry Giscard d'Estaing, President of France, 1974–81.

§ Diana Gould, ballerina (1912–2003); m. 1947 Yehudi Menuhin, violinist (1916–99;
cr. life peer, 1993).

other longer than most people had known us – for I knew her when she was the not very successful dancer Diana Gould.

Friday to Monday, 6th to 9th October

Flew to Stuttgart on Friday, returning Monday evening. Joined small party organised by Derek Hill. We stayed at Brenner's Park Hotel, Baden Baden, where Edward VII stayed, somewhat altered inside since. Extremely grand, comfortable, luxurious and expensive. Weather dark and cloudy, with some rain. Pity, for the setting, bedroom window overlooking arboretum and river below, very fine. Party consisted of dendrologists. A. is the dendrologist, not I, though I enjoy watching them as they pull and pore over leaves and argue about them.

Highlight for me was visit on 8th to Darmstadt to lunch with Princess Peg. Bus drove through narrow gateway of Schloss Wolfsgarten where she lives. Approached through suburbs. No lodges, which were deliberately pulled down by her husband so as to preserve anonymity. Short drive to *circa* 1700 house of dull sandstone. Tall, Dutch-like centre with cupola, and extremities added. Was until 1918 a shooting lodge, where royals could retreat to lead informal existence.

The Princess was on the steps to welcome us, and in the saloon made a pretty little speech. 'Please have a poor man's White Lady, or orange juice.' Some pretty furniture, and pair of handsome glass-framed mirrors on wall with deep blue borders. On windows the signatures of various celebrities, visitors to Wolfsgarten, had been scratched by diamond. I first noticed that of Adenauer,* carved in 1952. Princess told us that strangers remark on the dirty, broken windows which she must be too poor to have mended. She showed us dozens – Derek of course, Mick Jagger even, Julian Bream.† On other panes our present Queen, Queen Mother, David and Wallis (this pane cracked), Prince Charles, *et al.* And 'Nicky', the last Czar, dated 1895.

---

* Konrad Adenauer (1876–1967); Chancellor of German Federal Republic, 1949–63.
† Guitar and lute virtuoso (b. 1933).

A white-gloved footman handed round a tray on which were little slips of paper marked M[ann] and F[rau]. Mine taken at random resulted in my sitting on right of Princess. (Her slip said 'Die Hausfrau'.) She had Patrick Ford on her left, and I had Anthea Ford on my right. I had a long talk with the Princess. During the war she ran the Red Cross in Darmstadt until she and the Prince were confined to the house on Hitler's orders, as her Geddes relations were involved in the British war effort. She never met Hitler, though her wedding certificate was witnessed by Ribbentrop in London. (Her husband was born three months after me.) She said that, after 1918, all royal land, unlike that of ordinary private landowners, was forfeited by the Government, except for the immediate surroundings of a house. It was lucky that, when the Tsarevich* visited Wolfsgarten just before the 1914 war, an area of 150 hectares was fenced off for security reasons, and this was allowed to be kept. Most of the family's revenue came from their huge estate in Silesia, long since lost, but she still has a castle in Switzerland.

After lunch, she escorted us round the house. Several rooms filled with Jugendstil stuff collected by last reigning Grand Duke, very ugly I thought. In the park close to the house a very pretty baby cottage in Jugendstil built for little Princess Elizabeth, daughter of last Grand Duke and Princess Victoria Melita of Edinburgh (known as 'Duckie').† This poor little girl, result of a miserable marriage engineered by Queen Victoria and dissolved the moment the old Queen died, herself died aged eight of diphtheria. No grown-ups were allowed in the cottage or its tiny garden no matter how naughty the little girl may have been. Went into the cottage, full of photographs of the little Princess and the Romanov children. Full of pathos and sadness.

Princess P. is running a centre at Darmstadt to settle refugees from East Germany.‡ Says they are all young and skilled, and therefore most

---

* Crown Prince Alexei (1905–18); o. s. of Nicholas II of Russia and Alexandra of Hesse.

† HRH Princess Victoria Melita ('Ducky') (1876–1936), yr dau. of HRH Prince Alfred Duke of Edinburgh and Grand Duchess Marie Alexandrovna of Russia; m. 1st 1894 (diss. 1901) Grand Duke Ernst Ludwig of Hesse and the Rhine, 2nd Grand Duke Kirill of Russia.

‡ A flood of these had begun arriving, as the Communist East German regime tottered following the withdrawal of Soviet support. The Berlin Wall came down, and

welcome as there is a shortage of skilled labour in the West. When I asked if it was not difficult to house them, she said it was no problem at all.

Monday, 16th October

The *D[ictionary of] N[ational] B[iography]* have sent me a copy of a letter they have received from the killer of Jamesey Pope-Hennessy, sent from Parkhurst Prison. This person threatens to sue for libel on the grounds that he was never charged with murder, and I describe Jamesey as having been murdered in my *DNB* entry on him. I always understood that the case brought was of manslaughter because John P.-H., advised by Lord Goodman,* did not want a sensational trial full of relevations about Jamesey's sex life. They ask if I am willing to alter wording in future editions. I hope I do not get involved in this matter.

Another old friend not seen for a long time, Desmond Shawe-Taylor,† came for the night. We watched Mr Heath‡ being interrogated by Ludovic Kennedy. H. was asked rather bad-taste questions about his sex life which he parried without a quiver of annoyance or give-away. I admired him for this. Did he ever think of marrying? Yes, twice. Why then did you not do so? Were you not really in love? Heath's jowl is appalling, huge and pendulous; how does he shave it? Betrayed that he had a grievance. Out it came that Mrs T. had never offered him a cabinet post, though tried to get him to accept the Embassy in Washington in order to get rid of him. Desmond said that Heath has twice lunched at Long Crichel, necessitating many police in house and garden. Heath telephoned beforehand to ask if there would be any 'pomposos' lunching, odd word to use. On both occasions he was half an hour late, without apologising. Desmond says he is of almost professional standard as a conductor.

---

the German Democratic Republic effectively collapsed as a state, exactly a month later, on 9 November.

* Arnold Goodman (1913–95; cr. life peer, 1965); solicitor, known for his skill in handling sensitive matters arising from the private lives of public personalities.

† Music critic (1907–95); co-tenant of Long Crichel, Dorset.

‡ Sir Edward Heath (1916–2005); Conservative politician with musical interests; Prime Minister, 1970–74.

We talked of Jamesey, and A. asked Desmond if he had known anyone else who was murdered. 'Only my father,' said Desmond. This was in 1920, by Sinn Feiners. Desmond too young to be much affected, and bears no grudge against the Irish.

Monday, 23rd October

At midday to Bath Clinic to have lump removed by Clive Charlton. Was not alarmed, just slightly apprehensive. He talked throughout the operation to keep up my spirits. I felt nothing, just some tugging. 'You may feel a bit funny,' he said when it was all over. I did. Returned to the library to have something to eat, and took Folly for short walk on getting home.

Wednesday, 25th October

Clive rang before I set out for Bath. I think he expected to get A., who had gone to London for the day. I parried his irrelevant enquiries as to how I felt, and asked for the result of the test. 'Same as the cheek,' he said, giving the name of the growth. My heart sank. 'I am *not*', I said, 'going to submit to that radium treatment again.' He replied, 'Wait and see.' I thought about this blow all day, but with disappointment rather than wretchedness. Worked away at Chapter Six. Am determined to finish and deliver this book before I am bogged down with treatments. I did tell poor M. over the telephone, which was rather selfish, but I wanted to tell someone, and no one more understanding and sweet than he.

Friday, 27th October

Saw Dr King, who was extremely nice and sensible. He understood my disinclination to submit to further treatment, but said, 'You see, Jim, you are still worth patching up. In other respects you enjoy reasonable health, apart from your eyes, and your brain is still functioning.'

Saturday, 28th October

Darling A. left at seven this morning. Came into my room with Folly and kissed me goodbye. A day of terrible storms, 100 m.p.h. wind. Alex [Moulton] came to dine with me. While I was preparing dinner, the lights went out. Whole village blacked out for two hours. Had some difficulty finding torch and candles, Alex talking the whole time. Said Nigel Lawson* was a shit to waltz off during a crisis. Alex is to give a large luncheon for his seventieth birthday next April. During it, he intends to ask all guests who do not intend to support Mrs T. at next election to raise hands. To them he will say, 'It would be churlish not to let you finish your meal; but when you have done so, will you please leave my house.' Sitting by the gas fire by candlelight, Alex says, 'You look so well. How splendid that that horrid time of your cancer treatment is well behind you and you are as good as new.' I refrained from telling him the truth.

Tuesday, 31st October

Tony Mitchell motored me to Stowe,† where the National Trust launched an appeal for the park. Beautiful day after early rain; as we drove down the avenue, the sun flickered across the great arch like the lighting at an opera. We gathered at the Temple of Friendship and Concord.‡ A large crowd including many old friends. We followed George Clarke,§ the great Stowe authority, on a tour of the temples. I fell ignominiously walking up the steps of one. Given luncheon in a marquee, and listened to speeches begging for a mere £12 million.

---

* Conservative politician (b. 1932), who had just resigned as Chancellor of the Exchequer (a post he had held since June 1983) after disagreements with Mrs Thatcher and her economic adviser Sir Alan Walters; cr. life peer as Baron Lawson of Blaby, 1992.

† The former seat of the Temple and Grenville families, Stowe, Buckinghamshire, became a school in the 1920s. The splendid Georgian landscaped park with its decaying temples was transferred to the N.T. in 1989.

‡ In December 2003 it was announced that this atmospheric folly, long used by schoolboys for romantic trysts, was to be marketed by the N.T. as a venue for 'gay weddings'.

§ Stowe schoolmaster who wrote a history of its buildings and landscape.

Dame Jennifer Jenkins a charming woman, straightforward and enthusiastic. Is clearly devoted to the N.T. I sat near her on the top table, between George Clarke and Ralph Verney,* much aged and bent. Glynn Boyd Harte† opposite, speaking warmly of Julian Barrow, my other library portraitist. Headmaster of Stowe and others embarrassed me with praises of *Another Self*. Said they had never laughed so much, that there should be an A.S. Society, etc. What does this mean to me, under sentence of death?

Wednesday, 8th November

Before rising, in that semi-state of sleeping and waking, I now find myself consumed, not by despair, but utter languor and the certainty that I cannot 'carry on' any longer, and must die very soon. Yet exciting things are happening – the Bachelor coming to a close; the prospect of my diaries being dramatised (though I could not possibly attend a performance); and Nick [Robinson]'s offer to publish the first half of my novel as complete in itself. So odd to have a letter of praise and criticism from my dear great-nephew, almost incestuous. Now Jock Murray has asked me to write a brief life of Sachie. I am not at all sure that I want to do this, and a short biography would involve almost as much research as a long one, and possibly more labour. I would rather write something autobiographical or indeed another novel, which can be taken up and put down, rather than a biography, which is ceaselessly demanding.

Thursday, 9th November

Folly and I went in to the Bath Hospital. Dr Rees, looking overworked and unhealthy, chatted in the polite way specialists think patients prefer to straight facts. Was not in the least concerned about latest outbreak of malignancy. Suggests we just wait until another lump appears and deal with it accordingly. How do you feel? Fine.

---

* Sir Ralph Verney, 5th Bt, of Claydon, Buckinghamshire (b. 1915); chairman of committees concerned with conservation of nature and architecture.
† Artist, illustrator and dandy (1948–2003).

That's good – and off I go. F. sitting curled up on passenger seat just as I left her.

Saturday, 18th November

I do wish Hugh [Massingberd] would not bang on about an honour for me. Today's *Daily Telegraph* article on Bath refers to me in first and last sentence as a leading Bath conservationist. It is untrue. I have done the minimum for Bath.

Today A. and I lunched with Tanis [Guinness]* to meet A's first cousin Michael Menzies and American wife. Other guest was Maureen Dufferin,† who had brought with her some of Ava's last letters written from Burma shortly before his death. This was very sweet of Lady D., who clearly adores him still. The letters full of affection for her, the children and Clandeboye [Co. Down], which he begged her to keep intact for Sheridan. He clearly knew he might be killed. She said he was actually on some sort of secret mission when he died, and orders were on their way for him to return to London. She admitted his drink problem, and that she too drank to excess. I told her that F.E. Smith‡ was responsible for making that group drink at Oxford. The wicked thing was that F.E. claimed that when drunk his mind improved. This may have been true in his case, but it was not in theirs. The silly young things believed that by drink they would achieve greatness. I liked this old lady. Difficult to see how she was ever pretty. Her face looks as if someone had tried to press it down her neck. Strange to think that seventy years have passed since Tom [Mitford], Ava and I shared the top dormitory at Lockers Park.

---

* Thrice-married yr dau. (b. 1909) of Benjamin Guinness of New York.

† Maureen (1907–98), 2nd dau. of Hon. Ernest Guinness; m. 1st 1930–45 Basil, 4th Marquess of Dufferin and Ava, 2nd 1948–54 Major Desmond Buchanan, 3rd 1955 Judge John Cyril Maude.

‡ Frederick Edwin Smith (1872–1930), lawyer and Conservative politician; cr. Earl of Birkenhead, 1919; J.L.-M., an Eton friend of his son, sometimes visited his house near Oxford, and observed how his drinking habits influenced the young and clever.

Thursday, 23rd November

To London again. Was called for at Brooks's by Peregrine Worsthorne's[*] smart car and chauffeur and motored to *Telegraph* offices in Docklands. Ugly block in hideous mess of wasteland and skeletons of future blocks. Met at door by P.W.'s secretary, taken up in lift. P.W. received us in room with glass walls, sun streaming in. A party of eight, the others Frank Johnson,[†] nice jolly man of East End origins, Tony Hervey, Simon Blow, Geoffrey Wheatcroft,[‡] Ali Forbes and Lucy Lambton. I was treated like an idol, but owing to acoustics of room had difficulty hearing. Liked Worsthorne much, fine shock of white hair, neatly dressed with waistcoat and chain. We sat down to luncheon, not waiting for Lambton who was late. P.W. clapped his hands and said in authoritative tones, 'Please cease *tête-à-tête* talk, I want to hear the views of our guests on the National Trust. Is there a necessity for it? Cannot owners now afford to maintain their own houses? Is it N.T. policy to allow the families to continue in residence?' As soon as I tried to speak, Ali interrupted and talked ceaselessly. Eventually our host clapped again. 'Does not Mr L.-M. think that the aristocracy are returning to power and authority in England and Eastern Europe?' Mr L.-M. did not think. Then Ali made the remark of the day: 'As I once said to Pope Pius XII[§] at a cocktail party . . .' I can't understand why I was invited. Rather like the Queen's luncheon parties at Buckingham Palace. Filthy luncheon, hardly edible.

Monday, 27th November

Finished M's *The Reign and Abdication of Edward VIII* last night. It is fair, concise and moving, making a good case for Mrs Simpson and

---

[*] Writer and journalist (b. 1923; kt 1991); editor, *Sunday Telegraph*, 1986–9; m. 1st 1950 Claude de Colasse (d. 1990), 2nd 1991 Lady Lucinda Lambton (whom he met at the party described by J.L.-M.).

[†] Journalist on staff of *Sunday Telegraph* (1943–2007).

[‡] Writer and journalist (b. 1945), former literary editor of *Spectator*, then writing a weekly column in *Sunday Telegraph*.

[§] Pope, 1939–58 (Eugenio Pacelli [1876–1958]).

even the King. Today I got a postcard from him saying don't worry, Bachelor is good. Greatly cheered by this. Both of us slapping each other on the back. Have also heard from a Frenchman called Guillaume Villeneuve, asking to translate *Another Self* into French. I rang Debo this evening about getting Bachelor typescript to her to read. She is concerned about Diana's appearance on *Desert Island Discs*, which has become front-page news. Even the *Telegraph* has headline 'Lady M. loved Hitler', etc. M. fears she may be treated like Rushdie[*] and go in danger of her life.

Tuesday, 28th November

Went yesterday to see Paul Methuen's[†] exhibition at Victoria Gallery, Bath. Really excellent his pictures are. Sickert influence apparent in the oils. What a strange man, so abstracted, unworldly, socialist even, not really approving of private ownership, yet like old Sir Charles Trevelyan[‡] convinced that in the circumstances he was the best person to be curator of his long-inherited house. I never knew how much Paul cared for me. At times he was affectionate in a distant way. He was mightily attracted by women. A renaissance man in that he excelled at many things – music, botany, but above all painting.

Thursday, 30th November

An article in *Sunday Telegraph* quoting those country house owners who have never had it so good. Vulgarians like Francis Dashwood[§]

---

[*] British novelist of Indian origin (b. 1947), obliged to live in hiding after the Iranian leader Ayatollah Khomeini had called upon fellow Muslims in February 1989 to kill him for having insulted the faith in his novel *The Satanic Verses*.

[†] Artist (1886–1974) who succeeded as 4th Baron Methuen in 1932 and devoted himself to the conservation of country houses in general and his estate at Corsham, Wiltshire in particular; member of N. T's Country Houses Committee when J.L.-M. was its secretary.

[‡] Sir Charles Trevelyan, 3rd Bt (1870–1958); politician and landowner, education minister in Ramsay Macdonald's Labour Governments, who donated Wallington estate in Northumberland to N.T. after long negotiations in which J.L.-M. was involved.

[§] Sir Francis Dashwood, 11th Bt (1925–2000); tenant and restorer of West Wycombe

and Hugh Hertford* boasting of their cellars-ful of wine, their cuisine, the numbers of their guests, their *douceur de vivre* – and deriding me for writing (where and when?) that the country house is doomed for lack of servants. I might have asked them why it was that dukes needed to sell their treasures, Devonshire his engravings, Beaufort his Georges, Bedford his *Three Graces*. They can't be that rich if they live on capital.

Monday, 18th December

Have been suffering from influenza for past fortnight, and felt rotten. At one point ran a temperature of 103° [Fahrenheit], and could not speak, eat or even walk to bathroom. Today we learned that Joan Drogheda has died. She had been dead to all of us for some years already. Nevertheless sorrow rears its hoary head.

Thursday, 21st December

The shortest day, and a distressing one. Ian Dixon motored us through terrible rain to Joan's funeral, at Royal Chapel by Royal Lodge, ugly-pretty Victorian church with high-raftered roof. Full of friends – Jack Donaldson behind us, Julian and Gilly Fane† in front. Alexandra [Moore], who organised the whole thing, squeezed in beside me, and wept throughout. Joan's tiny coffin raised high in chancel, covered with a cascade of flowers. Most poignant moment was entrance of Garrett, wheeled in by nurse and doctor and hoisted, a lifeless sack, into front pew. Derry read from Gospel. I did not hear one word, nor the Dean of Chichester's address. Dadie [Rylands]‡ read from Wordsworth and Shelley, most moving. I was especially moved by

---

Park, Buckinghamshire, which his father Sir John, 10th Bt (1896–1966; m. 1922 Helen Eaton [d. 1989]) had donated to the N.T. in 1943.

* Hugh Seymour, 8th Marquess of Hertford, of Ragley Hall, Warwickshire (1930–97).

† Hon. Julian Fane (b. 1927); yr son of 14th Earl of Westmorland (and of J.L.-M's friend Diana *née* Lister); writer; m. 1976 Gillian Swire.

‡ George Rylands (1902–99); Shakespearean scholar and Fellow of King's College, Cambridge.

Benjamin Moore, aged six, playing unaccompanied Bach on the violin at foot of his grandmother's coffin. Yet he was not visibly moved, nor was Derry. We then drove to Parkside for tea. I am never happy at these death parties. Fabia Drake* told us that she was Joan's oldest friend, remembered her as a child, attended her first marriage. I asked if her childhood was wretched. Not wretched, she said, but neglected. The servants loved Joan, and were nearly in tears.

Monday, 25th December

What a Christmas. Clarissa and Igor staying with us for five days. I am enraged by this youth, without an idea in his head but extreme young-fogey snobbery. Mother sits with Cheshire cat-like grin of adoration. I can never go through such purgatory again. At breakfast Freda rings to say that Lennox is in a deep coma, looking like a beautiful boy, and not expected to survive the day. She is calm, sensible, relieved. Then Alexandra [Moore] telephones to announce that Garrett died this morning, just four days after Joan's funeral. A. comes into room weeping. He is a great loss to her.† When we left Parkside, he said to me, 'Look after yourself.' I replied, 'That's what I should say to you. Goodbye, old friend.'

Debo rang yesterday, in raptures about the Bachelor. Allowing for Mitford exaggeration, I honestly believe she is pleased. A great relief. Much still to do with this book, by which I am now bored.

Thursday, 28th December

The *coup de grâce* was another grandchild plus two greats for the day yesterday. Thank God we are alone again. Even A. is relieved.

Yes, what a Christmas. Lennox died on Christmas Day. Charlotte Bonham-Carter‡ also died, and Sybil Cholmondeley, both nonagen-

---

* Stage name of Ethel McGinchy (1904–90), actress known for her portrayal of *grandes dames* in films and television dramas; m. 1938 Judge Maxwell Turner (d. 1960).

† The Earl, as he wrote in his memoirs *Double Harness* (1978), had been in love with Alvilde as a young man, and counted himself as her oldest friend.

‡ Charlotte Ogilvy (1893–1989); idiosyncratic social figure; m. 1927 Sir Edgar Bonham-Carter (1870–1956), colonial civil servant and member of N.T. committees.

arians, and splendid women in their different ways. We both feel unmoved by Lennox's departure, not because he was a cabbage, but because we never quite got through to him. I suppose all saints are intangible.

Today we lunched at Tormarton with the Griggs. The Roy Jenkinses there. He very red in the face, and untidy. Was civil to me, and talked about my diaries. I wish they wouldn't. Asked if I thought Harold [Nicolson] 'important'. He didn't seem to think so, like many today. Asked about my Bath life. When I said A. gave me an egg or a pie for luncheon, he said he would not like that, and would have to go to the pub. His complexion suggests that. As soon as luncheon over, he dashed off with John to play ping-pong in the barn. A very curious mind. Now her I like tremendously – and I understand why the N.T. love her. She looks like a benevolent hedgehog, slightly drooping and hibernating-looking. Has prickles nevertheless, not shown to me so far.

Saturday, 30th December

Nephew Henry [Robinson] motored me to see Audrey. A melancholy visit. She has had several little strokes, and gone downhill. Extremely thin, and can't communicate. Just says yes or no. I tried reminding her of childhood days. During tea, she suddenly touched my arm, and said, earnestly, 'I wish, I wish', and again, 'I wish . . .' Then Dale, who had overheard, asked, 'What is it you wish, Mummy?' Slowly she said, 'I wish . . . to be a butterfly.' Now, what did this mean? The absurdity of it may have concealed a reluctance to share her confidence with the others. So I begged Dale to find out what she wanted to say, and let me know. Poor Audrey, I cannot wish her to linger on.

1990

1990

I am having an uninterrupted week in Bath, working on my novel. Nick is taking such trouble editing it that I feel I too must alter and improve. The beginning is embarrassingly awful; the middle better; the end again poor. Oh, what an effort.

Today I thought I might write a book about old age: on the one hand the inanities and indignities, the outward senility; on the other, the inner serenity, the ability to understand more deeply, the absence of the distorting influence of sexual feelings. Would have to be amusingly told, if not to be a catalogue of horror. *Yet Another Self*, perhaps? Meanwhile I have written to Jock Murray definitely refusing to undertake Sachie's biography. I do not believe I am up to it, and even if it is to be a brief life, the research and the reading of his ninety-odd books would be a labour. Greatly though I loved and admired Sachie, I found him intangible somehow. And shall I be alive in 1995?

Diana comes for the night, brought by Woman. Coote* joins us for luncheon. A. thinks I fuss too much over Diana. Probably true, because of what she meant to me in my extreme youth. I treat her differently from other mortals. We talked and talked. I said, 'Here we

---

* Lady Dorothy Lygon (1912–2000); yst dau. of 7th Earl Beauchamp; m. 1985 (as his 2nd wife) Robert Heber-Percy (1912–87).

are discussing Proust and Montherlant, just as in the Twenties we discussed Shelley and Keats.' She has a prodigious memory, retains all she has read. Like all Mitfords, she adores her friends, while not being very interested in their problems and domestic concerns. Sweetness on the surface. Remembers slights and grievances, e.g. Nancy's betrayal of her to Gladwyn Jebb,* and Woman's lack of sensitivity in writing to her in prison to announce that she had put down her horse and dog. So long ago too. A tigress in defence of her Kit [Sir Oswald]. Has his large framed photograph beside her when travelling. My affection for her is very deep; my joy in her company exceeds all joys, once the affectation barrier has been pierced.

Sunday, 21st January

We motored to Parkside to lunch with dear Derry,† Alexandra in Russia filming. Were shocked by his appearance. He has been through a dreadful time. Furthermore, trouble with Alexandra over where they are to live. D. adores Parkside and wants to stay there if he can afford the new rent, whereas she would prefer to live with her parents, the Nico Hendersons, at Combe,‡ which he is rightly determined not to do. I asked why Nico always disparaged Garrett. He thought simply jealousy – of his father's background, standing and good looks. I think true.

He took A. round the garden, asking her advice on how to reduce it. So sad here, memories of Garrett and Joan so vivid. When I was alone with D., he asked me if his parents had led separate lives. I said I thought not, for Garrett, whatever his harmless little flirtations, was always in love with Joan so far as I could see. He seemed surprised at this. He said that when at Eton he had never brought home other boys, except for a few who knew his parents, because he never knew what mood Joan might be in. Evidently he loved Garrett, whom he

---

* Gladwyn Jebb, 1st Baron Gladwyn (1900–97), diplomatist; m. 1929 Cynthia Noble (she d. 1990). In 1940, Nancy Mitford urged him to have Diana interned as a security threat (a fact which Diana only learned some years after Nancy's death).

† Now 11th Earl of Drogheda.

‡ The Hendersons had converted three disused school buildings in the Berkshire village of Combe, one of which had been used by the Moores.

considers a great man. G. very philosophical at the end; knew he was dying and didn't mind. Was never told he had lung cancer. Believed he was a failure. He certainly did not do well for himself, never seeking or receiving a golden handshake, unlike other captains of industry.

Sunday, 28th January

We dined at the House last night, in the large dining room. Twenty at table, silver spread over snow-white cloth, like banqueting chamber at Apsley House. No particular occasion, just family and friends. Talked with Tony Lambton afterwards. He has charm, though his dark glasses lend him what Lesley Blanch* calls 'sinistry'. Said the Prince of Wales had begun to read too late – one cannot become literate at the age of forty. Told hair-raising stories about sexual relationships in the Hope family between the Viceroy† and his brothers. And of Jamie Neidpath, who once picked up Lambton's foot and licked his sole, saying 'That was the best sole I have ever tasted.' Talked of second sons, of whom he said more than you would believe suffered from shoulder chips all their lives. Instanced David Herbert who loathed Sidney Pembroke (which I can't believe), and Andrew Cavendish who loathed his brother Hartington. When we repeated this to David this morning, he told us that Tony L. is himself a second son, his elder brother having killed himself; so is David, whose brother was killed in the war. When A. remarked that most sons would be relieved not to have the responsibility of inheritance, David replied, 'But no man likes to see his brother richer than himself. It all boils down to money.'

Tuesday, 30th January

To Chatsworth, travelling first class. Spent two nights alone with Debo and Diana. Absolute bliss. Chat, jokes and laughter in Debo's

---

* English travel writer (1904–2007) living in South of France, where the L.-Ms knew her in the 1950s; m. 1945–62 Romain Gary.
† Victor Hope, 2nd Marquess of Linlithgow (1887–1952); Viceroy of India, 1936–43.

little sitting room, with long processions to dinner through cold, empty drawing rooms and corridors, and walking in pleasure ground in biting winds. Debo becoming fat, with dewlap; Diana by contrast painfully thin. How I love these sisters. At tea on Wednesday, round tiny table, Debo said, 'Let's stay here forever. Why not?' Why not, indeed. A surge of love for them suffused my whole being.

When Andrew came, the temperature changed. A charming and attentive host – but his companions are impelled to please, and avoid topics. He says that the Queen is quite indiscreet about the Thatchers. She said to one of the equerries at the Palace while awaiting them, 'Don't make me laugh when Denis bows from the waist.' Says royalty all jealous of each other. If you invite one who fails, you may not ask another instead without causing grave resentment.

Saturday, 3rd February

Elspeth [Huxley] lunched with us [at Badminton]. Very spry for eighty-two. Told us she had been commissioned by the widow to write Peter Scott's biography. Thinks he was too decent and dutiful to be true, or to make interesting. But he is a hero, revered all over the world. I was telling her that Peter never liked me, and after K's death shunned me. Much to my surprise, A. suddenly said in front of Elspeth, 'If you don't mind me hazarding a guess why, it was because he disapproved of your affairs with young men.'* So what? I can hardly be said to have led a scandalous life. It is gallant of Elspeth to motor twenty miles to Slimbridge each day to research the Scott papers. Peter never threw anything away. He was a cold fish, his wife Jane leaving him because of his neglect. Never opened a book.

Wednesday, 7th February

A dark day of pouring rain. We drove to Bath Hospital where A. had to undergo a cardiac test. I waited in the car with Folly, as she would not let me accompany her. The test revealed that her heart valve has

---

* As J.L.-M. was to learn from Elspeth, Scott himself was homosexually inclined – see 17 May 1992.

diminished, impeding the circulation and causing the feeling of faint-
ness she experiences when doing anything which involves effort, like
climbing stairs or carrying heavy parcels. The doctor warned that she
could let things take their course, which would mean a steady decline,
or have an operation to install a new valve. She at once decided on
the latter. But it will be a hazardous operation. As she drives me home,
I look at her precious silhouette, so beautiful and calm, and am filled
with a terrible foreboding.

Thursday, 8th February

A. went to London to attend the Beits' dinner party. I refused to go,
but wish now I had accepted, for I don't like her out of reach. I telephoned her specialist, Dr Thomas. He explained that if the state of her
arteries proved to be unfavourable, she would be unable to have the
operation, and could not live two years. I put the telephone down,
aghast. Then I thought, we are both very old, and the chances of either
of us surviving much longer are slender. Nevertheless to have such a
term put to one's life is upsetting. Later A. telephoned. Listening to
her abrupt, no-nonsense voice, I shed tears. I must learn to control
them.

Saturday, 10th February

A. back from London, her normal brusque self. Forbids me to
commiserate or fuss over her; yet is telling everyone about the
forthcoming operation.

Monday, 12th February

Bruce Hunter writes that Murray's would be pleased to publish my
Bachelor Duke – on condition that they can cut it down to 85,000
words. Since I have written about 130,000, this would be a massacre.
I have replied to Bruce that I do not consider this an acceptable
arrangement. I know the book is too long, but not to that extent. It
is now more than two months since I finished the damn thing, and I
am fed up with it.

Wednesday, 14th February

To London yesterday, just to give luncheon to Derek [Hill] at Brooks's. He was charming, though his eyes swivelling towards Sir Martin Gilliat* at next table. Talked of his visit to Mount Athos with Bruce Chatwin, who was so moved by the experience that he could not write about it. He hoped to retreat to one of the monasteries, had he been spared. Derek agrees Bruce's fame has been exaggerated by the press – but what do they not exaggerate when it suits them? Derek full of self-pity – Debo does not like him, never invites him to Chatsworth; Virginia Surtees returned an expensive silk scarf he sent her and refused to overlap with him at a health farm.

Saturday, 17th February

Dined last night with Desmond Briggs and Ian Dixon. Such a kind couple they are. Nothing they would not do for their friends. When I told Desmond that Murray's wanted me to cut the Bachelor by a third, he asked as an old hand to give me some advice. It was to accept Murray's offer, as they were the most suitable publisher for such a book, having first got them to agree to 95,000 rather than 85,000 words. Once contract signed, cut less than agreed – they would not be in a position to argue much. What amoral conduct you are counselling, I said.

Thursday, 1st March

Sarah Bradford† came from London to talk about Sachie whose biography she is to write. I expected a precise, correct, middle-aged lady. On the contrary, she is pretty, youngish and flirtatious. She brought a copy of Regy, which I signed as her St David's Day friend. A day to be remembered, for it was fifty-two years ago today that I met Rick

---

* Lieut-Col Sir Martin Gilliat (1913–93); Private Secretary to HM Queen Elizabeth The Queen Mother, 1956–93.
† Sarah Hayes (b. 1938); m. 1959 1st Anthony Bradford, 2nd 1976 Hon. William Ward (b. 1948; succeeded 1993 as 8th Viscount Bangor); writer. Her *Splendours and Miseries: A Life of Sacheverell Sitwell*, appeared in 1993.

[Stewart-Jones]* in Queen Anne's Gate. Mrs Bradford is married to the future Lord Bangor of Castle Ward. She is bright rather than deep. I offered her a scratch luncheon, which she bravely accepted. We got on well. Much to be said for saucy ladies.

Tuesday, 6th March

A's energy over repairing the damage to the garden is amazing. She organises the gardeners, finds craftsmen to rebuild fence and wall, and chases the estate office. Yet what is in store for her? The pathos of it.

Wednesday, 7th March

Took darling A. to The Glen, Bristol, where she is to have artery test tomorrow. Saw her into a pleasant room with all cons, telly, telephone, etc. She at once threw open the window and turned off the heating. Then said to me, 'I would rather you left now.' So off home I went, with Folly.

Thursday, 8th March

Ian Dixon drove me to Bristol. Waited until six when A's heart doctor Vann Jones came to her room. Charming and direct. Made it clear that operation essential. Refusal to have it would mean heart attacks, black-outs, and a life of three years at most. A. thereupon agreed without reservation to have it in two weeks' time. She was so stoical, so serene, so beautiful sitting in bed that I was deeply moved.

Saturday, 10th March

Fetched A. from The Glen. She was already waiting on the doorstep. Once home she was in the garden, directing operations. She did not want me hanging around, so I went to Bath. Telephoned Midi to

---

* Richard Stewart-Jones (1914–57), architectural conservationist; one of the great loves of J.L.-M's life, whom (as described in *Fourteen Friends*) he had met on St David's Day 1938.

condole on the death of her brother-in-law Sir Julian Gascoigne.[*] We bemoan the appalling declension of standards in this country. The world was far better when we were young, we decide like all octogenarians. London was safe to roam around; people were basically honest. Yet our own young lives were both clouded by the fact that, although we came from well-off families, we were obliged to eke on miserable salaries and allowances, which prevented us consorting freely with our contemporaries.

Sunday, 11th March

Maureen Dufferin has invited us to dine on 29th to meet the Queen Mother. Now of course we cannot go. A. would have loved it. 'How pleased you must be,' she says. We lunch at the House. Caroline back from New Zealand, a beautiful country, though she was bored by her fellow dendrologists. Everyone solicitous about A's predicament. Then we motored to Wincanton to see Audrey in her home. Sitting like a pillar of salt by herself in large circular room. Knew us. Says 'yes' to everything, nothing more. Does not seem wretched. Accepts placidly.

Tuesday, 13th March

At breakfast telephone rings. A. dashes to pick up receiver. I overhear her say, 'Kind of you to let us know. A merciful release, of course', or words to that effect. Who, I ask? Selina, to say Rosamond [Lehmann] died last night while eating her dinner. Pneumonia. A. quite indifferent, as I might expect.[†] But I loved Ros deeply. Felt pleased that she is released. But very remorseful that I did not see her last week when in London. Selina has been more dutiful, visiting and taking little gifts of chocolates. Darling Ros, with whom I have been more intimate than with any other woman friend.

---

[*] Major-General Sir Julian Gascoigne (1903–89); Governor of Bermuda, 1959–64; Chairman, Devon & Cornwall Committee, N.T., 1965–75.

[†] Alvilde had broken off relations with Rosamond eight years earlier, as a result of an incident described in J.L.-M's diary on 11 May 1982.

Tuesday, 20th March

Joshua Rowley*, dearest of men, motored me in hired car to Putney Green cemetery [for Rosamond Lehmann's funeral]. Outside waiting room, I talked to Patrick Kavanagh† and Hugo Philipps‡ standing in the sun. Kavanagh said someone had taken me to task for having written [in *Independent* obituary] that Ros was a Christian. But she always strongly maintained that she was a follower of Christ. Hugo introduced me to his new wife, nice-looking, grey-haired lady. She amazed me by saying she had been reading my letters to Rosamond, amused by my accounts of this, that and the other. So dumbfounded that I could not reply. The idea of my letters to Ros being read before she is buried. We sat in the waiting room, Joshua, Selina and I. Decent but cold, clinical service. Old Wogan§ bent double and shuffling, supported by grandson. No emotion anywhere, but some good singing. The harrowing newness of the coffin, so carpentered and glittering – for what? Ros not so big as I imagined. I did not care to look. With head bent I hear a squeaking as though a door behind me opening; looked up and saw the coffin had slid away. Did not weep.

Thursday, 22nd March

I take A. to The Glen. Her activity prior to departure was amazing – giving orders to gardeners, buying food galore for me and writing instructions for its preparation, putting daffodils in Clarissa's bedroom. She makes me realise how useless I am.

---

* Sir Joshua Rowley, 7th Bt, of Tendring Hall, Suffolk (1920–97); Deputy Secretary of N.T., 1952–5.

† Writer, poet and actor (b. 1931); m. 1st 1956 Sarah Philipps (d. 1958), o. dau. of Rosamond by her 2nd marriage to Hon. Wogan Philipps, 2nd 1965 Catherine Ward.

‡ Hon. Hugo Philipps (1929–99); o.s. of Rosamond and Wogan; s. father as 3rd Baron Milford, 1993.

§ Wogan Philipps (1902–93); m. 1st 1928–43 Rosamond Lehmann, 2nd Cristina, Countess of Huntingdon; s. 1962 as 2nd Baron Milford (the only peer supporting the Communist Party).

Friday, 23rd March

Much telephoning from A. Has the carpenter finished the fence? Has the stone mason mended the wall? I meet Clarissa and motor her from Bath to the hospital, where we have tea and cakes with A. She is sitting surrounded by flowers and affectionate messages – the well-wishers including Mick Jagger and Jerry Hall, which greatly impresses the nurses. I write a note of love to A. and leave it on her pillow. We embrace rapidly. No tears, no emotion.

Saturday, 24th March

A day of anxious waiting. We lunched with dear Sally [Westminster], all kindness. The surgeon rings at 6.15. Very jolly. A total success, no complications. Clarissa threw her arms round me. I poured myself a whisky. Then I had an odd feeling as though of disappointment, can't understand why. We telephoned the good news to friends.

Sunday, 25th March

After lunching with the kind Barlows,* we drove to The Glen. A. in special care ward. Sitting, even talking, but tired and fretful. I am amazed she is so well, after dreadful ordeal of four hours. A horrid tube from some artery in her poor face. Surgeon told us she must stay a fortnight. Clarissa returns to London tomorrow, mercifully.

Wednesday, 28th March

When I arrived this afternoon, A. said, 'I am in a beastly mood.' A good sign. Although my only concern should be for her, I have been thinking of myself of late, wondering what I should do were she to die. Would I remain in Badminton, go to live in Bath, or chuck up everything and retreat to a 'home', or a religious institution if they would have me?

---

* Gerda Barlow and her unmarried son Nicholas at Stancombe Court.

Saturday, 31st March

Debo rang last night, as she does constantly now. Said I was very precious to her, possibly the greatest compliment I have ever received. A. is coming home next Tuesday; very cross with me for 'intriguing' with the surgeon to keep her there, for she wanted to come out tomorrow. Surgeon foolishly informed her of my talk with him on grounds of 'openness', another dotty liberal notion.

I dined at the House. The Michaels of Kent. Much groaning before they arrived by David and family. She has changed in looks – thinner in the face; hair unnaturally yellow, and frizzy. She sat on David's right, I on his left; Ali Forbes on her right, Caroline on my left. Princess very affected and flirtatious. After dinner she invited me to sit with her on an ottoman while she talked to me of her new book – on courtesans. She certainly seems to know much about the subject. Much complaint about her publishers. Ali asked her for details of Henri II's penile deficiencies and X's vagina troubles. She warded off these queries. Says Nell Gwynn* was a designing minx, not the open-hearted whore the history books presume. Royal couple did not rise until 11.30, by which time I was nearly dead. He, dear little toy soldier, politely regretted we had not had the chance to talk.

Tuesday, 3rd April

I fetched A. from Bristol and brought her home. She was fully dressed and packing when I arrived. For the first time ever, she asked me to drive slowly. On her arrival, she walked straight into the garden; then slept soundly for two hours.

Friday, 6th April

A. gets up, dresses, and wanders about the house, noticing what is wrong. Is depressed, tires easily, and is rather *exigeante* and cross at times.

---

* Hereford-born actress, mistress of King Charles II (1651–87).

Monday, 16th April

On Good Friday I motored to stay two nights at The Slade with Eardley and Mattei. Much agreeable talk and laughter. Mattei has become older; but the flaring temper of which E. complains was not shown during my visit, during which he was his old sweet-tempered self, charming and whimsical. I admire their carefree mode of life, though it would not suit pernickety me. Mattei's old mother present, a dear old pussy cat. Speaks not a word of English. He is sweet to her, chats and jokes. Eardley smiles and tolerates her benign and unobtrusive presence.

On Easter Sunday I went to Prior's Dean Church. Dear tiny ancient church, white plaster within and some pretty Jacobean monuments. Every pew filled with gentry. Friendly, old-fashioned vicar, a gent like the rest. Flowers everywhere, no Moyses Stevens[*] poshery, but nosegays of wild flowers in small pots and jars. Some curiosity over me. Who was I? Where was I from?

Sunday, 22nd April

I am disillusioned by Mrs Thatcher for several reasons. First, Hong Kong: absolutely wrong to admit half a million Chinese to this overcrowded island.[†] Second, Poll Tax: absolute disaster.[‡] Third, Lithuania: monstrous and cowardly not to stand up to Soviets.[§] Fourth, absolutely no steps being ventilated, let alone taken, to reduce birth rate. Fifth, Ireland: strong steps should be taken against that devilish island, e.g. dismissing all Irish citizens from England, and imposing sanctions. Sixth, the riot at Strangeways Prison [Liverpool]: madness to allow

---

[*] Mayfair florist.

[†] Following Britain's agreement in 1984 to return Hong Kong to Chinese rule in 1997, it had been announced that 500,000 of the colony's six million inhabitants would be allowed to settle in the UK.

[‡] The introduction from that year of a 'community charge' to finance local government, theoretically to be paid by every citizen, had led to rioting in London in March 1990.

[§] The Republic of Lithuania had unilaterally declared independence from the Soviet Union in March 1990, though Moscow refused to relinquish sovereignty and attempted to continue to exert control through military and economic pressure until August 1991.

criminals to hold police at bay for a month, whereas troops should have been sent in to sweep prisoners up and out on first day.

David Beaufort called at midday. Oh the charm of that man. Explained why he is selling his Italian cabinet, said to be the finest single item of furniture ever produced in that country. Needs to find £2 million to pay the tax on Master's estate and won't raise it from the sale of land; it would be unfair on the tenants and besides, tenanted land is not so valuable. Hopes Jacob Rothschild will buy it for Waddeson, which would be better than it going to a dreary museum. Jacob wants to live in the whole of Waddeson and keep the public out. Good for him – but will the N.T. agree?

Tuesday, 24th April

That charmer James Knox* came to see me in Bath to talk of Robert Byron. Very good-looking; slight; little cow-lick on side of hair. White teeth, white skin, white cuffs, thin white hands. Comes from Ayrshire; knows Arthur and Cunninghame relations.† Very keen on Robert, left job on *Spectator* to concentrate on biography. Can he write? Is clearly intelligent, with a quick grasp. We spent an agreeable three hours chatting, the recorder whirring the whole time. I fear I said too much. I enjoyed his visit, and think he was pleased.

Sunday, 29th April

In church this morning, instead of attending, I read the Commination Service. The phrase 'Too late to Knock' struck me as a good title for a last volume of memoirs.

Thursday, 10th May

To London for day after long interval. Chief objective to deliver revised typescript to John Murray's. A thrill to be published at last by

---

* Writer and art consultant (b. 1952); sometime publisher of *Spectator*.
† J.L.-M's mother's sister Doreen Bailey had married a Cunninghame and his own sister Audrey had married an Arthur, both families being distantly connected to J.L.-M's maternal grandmother Christina Thomson.

this Rolls-Royce of publishers. At Brooks's, John Saumarez Smith told me that my brother Dick once walked into the shop and said *Another Self* was a tissue of lies. I think a good title for a sequel would be *A Tissue of Truths*.

Saturday, 12th May

Dear Billa comes to stay for two nights, our first guest this year. Full of chat about the Prince of Wales, with whom she is going to stay next. Says that presents are expected, which seems strange. She has saved up to buy a watercolour for £300. As though the royal walls were not groaning with them. But she gets presents in return.

Tuesday, 15th May

Yesterday I drove Billa to Highgrove. We swirled off the main road down a tarmac drive. At newly built, stone sentry box, smiling policeman asked our business. I said I was chauffeur to Lady Harrod. Politely he telephoned through to enquire. By the farmyard, a second policeman stopped and inspected us before letting us through. A brand new barn in mediaeval style being erected; a meadow filled with glistening white sheep, very picturesque and Samuel Palmer-like.* At the front door, B. got out and was greeted by a smiling, youngish equerry. I got her luggage out of the boot and dumped it on the newly-built portico steps; then exchanged a friendly word with the equerry, embraced B., and drove off. What I could glimpse of the garden and park was most attractive.

Billa telephoned before dinner, overbrimming with content. She had been alone with the Prince. Said the house very correct inside; good furniture, no fantasy. The P's own room rather touching, filled with books he had no time to read, and decent watercolour landscapes (not his own). It rained the moment they stepped into the garden. We have not had a drop since March. He held a large umbrella over her head, telling her it was a delight to be with someone who really knew about gardens. She was in ecstasy.

---

* English romantic artist (1805–81).

Wednesday, 16th May

Nigel Nicolson lunched with me in Bath. Always a delight to see him. He is so full of chat. He sails into the room like a gigantic man-of-war, noticing nothing. He is compiling a book about all the houses known to have been stayed in by Jane Austen. Next work will be a selection of the letters exchanged by Harold and Vita. He is very happy that his son Adam[*] has overcome his qualms about inheriting the Carnock barony and the fortune of his cousin David.[†] Nigel is worried about the forthcoming BBC dramatisation of *Portrait of a Marriage*.[‡] They are concentrating exclusively on the Trefusis affair,[§] whereas the book's message is that the marriage was a happy one. 'I never thought the BBC would behave like this,' he says. This shows *naïveté*. Nigel asked why the backs of Georgian town houses, such as those in Bath, are so untidy. I explained that most of the untidiness was caused by additions of bathrooms, WCs and waste pipes by later generations. He was relieved to hear this, as he believes the Georgians could not go wrong tastewise in either architecture or furniture. He hates modern painting.

Friday, 1st June

The much-anticipated day on which I drive A. to Cornbury [Park, Oxfordshire] where she has been commissioned to do the garden. She endured it very well. Charlbury such a pretty village with still a remote feel. A lovely place where I first went in 1930 or even 1929 when Woman was engaged to that black stick Togo Watney.[¶]

---

[*] Only son (b. 1957) of Nigel Nicolson; writer, notably on walks and architecture; m. 1st 1982–92 Olivia Fane, 2nd 1993 Sarah Raven.

[†] David Nicolson, 4th Baron Carnock (b. 1920), to whom Nigel, his first cousin, was heir presumptive.

[‡] Nigel Nicolson's book about his parents, which dealt candidly with their homosexuality and created a sensation on its publication in 1973.

[§] The book centered on the 'elopement' in 1920 of Vita and her lover Violet Trefusis (*née* Keppel, 1894–1972), and the efforts of their respective husbands, Harold Nicolson and Colonel Denys Trefusis, to get them back.

[¶] Oliver ('Togo') Watney (1902–65), of Cornbury; engaged to Hon. Pamela Mitford in 1929; m.1934 Christina Margaret Nelson (whose sister married 2nd Baron Moyne, 1st husband of Pamela's sister Diana, as his 2nd wife).

Beautiful Webb-like gate piers between twin lodges. Drive leads straight to Nicholas Stone's stables which one thinks may be the house, but one swerves to the left and stops outside pair of shut gates at foot of steps to the terrace. Then the Hugh May façade of honey ashlar. Robin Cayzer* a charming young man, formerly in Life Guards, a mixture of Micky Renshaw[†] and Thomas Messel. Knows a lot about plants and trees, and loves the place. It should be a pleasant job for A., if not too arduous. We walked all round pleasure grounds of fifteen acres. He showed us the famous Hugh May chapel over which John Fowler had a row with Lord Rotherwick[‡] who wished to convert it into a squash court. Yet somehow the chapel is not nice, much of the wainscot and carving probably bogus. Carved on the west front of the house were the words *Deus Nobis Haec Otia Fecit. Otia* presumably means leisure, enjoyment, recreation, delight.

Saturday, 9th June

To Chatsworth for two nights. Missed train there from Gloucester and arrived late for dinner in a great fluster. On return journey, Debo delivered me into care of ticket man at Chesterfield station and told him to look after me, as I was slightly dotty. Ariane[§] came down for the day to help me select illustrations for *The Bachelor*. So attractive, sweet and clever. A joy to have her, and she was a great success with the Devonshires. Debo showed me a Royal Appointment for Bed and Breakfast she had received from the Prince of Wales. This shows humour.

On my return, A. and I dined with Miranda Morley. Lovely house and garden made for her by David out of three Badminton cottages.

---

* Hon. Robin Cayzer (b. 1954), er s. and heir of 2nd Baron Rotherwick (whom he succeeded as 3rd Baron, 1996); m. 1982 Sarah McAlpine.

[†] Michael Renshaw (1908–78); journalist and traveller.

[‡] Hon. Robin Cayzer (1912–96); succeeded father as 2nd Baron Rotherwick, 1958, and inherited his shipping companies.

[§] Ariane Goodman (b. 1955); publisher's editor, who (then at Collins) had worked with J.L.-M. on *Venetian Evenings*; now employed by John Murray; m. 1984 Andrew Bankes.

I sat next to Miranda, who is easy and amused. Charming party, the others being a granddaughter of Beaverbrook,[*] Charlie Morrison, and Colonel Parker Bowles.[†] The last assured me the army could destroy IRA by rounding up 120 well-known suspects and shooting the lot within twenty-four hours. Most other nations would do so, certainly the French.

Sunday, 10th June

Derry and Alexandra came for the day. We took them to Alderley garden which was open in the afternoon. Love of this house surged through me. Garden rather overgrown and romantic. Has a secret feel, though A. criticises it for being too full of shrubs. The poplars and limes we planted are now enormous. We peered inside the house, where the same quality prevails, but not so attractive as without — overcrowded and over-opulent.

Sunday, 17th June

Billy Henderson and Frank Tait lunched. Frank is a well-informed man, quick, amusing and a good story-teller. Talking of how French queers adopted their young lovers to enable them to inherit under the *Code Napoléon*, he said that Osbert Lancaster once drew a cartoon of a midwife carrying the swaddled baby Alan Searle up to Willie Maugham[‡] saying, 'Good news, it's a boy'.

---

[*] Maxwell Aitken, 1st Baron Beaverbrook (1879–1964); newspaper owner and politician.

[†] Andrew Parker Bowles (b. 1939); army officer; Lieutenant-Colonel commanding Household Cavalry and Silver Stick in Waiting to HM Queen, 1987–90; Director, Royal Army Veterinary Corps, 1991–4; husband (m. 1973) of the Prince of Wales's mistress (and eventual 2nd wife) Camilla *née* Shand, by whom he was divorced in 1994, the year he retired from army with rank of Brigadier.

[‡] The novelist and dramatist W. Somerset Maugham (1874–1965) bequeathed much of his estate to his companion Alan Searle under French legal arrangements which were challenged by his daughter Liza.

Sunday, 24th June

Nico Guppy* came for luncheon. A large teddy-bear with deep voice and precise diction. Told us his eldest boy, aged twenty-six, is now a commodity millionaire, with enough money to see him through life.[†] Began buying and selling at Eton; got a double first at Magdalen. Nico full of curious information: that Napoleon III invented the colour magenta from the mixture of mud and blood on the battlefield of that name; that Haiti once had a black monarchy, of which there still exist dukes of Marmalada and Limonada.

Bevis Hillier interviewed me for second volume of his John Betjeman, but I fear I was little use. It was one of my bad days, and he was not a good interrogator – polite and flattering, but too slick for me. He must have thought, 'This man is gaga.' Indeed, I sometimes feel that my mental processes are like a faulty electric wire, which sometimes flickers into life, and is sometimes detached.

Saturday, 7th July

Hugh Montgomery-Massingberd comes from London to spend day here. He wants to write a profile of me to coincide with the publication of my novel next month and my birthday. Alvilde takes to him warmly; likes his good manners, his hesitancy, his wide knowledge and cleverness. While she watched Wimbledon, he sat with me in the small room before the gas fire, for it was a perishing day. Has read the book. Asked questions about my extreme youth and what I remembered of the First World War, and the German prisoners working on the farm. I trotted out the old and worn memories. But he is a good, casual-seeming interrogator, and makes talk easy. After he left, I told A. that I now rather dreaded publication of this novel. She replied, 'Well you do ask for it, don't you?'

---

* Underwriting member of Lloyd's, then undergoing difficulties owing to the insurance crisis.

[†] Darius Guppy, who had become a celebrity after acting as best man at the wedding of his Eton friend Earl Spencer (brother of Princess of Wales) in 1989, had in fact made his recent fortune through an insurance swindle for which he would eventually be sentenced to six years in prison.

Saturday, 14th July

Although I have never cared much for Nicholas Ridley, I am sorry for him.* He got carried away in talk with Dominic Lawson – just as I did the other day with the *Daily Mail*. The pity is that he retracted what he said about Germany, which deprives him of the sympathy of those millions who agree with him (not including myself). Meanwhile he is being hounded by his many enemies – and I detest the baying of hounds.

Sunday, 15th July

In our snobbish way we lunched today with the Michaels of Kent instead of going to Sally [Westminster]'s memorial service at Wickwar. But the service was given contrary to her wishes, for she was a total unbeliever; and I did go to her funeral in Cheshire. So we lunched with the Prince and Princess, though I warned A. what this luncheon would be like, and indeed it turned out to be exactly like the two last I attended on my own.

We arrived punctually at one. Met by her in the downstairs hall. Much friendliness, embraces moderated by A's bob and my bow. I had taken the precaution of bringing straw hats. They were needed, for the heat was stifling. Drinks under mulberry tree on lawn. Usual strange assortment of guests. A nice decent couple called Biddulph, he a son of Mary Biddulph, unknown to us and to our hosts. It transpired the secretary had invited them by mistake. Lynn Seymour,† dancer who has just played Marie Antoinette in a film; Lady Northampton, *divorcée*. Luncheon was outdoors in the sun, and even under our hats the heat was terrific, the flies tiresome.

The Prince's manners beautiful as always. He is becoming less shy with me, and tells nice tales of 'my grandmother' and 'my great-uncle'. They have been in Hungary visiting her grandmother's castle,

---

* Ridley had been forced to resign from the Government after casually remarking to Dominic Lawson, editor of the *Spectator*, that European Monetary Union was 'a German racket designed to take over the whole of Europe'.
† Ballerina (b. 1939).

now a terrible computer factory, all coffins in the family mausoleum vandalised. She is determined to build a small property nearby for themselves. The Princess sets out to please and entertain. Her taste is good – lovely china, and two charming silver wine carafes in the shape of Chianti bottles. But there is a feeling that everything is just a little unreal and Ruritanian, and may dissolve. She was sharp with the poor young footman, borrowed from Buckingham Palace, when he trod on the cat's paw carrying heavy trays in the sweltering sun. Told me she was having a row with the publisher of her book. She asked me if she ought to consent to newspaper serialisation – 'not that I need the money'. I cautioned against, as they always highlighted the scandalous. 'There's nothing scandalous about my book', she said of her history of royal mistresses.

Monday, 23rd July

Yesterday we lunched at Barnsley Park. Some fifty assembled. Two hours of sheer banality, during which I heard not one single remark worthy of remembrance. It is ghastly that I never see intellectuals and spend so much time with idiotic society people – though our host, Charles Faringdon, is decent and good-natured. How rich the rich are today. Grandest house, enormous garden and park, wine flowing. Is 'society' on the edge? Can it last – and should it?

Thursday, 2nd August

August is once again proving a dangerous month. Brightest, sunniest weather, as in 1914, 1938, 1939, 1940 . . . Now the Iraqi aggression, which is world-shaking.* The unbroken heat brings with it an invisible worm of fear.

Monday, 6th August

My eighty-second birthday. Heralded by Hugh Massingberd's interview with me in yesterday's *Sunday Telegraph*, which I can't fault for kind-

---

* To international uproar, Iraqi forces had invaded and occupied Kuwait in the early hours of that day, Saddam Hussein proclaiming the territory annexed as the nineteenth province of Iraq.

ness and understanding. A. gave me *The Oxford Companion to French Literature*, a green jersey and a white dust-proof jacket. A luncheon for seven – Caroline, Woman, Billy [Henderson] and Frank [Tait] – and Nick, who came down from London bearing the first six copies of the dreaded novel [*The Fool of Love*], which looks very well. Billy very aged and frail. We agreed that with the best will in the world we could no longer sparkle or even keep up.

Thursday, 9th August

To John Murray's where I went through illustrations with Ariane. How she enchants me. Jock [Murray] joined us for sandwiches, jolly and jokey. I watched Ariane, the dutiful, admiring subordinate, responding deferentially to the spate of jokes. Jock showed me Paddy [Leigh Fermor]'s manuscript, a spider's nightmare of corrections which he goes over again and again. Jock says Byron's are the same. He says a Byron letter will fetch as much as £3,000 if unpublished, otherwise only half that amount. Jock showed me letters from his friend Axel Munthe,* who told him how bored he had become by his weekly audiences with King Gustav.† When the King arranged for him to be buried in the royal mausoleum, Munthe was horrified to think he might continue to be bored by the sovereign for all eternity. After his death, his son secretly disposed of his corpse at sea, and an empty coffin was interred in the mausoleum. When I left, Jock said, 'Now do one thing for me. Make a list of all those friends you want invited to the party I shall give for the publication of *The Bachelor Duke*.' Terribly kind, but the last thing I want is a cocktail party.

In asphyxiating heat, I stumbled to Burlington House to see the Edwardian paintings exhibition. A pretty poor lot, barring Sargent and [Paul] Nash. Then crossed the road to Fortnum & Mason. While I was waiting for the lift a woman with a jolly face and charming smile

---

* Swedish doctor and writer (1857–1949), who became physician to the Swedish Royal Family, and spent much of his life on Capri; known for his autobiography *The Story of San Michele* (1929).
† Gustav V Adolf, King of Sweden, 1907–50 (1858–1950).

turned to me and said, 'Am I right?' It was Mrs Nuttall, widow of my recently discovered half-brother. A delightful lady, a Mrs Miniver; very slight accent, which might be Australian or North London. Over tea, she was able to tell me more than I already knew of my father's affair with her mother-in-law, the Crompton Hall coachman's daughter. Said that her John minded the bastardy much when a boy with his mother in Sydney, and made her buy a wedding ring and pretend to be a war widow. No future in this connection, and after an hour I was relieved to depart for Paddington. But I liked her.*

Tuesday, 21st August

I wonder how many people recall the birthday of an uncle who died seventy-three years ago. If only my Uncle Robert† had lived he would surely have guided my feet into the way he saw most fitting for me, have encouraged my desire to learn, have smoothed my relations with my father, have taught me to be filial and not reproachful, have inculcated courage in me and turned me into a more worthwhile character.

Thursday, 23rd August

In the car this morning I run into hounds in the village. I stop patiently and wait. The Master, Ian Farquhar, comes up to the window and we chat politely. I ask when they will start cubbing, feigning interest and goodwill. Two discreet huntsmen, in square billycock hats and green, traditional livery, touch their hats and thank me. Well, I like all this tradition, just as I like the old builder saying, 'Yes, Sir', 'No, Madam'.

---

* Going through the effects of John Nuttall (b. 1907), an Australian banker, following his death in February 1990, his widow and stepson were intrigued to come across papers suggesting that he had been the illegitimate son of J.L.-M's father George Lees-Milne. (His mother, Katherine Nuttall, had been the coachman's daughter at George's property of Crompton Hall near Oldham, and had emigrated with her son to Australia in 1916.) They had written to J.L.-M. in an effort to find out more about the connection, enclosing photographs which showed a strong family resemblance.
† Robert Bailey (1880–1917); only brother of J.L.-M's mother; a clerk to the House of Commons; died of wounds received while fighting the Turks in Palestine.

Wednesday, 29th August

One Peter Mandler came to interview me about a book he is writing on the history of public access to country houses.* I had at first declined to see him, but then he sent me a copy of his book *Whig Government*, by which I was impressed. He had already seen Howard Colvin,† who barely unbuttoned, and John Summerson,‡ who was full of information of every kind, including details of his successes with women. When Mandler asked Summerson how well he knew me, he replied, 'We have always got on, but he is too patrician for me.' I began to worry about what Mandler might have heard about me, and was alarmed to see the ubiquitous tape recorder, though as usual I soon forgot about it and said too much. He asked me when and by whom I was first inspired to love country houses. I mentioned John Betjeman, Osbert [Lancaster], Gerry Wellesley, Robert Byron, and my colleagues at the National Trust and the Georgian Group. Oh, he replied, I thought it was at Oxford when you experienced the awakening at Rousham.§ Kept pulling me up. Although he made a favourable impression, I did not enjoy the interview, which I fear was not much of a success for him.

Tuesday, 4th September

Having made a copy for myself, I am sending my unpublished manuscript diaries up to 1978¶ to Rota to sell with the rest of my papers. Why am I exposing myself gratuitously to eternal obloquy, when I could destroy the lot and keep my reputation unscathed? Is it vain of me to suppose that my papers may be of some interest two hundred

---

* *The Fall and Rise of the Stately Home* (Yale, 1997).

† Sir Howard Colvin (1919–2007); architectural historian.

‡ Sir John Summerson (1904–92); architect and architectural historian.

§ In *Another Self*, J.L.-M. claims that his interest in architecture was 'awakened' when, as an Oxford undergraduate, he was invited to dinner at Rousham on the Cherwell, and watched in horror as the drunken tenant, cheered on by fellow guests, damaged the family portraits with a horse-whip.

¶ These were edited by J.L.-M. himself during his lifetime and published by John Murray as *A Mingled Measure* (1994), *Ancient as the Hills* (1997) and *Through Wood and Dale* (1998).

years hence, as those of an ordinary man of his time who kept his letters and recorded his own insignificant and not very estimable life?

Wednesday, 5th September

We made an expedition to Wickhamford. While A. sat with Folly in the car, I went into the church. Two nice elderly ladies therein, looking around. The head one told me they visited it once a year. I told her I did too. When she said I seemed to know a great deal about it, I explained that I had been born and brought up there. 'You are not James Lees-Milne, by chance?' she asked. When I confessed to this, she clasped her hands, bowed, and said, 'Well, I never.' When the dear things left, I inspected the panels of the box pews, which are Henry VII or earlier. Paid my respects to this beloved building and Reynolds [Stone]'s lovely tablet commemorating my parents.

We then called by arrangement on Frederick Mason and his wife at Ashcroft, a bungalow the far side of the Sandys Arms. He wrote to me recently to say he had been employed as the boot boy at the manor from 1924 to 1927, at twelve shillings a week. He is one year younger than myself, and remembers how I used to sit with a pile of books under the mulberry tree while brother Dick messed about with his motor-bike. He is tiny (from early lack of nourishment perhaps), rather toothless, well-dressed, with very nice manners. Wife a dear, dressed in her best. They declined our invitation to come with us to a tea shop in Broadway, and insisted on giving us tea in their parlour, a room which they admitted they used rarely, as neat as two pins with hideous suite in orange and gold. Delicious home-made sausage rolls. He talked much about the servants at home – Copeland the cockney butler, and Paddy the Irish groom who used to bet on my father's horses (Mason taking the betting telegrams to Badsey post office, running across the fields). He referred to my father as 'the boss'. I would have loved to know what he really thought of my parents, but could not ask.

Saturday, 8th September

Tony Scotland and Julian Berkeley to luncheon. Both delightful. Julian has lost his giggly, looking-into-stomach habit, and is now adult, gentle, soft-spoken and wise. Tony his usual bubbling self. Said the director of Radio Three now urges announcers to make personal comments on the music they present – surely a mistake. He talked of the book he is thinking of writing about his adventures in Europe during a three-month sabbatical. He agreed with me that one should not go into too much detail about experiences, but rely on under-statement, suggestion and innuendo.

We dined with Charlie and Rosalind Morrison at Luckington, another enjoyable reunion. Charlie says the proceedings in the House of Commons over the Gulf crisis this week showed the chamber at its best. All contributions deadly serious, even Kinnock's first-rate. Saddam is totally unpredictable, and no one has the slightest idea what the outcome will be. He talked to me of the overpopulation problem, which is at last sinking into the minds of ministers, includ-ing Chris Patten. Poor Charlie is on the 'hit list' both of the IRA and the Animal Rights people, and spent this afternoon with the police, who warned him of bombs not only under his car but in his rubbish bins. He will be glad to step down as an MP at the end of this Parliament.

Monday, 10th September

To London, to deliver to Rota's my diaries from 1953 to 1978, along with the letters I have accumulated in recent years. At Brooks's, when John Saumarez Smith made no mention of my novel, I did not refrain from telling him that a film producer had asked for a copy to see if he might make something of it. Jamie Fergusson dined at Brooks's. He exhorted me to write a book about what he called 'my babies' – that is, those houses which the National Trust acquired largely through my efforts.* But I have to overcome my current apathy, and sense of disappointment at the total ignoring of my novel, before I can write again. Jamie looking most distinguished – tall, collected, morose, companionable, clever.

---

* As described below, he undertook this in 1991 and it was published by John Murray in 1992 as *People and Places*.

Tuesday, 11th September

I had a long talk with Nigel [Nicolson] who is appalled by the television version of *Portrait of a Marriage*.* He says the 'seduction' of his mother by Violet [Trefusis] is horrifying. He has written an article for *The Times* criticising the production, and is going to America for six weeks to avoid the consequences. Nigel really ought to have known what he was letting himself in for with the modern media.

Thursday, 13th September

My French translator Guillaume Villeneuve spent the day, coming all the way from Fontainebleau by car. I had tried to put him off, but he was most insistent on meeting me. He was not the established literary man I had envisaged, but youngish and touchingly modest. The day not a great success. Our luncheon in a Bath wine bar was filthy; I took him to see Dyrham, which turned out to be closed; then I gave him a cup of tea at home and took him to see the House, which was shut up, David and Caroline both being away. Although conversation was not easy, as his spoken English is not much better than my French, we ended friends. Spoke to me of his background. Only child of separated parents; father from Mauritius (hence swarthy appearance); devoted to mother. Familiar story. Said he always felt an outsider, whatever the company. Asked me direct questions, to which I gave hesitant answers. Has read all my books and can quote long passages by heart, illustrating my views on politics, religion and all other matters. I was touched that he had come all this way just to see me. He told me he had a mania for neatness and tidiness; preens and polishes all day long; can't abide anyone being in his flat for long because of the disorder engendered. Guillaume – I suggested we use first names as he already knows me so intimately – is one of those foreigners fascinated by English literature, architecture and social distinctions, like Stuart Preston.

---

* See 19 September below.

Wednesday, 19th September

Tonight on BBC 2 the first part of *Portrait of a Marriage*. A. refused to watch and went up to bed. I turned on to see a (recognisable) impersonation of Vita in her actual tower room at Sissinghurst, huddled over a bottle of gin (she only drank sherry), dead drunk. Then a series of flashbacks – Vita playing with Violet in the Knole galleries; Vita and Harold getting married; Lady Sackville,* looking like a common tart with red hair, explaining her husband's sexual inadequacies to her dinner table while three liveried footmen stood silently to attention. Then V. driving her car in Kent on the right-hand side of the road, passing a horse-drawn cart, making the horse rear, getting out to bark a haughty apology. Harold portrayed as a feeble, whingeing wimp, like a bank clerk with Hitlerian moustache; shown writing with left hand. Then back to V. swigging gin in the tower, her manner unbelievably haughty. Then Harold confessing at her bedside that he cannot sleep with her as he has caught the clap, and blubbing. I turned off, disgusted that these two distinguished, beloved friends should be so degraded and misrepresented in a film which will presumably be watched by millions. Nothing to suggest they were creative artists, with a life of the mind.

Sunday, 30th September

Derry arranged [at Windsor Castle] for us to be shown round Frogmore this morning by Hugh Roberts,† deputy keeper of the royal works of art. Delightful man like most courtiers. Said the Queen had had to be consulted, and give her approval of us. This house most evocative of past inhabitants. Marvellous restoration of original contents, including curtains, carpets and even chandeliers. Rooms restored are of three main periods – Queen Charlotte; Duchess of

---

* Victoria Sackville-West (1862–1936); illegitimate daughter of 2nd Baron Sackville and Pepita, a Spanish dancer; m. 1890 her cousin Lionel Sackville-West (1867–1928), who, following a sensational court case, was deemed to have succeeded 1908 as 3rd Baron; mother of Vita Sackville-West.
† (Sir) Hugh Roberts (b. 1948); Deputy Surveyor (later Surveyor) of Queen's Works of Art, 1988–96.

Kent; Queen Mary.* The last the least tasteful, it must be said. The Gallery restored to resemble a plate in Pyne's *Royal Residences* [1819]. A wondrous and moving display.

Monday, 1st October

We motor to Petersham Lodge, Richmond, stopping on the way at Chiswick. Here is another example of restoration on the grand scale. A marvellous recreation, for unlike Frogmore, the house and garden at Chiswick constitute a work of art created at one period, by Lord Burlington† and William Kent.‡

Petersham, where the Loewensteins have now been living for a year, is very luxuriously appointed. I was envious of Rupert's magnificent library, which has every convenience; likewise his bedroom and dressing room. Yet the house is too posh and overdone. The yellow drawing room with its gilded furniture gives a feeling of being empty and unnatural. The floor of the staircase hall is of shiny black marble; it should be of stone. The building a fake from top to bottom, the interior completely reconstructed by the Ls at huge expense. A large garden by metropolitan standards, in fact an untidy little park. Portuguese couple, butler handing out cocktails. Princess Margaret a frequent visitor. Too snobbish they are; but lovable.

Wednesday, 24th October

Last night Dale telephoned to say that poor little Audrey had died at 3.30 in the hospital. She developed a slight cough, then faded away. Dale was with her, holding her hand. No mother could have had a

* King George III bought Frogmore House and its grounds in 1792 as a pleasure retreat for his wife Queen Charlotte (1744–1818). In 1841, Queen Victoria presented it to her mother, Victoria, Duchess of Kent (1786–1861), as a residence. The future King George V and Queen Mary lived there as Prince and Princess of Wales from 1902 to 1910.

† Richard Boyle, 3rd Earl of Burlington (1694–1753); statesman and architect in the Palladian style.

‡ Artist, architect, furniture designer and landscape gardener (1685–1748), who worked closely with Burlington from their first meeting in 1715.

more devoted daughter. I rejoice that she went peacefully, yet feel desperately sad, my grief tainted with the usual remorse. For I was often unkind to Audrey; she irritated me and I snubbed her, an unforgivable thing. She was as good as gold, and never harboured an ungenerous thought or did a mean thing, which cannot be said of me. And let's face it, goodness is greatness; nothing else counts for much in the sight of God. I shudder to think of the many occasions when I was horrid to her. I never responded to her harmless whimsies, e.g. that I call her 'Minty'; I was self-righteous over her ghastly husband Tony,* on whose account she suffered torments; I was never generous or protective towards her as I should have been. Before she married Matthew, I remember Ralph Jarvis† fancying her, which I discouraged for no better reason than that I thought her too simple for him. I am now the last of the Wickhamford family, and feel like a plant torn out of the earth. Although Audrey was not at all religious, yet she seemed to be disembodied somehow, a spirit rather than a terrestrial being.

Thursday, 25th October

J.K.-B. lunched at Brooks's. Angus Stirling‡ came and sat with us. Very distinguished looking, one of nature's ambassadors. Much exercised by a move among the membership to ban hunting on N.T. land. If this goes through, it will deter landowners from giving their estates to the Trust in future, and make great inroads on the country way of life. I feel divided myself, for instinctively and rationally I do not approve of hunting; yet I believe that it renders more good than evil.

Tuesday, 30th October

This afternoon A. accompanied me to Audrey's funeral at Bagendon. Nice little service in this pretty church. I tried hard not to be moved,

---

* Cecil ('Tony') Stevens. On his death, J.L.-M. wrote (19 December 1972): 'He was a bounder, and boring . . . Yet he was an object of pity, a failure, and like most people I suppose he had his pride.'
† Colonel Ralph Jarvis (1907–73) of Doddington Hall, Lincolnshire; Eton contemporary of J.L.-M.; m. Antonia Meade.
‡ Director-General of N.T., 1983–95 (Deputy Director, 1979–83); (b. 1933, kt 1994).

but of course was, especially when her tiny coffin passed me in the aisle. Could not bring myself to go to the graveside. Try as I might, all memories of our childhood at Ribbesford and Wickhamford surged, days when I was as close to her as she always was to me. She is to be buried next to Prue and Ted.* How much would the poor darling have relished Ted's eternal company? Then tea with the Henry [Robinson]s at Moorwood. I suppose I ought not to be ashamed of weeping. How I admire Dale, who was wonderfully controlled.

Tuesday, 13th November

Have just watched Sir Geoffrey Howe† on television speaking damn-ingly in the House of Mrs Thatcher. The attacks on the poor woman from her own side do not augur well for the Conservatives' chances of survival. Personally, I think she is right to go cautiously over Europe – though I believed in the ideal of a continental federation during the war, under the influence of Robert [Byron].

Thursday, 22nd November

Mrs Thatcher fell this morning. The great and glorious woman has resigned. The media are now full of her praises, as are her enemies. Really, the lack of loyalty and integrity among politicians is unbeliev-able. Even A., the least politically-minded of beings, says she has not been so upset since Kennedy's murder. Mrs T's speech in the House this afternoon was one of the most admirable displays of courage I have ever witnessed. Making light, pulling no punches, teasing, damning, edifying, exhorting; a splendid display of nerve and dignity.

---

* Audrey's dau. by her 1st marriage, Hon. Prudence Arthur (d. 1976), and her husband Major Edwin Robinson MC of Moorwood (d. 1985): parents of the Robinson brothers.

† Conservative politician (b. 1926); Foreign Secretary, 1983–89; resigned as Deputy Prime Minister and Leader of the House of Commons, 1 November 1990, owing to disagreements with Mrs Thatcher over 'Europe'; cr. life peer as Baron Howe of Aberavon, 1992.

Sunday, 25th November

The country is plunged into a state of shock, and the Tories into dismay and shame. The greatest Prime Minister this century toppled for no good reason, by pygmies.

We had the Badenis* to luncheon. He talked of his recent audience with the Pope. Tactlessly I asked him whom he was representing. 'Old Poland,' he replied. They talked in Polish. Jan says there is something about the Pontiff which transcends charm or even holiness and is almost supernatural. I said I experienced similar feelings with Pius XII, and supposed that one's awe of the office induced it. No, he said, it was a special gift. He said the Vatican is just as splendid as ever. Nothing is second-rate or shoddy. Halberdiers, Swiss Guards, flunkeys at every turn. He then said to me, 'You must come back to the Church', as if I had left it because of the lack of panoply. There is an Oundle master who is trying to persuade me likewise.

Monday, 10th December

Walking through Bath this afternoon, almost dark at 3.30, I looked through uncurtained windows at the interiors of Queen Square, Gay Street and Brock Street. Every single building is now an office with strip lighting. Not a vestige of Georgian decoration to be seen; only the façades left. What has happened to the people who used to live here? Why have they been driven from this beautiful classical setting? What is the point of it all?

Friday, 21st December

Before driving home in the dark, I sat in my library with the lights on, imbibing the opulence of the rich colours – the yellow curtains, the green lampshades, the silver and brass lampstands, the mahogany, the gilding, the bindings of the books. I love this room, which I ought now to leave and get rid of. And I felt lonely and empty, without

---

* Count Jan Badeni (1921–98); wartime Polish aviator; High Sheriff of Wiltshire, 1978–9; m. 1956 June Wilson.

purpose, no book ahead of me, unable to get down even to the short article I am supposed to be writing for *Country Living*.

Sunday, 23rd December

Coote Lygon, who is staying with us, told me that, during her childhood and early youth at Madresfield, they had family prayers daily in the chapel. When her father was present, he read them. When he was absent, the Vicar officiated. After Lord Beauchamp was obliged to go abroad, the prayers continued. By this time only the children were in residence, Lady Beauchamp having been taken by her brother Bendor to live at Saighton Grange. The Vicar continued to officiate, and Coote played the organ. This continued right up to 1939. None of the children was religious. All drifted away. I was surprised to hear this, as I imagined that family prayers only survived in middle class families after Edwardian times. I recollect that the Chutes still had them at The Vyne [Hampshire] during the last war; but then they *were* rather middle class. I asked Coote if Lady Beauchamp was deeply shocked to learn of her husband's peccadilloes. No, she said, her mother was extremely simple and never understood what homosexuality meant.*

Coote also spoke of Zita and Teresa [the Jungman sisters],† who have sold their house and moved to Aynho.‡ They first applied for rooms in a convent, and were presented with a questionnaire. The first question was, 'Are you incontinent?' They had no idea what this meant, but imagined it must be a good thing and answered, 'Yes, very.' Both were refused admission.

---

* Coote's father, the Liberal statesman 6th Earl Beauchamp (1872–1938; m. 1902 Lady Lettice Grosvenor [d. 1936]), was obliged to resign his offices in 1931 and flee abroad to avert an imminent scandal arising out of his homosexual life, which his vindictive brother-in-law 'Bendor', 2nd Duke of Westminster, was threatening to make public. Only when near to death could he safely rejoin his family at Madresfield Court, Worcestershire – see 23 December 1994. Evelyn Waugh's portrait of Lord Marchmain in *Brideshead Revisited* carries echoes of the affair.

† Zita James (1903–2006) and Teresa ('Baby') Cuthbertson (b. 1907); daughters of the socialite Mrs Richard Guinness by her first husband, Dutch-born artist Nico Jungman; survivors of the 'bright young people' of the 1920s.

‡ Country house in Northamptonshire, former seat of Cartwright family, converted into sheltered accommodation.

Sunday, 30th December

I mentioned to Selina what Coote had told me – that Evelyn Waugh's last years, though he would not admit it, were made miserable by the loss of faith consequent upon Pope John's disastrous Vatican Council II; that this contributed to his being so bad-tempered and difficult and may even have killed him. Selina showed the insensitivity of the non-believer by saying, 'But Evelyn ought to have been happy not sad to have lost his faith.' I tried to explain that it is not so, when a man loses what he found for himself.

1991

1991

Tuesday, 1st January

We have rather a grand luncheon party to which come the Beauforts, the Loewensteins, and Archduke Ferdinand of Austria.* Not terribly enjoyable. Caroline shouts; David spouts gossip; Josephine's talk is dull and pointless. Rupert who can talk doesn't, attending obsequiously to the Archduke. In the sitting room after luncheon, I try to steer conversation to the Austro-Hungarian Empire. Do you live in Austria? Yes, a flat in Salzburg. I suppose your family were unable to live in Austria for some time after 1918? No response. I offer chocolates, wondering how many one could eat before feeling sick. 'Five,' suggests the Archduke. End of contact.

I am re-reading *The Bachelor Duke* in preparation for the dreaded luncheon the Devonshires so generously offer to give at Chatsworth for booksellers. I have found a few misprints, and many infelicities in syntax. I fear it is not a good book, and that I cannot write now.

Thursday, 3rd January

Reading through old family letters chucked helter-skelter into the bottom drawer of the Sheraton bureau, and trying to sort them for posterity (who are they?), I come across a pathetic little torn notebook in which Mama, a few months before her death [in 1962], wrote directions as to how she wanted her possessions divided between us three. Touching little requests. Jim, do keep this, not that it is valuable, but I remember it at Coates [her father's estate near Cirencester]. And

---

* Archduke Ferdinand Karl Max Frank Otto Konrad Maria Joseph Ignatius Nikolaus, also known as Count von Kyburg (b. 1918); nephew of Karl I, last Austro-Hungarian emperor.

apologies for being cross and difficult when she feels so ill. And the agony of having Alice (whoever that was) foisted upon her when she longs to be alone. O the sadness of it.

Sunday, 6th January

Clarissa staying the weekend, brought by her lover Billy. She tells us that every full moon he becomes a different character, abstracted, moody and somnolent – a 'lunatic', so to speak. This may explain the slightly odd look in the eyes which Oenone noticed in him.

Tuesday, 15th January

Tonight at midnight we shall know for certain what seems ineluctable. It is clear that Saddam is bent on war, while the Western countries have done all in their power to prevent it. He seems mad to defy the United Nations, unless he really has some secret weapon. The only hysteria in Britain seems to be an obsessive listening to the news with its repeated platitudes. There is none of the jingoism of 1914 or even the Falklands, rather a sense of resignation. If the world survives, I suppose the outcome may be some system of universal peace-keeping in future.

Thursday, 17th January

I turn on news at 7 to learn that the Allies have bombed Baghdad, with no casualties to us. I later speak to M. who watched the bombing throughout the night on television, moved to tears with excitement. How different from 1939, when all was mystery and concealment of facts; now even troop movements are mentioned.

Saturday, 19th January

The euphoria is over, and we are warned that the war may last four months. Israel has been attacked and persuaded to refrain from retaliation, but she will certainly strike back if attacked again. Then the Arab world may shift and the Alliance dissolve, so we are warned.

Saturday, 26th January

Charlie Morrison, with whom we dined, said that Mr Major* was a great success. Everyone liked him, and even the Labour Party found it hard to be beastly to him.

Sunday, 27th January

Elspeth [Huxley] lunched. Full of gloom about the flooding of the Gulf with oil by the demon Saddam. She showed me an entry in K. Kennet's diaries in which she writes that she 'picked up a beautiful boy', and then describes his pyjamas and what he was wearing at breakfast. I remember K. talked like this, and that 'picking up' did not quite mean to her what it means today.

Saturday, 2nd February

We are in a spell of great cold. I have started on my new book [on country houses donated to the National Trust], which is not proving too difficult. Have done the piece on Brockhampton [Herefordshire], and am now tackling Blickling [Norfolk]. Nice to be occupied again. Am writing by hand, and a nice elderly Miss Anson from New Zealand who lives in Lansdown Terrace will type for £7 an hour.

Tuesday, 5th February

Nasty 'mare last night. I was at some college where the students were given an essay to write by a certain time. Time came. We were all assembled in a large room to read our contributions. I was in a great scare of the headmistress, and endeavoured to hide behind a grand piano lest I be called upon. Woke just before the dreaded moment, by which time it was no longer a mere essay demanded of me, but something more in the nature of a sexual performance.

---

* Conservative Prime Minister, 1990–7 (b. 1943; KG 2005).

Sunday, 24th February

When I spoke to Jock Murray on Thursday, he said he had something important to tell me, but not then, having had a hard day dealing with Candida [Lycett Green] and Paddy [Leigh Fermor]. Oh dear, I thought, he is going to tell me, as Nigel [Nicolson] had to tell Harold, that I am gaga and that the first instalment of my N.T. book is gibberish. This evening he rang. He said, 'You know Freddie Stockdale,* who produces opera in country houses.' (I don't.) 'He is a great friend of Ariane. Well, they are afraid to approach you directly, but they have asked me, as your old friend, to tell you that they want to write your biography.' I was aghast and replied, 'You must be mad. I have never heard anything so preposterous. It's out of the question.' Jock laughed and said he understood my reaction, adding, 'But you wouldn't oppose the idea out of hand?' Yes I would, I replied. Just imagine being interviewed by dear little Ariane whom I adore, and a man completely unknown to me, about my love life, my relations with my father and mother, my inmost thoughts. I discussed it with A[lvilde]. She said why not, someone will do it one day anyway. I don't believe this for one minute, and have written to M. to warn him as my literary executor.†

Monday, 25th February

Woke to the news that the ground battle in the Gulf had begun.‡ I wonder what makes British soldiers fight this war. They are fairly sophisticated, and can't be fired with a desire to free Kuwait. Like the majority of Brits, they probably disapprove of war unless it were to defend their own shores. I am amazed by their loyalty and courage.

Tuesday, 26th February

A beautiful day; mild too. My first whiff of that elusive, disturbing Spring which used to cause me such distress – that far-off enticement

---

* Frederick Minshull Stockdale (b. 1947), yr s. of Sir Edmund Stockdale, 1st Bt; writer, and founder of Pavilion Opera (see 2 December 1992).

† A biography by Michael Bloch is due to be published by John Murray in 2009.

‡ The offensive was instantly successful: Kuwait was liberated on 27 February and President George Bush declared a cessation of hostilities the following day.

by unseen sirens towards *Wanderlust*. In the garden here, a bunch of primroses is out; lots of snowdrops; no crocuses yet, but euphorbia in flower, and one violet.

We dined at the House, just the four of us. Caroline complained she was the only duchess who had not been painted, and wanted a full-length of herself. David said he was perfectly agreeable. We suggested her son-in-law Matthew [Carr]. C. objected, saying he had made Anne look 'like a houri'. A drawing of Anne was produced, the first work of Matthew I had seen. Simply excellent, giving her an air of hawk-like power and intellect. C. said she didn't think it reflected her own character. Of course not, we said, he would depict you as you are. 'I don't want to be depicted as I am', C. replied, 'but as I was when young and pretty. I want someone to do a portrait of me from a photograph of twenty-five years ago.' In that case, said David, he would not pay for it. He asked me whether the upper classes spoke with regional accents a century ago. I said many of them did, instancing Tennyson's Lincolnshire burr.

Wednesday, 27th February

To London for the day. Lunched with Hugh Montgomery-Massingberd at Travellers. Admired the dining room which has been richly redecorated by Gervase and others, canary, red and gold on pale yellow ground. Hugh very greedy, ate one of my cutlets as well as his own. Is going to write front page of Saturday's *Telegraph Review* on *The Bachelor*. No need to talk to me, he said. 'I know you so well I shall just invent your replies. Do you mind?' 'All the same to me,' I said. He said his fascination with the stage and the green room had become a mania of which he was almost frightened. Not actresses but actors he is interested in − their vanity, their patter, their history.* Hugh looking spruce, if not exactly slender, in smart blue London suit.

Struggled in pouring rain to National Trust offices in Queen Anne's Gate. Had a security tag attached to me. Shown by secretary to Martin Drury's room, where until 5.30 I looked through old files on Blickling and Attingham [Park, Shropshire]. Odd to be reading

---

* As he fascinatingly explained in his memoirs *Daydream Believer* (2001).

my correspondence with the Berwicks* of half a century ago. When Martin came in, he asked if I recognised the tall lampstand. It is the one I was photographed under as Historic Buildings Secretary, sitting at the same writing-table before the same inkstand. Robin Fedden† and Bobby Gore retained these items, which are now historic souvenirs. Martin charming. We arranged a tour of N.T. properties in June.

Talking of obituary-writing, Hugh M.-M. said, 'It is not one's friends' virtues but their foibles which endear them to one.'

Wednesday, 6th March

I went to Hanbury [Hall, Worcestershire] at invitation of Jeffrey Haworth,‡ who thought I would be interested to see the improvements being effected. Nice of him, but they depressed me to extremes. Horribly drizzly day and Hanbury surroundings *triste* and *morne*. The house entirely gutted except for Thornhill staircase and ceilings.§ Floors up, walls stripped to plaster, not a vestige of furniture to be seen. This house which I love has lost all its magic, and indeed its antiquity too. It might now be a building of any date. Sad, sad, sad. There must be something deeply wrong with the National Trust, spending so prodigally on this building, which has no endowment, and which was restored in 1952 by an anonymous benefactor for an enormous sum. Why within thirty years should another drastic restoration be necessary?

Sunday, 10th March

We lunched with the Acloques at Alderley. How I love this house and garden. Seeing this couple who have now been here fifteen

---

* Attingham came to the N.T. on the death of 8th Baron Berwick in 1947 – largely owing to the initiative of his wife, who lived there until her own death in 1972.
† J.L.-M's successor (1951–68) as Historic Buildings Secretary of N.T. (1909–77).
‡ N.T. Historic Buildings Representative for Severn Region, 1981–2002 (b. 1944).
§ Sir James Thornhill (1675–1734) had decorated the walls and ceilings of this part of the house with mythological frescos.

years, bringing up a son and twin daughters, and thinking that we were here fifteen years, almost makes me wish we too had a son and heir, and could have remained. The garden, with its view of the wooded hill above Ozleworth Lane, is a dream of beauty and tranquillity. The Acloques have some splendid things. The house is too tarted-up, but never mind; they adore the place, and he is a good gardener.

The prospect of Murray's party on Wednesday is like a rat gnawing at my vitals. I have nightmares of being hemmed in by a multitude of faces, recognising no one, hearing nothing, panicking.

Wednesday, 13th March

The dreaded day. Found the Sarge* at Brooks's lunching with his handsome French protégé Didier.† They accompanied me to a silly 'Cupid and Venus' exhibition at Wildensteins. I lay down during afternoon to prepare self for coming ordeal, then collected A. from Lansdowne Club and we went together to Murray's. Although the two rooms were packed – apparently more had accepted than ever before – I actually enjoyed it. Numerous friends old and new, plus critics and celebrities. Everyone enthusiastic about the book and congratulating. Many came with book in hand asking for signature. One woman asked me to write, 'To Jacqueline Onassis‡ from J.L.-M.' Instead I put, 'For J.O. and *by* J.L.-M.' Much photography, I suspect for *Tatler*. ('Jennifer'§ there taking notes.) Certainly I have never before been fêted in this way. At nine Jock gave a dinner at Brown's Hotel for eight, Devonshires, Murrays, Ariane, Gervase [Jackson-Stops] and L.-Ms. I praised God that it was all over

---

* Stuart Preston.

† Didier Girard (b. 1964); French scholar interested in English eccentrics, then writing a doctoral disseration on J.L.-M's Eton contemporary Edward James; he later edited a French edition of the works of William Beckford.

‡ Jacqueline Bouvier (1929–94); m. 1st 1953 John F. Kennedy (1917–63; President of United States, 1961–3), 2nd 1968 Aristotle Onassis (1906–75).

§ 'Jennifer's Diary' was a society column, then appearing in *Harper's and Queen*, written by Betty Kenward (1906–2000), notorious for its carefully graded lists of names of those attending various parties and ceremonies.

and had been without embarrassments, feeling rather pleased with myself.

Monday, 25th March

Left Chatsworth this morning after a lovely visit.

Every other left-hand page of the Chatsworth visitors' book bears the Prince of Wales's signature. He stayed for three nights lately. I asked Debo how he spent his time. He disappears unaccompanied for long solitary walks across the moors. A fairly unhappy man, full of passionate beliefs, over-sensitive, trusting, anxious to learn. Has no friends among his family, apart from Queen Mother whose departure will be a terrible wrench. Not many men friends; Colin Amory* drafts speeches and advises, but hardly an intimate. His friends mostly women, including Candida [Lycett Green].

Wednesday, 3rd April

A. being in France, Folly and I were alone after Easter with Clarissa and her fancy boy Billy, who is a decent fellow, extremely good-looking and stupid. Asks countless questions without listening to answers. 'What exactly do you mean by squirearchy?' 'Is the aristocracy no longer rich?' Then Clarissa: 'Jim, do tell Billy about the man who lived at No. 19 before you.' 'You mean Lord Strathcona?' She was thinking of William Beckford, of whom she knew nothing and he had never heard.

Thursday, 4th April

Bamber [Gascoigne]† telephones this afternoon. 'I have got news,' he says in his cheery voice. 'It is good. Mother had a stroke a week ago, but is now rather better. Actually she was better yesterday but has relapsed a bit today.' Really, he is extraordinary. Apparently Midi is

---

* Architectural historian (b. 1944).

† Arthur Bamber Gascoigne (b. 1935); writer, broadcaster and publisher; son of 'Midi' Gascoigne; m. 1965 Christina Ditchburn.

dying, for I asked, 'Please tell me, Bamber, should one hope for recovery or not?' and he replied, 'Well, I would give her a fortnight. I am sure she would be glad to see you on a good day. Do ring up when you are next coming to London.' Darling Midi, lying there gazing into space. Yet Bamber is not heartless. What is he?

Tuesday, 9th April

Selina who dined with us said that when she had finished [Evelyn] Waugh's life she would start on Rosamond [Lehmann]'s. She said she was relying on me to let her have Ros's letters to me. I murmured that I hoped they had not gone to Yale with the rest of my papers, aware that they probably have. I'm not sure how much I want Selina to see Ros's letters, which are sure to contain much about the differences between A. and myself in the past. And Selina gossips.

Wednesday, 10th April

In London Library, someone came up to me to say that Reresby [Sitwell] had lent him a copy of my *Heretics** to read at Renishaw. Said he, 'It made me feel absolutely sick.' What is an author to reply to such a remark? I said nothing.

Worked all day at N.T. papers, then to see Midi. Terribly downcasting experience. Midi lying on back with mouth open and teeth out, unrecognisable. More like a corpse than anyone I have seen. Kept mumbling as if wishing to say something, but words unintelligible. I did not know what to say. She knew me, held up an arm which looked like a stick, and gave a ghost of a smile. Eyes staring, blank and watering. A terrible sight to see. What have we humans done to deserve such an end? I took her warm hand, pressed it and slunk away. Poor darling Midi, my oldest woman friend.

---

* J.L.-M's first published novel *Heretics in Love* (Chatto & Windus, 1973), which dealt with incest, homosexuality and necrophilia, amongst other peculiarities.

Friday, 19th April

Reading through reviews of *The Bachelor*, I feel I have been treated better than my subject. The general view is that he was a bore. In fact he was extremely funny, and his character complex and interesting. It is my fault for failing to reveal him.

Saturday, 25th May

A. gave a party for sixteen gardeners. Tables out of doors. Rain kept off. Garden looking splendid. Apart from Melanie Cairns and the two retired '*Mädchen*'* from Sissinghurst, all the gardeners were young men, and mostly queer I should say. Mostly head gardeners to great houses, calling each other Nick, Mick, Jack, etc. Clarissa [Luke] and Pat O'Neill† also present. I am fond of old Pat for the sake of Rory and past glories of Cap Ferrat, which I never really enjoyed at the time. She is incensed by a vicious article about her mother in one of the glossies, alleging that Enid murdered all four of her husbands.‡ Enid used to say this of herself in jest, but the author of the article takes it quite seriously.

Monday, 3rd June

Noticed in *Times* list of deaths that of Berkeley Villiers§ who was the first boy to seduce me at McNeile's [House, Eton]. I remember

---

* Pamela Schwerdt and Sibille Kreuzberger, who went to Sissinghurst as head gardeners in 1959.

† Sister of A.L.-M's friend Rory Cameron; owner of a stud farm in South Africa, where the L.-Ms had stayed with her in 1983.

‡ Enid Lindeman of Sydney, NSW; m. 1st 1913 Roderick Cameron of New York, 2nd 1917 General the Hon. Frederick Cavendish (d. 1931), heir to 6th Baron Waterpark (their son succeeding as 7th Baron), 3rd 1933 (as his 3rd wife) 1st Viscount Furness (d. 1940), 4th Jan. 1943 (as his 2nd wife) 6th Earl of Kenmare (he d. Sept. 1943). As Countess of Kenmare, she was sometimes known as 'Lady Killmore'.

§ Lieut-Col (Francis) Berkeley Hyde Villiers (1906–91); connection of Earl of Clarendon; sometime senior executive of ICI; married an Austrian; art collector at his house near Kidderminster. J.L.-M. had referred to him anonymously in his diary for 13 November 1947, after meeting him at a concert: 'X, and I suppose his wife, were in the box. His proximity made me feel self-conscious. I must have been no more than fifteen . . . when I met my "undoing" from his hands . . . I rather enjoyed it, though of course pretending not to.'

the incident extremely well, I aged fifteen at most. In the middle of the performance Michael Rosse, then his great friend, came into Berkeley's room and like the perfect gentleman he was fetched something he had left on the mantelpiece without turning his head in our direction. Michael never referred to the incident in later life, nor did B.V. whom from time to time I ran across. A prissy, affected fellow. I never had the opportunity to talk to him and would have liked to. The smell of his Roger & Gallet Carnation Soap never fails to remind me. Thrilling, alarming, wicked-seeming and delicious it was.

Wednesday to Thursday, 5th to 6th June

Martin Drury, a charming man and perfect for his job, took me on a two-day tour of Midlands. Lower Brockhampton our first call. This beautiful setting much the same. The old Manor lies snug behind the gatehouse, farmyard still next door and good old smell of pigs. Delightful volunteer lady administrator received us, treating me like something pre-historic from the Ark. Much-fingered copy of *Caves of Ice* lying on long table. The Hall is now rented by insurance company as offices. Fitted carpets, telephones in every room. Still traces of what went before, original door hinges and fireplaces *à la* Pritchard. Bluff caretaker assured us that the house was haunted by a child of nine, who bangs doors, opens windows and sneezes in the night.

Thence via Hanbury Hall to Little Moreton Hall [Cheshire]. Hanbury has advanced since my last visit, but Little Moreton swathed in polythene sheets from gallery roof to ground. Not possible to get any idea of what it now looks like. New compartmentalised garden on east front, too well-kept for the dear old farmhouse I remember. Here joined by Julian Gibbs* who took us to stay the night at their nice, plain rectory in Shropshire. A dear couple, he a simple soul like his father Christopher but without the business acumen, she, picture restorer, more sophisticated and beguiling, very pretty with dark hair

---

* Son (b. 1949) of J.L.-M's former colleague Christopher Gibbs (d. 1985), Assistant Secretary of N.T., 1935–66.

and fresh complexion, and slightly Tartar cheekbones from Greek mother.

We continued to Charlecote, dismayed at appalling ruination of Shropshire landscape by motorways, pylons, factories in fields. Welcomed by nice custodian and given coffee by Edmund Lucy in his studio. A charmer, his face Alice's, his frame and slouch Brian's. I coveted his paintings of Venice, and wish I could afford one. He gets irritated by the public milling outside his window, and is happier here in winter. Then to Coughton [Court, Warwickshire]. Much the same, but too many cars in front of house. Met husband of Robert Throckmorton's* niece who is heiress to contents. She evidently believes that I talked her grandmother into donating Coughton.

Sunday, 9th June

We lunched with Chiquita [Astor]† to meet the Jenkinses. Roy (as he now is to me) said that to understand the value of money in 1941 one has to multiply by forty. When I said that my great-aunt Isabel lived in No. 5 Royal Crescent, Bath with cook, parlourmaid and house-maid on £600 per annum, he admitted that no one would get far on £24,000 today. I had to keep off politics, for both were ready to bash Thatcher. When I said, in retort to his mockery of House of Lords debates, that the Lords showed more wisdom than the Commons in opposing the trial of old war criminals, he agreed the idea was ridiculous and wrong, adding that it was started by Mrs T. Jennifer is gentle, wise, moderate in her views and infinitely sympathetic, far more so than he. When I told her of my shock at the ruination of Shropshire, she said it had all happened within the past ten years – i.e., under the Thatcher régime. Roy is easily bored. I could see the film across his eyes and the fidgety hands while I was trying to reply to a polite question he had put to me. Talking of atrocities in Europe since 1939, both

---

* Sir Robert Throckmorton, 11th Bt (1908–89), whose mother, Lilian, Lady Throckmorton (*née* Brooke, d. 1955), had set in motion a long legal process resulting in the donation of Coughton to N.T.
† Ana Inez Carcano; m. 1944–72 Hon. John Jacob Astor (d. 2000), yst son of 2nd Viscount Astor.

Jenkinses insisted the Germans were worse than the Russians. Now this is just not true; they were of equal horror; but it is a socialist article of faith that Hitler must have been worse than Stalin.

Tuesday, 18th June

To Sissinghurst for the night. Nigel had asked Arland Kingston,* the N.T. regional agent, to meet me, along with Anthony Hobson.† We all lunched in the restaurant. I remember Arland as a very young member of staff in my day; very handsome still, as well as clever and bright. He said burglaries at N.T. properties had lately increased twofold.

Nigel motored Anthony and me to Smallhythe.‡ Same isolated situation on edge of the Level with Isle of Oxney to the south. Charming Mrs Weare and husband custodians. Just the right type, being stage-connected, and very knowledgeable about Ellen and Edie. House beautifully kept. Pretty cottage-like garden on north side. We went on to Rye to see Lamb House.§ I would like to live in this town. Unspoilt, overlooking the Level which can't be built over because of flooding. Mrs Martin, late tenant of Long Barn,¶ which she showed me over when I was writing my *Harold*, is the N.T. tenant. Nice, clever woman. Showed us round house, upstairs where the public do not go, and round garden. Large garden, lawns and brick walls, like the Meteyard painting we have of Mrs Meteyard there, sitting in

---

* Joined N.T. staff in 1961; N.T. Regional Director for Kent and East Sussex, 1973–93 (b. 1935).
† Bibliographical historian (b. 1921); m. Tanya Vinogradoff.
‡ This small but ancient Kentish property, subject of a chapter in J.L.-M's book, had belonged to the actress Ellen Terry, whose daughter, Edith Craig, wished to preserve it as a shrine to her. J.L.-M. visited it on behalf of the N.T. in 1938 and was 'wholly captivated . . . I have seldom walked through rooms more nostalgic of a particular owner.' After its acceptance virtually without endowment, Vita Sackville-West kept a benevolent eye on Miss Craig, who lived eccentrically with a group of lesbian friends.
§ Residence of Henry James, whose niece-in-law donated it to N.T. after Second World War.
¶ Property at Sevenoaks, part of Knole estate, lived in by Harold Nicolson and Vita Sackville-West prior to their purchase of Sissinghurst in 1930.

deck-chair. Relics of Henry James accumulate as the house is visited by thousands.

Wednesday, 19th June

Anthony leaves Sissinghurst early for a funeral. I wander round garden, sun half out. Actually heard a cuckoo towards the lake. Greatly enjoy being with Nigel. He brushes aside obstacles, and gets things done. Telephones Bateman's, Kipling's house, to warn we were coming. Telephones Max Egremont* to ask if we may lunch at Petworth [West Sussex]. Bateman's unchanged, and coping with huge influx of visitors. We go quickly over the house, and on to Petworth. On greeting us, Max says the butler is away today, and we shall eat in the kitchen. Lady Egremont repeats this when she receives us in the rococo drawing room. I wonder if this is a dig at me for something I wrote in my beastly diaries? What a charming couple they are. He is grand yet simple, unlike his horrid father John and portentous great-uncle Leconfield.† She is very easy and intelligent. Nigel and I whisked round the state rooms, enabling me to refresh my memory of the pictures and architecture. The N.T. are spending millions on redecorating the vast North Gallery because the Egremonts don't like John Fowler's vivid orange walls. Enjoyable conversation over luncheon. Which authors do we consider will be read in a hundred years? Which living politicians do we respect, if any? Nigel drops me at a wayside station. I get a train for Waterloo, and am home in time for dinner.

Sunday, 23rd June

This morning, Folly, who had not seemed well of late, was making funny little noises, and could hardly stand. We were both very worried

---

* Max Wyndham, 2nd Baron Egremont and 7th Baron Leconfield (b. 1948); writer and farmer; m. 1978 Caroline Nelson.
† Charles Wyndham, 3rd Baron Leconfield (1872–1952), with whom J.L.-M. (as described in his diaries) had some unedifying wartime encounters to discuss the future of Petworth.

and telephoned Riley the vet, who told us to bring her in at midday. We agreed that, if he advised it, we would let her go. A. had to prepare luncheon for Hardy [Amies] and Rosemary, and I dreaded going alone, so A. telephoned Ian [Dixon] who like a brick accompanied me and Folly, waiting in the car while I carried her in. Riley took a grave view and thought her case hopeless – spinal trouble with no hope of cure – so I took the decision. He gave her an injection while I held her in my arms; I then bolted, brimming with tears. Ian motored me back. I said to A., 'I have long known that, after you, the creature I love best is Folly.' She said, 'It is the same with me. I think we made the perfect trio.' After fifteen years of close companionship I feel empty, as though rats had consumed my innards.

Monday, 24th June

I see Folly everywhere – in my car, at No. 19 despite my removing all her dear relics. The silent little presence, so forceful, demanding, uncompromising about the time for her dinner, her walk, her desire to go to bed. Her different barks indicating different emotions – for wishing to go out, fear, suspicion, detection of intruders. So wise in her responses, so clever in sensing our moods. And what wrings the heart is the memory of her affectionate little habits – laying her head on my shoulder, nosing my leg from behind to indicate she was there. Never bearing resentment; sometimes irritating, never boring. And her morning welcome of me when she slept with A., and would jump on my bed and lick my face. She was a catalyst, a joy, someone to talk to, always the best companion. How to bear the house alone now when A. is away?

Monday to Tuesday, 8th to 9th July

By train from Bath to Bodmin, changing at Bristol and Plymouth. Welcomed by Michael and Elizabeth Trinick and motored to Newton House for cold luncheon in kitchen. Michael takes me to Lanhydrock. Beastly day, mist and drizzle. House shut today but Michael conducts me around every room alone. We draw back blinds as we go along. He is justly proud of the house and what he has done. Another late

Victorian specimen. He has ingeniously preserved the crinkly brass
electric light switches by putting them on hinges which swing open
revealing the horrid modern switches which are now mandatory.
Who else would have thought of this refinement? In the late Lord
Clifden's* bedroom, bottles on his dressing table of Bay Rum and Eau
de Portugal from Trumper's, no longer obtainable.

On our return at six, two N.T. boys join us for drinks – Michael's
successor [Jeremy] Pearson, shy and nice, and Giles Clotworthy,† frisky
and facetious. An old colonel to dinner, who tells a funny story of
how he had gone into Hatchards and told a terrified young lady assistant that he had come for *You Bloody Women* – in fact a book about
three Englishwomen in the Boer War protesting against the concentration camps.

Next day Michael motors me to Cothele.‡ Told me that, when the
last Lord Clifden§ succeeded his brother, he received letters addressed
to him as Lord Mendip, summoning him to sit in the House of Lords.
He returned these to the post office, marked 'not known at this
address'. Michael had to explain to him that the Clifden viscountcy
was Irish, and it was by virtue of the Mendip barony that he held his
seat. At Cothele he shows me the Quay, the docked *Shamrock*, the Mill
grinding away – all features developed by Michael – then garden
and house, all in mint condition, almost too tidy. He has opened
the kitchen, every detail thought out, a spit brought from some
demolished house in Plymouth. A wonder of a man, really a treasure
to the National Trust.

Saturday, 13th July

This morning A. confessed she was lonely without her constant companion. I already knew this – I could hear it in her voice yesterday

* Francis Agar-Robartes, 7th Viscount Clifden (1883–1966); bequeathed Lanhydrock, Cornwall and most of his fortune to N.T.
† Former MI6 officer who joined Cornwall staff of N.T. in 1983 (b. 1944).
‡ Tudor house donated to N.T. by Edgcumbe family.
§ Arthur Agar-Robartes (1887–1974); s. brother 1966 as 8th and last Viscount Clifden (the remainder to Barony of Mendip passing on his death to 6th Earl of Normanton).

when she called to her wild doves at the end of the garden. I know I am not often a bright companion for her, and anyway out most days when she needs companionship. Her need of animals is very great. We discussed a cat, but neither of us really likes cats, though I was flattered when one of the Trinicks' came to my room while I was dressing and roosted on the pillow. And it may be awkward for us to get another whippet, even a middle-aged one from the Dogs' Home. We can do nothing anyway until the autumn.

Monday, 15th July

I went to PCC meeting in Badminton Village Hall to discuss women priests. Vicar vehemently against. Penny Wood and Dorothy Lane, both on Synod, in favour. Object to find out what the rest of us thought. To my surprise, the majority were in favour. I declared myself so, though deprecating pursuing the matter at this delicate juncture in history of C. of E. Was told that every moment in the history of the Church was delicate. I nevertheless feel that, since recruits to the clergy are now hard to come by, and females are naturally more devout than males, we must admit them sooner or later. Vicar upset. I must have it out with him.

Monday, 29th July

Another expedition. Hugh Massingberd greets me on platform at Grantham [Lincolnshire]. It is torrentially hot. He opens the roof of his car, and lends me his panama. As we leave the town I say, 'That little corner shop might be Mrs Thatcher's birthplace.' 'It is,' Hugh tells me, pointing out nice little neo-Grecian Methodist chapel opposite. We get to Marston at 1.30. Henry Thorold is an amazing spectacle, long flaxen hair falling over temples, belly like a pregnant elephant, walking not on the soles of his shoes but the sides. A young couple called Thorold from South Africa call without warning. He talks to them in a friendly, condescending fashion, and sends them to eat in a pub. They return while we are eating a massive lunch prepared by Hugh, and share our strawberries. We talk about churches and genealogy, and are then shown round the house and garden. Henry tells us about the wonderful couple who look after him and even decorate the rooms for him. Their taste is naturally ghastly.

Accompanied by Henry we drive, seemingly for hours on small roads, to Gunby. I am delighted with this dear old house. Had forgotten it stands within a substantial park. Hugh's wife* there, whom I had not met before – delightful, good-looking and distinguished, but painfully thin. Very sweet, but strange. Looks adoringly at Hugh. They seem very happy. I like her much. We have a large tea on the steps of the west front in blazing sun, I still sweltering under Hugh's hat. Then we amble around the walled garden, which is very pretty, in full midsummer bloom. And into the wilderness, and the churchyard where we pay our respects to the Field Marshal and Lady M.-M. I press £5 note into the eleemosynary box out of love for Gunby and them. We then dine very late in the kitchen off good food bought by Hugh from Marks & Sparks, for wife neither cooks nor eats. At 11.15 I say I must go to bed. Hugh then motors Henry all the way back to Marston, not returning until 1 a.m.

Tuesday, 30th July

Arrive at Flintham for tea. I rejoice to see Myles [Hildyard], looking a sight with blotchy complexion and parti-coloured boiler-suit. We have tea in the library. It and the conservatory in which we later dine are splendid Victorian specimens. Myles has done wonders with this house. All portraits cleaned, furniture sparkling. Likewise the garden is very good indeed. All better than when I last was here. Myles is to Nottinghamshire what Henry and Hugh are to Lincolnshire. I could not have been treated more kindly by this beloved old friend.

Wednesday, 31st July

Spent morning going round the house with Myles, stopping before each picture or relic and hearing its story. A country house like this is my natural element – blinds down, the sun percolating mischievously

---

* Catherine Ripley (b. 1947), er dau. of Sir Hugh Ripley, 4th Bt (1916–2003); fashion model; m. 1983 Hugh Massingberd as his 2nd wife.

through crannies, the sense of a green world shut out, the musty smell of ancestral belongings, the blind stare of their faces on the walls.

Saturday, 10th August

Eardley [who had been staying at Essex House in Alvilde's absence] departed yesterday morning, rather to my relief. I was aware of something indefinable in his manner, a dismissiveness of my enthusiasms, a lip-curling disapproval of my writing (as when I showed him some chapters of my N.T. book), a contradictory manner as if determined never to admit that I can have an original thought or make an amusing remark.

Saturday, 17th August

Dined with the Norwiches at Castle Combe. Mollie is very pretty, and fun alone. John Julius makes me feel inferior, not by his manner but by his accomplishments. He is organising a V&A exhibition about the Queen, preparing to tour Japan, finishing his history of the Byzantine Empire, presiding over Venice in Peril, writing introductions to three books, and constantly appearing on television. He also cooked the pudding.

Monday, 19th August

Kind Tony Mitchell motored me to Attingham [Park, Shropshire]. Spent whole day there under guidance of Betty Cousens, the efficient and charming representative who manages the N.T.'s historic buildings in these parts. The house makes a splendid impression from the bridge, vastly spread out to impress the world with the new lord; yet the architecture does not bear examination. Spent morning going over state rooms. Rather barren, otherwise very good. Since the [Shropshire Adult] College left in 1986, the Trust has been repairing furniture and redecorating along most conservative lines. Snack lunch under east colonnade in the wind. Met Julian Gibbs, new area organiser, and Mr and Mrs Walker who are studying and cataloguing the miniatures and landscapes respectively. Continued during afternoon in nether regions and upstairs, and drove to look at the mausoleum in the park for which I in a sense was responsible. I think Gerry Wellington first suggested a [Berwick] mausoleum with deer grazing from Constable's painting in National Gallery. The large rear court-yard has been brought back to what it was, and is probably the best feature of the exterior.

Tuesday, 20th August

I motor self to stay the night with Christopher and Francesca Wall* at The Apple Orchard, Bradenham. Charming their house has become, walls crammed with paintings. Friendly welcome, though C. rather morose. Daughter and new husband Charles Ernle-Erle-Drax, nice young man, not outstandingly bright. Dine in garden by candle and mosquito, sitting in uncomfortable low chair, but fun. I hope they did not think me rude when I asked to go to bed at ten.

Wednesday, 21st August

Extremely hot day. Join Christopher in the morning at the office in Hughenden. Went round the house, like all N.T. houses immaculately kept.† Has anyone been living here since Dizzy died? No one seemed to be when I first visited from Oxford in 1930 with Arthur Rathbone,‡ he being a friend of Major Coningsby Disraeli's sister Mrs Calverley. I remember Coningsby stalking about the library wearing a skull-cap, bored by us visitors. Sister pale and prim. Christopher accompanies me in afternoon to West Wycombe. Dashwoods away. Great number of public going round in parties every twenty minutes. C. escorted

---

* Christopher Wall (b. 1929), N.T. Historic Buildings Representative for Thames and Chiltern Region, 1956–94; m. 1961 Francesca Fummi (b. 1935; her mother Lady Cynthia was the sister of David Lindsay, 28th Earl of Crawford, Chairman of N.T., 1945–65).

† Hughenden was the seat of the Prime Minister Benjamin Disraeli, Earl of Beaconsfield, from 1847 until his death in 1881, when it passed to his nephew Coningsby. Coningsby's sister sold it to Major W.H. Abbey, who presented it to the N.T. in 1946.

‡ Arthur Benson Rathbone (1853–1933); member of Liverpool shipping family.

me at our leisure. Many changes since I was here during the war, mostly for the better. Francis, with financial assistance from the Government, has transformed the whole place from seedy dilapidation to poshness, just missing a *House and Garden* standard of fashionableness. He has done well in restoring the original marbling of dining room and hall. Temples restored. Saddest thing is Francis's development on far side of valley, mean terraces of worst sort visible from drive as one approaches front door.

Thursday, 5th September

To London for the day, working in N.T. registry until tea time. Rushed through the Hatchlands[*] file, and finished it and the archive research for my book. So engrossed that I felt no pangs of hunger, though I had breakfasted at seven. Worked at full steam, reading letters and taking notes – not brain work, but requiring intense concentration. Felt happy. Called on M. for tea, just returned from Paris where his beloved Maître Blum has miraculously recovered from her accident. He is now engrossed in his *Ribbentrop*. Walked with me to Paddington. *Eheu!*

In the train, an extremely handsome and pleasant young man was sitting in the reserved seat opposite to mine. At Reading, the seat next to his became vacant and was taken by a very pretty girl with a sweet smile who had been standing in the passage. For a time there was no sign of recognition between them; but when the girl rose, the young man said to her, holding out money, 'Will you please get me a coke?' Yes, she said, and smiled. When she returned with the coke and a sandwich for herself, they began an animated conversation. Their eyes were sparkling with desire and that peacock-preen look which lovers assume. When I got out at Chippenham they were still deliciously flirting – or so it seemed, for I did not hear what they said. I could not make out whether they knew each other before meeting in the carriage. I assume not, for surely the young man, who was gallant and attentive, would have given up his seat to her? Do the young instantly assume intimacy of this sort? I left them with an unuttered benediction.

---

[*] See 11 September 1991 below.

Saturday, 7th September

O lack, lack, lackaday. Was about to sit down to luncheon, the old Coopers[*] here, when telephone rang. A. said that Mattei wanted to speak to me. At once I feared that something must be wrong with Eardley, for Mattei never rings me up. 'I have to tell you', he said, 'Eardley is dead.' A week ago he had palpitations at The Slade. Motored himself to London, saw doctor, took pills, seemed to recover completely. But no reply when Mattei telephoned yesterday, and none this morning, so he went round and let himself in with spare keys. Found E. slumped half on floor, half on bed, his blue eyes open. Doctor came and said E. must have died instantly. But how instantly? Poor Mattei is dreadfully upset. And I? What do I feel? I returned to the kitchen where we ate and I tried to tell stories and make jokes. What is life?

Sunday, 8th September

Eardley hated churches; would seldom visit one, even to sightsee. Hated religion, a subject we never discussed. The other was his health. And how beastly I was when he stayed last month. Walking down the Centre Walk, I strode ahead, deigning to turn my head from time to time. He was without doubt my best friend these fifty years, for we met at the National Trust towards the end of 1941. All those wartime and postwar years when we visited properties together, laughing, gossiping; he forever patient and tolerant, someone I could always turn to in moments of near-desperation; and we went abroad together year after year. Latterly a change in us both, no doubt. Old age and bad temper. Yet he wrote to me how much he enjoyed his visit. After Communion this morning, while the Vicar was talking of his summer at Lake Como,[†] I kept saying, 'Yes, how interesting', my thoughts concentrated on E.

---

[*] Sean Cooper, conservatory designer, and wife Evelyn.
[†] Where he had a seasonal appointment as the Anglican chaplain.

Monday, 9th September

Have finished *Paradise Lost*. It was a grind in anticipation more than in reality. Middle sections boring; end ones retrieve the sublimity of the earlier. At times the story grips. How much did Milton believe? What did he mean by it? Was it considered shocking by Commonwealth folk? I believe it was not published until the permissive years of the Restoration were well established.

Tuesday, 10th September

John Saumarez Smith for luncheon at Brooks's. He is overjoyed that Andrew Devonshire has bought 51 per cent of the shop [Heywood Hill]'s shares, saving his bacon. Most satisfactory solution, and another interest for Andrew. Then to Tate Gallery for the Constables. Far too large an exhibition. Somehow the great six-footers are pompous rehashes of the first inspired little canvases of twenty years earlier. J.K.-B. and nephew Nick dined at Brooks's. Nick charming and handsome, never a banality even when discussing art subjects which are not his.

Wednesday, 11th September

By train to Leatherhead. Met by Christopher Rowell* who drove me to Polesden [Lacey near Dorking] to look through some papers and see Mrs Greville's† tomb. We went on to Hatchlands [near Guildford], where Alec Cobbe‡ took us round. Curious sallow face, deep dark eyes. Something of a genius there. Amazing the opulence of the rooms

---

* N.T. Historic Buildings Representative for Southern Region, 1986–2002 (b. 1952).

† Margaret McEwan, illegitimate daughter of the brewer William McEwan; m. 1891 Hon. Ronald Greville, yr s. of 2nd Baron Greville. She bequeathed Polesden Lacey to the N.T. on her death in 1942.

‡ Richard Alexander Charles Cobbe (b. 1945); artist and designer, arranger of pictures and interiors for N.T.; m. 1970 Hon. Isabel Dillon. In 1987 he became tenant of Hatchlands, which he theatrically designed in Regency style, filling it with his family pictures from Newbridge House, Co. Dublin and his collection of early keyboard intruments.

compared to the sparsity of Goodhart-Rendel's[*] time. Jamie Fergusson caught me at Brooks's and persuaded me to write a supplement to the two obituaries of Eardley in today's *Independent*, dealing with his N.T. side. I wracked my brain and scribbled in train home, typing out before going to bed.

Wednesday, 25th September

Spent day with Guillaume Villeneuve, my French translator. He is a touching little fellow and I cannot but like him much. Fancy his motoring from Fontainebleau just to spend a few hours with me. Brought first copies of *Un Autre Moi-Même*. I am not sure about the title, or the melancholy 1920s photograph on the cover. I try to appear delighted and am indeed appreciative of his trouble. He drives me to Stourhead which he wishes to see, and we walk into the gardens and round the lake. A glorious late afternoon, few visitors. He knows me better than I know myself, being familiar with every word of my four diaries and *Moi-Même*. Quotes what I said, what I thought, how I acted. Most strange. Confided in me about his unrequited passion for a youth of twenty-one. Lives entirely upon translating. Wants to tackle Walter Pater,[†] but I discourage for no French will be bothered with him now. I feel almost paternal towards him, for there is something vulnerable about him. I like his humour, his brightness and sympathy, his curiosity for all that is beautiful and civilised. Was moved to embrace him on parting. He is anxious for me to present myself at some Parisian bookshop and meet French writers, but I tried to explain I cannot do this. Yet I ought to help him, for he needs the money.

Sunday, 20th October

I have decided that, whereas an old person may become a friend of a young person, a young person cannot be a friend of an old person. It requires working out; but I think I am right.

---

[*] Harold Stuart ('Hal') Goodhart-Rendel (1887–1959); architect, donor of Hatchlands to N.T.

[†] English critic and essayist (1839–94); Oxford mentor of Oscar Wilde.

Yesterday we went to Hanbury, which I wished to see now the contents have been put back after the major refurbishment. Crowds, which made the occasion sorrowful. It is over-decorated. No longer a squire's country house. Pretentious curtain-hanging, and not quite right – shallow pelmets and garish fabrics. I was reminded of what David Crawford* once said to Christopher Wall at Hardwick [Hall, Derbyshire], that within a generation there would not be a soul left who knew what a country house really looked like.

Tuesday, 22nd October

Billa [Harrod] motored me to Blickling where we spent the day. The Administrator approached us with outstretched arms and said, 'I am taking you under my wing.' Quick as lightning Billa, with whom I had hoped to go round house alone, said, 'Not too much wing, please.' I feared this nice man, bearded like St Luke, would be affronted, but he joined us at the end of our tour and took us to see the conservation department. The bedrooms at Blickling are just like the pre-war bedrooms to which one was ushered on arrival. Whole house beautifully arranged and kept.

Thursday, 31st October

Invited to State Opening of Parliament by Patric Dickinson. Walked there after giving breakfast to Nick, who says he may get Nicky Johnston to build him a house near Tisbury. Arrived punctually at ten o'clock, queueing at Norman Arch. Ladies in best clothes. In Royal Gallery found Patric with co-heralds, looking out for me. Given seat at back, near entrance to Robing Room. A joy the whole thing, pure *Alice in Wonderland*. May the beauty, tradition and symbolism be preserved forever. Much to look at during hour before ceremony began. Duke of Norfolk† like genial teddy bear talking to daughters in row below me, they straightening his shaggy robes. Men in

---

* David Lindsay, 24th Earl of Crawford (1900–75); Chairman of N.T., 1945–65.
† Miles Fitzalan-Howard, 17th Duke of Norfolk (1915–2002); Hereditary Earl Marshal and Chief Butler of England.

black tailcoats, medals round necks. Then the toy soldiers, Queen's Bodyguard of Yeomen of the Guard, their hatbands seemingly interwoven with wild flowers, marching through to Prince's Chamber. Then Gentlemen at Arms, swan plumes waving from helmets, march through slowly, canes tapping rhythmically on carpet. Then Cap of Maintenance, Sword of State and Imperial Crown borne in, the last on a cushion by a page under escort. Then the Crown borne by Lord Great Chamberlain, the handsome young Lord Cholmondeley, looking slightly awkward and not carrying himself quite straight. Princess Margaret in dark velvet, Duchess of Gloucester looking distinguished. The Queen's three ladies, Fortune Grafton* in middle looking old and tired, flanked by fat Mrs Dugdale,† and Lady Airlie‡ looking very distinguished with bare back and fine high diamond collar. Queen looking bored, in spectacles, but splendid. A rustle as she enters, but no lights lowered or raised. Lord Chancellor§ robed in gold and black, the old robes of the peerage. Most males rather ugly. Heralds little better, except for naughty Terence McCarthy,¶ with his jolly, wicked face. I had a word with him when I arrived, he already tipsy at 10 a.m. He is a great embarrassment, Patric whispered, much as they love him. Hubert Chesshyre** also handsome though over fifty, and charming to talk to, which I did at stand-up luncheon at College of Arms to which Patric drove me afterwards in hired car. There I stood first on one foot then the other until hernia started playing up and leg ached.

The Royal Gallery is frankly ugly, all glittering gold, with that cheap, cardboard quality in which the mid Victorians sometimes indulged.

---

* Fortune Smith; Mistress of the Robes from 1967; m. 1946 11th Duke of Grafton.

† Kathryn Stanley (b. 1923; DCVO 1984); m. 1956 John Dugdale (b. 1923); Woman of the Bedchamber to HM The Queen from 1955.

‡ Virginia Ryan of Newport, R.I. (b. 1933); m. 1952 David Ogilvy, 13th Earl of Airlie (b. 1926; Lord Chamberlain, 1984-97); Lady of Bedchamber to HM The Queen from 1973.

§ Lord Mackay of Clashfern (b. 1927); Lord Chancellor, 1987-97.

¶ Terence McCarthy (1954-2003); Bluemantle Pursuivant, 1983-91; elder brother of John McCarthy (b. 1956), hostage in Beirut, 1986-91.

** Chester Herald of Arms, 1978-95, and Secretary to Order of the Garter, 1988-2003 (b. 1940).

But I am haunted by the fluttering (for it was a stormy morning and the wind blew straight up the stairs into the antechamber) of the swan feathers, snow white alternating with mauve grey; and the bustiness and aplomb of the Queen as though she did this daily, her voice a little deeper than usual in keeping with the dignity of the ceremony.

Saturday, 16th November

Today we lunched with the Richard Robinsons at the Old Mill, to see Julian Barrow's conversation piece of us two hanging. Visit spoiled by constant yelling of their child, a pretty little girl. I will never lunch again with my great-nephews, nor allow them to bring their bloody children to us. They can come and see us on their own, and I shall not go to their houses so long as their children are present.

Monday, 18th November

Tomorrow is our Ruby Wedding Day for which A. is making tremendous preparations, though we are merely having a few friends to dine. She said at breakfast how disappointed she had been by our honeymoon in November 1951, after that rather dismal wedding at Chelsea Registry Office, only attended, as I recall, by Harold and Vita, Freda and Lennox. We went to see my Aunt Deenie at Stow-on-the-Wold and then my mother, both in a bad way. Neither liked A. which put me in an embarrassed mood, I not having the character to rise above such things. Then we stayed the night at the Lygon Arms in Broadway [Worcestershire], whereas we should have gone abroad (in November?) to some delectable Mediterranean shore. It was a cloud upon our marriage, one of several that I now prefer not to dwell upon. She admitted that honeymoons were perhaps only really for young newlyweds, and we had after all enjoyed several 'pre-moons' during the preceding two or three years.

Tuesday, 19th November

We got out the best silver we have, scrubbed and polished, and prepared kitchen table for nine, rather a squash. Guests were the

Droghedas, Michael and Isobel Briggs, Nicky and Susanna Johnston, and Caroline [Beaufort]. It went all right, except that A. was worn out before it began. Dinner held up because Derry, who came by road, had to meet Alexandra's train, which was late for some reason. Caroline sensibly slipped away without goodbyes; the others stayed until 11.30, too long; Droghedas staying the night upstairs. No memorable conversation. I dislike artificial celebrations on the whole. A matter between us, and I believe we are made happy by it.

Wednesday, 4th December

Selina lunched with me in Bath, on her way to see a daughter of W. W. Jacobs* who was a childhood friend of Evelyn Waugh. She said there was no doubt that the aristocratic intelligentsia was the most desirable milieu in the civilised world; that it was not snobbish to want an entry, but a sign of sensibility and intelligence. Well, we have all known that, but she put it in a charming and forceful way which surprised me. I said, 'You were born into it.' No, she replied, for her father, though an earl, had little money and no country house.

Saturday, 14th December

Am reading in Painter's biography of Proust about the frightful misunderstanding between Proust and his mother. She, knowing that death is not far off, wishes to warn him without alarming him, and asks brightly, 'If I were to go away for a long time, and possibly not return, how would you manage?' Fearing to confirm her anxiety, or show how much he would mind, P. replies in a casual way, 'I would do fine, I wouldn't turn a hair.' With the result that both were made miserable. A vain attempt to achieve content by downright lying. I must say I was unaware of the depths of Sodom to which Proust descended, the cruelty too.

---

* Novelist and short story writer, author of *The Monkey's Paw* (1863–1943).

Thursday, 19th December

Grant McIntyre* rang me as soon as I arrived in Bath, to say he had read half of *Donors & Domains* in bed last night and is delighted with it. Looks forward to discussing it with me in new year. Well, this is the best Christmas greeting I could have had, and such a quick response too. Told M., who has had a similarly rapturous reception of the first half of his *Ribbentrop*. So both of us are pleased.

Sunday, 22nd December

While reading *Portrait of a Lady* – and I don't much care for the heroine Isabel – in a dreadful flash I suddenly saw no future whatsoever. My book is finished. I have no plans for another. The past stretches behind me longer than ever. The future is like an inch-long white ribbon before my nose.

Saturday, 28th December

Igor comes to stay on Christmas Eve. On Xmas Day, as we drive to luncheon at Stancombe, he asks, 'Are the Barlows aristocratic?' I tell him not to be snobbish, and that this is not a question one asks of anyone's friends. Interminable questions. 'How old are these Cotswold houses?' 'Do you think Tracy will make a good Duchess?' Having read my account of meeting and losing Theo† in that ridiculous book *Memorable Dinners*, he claims that he too has lost dozens of girls by writing his name and address on a piece of paper, failing to give it to the girl, and finding it in his pocket next day.

Today we lunch at Dyrham [Park, Gloucestershire] with the Mitchells, taking Igor who makes himself very agreeable, is well turned out and looks distinguished even. The other guests the Peter

---

* Director of John Murray, 1987–2003, and J.L.-M's editor there (b. 1944).
† Mysterious man whom the young J.L.-M. (as recounted in *Another Self*) met in London and with whom he formed an instant romantic attachment – though they accidentally returned their exchanged addresses to each other in the course of parting embraces, so never met again.

Levis,* both of whom I like much. He has had a small stroke, but is
mentally alert and full of anecdotes. Is three-quarters way through
biography of Tennyson. She is plain, with projecting teeth like the
eaves of a medieval cottage and eyes like a bloodhound's. She said that
Robert Heber-Percy would never meet her husband, he was so anti-
Semitic. Horrible man he was.

---

* Peter Levi (1931–2000); Jesuit priest (to 1977), Oxford classics don, archaeologist,
writer and poet; Professor of Poetry at Oxford, 1984–9; m. 1977 Deirdre *née* Craig,
widow of Cyril Connolly.

1992

1992

To Chatsworth, where I am given a tiny bedroom on top floor overlooking court. Diana [Mosley] staying, with son Ali and wife Char. Ali delightful and extremely intelligent, though unacquainted with nature and the country, Debo says. Char busy editing Nancy [Mitford]'s letters, from eight thousand of which she must select five hundred or so. Here I over-eat, sleep better than at home, and walk within the Kremlin walls.

Friday, 17th January

Two Sotheby's men lunch [at Chatsworth], James Mitchell, breezy and buoyant and telling me how pleased he is to renew an acquaintance which I have to dive into the memory to extract some clue to, and Lord Something Kerr,* small, docile man divorced from Grafton daughter. They leave after luncheon, and two visitors arrive for weekend, Dudley Poplak† and Lanto Synge.‡ Former South African, decorator of the Prince of Wales's houses. He shows us photographs of a house near Cape Town he has just done up, which both Debo and I deem awful. He talks about reincarnation, his pet subject. Debo says the P. of W. is coming tomorrow, and asks me to stay on. I hesitate, saying I had better get home. Then regret missing opportunity to observe at close quarters.

---

* Lord Ralph Kerr (b. 1957), yr s. of 12th Marquess of Lothian; m. 1st 1980 (diss. 1987) Lady Virginia FitzRoy, dau. of 11th Duke of Grafton, 2nd 1988 Marie-Claire Black.
† Interior designer (b. 1930).
‡ Antique dealer (b. 1945); great-nephew of J.M. Synge, Irish poet and playwright.

Saturday, 18th January

Again at breakfast Debo says, 'Why not stay on?' so I say yes, gladly. Truth is I don't want to be thought pushing where royalty is concerned.

After tea we all wait in the drawing room, uneasily. Escorted by Andrew and Debo, the Prince enters in breeches, stock and stockinged feet. Andrew whispers that he has had a good day [hunting], so thank goodness will be in a good temper. We stand in a circle. To me he says politely, 'Nice to see you again.' He proffers a hand, I grip fingers and bow. He subsides onto a sofa and whispers confidences to Debo. Then retires to change for dinner. We all rise, bow and curtsey, then relax. At dinner I sit between Synge, young-old man who has little to say to me, and Diana, fully engaged with Andrew. I hear the Prince opposite talking to Debo. When women leave the table, Dudley talks to the Prince about reincarnation, to Andrew's displeasure. Conversation turns to world situation. Prince laments that Christians are so disunited. Was upset by the outcry which prevented him accepting the Pope's invitation to attend a Catholic mass. Says he dearly loves the Italians, 'who are so nice to me'. He seems harassed and unhappy; also shy, with nervous mannerisms. We move to yellow drawing room, where Debo has displayed John Webb drawings of Whitehall Palace and Henry VII's Bible. We flip cursorily through these most precious things. Prince goes early to bed, whereupon everyone relaxes. There is no doubt that royalty causes constraint. When in my bath I decide that my remaining here has not had much reward; that the last few hours have been of dross.

Sunday, 19th January

Henry [the butler] calls me at 8.15 to say that breakfast will be earlier this morning, at 8.45. I hurry. On my way down meet the Prince issuing from centre bedroom. We greet and walk to dining room. He hopes I slept well. I thank him, wish him the same, and add, 'I believe you had a good day yesterday, Sir.' He says Yes, and there were no 'antis' for a change. Breakfast of all the men, joined by Debo. She must have thought I was not asserting myself, for she said, 'Sir, we owe more

to this man for the preservation of country houses than to anyone.'
For rest of breakfast we have a jolly talk. I feel this very sweet man is
deadly serious and worries more about the devastation caused to the
world's face than any other problem. He says he feels John Betjeman's
mantle has fallen on his shoulders. This is rather touching, but alas he
is too ignorant, groping for something which eludes. I somehow feel
that all his interests and commitments and speeches and writings are
too much for him, that he may have a breakdown. And the sadness of
his marriage. No one to share thoughts with. After breakfast Andrew
said that, had the Princess been present, we could never have had the
interesting conversation we had this morning.

Thursday, 23rd January

Dudley Poplak has sent me a book by George Trevelyan* on reincarnation and other psychic matters. A sort of erudite madness. The truth
is I don't know how much I want to re-establish contact with friends
of long ago. There would be little left in common, and juvenile links
and affections would surely be outdated.

Friday, 7th February

Last night we watched the film about the Queen for the fortieth anniversary of her accession. She is perfection, with her little understated
asides of wit, and such tact. Humorous, sensible, wise, wise. No intellectual could put up with her unenviable life. How lucky we are to
have her.

Tuesday, 25th February

We got back from our trip down the Nile yesterday, both utterly
exhausted. Sunshine all the way, and not too hot. Excellent Cook's

---

* Sir George Trevelyan, 4th Bt (1906–96); e. s. of Sir Charles Trevelyan, 3rd Bt,
donor of Wallington to N.T.; furniture maker, Alexander teacher, schoolmaster, and
Warden (1947–71) of Shropshire Adult College, Attingham Park; interested in the
beyond.

boat, with first-rate guide and scholarly Egyptian lecturer. The impression one gets is that Egypt is heading for disaster. Population increase appalling, one Egyptian born every second. Since our last visit in 1975 the building development along the banks of the Nile has increased tenfold. We moored at Luxor alongside 150 other boats. Tombs packed with sightseers, paintings and carvings suffering. And is the Nile drying up?

Saturday, 7th March

We dine at the House. David gloomy about world's future. Is sure that within a few years everyone who is 'comfortable' will need a permanent security guard, as in Brazil. Agrees that the great menace, next to the population explosion, is Muslim fundamentalism. Thinks the present Pope a remarkable man, who brought about the fall of world Communism; but the irony is that the world is a more dangerous place than before the fall of the Iron Curtain, with nuclear proliferation, the rise of nationalism, and the flood of refugees from East to West.

On Tuesday, 10 March, A.L.-M. felt unwell, with a pain in her left leg. Having been diagnosed as suffering from a heart-theatening virus, and fallen into a coma, she was sent to the intensive care unit of the Royal United Hospital in Bath, the doctor in charge putting her chances of recovery at fifty per cent.

J.L.-M. had grown close to his wife in recent years, and was distraught at her sudden collapse and the thought that he might be about to lose her. He continued to keep his diary 'to mitigate somewhat the agonising worry ... the worst misery I have ever endured'. For the next few weeks it consists largely of medical bulletins and accounts of her distressing condition, while noting the kindness and concern shown by many friends. He had gone so far as to start planning her funeral, when he was amazed to be telephoned by the hospital on the 21st with the news that she was 'waking' from her ten-day coma. He was still more amazed to find her sitting up and talking in French, a language she had not spoken regularly for thirty years. 'The change is stupendous.' A few days later, however, she suffered a relapse. On the 26th the doctor warned that the virus was attacking the replacement heart valve installed two years earlier, and J.L.-M. would have to decide whether to authorise intensive treat-

ment with antibiotics which risked leaving her brain-dead, or to let things take their course. With a heavy heart, he chose the latter alternative. However, during the following days A.L.-M. again rallied remarkably, and by the beginning of April it looked as if she might recover to lead a reasonably normal life.

Thursday, 2nd April

The head-doctor Dr Hall saw her this morning, so I went to hospital with Freda [Berkeley] to lie in wait. Imagine our amazement when he sallied out of her room to say, 'Well, it is almost a miracle. From death's door she is doing well. Heart and valve perfectly all right, also kidneys; the knee infection gone, the swelling being septicaemic arthritis. She can put on clothes tomorrow, and go to a convalescent home quite soon . . .' F. and I were *bouleversés*, not knowing what to feel or where to look, fearing to rejoice. When we got home I went for a two-mile walk along Luckington Lane, picking primroses growing in the ditches over the streamlets to take to A. next morning.

Friday, 3rd April

I take Freda to station. Never could I imagine a better friend or greater consolation in unhappiness than she. Then to A., complaining much and very sleepy. Sit beside her while she sleeps.

Grant McIntyre comes at 1 for a snack lunch. I surrender to him my corrected copy of N.T. book, now to be called by title of my original choice, *People and Places*. We go through the photographs, with which he is pleased. I like this charming, shy, clever man more than ever.

Saturday, 4th April

To A. at 10, she demanding things I have not brought and rejecting those I have. Good signs. I arrange with her hairdresser to come tomorrow at 2.

Monday, 6th April

Mrs Weideger,* American lady writing about National Trust, called in Bath by appointment made before A's illness. Smart, well-dressed woman, bringing huge poodle on leash. Said that Commander Rawnsley† – the dreadful man is still active, it appears – criticises my period at the Trust for being 'obscured by homosexual and snobbish elements'. He also accuses Bobby Gore of supplying vintage wine to his upper class friends and plonk to lower grades. And Len Clark,‡ proletarian busybody on Trust committees, describes Robin [Fedden], Bobby and myself as 'courtiers of the Establishment'. I have always been aware of having enemies in Trust circles.

[Clarissa's boyfriend] Billy has gone into a deep depression; sits silently, head in hands, speechless, with curtains drawn, gazing at television and not taking in, a spectre at the table. Clarissa explains that such moods may last two months. Thank God they both leave tomorrow for a few days. C. is being very good with her mother I must admit. It is now my intention to devote my entire life to A., subordinating all other interests.

Wednesday, 8th April

A. is better still. Really in good form, reading letters of commiseration received during her illness, though too quickly to convince me that she properly takes them in. She had her first meal today of meat and veg. When I got home I walked for a mile up Luckington Lane to throw off cobwebs, and after supper listened to Vivaldi's Flute Concerto Op. 10, most wonderful.

---

* Her book was *Gilding the Acorn* (Simon & Schuster, 1994).
† Commander Conrad Rawnsley (1907–97), grandson of a co-founder of the N.T., and director of its successful 'Enterprise Neptune' to save a thousand miles of unspoilt coastline, had issued a violent public attack on the organisation in the autumn of 1966, claiming that it was run by aristocrats for aristocrats and ignored 'the leisure pursuits of the people as a whole'. He was heavily defeated when he proposed radical reforms to the N.T's constitution at an E.G.M. in February 1967 – though his criticisms did encourage a trend of substantial changes over the ensuing years.
‡ He was the link between the N.T. and the Youth Hostel Association, and much appreciated by both institutions.

Friday, 10th April

This morning I turned on TV news to hear about the predicted Labour victory.* When they spoke of re-election of Tories, I at first thought a joke, and turned to wireless for confirmation. It just shows that the majority of the population is now middle-class aspirant, for it is the money in their pockets which governs the way people vote.

Saturday, 11th April

On leaving A., Freda and I drive to Castle Combe to dine with John Julius and Mollie [Norwich]. In the spring evening sunlight their little house is very enviable, set in its secret dell where no officious journalists or teasers can find him. J.J. says it is a treat to hear Princess Margaret sparking up the Queen. The Q. then plays Princess M. up, and both are incredibly funny and witty, parodying pompous royal pronouncements of long ago.

Monday, 13th April

Freda returns to London and I to my library. Feel desperately lonely. I realise that I was never lonely in the past because I knew A. was there twelve miles away and I was going to rejoin her in the evening. However, I shall see her this evening in hospital. Finish letter-writing and think of beginning my piece on Sachie [Sitwell] for *DNB*.

Wednesday, 15th April

It was five weeks ago today that A. was taken to Bath Clinic. During the afternoon Princess Michael telephones, full of sympathy and asking me to lunch on Sunday at Nether Lypiatt. Charming of her and I accept, though it will be Easter Sunday.

---

* The general election on 9 April confounded the pollsters by returning John Major's Conservatives to power with a majority of 11.

Thursday, 16th April

Clarissa and Billy come to stay, self-invited. Over dinner I tell C. that her mother, now she is in full possession of her wits again, is irritated by her attitude, lovey-dovey stuff interlarded with endless 'darling Mamas'. Clarissa bursts into tears and leaves the room. I am left with the 'lunatic', who by way of making conversation asks me whether I don't think a little selfishness is a good thing. No, I say, any more than cruelty and spitefulness are good things.

Saturday, 18th April

At 1.20 Princess Michael rings me up in Bath to ask why I have not turned up for luncheon. Horrors! I grovel and say I thought she said Sunday; indeed, I was puzzled that she should have asked me on Easter Sunday. She is charming and assures me I will be welcome tomorrow, although they will have a large family party. Why do I get involved with these people? I have been reading her *Cupid and the King*. A poor show for a Royal to write such half-baked pseudo-porn.

Sunday, 19th April

I get to Nether Lypiatt with plenty of time to spare. A smiling young pansy butler greets and takes coat and ushers. Party consists of father, mother, son[*] and daughter;[†] also the Princess's mother, charming and distinguished Madame Zippari who talks little but listens. And a nice, jolly, bright American couturier called Roberto Devorik, friend of the family. Luncheon in dining room with rare plates in every panel of the white-painted wainscot. Princess kisses me and accepts peace-offering of expensive chocolates. 'Oh, more chocolates, how kind.' Indeed the table groaning with Easter eggs, chocolate rabbits, etc. The poor children bored throughout, as we sat from 1.30 to 4 while the Princess discoursed, almost lectured, on the subject of Mariolatry, how the rise of culture coincided with the enslavement of women and

---

[*] Lord Frederick Windsor (b. 1979).
[†] Lady Gabriella Windsor (b. 1981).

its fall with their emancipation, the current age of women's lib being the age of the yob. She quoted from Aristotle, early Church fathers, Renaissance sages, down to present day. Then told us about a book she is reading about the Duke of Clarence,* suggesting that he did not die of typhoid as supposed but was murdered as he had secretly married a Roman Catholic. (How can they believe this tosh?) She gave me a copy to take away, along with two bottles of her own home-made jam. She is kind, well-intentioned and affectionate. But of course bossy, picks on daughter who may later turn against her. Boy is handsome and clever with excellent manners, hopes to get scholarship to Eton. Prince Michael adores the children who clearly worship him. We had everything but crackers on the table, a kind of mid-European, Orthodox Easter. Princess Michael still beautiful with remarkable clear skin and fair hair, very fresh and appealing. How good they were to welcome me, a comparative stranger, in their Easter midst.

Tuesday, 21st April

While I was sitting with A. this evening, a nurse told her that she could have her own room if she wanted. A. immediately said No, she preferred to stay where she was. Before this illness she would never have said such a thing. But the darling is right. She would be lonely shut up in a little room, whereas in the ward there is perpetual coming and going.

Friday, 24th April

So the days pass, one like another, no weekend breaks to punctuate. I go to Bath every day, see her in the morning and the evening, fetch the things she asks for, try to work during the afternoon in my library. I hold desperately on to my wits as a man holds on to his hat while

---

* HRH Prince Albert Victor, Duke of Clarence and Avondale (1864–92); e. s. of Albert, Prince of Wales (the future King Edward VII); died soon after engagement to Princess May of Teck (the future Queen Mary). Much speculation has surrounded the demise of this weak and debauched character, who appeared far from suitable as future monarch.

crossing a desolate moor in a whirlwind. I am all right left to myself, but frustrated by the chores with which A. normally copes, especially dealing with gardeners. And I have hardly had the chance to look at the garden this glorious spring, with crown imperials fully out and even cowslips. It is no earthly pleasure to me, but has to be kept going for darling A., who may never see it again. I must not beef but count my blessings, as I used to say to myself during the war at times when the overhanging clouds seemed to darken every pleasure.

Tuesday, 28th April

Nick [Robinson] came to dine. We had finished the shepherd's pie and were about to begin on the strawberries when the telephone rang, and a voice said that A. had had a fall, but I was not to worry. I said that since they saw fit to tell me at 9.15, I did worry. Angelic Nick motored me to the hospital where A. was fast asleep, face serene and so pretty. We decided not to wake her. We left on tiptoe, I gulping with sorrow, and returned to Badminton for cake and coffee.

The following day, A.L.-M. was moved to Malmesbury Hospital for her convalescence. This was an inconvenience for J.L.-M., involving as it did a twenty-five-mile drive from Bath.

Thursday, 7th May

The doctor in Malmesbury reads me a letter from the doctor in Bath to say that A. now seems to have no infection of the leg or any other part, and he sees no reason why she should not in time recover to her condition before this devastating illness, and walk again. Almost too good to believe.

In state of elation I take train to Paddington for my first night in London for more than two months. Object of visit the Pavilion Opera's *Elisir d'Amore* at Brooks's. I take Freda in lieu of poor A. Very good indeed, perhaps slightly too noisy for the small rooms. We then have a not very good dinner, sitting at a table with Lionel Sackville's brother and shy wife. Derek [Hill] came for a drink before Freda arrived, and catalogued the smart friends he had been consorting with.

1992

Friday, 8th May

In the morning I go up the street to John Murray's to hand in final typescript [of *People and Places*] to Gail Pirkis.* Why Gail, I ask, so cold, misty and Scandinavian? She says short for Abigail. Nice young woman, married with children,† and good over punctuation. Extravagantly I buy expensive cardigan made of silky wool, and some French socks. Lunch alone at Brooks's. I catch an afternoon train and motor from Chippenham to Malmesbury. So I have not missed a single day's visit to A. since her illness began two months ago.

Saturday, 16th May

I drove to Malmesbury and stayed about an hour. Then drove to Bath. Having opened door of flat I went to fetch something from motor. Front door slammed behind me, keys within. No other inmate present at No. 19. Had to motor home to Badminton to fetch spare keys. Then to Union Street for Clarissa's picture opening. One large room, formerly part of Owen & Owen's shop. Clarissa stunning in white dress. Paintings well-hung – Billy's work – but mostly rubbish. Young artists milling self-consciously. C. introduced 'my stepfather' to sub-editor of *Daily Telegraph*, one Connell.‡ I bought a little painting of three Turkish women like Byzantine icon, and left. Felt like Lady Catherine de Burgh swanning in and out. When I got home I estimated I had motored more than a hundred miles this afternoon.

Sunday, 17th May

Lunched with Elspeth [Huxley], who asked my advice. She had discovered that Peter Scott was passionately in love with a Cambridge friend called John. When John became engaged, Peter was distraught. He wrote to a third friend, Michael, that John's marriage meant the end of existence for him. John is still alive. Should Elspeth mention

---

* Managing Editor, John Murray, 1987–2003 (b. 1957).
† Her son, Max Pirkis, was to achieve fame as a boy actor in films.
‡ Jolyon Connell; deputy editor, *Sunday Telegraph*; subsequently founding editor of *The Week*; m. 1989 Lady Alexandra Hay, sister of 24th Earl of Erroll.

the affair in her biography? Should she reveal that her hero had feet of clay? But why clay, I asked. It makes him more human than I thought he was. One might have expected the affair to have been platonic in that pre-1914 way, although Peter's widow maintains this was not the case. However Elspeth does it, it is sure to be well done.

Tuesday, 19th May

James Methuen-Campbell* came to tea, bicycling from Corsham. He is a cousin of the dreaded John,† and great-nephew of Paul whose memory he venerates. Nice man of thirty-five, plain oval face reminding me of Terence O'Neill,‡ similar self-deprecatory manner. Has been music critic of *The Times* and other papers, and written a book on Chopin. His biography of Denton Welch§ comes out this autumn. He met dozens of people who remember Denton, including a doctor with whom D. was passionately in love. Doctor did not reciprocate, but was fond of him. After D. died, doctor married a woman who goes into a towering rage whenever D's name mentioned. Really, the idiocy and jealousy of which women are capable.

Thursday, 21st May

I dined with the Morrisons. It would be difficult not to fall in love with Rosalind if one were younger. She said the Lygons had made an offer for Madresfield (they already own a life interest in 60 per cent of the contents) and the Danes had to decide whether to accept. If they refuse, Ros will not have the chance of getting the estate for another thirty years, the Danish grandson of old Lady Beauchamp being still

---

* Grandson (b. 1952) of Hon. Laurence Methuen (yst bro. of Paul, 4th Baron Methuen) and Hon. Olive Campbell (only dau. of 4th Baron Blythwood); inherited Corsham estate on death of John, 6th Baron Methuen, 1995; heir presumptive to 7th Baron Methuen from 1998; writer and musicologist.
† John, 6th Baron Methuen (1925–95); nephew of Paul; scouting enthusiast.
‡ Hon. Terence O'Neill (1914–90); brother of J.L.-M's friend 'Midi' Gascoigne; Prime Minister of Northern Ireland, 1963–9; cr. life peer, 1970; m. 1944 Jean Whitaker (sister of J.L.-M's friend Billy).
§ Novelist and diarist (1915–48).

fairly young (as well as odious). If they do go to Madresfield they will sell this house which they have made so delightful and pretty. They know few people in Worcestershire, yet Ros longs for her native seat. Charlie delighted to be free of Parliament. He conveyed good news that his father* is at last repairing the marvellous boathouse which Alderman Beckford built at Fonthill and which I tried so hard years ago to get this philistine old man to save from perdition.

Friday, 22nd May

A. home at last after ten weeks, driven from Malmesbury by efficient lady officer called Bridget. I pushed her in her wheelchair around the garden, which looked green and lush and I think pleased her. Not only is she immobile, but she can do practically nothing for herself. Things are out of reach, telephone has to be answered by me and she asked if she wishes to speak. By end of day I was absolutely whacked, having gone up and down stairs a million times. Dreadful to admit, but by 10 p.m. I showed irritability, and told her she was very demanding. Awful of me, but true.

Tuesday, 26th May

Tropical weather for past week. A. doing wonderfully. I have to recognise that I am no longer an independent being. My day begins at 7.15 when I rise, draw back her blinds, empty her commode, descend to fetch her orange juice. Having shaved and dressed myself I boil her egg, lay tray, carry her breakfast up to her in bed. Then dear Peggy comes and gives her a bath.

Saturday, 30th May

And so the days go on. Dreadful for her not to be able to fetch a book from a shelf, a cushion to sit on the terrace, anything. I confess there

---

* John Morrison (1906–96) of Fonthill House, Wiltshire; Conservative politician, MP for Salisbury, 1942–64, Chairman of 1922 Committee, 1955–64; MFH, 1932–65; m. 1928 Hon. Margaret Smith, yr dau. of 2nd Viscount Hambleden; cr. 1st Baron Margadale, 1965.

are moments when the devil gets into me and I am tempted to take revenge on her in little ways. I lack all intellectual stimulus, and physical exercise apart from endless climbing of stairs. I am miserable at not being able to get down to work. In between her calls for aid I have been trying to finish Sachie's *DNB* entry. Much trouble to make it concise. I asked the editor to allow me more than 750 words; she has conceded 900, but I have still not got down to that figure. Am sending draft to Francis [Sitwell] to check.

Sunday, 14th June

We lunched at the House, A's first meal away from home. She walked from the motor through the House to the east lawn where we ate under two enormous umbrellas. Unfortunately David lost his temper with Caroline for muddling the seating arrangements. C. said not a word in return, and we shunted round, looking down our noses at our feet. My neighbour, friend of Anne and Matthew [Carr], said that a famous New York decorator had had a room copied from my library in Bath. Must have been from Julian Barrow's painting, I think.

A's sole interest is now the garden – her own, not others'. She doesn't seem interested in anything else. She sits with a pad on her knees, making notes of orders to give the gardeners.

Monday, 22nd June

Midsummer already, but cold. Went to London to return corrected proofs to Murray, along with postscript. So the book is at last done. Young John* came into the room and made polite conversation, saying he had read and enjoyed. Then J.K.-B. and Jamie Fergusson lunched at Brooks's, not a great success. Jamie, very spruce in new suit and haircut, thought Murray's were in a precarious condition and living on expectations from Paddy L.F. I fear Jim L.-M. will not help them much. Their great asset is their freehold of No.50. How tragic if they had to sell.†

---

* John Murray VII, heir to publishing house, then running the marketing department.
† In 2002, the family sold the firm (to Hodder Headline) and kept the house.

Wednesday, 24th June

Hugh Massingberd rang to announce that Johnnie Churchill died yesterday, and ask if I would write a short appreciation. Dear Johnnie, so eccentric and absurd. What memories – of Didbrook and Stanway in 1928,* and Rome in 1930 during the royal wedding.† We used to laugh endlessly. He never grew up. Was always clowning, 'the parlour-trick man' as Lady Chetwode called him. He irritated my father at tennis, for he would not take the game seriously, yet generally won. Signed his letters to me 'Chunluli' after some foreign hotel porter's misreading of his surname. He was affectionate and unwise; a gallant lover; a terrible boozer which made him difficult to meet in later years, for he would embarrass one in a stuffy club with his outrageous behaviour. Yet his blue eyes spelt honesty and courage. (His uncle Winston once assured me he was full of guile, but I didn't then and don't now believe it.)

Tuesday, 30th June

Motored in terrific heat to Johnnie's funeral at Bladon [near Blenheim Palace, Oxfordshire]. Church full of strangers in dark suits. No familiar face. Goodish address. Two Crewe grandchildren read extracts, but too hurriedly, as if wanting to be done. Followed coffin to graveyard, passing graves of Lord Randolph, Winston and our Randolph,‡ all with placards for convenience of tourists. Johnny buried against far wall next to his last love. I could not face beano at The Bear, Woodstock. Instead drove to Asthall to look at the Manor, so beautiful looming over the Norman church. Then stopped at Swinbrook to

* As J.L.-M. relates in *Another Self*, he and Johnnie Churchill crammed for Oxford with the eccentric Vicar of Didbrook and Stanway, 'benefices in the patronage of Lord Wemyss'.

† The marriage on 8 January 1930 of Prince Umberto, only son of King Victor Emmanuel III of Italy, to Princess Marie José, only dau. of King Albert of the Belgians.

‡ Lord Randolph Churchill (1849–95), yr s. of 7th Duke of Marlborough, Unionist statesman; his son Sir Winston (1874–1965), Prime Minister and indomitable war leader; Sir Winston's only son Randolph (1911–68), J.L.-M's Eton and Oxford contemporary.

see Tom [Mitford]'s memorial, 'a very perfect son and brother', and Nancy's little gravestone, her name and mole insignia almost obliterated by moss and elements.*

Wednesday, 1st July

Today the *Daily Telegraph* asked me for a paragraph on my favourite country house. I said that I would have chosen Stanway, had not Hugh Massingberd already praised it last Saturday; instead selected Moccas [Court, Herefordshire] for its remoteness and melancholy. I wrote rather a silly letter to Sally [Ashburton],† excusing myself for having been such a hopeless godfather. Explained that her christening and upbringing in the C. of E. coincided with my becoming a Catholic. As I subsequently left the R.C. church, this hardly justifies my neglect.

Friday, 3rd July

Spent much of the day in Bath pasting old snapshots of Johnnie Churchill into my photograph book. When I got home, Thomas Messel rang to announce that Anne Rosse died at midday. Heart attack, aged ninety. No surprise, nor do I feel any particular sadness. Funeral next Thursday at Womersley [Yorkshire], all arranged by Anne. A. mentioned that Hugh Massingberd had rung earlier, doubtless wanting an obituary. A., who never liked her, said I would have lots to write, mentioning her considerable horticultural knowledge, and sparkling personality which could never be ignored. Yes, I said, but I hope I won't be asked.

---

* Two Oxfordshire properties inhabited by Mitford family between the wars. In 1919 2nd Baron Redesdale bought the Jacobean Asthall Manor on the River Windrush, where J.L.-M. stayed as a schoolboy with his friend Tom. It was sold in 1926, and Lord Redesdale built Swinbrook House, described by his grandson Jonathan Guinness as 'an unremarkable, rather insipid square building in Cotswold stone, such as councillors might have erected as a cottage hospital' (*The House of Mitford*, p.289). It was sold in 1938.

† Sarah ('Sally') Churchill (b. 1935); o. dau. of Johnnie Churchill and Angela Culme-Seymour; goddaughter of J.L.-M.; m. 1st 1957 James Colin Crewe, 2nd 1987 John Baring, 7th Baron Ashburton.

Wednesday, 8th July

To Eton for the day to meet Michael Meredith,* who met me on the steps of Timbrall's House (which was Slater's when I was up, and has been much improved since then). Delightful man, bachelor house-master, brimming with enthusiasm and a great expert on literary anecdotes and holographs. Has formed the finest collection of Browningiana, including rare photographs and possessions of the poet, all paid for out of his income as a schoolmaster. Boys away on holiday, for which I was glad. He gave me luncheon in the cheerful dining room. He said that Martin Charteris and Eric Anderson formed a perfect combination the like of which Eton may never see again. Why, I asked, was Martin so remarkable? Because of his enthu-siasm, and wise adoption of all good schemes. Meredith seemed genuinely delighted with my gift of lockets of Byron's and Dickens's hair, and especially with the authenticating letters from Augusta Leigh and Georgina Hogarth. By the time we had seen the School Library and looked at the treasures he had kindly got out to show me, it was 4.30 and time to return.

An enjoyable visit and I feel I have found a new friend. Meredith is not an Etonian himself I fancy, though he is dedicated to the school, and has undoubtedly done wonders for the Library, which he loves. Said his brother was a master at Stowe, where they have had much trouble since the school went co-educational. When girls get to sixteen or seventeen they become tiresomely flirtatious and cause much mischief; sex behind bushes and abortions ensue. Luckily Eton has not yet committed itself, the Headmaster against.

Thursday, 9th July

To Anne Rosse's funeral at Womersley [Park, near Doncaster], the *Independent* having published my obituary yesterday which I fear the family will not have liked overmuch. By train to Doncaster with the Thomas Messels, from where we taxied to Womersley, where

---

* Head of English, housemaster, and School (later College) Librarian at Eton (b. 1936); President of Browning Society.

mourners assembled for stand-up luncheon. Martin* looking like Mervyn the Badminton gamekeeper, florid-faced, thickset and bois- terous in charming puppylike way; William Rosse by contrast frail and slight, and very Irish. Having not seen them for so long, I had little to say to them, though they were very sweet to me. Lucy Snowdon a darling, and William's wife nice and unassuming. Service done in great theatrical style of which I approved. Tony [Snowdon] had arranged a marvellous display of white flowers in front of the Bodley roodscreen. Two priests, one Irish swinging a censer. Anne's coffin invisible under a golden pall smothered with wreaths and raised on a catafalque. Three lessons read by the three sons, all beautifully. John Cornforth† gave a long address of which I heard little, being the far side of the nave. People said it was good, but what I heard sounded rather conventional to me. He is a stiff pudding. Six young men, one a grandson wearing pony tail, carried the coffin slowly down the nave through the west door, across the graveyard into the grounds of the house, where they put it into the hearse, a handsome, streamlined, modern motor. From her own front door Anne was driven away for the last time, with great dignity and in total silence. Moving moment.

This sympathetic, unknown, beautiful, simple old house within its white limestone park walls has no land left to speak of, and is too large one would suppose for the impoverished Martin and his family. I shall never go there again. I had a last look at Anne's little boudoir wherein she lived during the war, with Oliver [Messel]'s dazzling portrait of her, and the great, stiff, rather gloomy neoclassical room redolent of 'that splendid monster Lois', as Anne's friend Phoebe Davis described Lady de Vesci.‡

Anne had the distinction of having two sons who were earls and three grandsons who were viscounts or barons at her funeral, along with ladies and hons galore.

---

* Hon. Martin Parsons (b. 1938); yr s. of 6th Earl of Rosse and Anne Messel; lived at Womersley.

† Architectural historian (1937–2004) on staff of *Country Life*.

‡ Lois Lister-Kaye (1882–1984); m. 1st 1905 5th Earl of Rosse (d. 1918), 2nd 1920 5th Viscount de Vesci (d. 1958); mother of Michael, 6th Earl of Rosse (d. 1979).

Wednesday, 15th July

A party of Irish ladies came to see the garden. They were most appreciative. One of them said to me, 'This of course is the house where *Winnie the Pooh* was written.' I had to tell her that regretfully this was not the case, nor was I Christopher Robin.* I heard one lady ask another, 'Who are they?' to get the reply, 'They made their money out of tassels.' Tassels is rather nice; but *what* money?

Monday, 20th July

These days, I find I can seldom discuss a subject with A. which is not concerned with our household affairs. She seems not to listen if I try to talk about anything else. Or rather, she is not interested in anything apart from the garden and her grandchildren, of which I can only admire the first and am bored and irritated by the second.

Thursday, 6th August

My birthday. A shock to see announced in *The Times* and *Telegraph* that I am eighty-four. A most beautiful day, with just a suspicion of crisp lawn, and slanting golden sunshine. I motored to Wickhamford with A. and Clarissa. While A. remained in the car I made C. climb the gate to the field facing the manor and we walked to the hedge between field and pond. She seemed to enjoy this, and when we went round to the church she claimed to be overwhelmed by the beauty of the nave and monuments. Door still kept unlocked. How much longer before the tombs are vandalised? The tranquillity of the graveyard. I think I would like my ashes scattered here.

At dinner, Clarissa announced to us both that she was considering marriage to Billy. What did we think? A. said she thought it a good idea. I said Billy was too unstable, with the full moon and all. A. later came round to my opinion and said that on reflection she opposed the marriage. C. will pay no heed of course. Why should she?

---

* They were presumably confusing J.L.-M. with the children's writer A.A. Milne (1882–1956).

Friday, 14th August

Ian Dixon drives us to Chatsworth, where Debo presses him to stay to tea. This he does not do, I imagine from shyness. I accompany him to the door and give him a cheque for £80 to cover his kind service and the petrol. I am given the centre bedroom in which Dickens and Prince Charles have slept. Am fascinated by the bed canopy, with pink dome of either bees swarming or little roses. The sheets of the beds are starched at the top ends in the old-fashioned way. My hand towel dated 1907. A. is given the centre dressing room which I usually have, because the bed is low and nearer to the bathroom. Also staying for the weekend are Woman and her friend Margaret Budd,* E. Winn† and Peter Maitland.‡

Monday, 17th August

Young Patrick James§ comes [to Chatsworth] for the night. He wishes to talk with me about the National Trust, for he is writing with Jennifer Jenkins yet another book, to appear in the centenary year of 1995.¶ A delightful boy, aged twenty-three or so and extremely bright. Beautiful manners and asks very pertinent questions. We sat after dinner in the yellow drawing room talking till late. He said he had seen a photograph of me staying at his great-grandmother's house in Yorkshire, as a friend of his grandmother, Helen Baring.** I only just remember, though don't recall the name of the house. Lady Ulrica was a sister of the beautiful Lady D'Abernon; the daughter was dark and plain, but nice.

---

* Margaret Cross (b. 1917); friend of Pamela Jackson; m. George Budd, who had served in the same wartime RAF squadron as Pamela's ex-husband.

† Interior designer (b. 1925), renowned for her mimicry.

‡ Group Chief Executive, Mallett plc, 1993–97 (b. 1937).

§ Patrick Esmond James (b. 1967); landscape expert.

¶ *From Acorn to Oak Tree: The Growth of the National Trust, 1895–1994* (Macmillan 1994).

** Helen Baring (b. 1906); er dau. of Brig.-Gen. Hon. Everard Baring, yr s. of 1st Baron Revelstoke, and Lady Ulrica Duncombe, yst dau. of 1st Earl of Feversham; m. 1939 Major Gordon Foster; their daughter Rosanna (b. 1941) m. 1965 Professor Hon. Oliver James.

Tuesday, 18th August

Feeble comes to luncheon, bringing Frank Tait and a couple called Hubbard – she a Trustee of National Gallery, he a gardener and painter. We motor up the hill and walk round the lakes. Beautiful day, sun and cloud and long shadows. Hardy Amies comes for the night. He is very bent, but brain very much all right. Full of smart talk and amusing stories. At dinner he speaks fascinatingly about men's fashions since the eighteenth century.

Andrew eats little, and looks thin and drawn. Is inclined to be moody. Told A., only half in jest, that she was being disagreeable; and when I mentioned the Glorious Revolution, said sharply, 'If it hadn't been for it you wouldn't be sitting here now.' I don't feel altogether at ease, yet we get on. When we leave he protests that our visit has brought him joy and presses us to come for Christmas.

I have been reading a proof copy of M's *Ribbentrop*. A marvellous biography, absolutely first rate. Perhaps a bit too long towards the end. He tells me it is already shortlisted for the *Yorkshire Post* prize, though only estimated to sell 2,000 copies.

Monday, 24th August

Francis Sitwell called at No. 19 this afternoon and took away some eight of Sachie's books. I said I would not part with them to anyone else. At the last moment I witheld *Southern Baroque Art*, which I could not bear to part with. Francis now a beefy middle-aged man. He venerates Sachie, and wants to build up a library of all his books. Told me he believed that his father's Alzheimer's was caused by the kitchen at Weston using aluminium saucepans. Apparently stewed fruit, which Sachie liked to eat most days, causes dangerous effects on the brain when cooked in this metal. Also believed S. was not awarded an honour until so late because Michael De-la-Noy* quoted in the press S's remark to him in private that Queen Victoria purposely employed homosexuals in her household as they were unlikely to interfere with the ladies-in-waiting and maids of honour.

---

* Writer (1934–2002), interested in royal and ecclesiastical subjects.

Wednesday, 26th August

A most enjoyable day. Tony Mitchell motored me to Herefordshire, that nostalgic county. A relief to be away from the stone-wall country for a change. Tall, lush hedgerows engulf narrow lanes. We first visited Hope End. Much improvement since I was last there. It has been bought by a couple called Hegarty, she the daughter of a prosperous local farmer. They have constructed a small and exclusive hotel out of the back regions, where we had coffee and bought her cookery book. Few remains of the house known to Elizabeth Barrett, though the minaret still conspicuous. Such a charming setting, in a hollow with stream at east boundary. How Eardley would have loved it. Then back to Ledbury, still a beautiful small town surrounded by country. Visited huge church with detached tower and spire to inspect Biddulph monuments. One, a figure under a canopy of flowing drapery, is dated 1630 and must be about the first Baroque sculpture in England.

After lunch we drove to Eastnor where we lingered long. The castle an unromantic structure, which looks as if machine-made. Smirke was not an imaginative architect. Great hall frankly hideous and splits the house in twain. Family still resides, youngish couple who seem to be doing well. The best room is the fan-vaulted drawing room by Pugin. Splendid Pugin chandelier of mock brass; splendid views from windows of unspoilt country. Tony an admirable companion on such an expedition. How bored our wives would have been, we reflected. In Eastnor churchyard we saw terracotta figures by the infamous Lady Henry Somerset, David Beaufort's great-grandmother. Rather beautiful, with a whiff of Pre-Raphaelitism. (Indeed, her family, the Somers, had a connection with the Pre-Raphaelites through Mrs Cameron.*)

I have decided that, as one of my recreations in *Who's Who*, I might include 'Visiting the haunts of illustrious writers and artists'.

Wednesday, 2nd September

Whenever a radio announcer refers to the millions in East Africa dying of starvation, hoping to wring my heart strings and get me to

---

* Julia Margaret Cameron (1815–79); photographer and Pre-Raphaelite artist; aunt of Lady Henry Somerset.

send some money, a dreadful elation rises within me. Fewer people, I say to myself, no bad thing. Then I feel slightly ashamed of myself, though not as much as I should.

Monday, 14th September

Went to see Clive Charlton at Bath Clinic. He said, 'At your age you can't expect to be wholly sane. Stop fussing, you have had a very good innings.'

Misha comes from London for picnic luncheon. I enjoy having him. He has developed the eccentric trick when making a profound statement of twisting his head to one side and lowering it towards the floor, then raising it, looking one straight in the eyes, and lowering it on the other side. He brings me the first copy of his *Ribbentrop*, handsomely produced. I say his illustrations are better than mine. Yes, he says, but then my book costs a penny more than yours.

Tuesday, 15th September

Went blackberrying. Most heavenly evening, still and golden with mist. Glowing ball of sun casting woolly shadows. The park never more beautiful. I stop at the circular wood I call Folly's Spinney, from which I fill my plastic pudding bowl full of foaming jet blackberries. My thoughts are all of darling Folly, sensing her a little ahead of me, plucking the fruit and eating it in the way she alone of dogs used to do, and looking up with those beseeching golden eyes. It is a year and a half since she died and I still adore and miss her more than Anne Rosse, Johnny Churchill, Sheila Birkenhead or any of the friends lately gone.

Monday, 21st September

To London for the day. At Murray's I signed sixteen copies of *People and Places* for them to send. [Young] John spoke bitterly about the refusal of the National Trust to sell the book in their shops or even review it in their magazine. He is sending copies to the Chairman

Lord Chorley* and Director-General Angus Stirling with letters of protest. He also talked of Jock's illness, hip trouble on top of prostate trouble. Poor Jock, always so jokey and debonair, has gone into deepest depression from which they fear he will not recover.

Thursday, 1st October

I never liked Francis Watson† much, though he was good company. Always in good cheer, gossipy, mischievous, informative. Pleased with himself, very. Always the society man, but scratch the surface and there was a little bounder. One was pleased to see him, while dreading what he would say about one at the next party he attended. Undoubtedly very clever, and an expert on French artefacts. Not Keeper of the Wallace Collection for nothing. Jane a rather dreadful woman, who revelled in the discomfiture of others. Why they married God alone knows; presumably both wished to keep up the pretence of being the marrying sort.

Wednesday, 21st October

I lunch with Hugh Massingberd at Travellers. He is flattering about *P. and P.*, which he is reviewing in *Sunday Telegraph*. Is enormous; eats voraciously, ending with rice pudding. Recently had a cancerous growth removed, almost disappointed not to be told he had six months to live. So is writing an article on death.

Saturday, 31st October

All this week I have been having a swimgloat over reception of *P. and P.* Splendid notice on *Times* middle page; first-rate review by Peter Levi in *Spectator*, *Country Life*. Much fan mail from friends and strangers. When the girl called my name in the dentist's waiting room, a man came up to me and asked to shake my hand. *House and Garden*

---

* Roger, 2nd Baron Chorley (b. 1930); accountant, member of government committees; Chairman of N.T., 1991–6.
† Sir Francis Watson (1907–92); Director, Wallace Collection, 1963–74; Surveyor of Queen's Works of Art, 1963–72; m. 1941 Mary 'Jane' Grey (d. 1969).

has asked to interview me. *The Field* has begged me to write to the
new head of English Heritage protesting at their decision to shed half
their historic monuments to local authorities. At moments euphoria
has wafted me to such heights of confidence that I feel I can still write
almost anything.

Freda much upset by the proofs of Carpenter's life of Britten.* She
has asked for two nasty references to Lennox to be removed, one to
the effect that Britten objected to being buggered by L. The usual
over-emphasis on sex in this book.

Thursday, 12th November

Papers today are full of Alan Clark,† and his role in the Arms for Iraq
affair‡ when he was a minister in the Tory Government. *The Times*
contains a full-page article in which Alan states his views, which are
totally cynical. He ends by saying that he is publishing his diaries next
year, adding that he will make a contrast to the outstanding diarists of
the mid-century – Chips Channon, Harold Nicolson, James Lees-
Milne – all of whom were homosexuals. This does not please me, the
only survivor. I spoke to M., who counselled against my remonstrat-
ing. But I thought I would write Alan a line on a postcard, just to
remind him I am still alive.

Wednesday, 18th November

Two letters this morning which I have kept from A. First from Alan
Clark in reply to the line I wrote him, charming of course but evading

---

* Humphrey Carpenter, *Benjamin Britten: A Biography* (Faber & Faber, 1992).
† After a decade in government, Clark had (temporarily, as it turned out) retired
from politics at the 1992 general election. His diaries of his years as a minister in the
Thatcher Government, also revealing much about his private life, were to cause a
sensation on their publication – see 5 August 1993.
‡ The affair concerned the prosecution of directors of the Matrix Churchill firm for
the alleged illegal export to Iraq, prior to the Gulf crisis of 1990–1, of machine tools
for munitions. The case collapsed after it emerged that the Conservative Government
(in which Clark had been minister responsible for the arms trade) had been aware
of, and possibly encouraged, the exports.

(as one would expect) the matter which led me to write to him. The second from Downing Street asking if I would agree to my name being submitted to the Palace for a CBE.* I deliberated about this on my way to Bath, and as soon as I arrived replied declining it. At my age, I can't face up to all the bother – the congratulations from all and sundry, the letters to be replied to, the investiture ceremony and celebratory dinner. It is too late. I am not interested, and quite content to be just plain me. I daren't tell A., for she might press me to accept. It might have been different had I been offered a knighthood in which she could have shared, or one of the honours in the personal gift of the Queen. The CH† is the only honour I really covet, but that would be beyond my deserts.‡

Friday, 20th November

Tragic news of the burning of Windsor Castle. A chunk of English history wiped out in an afternoon. It seems most of the treasures saved, but George IV's rooms all gone. Poor Christopher Lloyd§ has had a heart attack from the shock.

Saturday, 21st November

I lunch with Peter and Deirdre Levi at Frampton-on-Severn, in a workman's cottage at the end of a pretty street with wide grass verges. Main object to meet Jeremy Lewis¶ who is writing Cyril Connolly's**

---

* Commander of the Order of the British Empire.
† Companion of Honour (founded 1917 and restricted to 65 members); generally considered the junior branch of the Order of Merit (founded 1902 and restricted to 24 members).
‡ Another factor in J.L.-M's refusal (as he told the editor) was that he had been due to receive an honour on his retirement from the National Trust's staff in 1966, but this had been withheld owing to known complications in his private life at the time.
§ Christopher Hamilton Lloyd (b. 1945); Keeper of The Queen's Pictures from 1988.
¶ Writer, publisher, journalist and literary editor (b. 1942).
** Writer and journalist (1903–74); editor of *Horizon*, 1939–50.

biography. Matthew,* the son of Cyril and Deirdre, is a prettier version of Cyril (if not a contradiction in terms), but says little. I try to engage by asking him if he is still at school. He replies haughtily, 'I have retired from working in a bookshop.' Deirdre is a good cook, friendly, quick at repartee. He very clever and donnish. Does imitations – Maurice Bowra, the Queen Mother – demanding laughing rejoinders. Yet I like him immensely. No inhibitions here. For half an hour Jeremy and I talk 'dirt' about Cyril. I tell him he is brave to tackle such a deep and devious character, with no life outside friendship and letters. I leave him with two quotes from my diary when I learned of C's death in 1974.

I asked Peter how the old-fashioned Papists reacted when he left the Jesuits. He said he had been fearful of the reaction of Monsignor Gilbey,† who expressed regret but said he would not allow it to interfere with their friendship. Deirdre said that, when she was living in sin with Cyril, she was cut dead by Evelyn Waugh, who told Cyril that adultery was all right for a man but not for a woman. When Cyril was in America, he visited the library which holds Evelyn's diaries and asked to look through them. He found such appalling entries about himself that he never got over it.

Saturday, 28th November

Julian Berkeley and Tony Scotland came to luncheon, bringing gift of precious orchid for A. Too much kissing for her liking, otherwise both enchanting. Tony told us how by devious means he tracked down pretender to the imperial throne in China, whom he found living in a sort of mud hut and doing lowliest jobs such as cleaning public urinals. He was nominated by the last reigning Emperor. Tony could only meet him accompanied by official interpreters, and was obliged not to say anything which might either embarrass him or annoy the Communist attendants.

---

* Matthew Connolly (b. 1970); genealogist; editor of *The Selected Works of Cyril Connolly* (2002).
† The Rt Revd Monsignor Alfred Gilbey (1901–98); Roman Catholic Chaplain to Cambridge University, 1932–65; resident at Travellers Club, Pall Mall.

We dined at the House, Tony Lambton staying. Very praising of *P. and P.*, but told A. that I should now concentrate on diaries, for I was above all a chronicler. When the women left the room, David recalled A's illness and how he, Caroline, Freda and I sat in gloom one evening in anticipation of her imminent demise. Merriment ensued in which I joined while feeling bitter sadness in the recesses of my heart.

Monday, 30th November

A letter from the Honours Secretary at 10 Downing Street saying the PM regrets my decision but respects my wishes. I am certain I have done the right thing. Another reason for refusing this absurd decoration is that many regard me as a snob. Yet I am not their sort of snob, and content to be an ordinary esquire, to which I am entitled by virtue of being armigerous. An ounce of heredity, as Olive Lloyd-Baker used to say, is worth a pound of merit.*

Wednesday, 2nd December

Lunched at White's with Freddie Stockdale. Absolutely charming early forties, healthy complexion and thick black hair, abounding in energy and enthusiasm. Tells me he is to remarry next week. Laughs off his success producing opera in clubs and country houses; says he is totally unmusical, though he turns the pages for the pianist at every performance. Said that, at Eton, he looked forward all week to Sunday evening chapel, just as I did; loved the frescoes, the Hone windows, the candlelight. His greatest friend was Charlie Lloyd.† One day, C.L. ashamedly and wretchedly admitted to him that he had fallen hopelessly in love with a boy living on a Hebridean island. F.S. said, that's all right, let's discuss it next time. Two days later, Charlie committed suicide in the woods at Clouds Hill [Hertfordshire]. F.S. has a roguish

---

* Owner of Hardwicke Hall, Gloucestershire (d. 1975); she had made her celebrated remark on the spur of the moment lunching with J.L.-M. and John Betjeman on 19 March 1972.

† Grandson (1949–74) of J.L.-M's former employer George, 1st Baron Lloyd, whose suicide led to the extinction of the peerage.

smile, rather like Francis Dashwood's. A remarkably attractive person whom I take to enormously.

Tuesday, 15th December

As Chloë and her offspring have arrived to see A., I stay with Alex Moulton for the night. He has three friends to dine who are pheasant-shooting on his land tomorrow, all decent fellows. One of them, Derek Strauss,* is big in the City and knows everyone in the business world. Told me that Lord King† longs to be made a heredi-tary peer. Tiny Rowland is a rogue but not as bad as his arch-enemy, the shit Fayed;‡ he exercises enormous influence, and could probably get Gaddafi to hand over the two assassins who brought down the airliner, if only the Government would ask him.§ I recommended my Italian tailor in Bath to Alex, who said he would send for him to The Hall. 'I always send for my tailor. Wouldn't think of going to his shop.' I know my grandfather sent for his Jermyn Street tailor to Bewdley, but that was in 1908. When I asked Alex whether his CBE had stood him in good stead these past nineteen years, he replied, 'None at all. A perfectly useless honour. But it would have been churlish to refuse.' After dinner we sat in Alex's stiff upstairs drawing room while they drank port and smoked cigars. All rather a strain.

Friday, 18th December

Driving along I hear Radio Four announcer say, 'And now we are on the subject of mortality, here is an extract from the diary of

---

* Old Etonian City man, sometime Chairman of Strauss Turnbull.

† John King (1917–2005); Chairman, British Airways, 1981–93; cr. life peer as Baron King of Wartnaby, 1983.

‡ Egyptian businessman, accused of 'dishonest misrepresentation' in a Department of Trade report.

§ Western intelligence suspected named Libyan agents of being responsible for the explosion which destroyed Pan Am Flight 103 over the Scottish town of Lockerbie on 21 December 1988 – though the Gaddafi regime refused to hand over the suspects at this time.

today's date for 1947 of James Lees-Milne.' I listen, without great interest, to an incident I had totally forgotten, in which I visit a sad, truculent old lady who wished to bequeath her worthless collection of bric-à-brac to the N.T. I am glad I was compassionate at the time.

I no longer have sexual twinges of any kind, only revulsion. And I far prefer the society of women to men. Does this mean that, were I still to have a propensity to sex, I would now be predominantly heterosexual? In fact I am now like any little prudish octogenarian spinster, turning away from the mere mention of the word sex.

Communication with A. is no longer easy because of her deafness. Also she is less on the uptake. Her mind, still so sharp on everyday affairs, has no interest in matters cerebral, or artistic or musical come to that. She never listens to music now unless I suggest it. Yet it was she who taught me to enjoy it.

Wednesday, 23rd December

At breakfast I told A. that I had been offered an honour by Downing Street, and turned it down. I had put off doing so fearing she might be upset and rebuke me. On the contrary, she received news with unconcern. I was surprised by her lack of surprise. When I gave my reasons, she agreed. There has been no further mention.

Sunday, 27th December

Coote who stayed the night [on 23rd] motored us to Chatsworth. Traffic awful and long delays.

For three successive days, Chatsworth was white with hoar frost. Only the gravel paths uncovered. Far whiter and more beautiful than snow. Grass sparkling like jewelry. Trees fairylike. Intense quiet. Not a breath of wind. Evenings misty of powdered blue, the lemon skyline reflected in the still river.

Clarissa [Luke] came from London, as did Woman's friend Margaret Budd. Woman herself of course, and Diana [Mosley] to my joy. We have long talks. She extremely thin, that soulful look, wonderful eyes and silhouette, sweetness of expression. Talks of the Duke of

Windsor* whom she loved, 'dear little man' with his wonderful manners. He so funny too, and she the best hostess imaginable, going out of her way to bring the shy into conversation, also funny at times, and always sharp.

We all attended Communion on Christmas morning, even Diana, a rare thing. She explained she was grateful to Edensor Church for the prayers for her recovery when she had her brain tumour years ago. To church again on Sunday. We walk up to front pews just after start of service, and are the first to leave. Debo and Woman go first to altar rails. This feudalism embarrasses me. Memorable sermon by old Mr Beddoes, who welcomes a robin in the church 'which some of you may notice'. A. noticed it was not a robin but a wren.

On Christmas Day, the Ds dispensed gifts to the staff by the enormous illuminated Christmas tree at the end of the South corridor. Suitable murmurs of gratitude and satisfaction. Andrew surreptitiously slipped envelopes into the hands of Henry and the footmen, all done with the greatest friendliness and affection. Absolutely no condescension, yet feudal – as was the reception of the carol singers on Christmas Eve, who came in by the wicket letting through sharp stabs of freezing air, and sang light-heartedly. We sat on the stairs and on benches round the central hall, the oldies wrapped in rugs, A., Woman and Coote having thrown their sticks on the floor.

Monday, 28th December

We leave for home. A. much enjoyed visit, which Coote thought far better than two years ago. Andrew and Debo seem totally content, in fact Derby and Joan. At breakfast she told us it was the eighth anniversary of his giving up the bottle. And what, she asked him, made you do it? He answered succinctly and fervently, God. Debo very sweetly said to me, 'Supposing Alvilde should die before you, you can always come up here to live. Just get rid of everything but your books. You can have a large room somewhere.' I told A., who was touched.

---

* The Windsors and the Mosleys had been country neighbours in France in the 1960s.

1993

1993

Now that I tend to fall asleep over novels, a curious thing happens. I doze off and briefly continue the story I have been reading in a sort of dream, before waking with a jolt. I then read on and find, not surprisingly, that the next passage does not coincide at all with the dreamed continuation I have just experienced.

Saturday, 9th January

A. made a superb effort and gave a luncheon party for Diana Mosley, Woman and Hardy Amies. Hardy has a pro to play tennis with him every Saturday if the weather is fine. As he is bent double, I asked him how he managed to play. He replied that it was possible to perform every action with the body bent except service, which he has to do pat-ball. He seems a happy man, delighted with an article in today's *Telegraph* in which he gives his idea of the perfect weekend. Diana asked him how his firm was standing up to the recession. He said that never in his sixty years as a couturier had he experienced a better year financially, for the rich understand that the best clothes endure. All very fine for the rich who can afford the best, but will they continue to do so if the recession endures? Diana said that Heywood Hill's bookshop have also had their best year, and that *People and Places* was their best seller.

Today's *Telegraph* also contains a review by Nicky Mosley[*] of a book on wartime internment under 18B,[†] in which he defends Sir Oswald,

---

[*] Hon. Nicholas Mosley (b. 1923); writer; er. s. of Sir Oswald Mosley and his 1st wife Lady Cynthia Curzon (d. 1933); s. aunt 1966 as 3rd Baron Ravensdale.
[†] The Defence Regulation which, during the Second World War, authorised internment without trial of anyone suspected of enemy sympathies.

emphasising his deep patriotism. This pleases Diana, who nevertheless refuses to forgive her stepson for writing that book about his father.[*] But oh how I love her.

Saturday, 16th January

A. is not very well, having recently given up the drugs she is supposed to be taking in favour of homeopathic treatment. However, today she managed with help from Peggy and me to prepare lunch for the Norwiches and Droghedas. This passed well, though she was very bent and breathless. When the guests left, I took her for a drive round by Sopworth and Didmarton; as soon as we got back, she went to bed. I tried to read downstairs by the fire, but felt tormented with forebodings as I looked at her empty chair. All I can do is minister to her every whim and pour love into her.

Sunday, 17th January

Despite A's continuing frailty, we lunch with the Briggses at Midford, having ascertained beforehand from Isabel that the only other guest would be Bill McNaught,[†] a harmless individual. I watch her struggling to respond to McN's and Michael's conversation, she normally so bright and responsive. On way home she says she cannot go out to another meal until she is better. Conversation at Midford mostly about the so-called Camillagate affair and the infamous publication of the Prince of Wales's taped conversations.[‡] All I have talked to on this subject are unanimous in condemning the press's behaviour. Michael Briggs however is critical of the Prince, who he says is so devoid of humour as to be devoid of human understanding. Told us of some function at which HRH, Bishop Stockwood,[§] the

---

[*] The two-volume biography *Rules of the Game* (1982) and *Beyond the Pale* (1983).
[†] William P. McNaught; Curator of American Museum at Claverton near Bath.
[‡] An intimate telephone call from the Prince of Wales to his mistress Camilla Parker Bowles on 18 December 1992 had been monitored and recorded by a 'scanner' and subsequently published in the tabloid press.
[§] Anglican clergyman (1913–95), who as Bishop of Southwark from 1959 to 1980 was renowned for his humanitarian ideals and love of Society and good living.

Lord Lieutenant and Michael were all present. Stockwood was saying how he adored watered silk, fondling his episcopal garment; the LL riposted that he had a fetish for feathers, drawing attention to his plumed hat. Overhearing this, the P. puckered his brow, became indignant, and asked them if they were serious. Totally at sea.

Monday, 18th January

Today I made three trips to Bath and back. First to dentist to have my plate adjusted. That was put right and I returned to find A. still in bed, her cheek and neck swollen and red. I fixed urgent appointment with her specialist Dr Thomas and drove her to Bath Clinic. He said at once she must go into hospital. A. surprised by this, I not in the least. While they put her through tests, I returned home and with Peggy packed her little bag and drove again to Bath. Thomas thinks her swelling may come from infected collar bone. He was worried I could see. I am miserable but determined to adopt a resigned and non-emotional attitude, reconciled to whatever fate has in store.

Tuesday, 19th January

At A's insistence, I go to London for Alfred Beit's ninetieth birthday party at Brooks's. Over tea there I am joined by Francis Sitwell who is delighted with Sarah Bradford's life of Sachie, as is Bruce Hunter. His only reservation is about some revelations of S.B. concerning Sachie's love life, particularly relating to Bridget Parsons.* Apparently Georgia came upon them *in flagrante delicto*.

Alfred's party huge, sixty-eight guests. Nearly all from the old *gratin,*† with sprinkling of young *gratin* like Tatton Sykes. Alfred arrived from hospital in an ambulance, carried upstairs in wheelchair, and pushed into dining room where guests assembled. I seated happily

---

* Lady Bridget Parsons (1907–72), o. dau. of 5th Earl of Rosse; a great heart-throb also for J.L.-M., who had been in love at Eton with her brother Desmond.
† 'The upper crust'.

between Mary Roxburghe[*] and Kitty Giles.[†] I have never known the Duchess well, but we have many links. She is Bamber [Gascoigne]'s great-aunt and finds him almost too good to be true. Spoke with admiration of Jamesey [Pope-Hennessy]'s life of her grandfather Monckton Milnes. Appreciated that J. had a problem writing about her parents, her father a stereotyped character, her mother inclined to be rude to her inferiors through shyness.[‡] (Shyness hardly seems the right word for Lady Crewe's predicament.) Told of the brutality of her Aunt Sibyl Grant[§] to her son, whom she persuaded her husband the General to disinherit. Kitty Giles talked of her prison-visiting at Brixton. Knows the prisoners intimately, visits them in their cells. She concerns herself with their rights to be treated as civilised beings, though their reform is generally out of the question: seventy-five per cent of those discharged return.

Afterwards chatted with a host of forgottens. John Nutting,[¶] so handsome, who has reviewed my book for *The Field;* John Bellingham,[**] who always greets me as a cousin; the Brudenells.[††] Derek Hill

---

[*] Lady Mary Crewe-Milnes (b. 1913); dau. of 1st and last Marquess of Crewe; m. 1935–53 9th Duke of Roxburghe (d. 1974).

[†] Lady Katherine Sackville (b. 1926), o. dau. of 9th Earl De La Warr; m. 1946 Frank Giles, journalist.

[‡] Mary Roxburghe's grandfather Richard Monckton Milnes (1809–85), writer, poet, statesman and philanthropist, cr. Baron Houghton, 1863; his son Robert (1858–1945), 2nd Baron, Liberal Party statesman and HM Ambassador to Paris, 1922–8, cr. Marquess of Crewe, 1911, m. (2nd) 1899 Lady Margaret Primrose, dau. of 5th Earl of Rosebery (Liberal Prime Minister 1894–5), at whose instigation J.P.-H. wrote biographies of her husband and father-in-law.

[§] Lady Crewe's sister (1879–1955); m. 1908 General Sir Charles Grant (1877–1950); described herself in *Who's Who* as 'poet, writer, designer and artist'; interested in 'the beyond'; lived at Pitchford Hall, Shropshire, where J.L.-M., visiting her during the war, found her eccentric almost to the point of insanity, but 'with a mind as sharp as a razor's edge'.

[¶] Barrister (b. 1942; QC 1995); e. s. of Sir Anthony Nutting, 3rd Bt (politician who famously resigned from Eden Government over Suez, 1956), whom he s. as 4th Bt, 1999; m. 1974 Diane, widow of 2nd Earl Beatty, châtelaine of Chicheley Hall, Newport Pagnell, Bucks.

[**] Old Etonian genealogist living in Ireland (b. 1929); m. 1989 Fiona Nugent; his mother, *née* Arthur, came from an Ayrshire family connected to J.L.-M's.

[††] Edmund Brudenell (b. 1924) of Deene Park, Northamptonshire; m. 1955 Hon. Marion Manningham-Buller, dau. of 1st Viscount Dilhorne; the L.-Ms had stayed

told me that he told the Prince of Wales last week, 'Sir, I don't know how you go on.' HRH replied that that was not something he ought to be told – though there was worse to come. Derek says that bitch Kitty Kelley's* book on Prince Philip is going to be an absolute brute, revealing the names of the women involved in his life. All I can say is that he is a man of discretion, concerning whose private life I have never heard a word of criticism.

Thursday, 21st January

The Beits' guests are a gathering of the clan. They are tribal just like the African negroes. What makes them so conspicuous? Not so much their breeding or their appearance, rather their money and security. Their physical comfort and lack of financial worry leads to self-confidence, sophistication, good taste, in many cases a knowledge of the arts. It also explains their good manners, tolerance, iconoclastic brand of humour, self-deprecation, and willingness to accept those outsiders wishing to be received whose manners make them acceptable. They are for the most part kindly and compassionate – yet withal proud. They won't admit to being superior, yet consider themselves so. Their society is undoubtedly agreeable, and it is possible for intellectuals to bask in it without becoming corrupted by their *train de vie*.

Debo rang. Long talk. Full of solicitude for A., about whom she had heard through Woman. Said the Prince of Wales was to stay with them tomorrow, and wondered what they would talk about. I said, 'You will have to talk about the crisis for it will be on the tips of all your tongues. Be frank.' She said she had just lunched with Andrew Parker Bowles, and was surprised to see no journalists outside the house. After ten minutes of mutual deploring, I said, 'I suppose we are being bugged.'

---

with them on several occasions during the 1980s and been amazed at their ante-diluvian lifestyle.

* American writer of scandalous biographies (b. 1942).

Sunday, 24th January

Clarissa came last night, and was very sweet. We went to fetch A. from the Clinic. Her recovery is striking, though swelling of leg and neck not yet entirely gone.

Thursday, 4th February

On Monday, John Harris telephoned that Geoffrey Houghton-Brown had been sent to a nursing home in Wimbledon, next to the house where he was brought up. John has been kind in visiting and caring, for G. was his first protector in London, who gave him a room at 20 Thurloe Square and a job in his shop. I telephoned G. and could barely hear his tiny voice, but he seemed pleased to be remembered. This morning, I heard from John that G. died last night on the eve of his ninetieth birthday, having quietly fallen asleep, his friend and minder Fisher by his side.

Geoffrey was gentle and unassuming, too much so, yet a man of deep sensibility and conviction. An extremely pious Catholic until Vatican Council II when his faith, if not shattered, was so dented that his religion meant little to him thereafter, and he felt betrayed. He was very kind to me, letting me take a floor in his house in Alexander Place when I came out of the army during the war. I dare say I rather traded on his good nature and generosity, but we were always good friends. He was as good as gold and quite a respectable artist, being a friend and disciple of the Australian painter Roy Le Maistre* who claimed to be the rightful King of England through the Stuarts. G. was an authority on eighteenth-century French furniture, but never wrote down his views on the subject. He lived all his adult life with the rather absurd Ronald Fleming, decorator, until the latter's death.

While sad about Geoffrey, I found my hateful thoughts veering to speculation as to whether he had left me Henrietta Maria's heart in a small reliquary, knowing as he did of my interest in the Stuarts. I quickly brushed aside this selfish, acquisitive, beastly thought, as though at my age I needed or even wanted a token. One cannot prevent such sinful thoughts arising, only try to batten them down.

---

* Australian Post-Impressionist artist (1894–1968); resident from 1930 in London, where his other disciples included Francis Bacon.

Saturday, 6th February

Susanna [Johnston] lunched, full of gossip about Camillagate. She is furious with her brother* for having mocked the Prince in his *Times* column, which she considers almost as bad as the persecution of Camilla's children at school. When Sir William Hayter† told S. that he was so disgusted with what the Prince had said that he could no longer have any respect for him, S. retorted angrily that the conversation was not one he was ever meant to hear. Quite right too – sex chat between participants is no more the business of others than how one behaves on the lavatory seat. No one should be judged by it.

Tuesday, 9th February

Father Michael Crowdy,‡ nice old boy but slightly cracked, called on me in Bath yesterday, hoping to reconvert me to Catholicism. He is a 'freelance', having quite rightly quarrelled with the bishops over the Latin Mass *et al.* I had to tell him that I had returned to the C. of E., and couldn't stomach the Catholic Church's opposition to birth control. He argued that few Catholics observe this ban, and that practising birth control is rather like telling lies – something we ought not to do, yet nevertheless do all the time. He then fell in my esteem by claiming that the population of this country is decreasing. I said that only that morning I had received a letter from the CPRE§ warning about government plans to build two million more houses as soon as the economy permitted. We parted in a friendly spirit, but I hope he will leave me alone.

After he left I drafted my obituary of Geoffrey for the *Independent*. As I dictated it down telephone to bedint-sounding transcriber, I felt rather disloyal to have described G. as a collector of reliquaries

---

* Alexander Chancellor (b. 1940); journalist; editor, *Spectator*, 1975–84; columnist on *New Yorker* and *The Times*.

† Diplomatist and scholar (1906–95); HM Ambassador to USSR, 1953–6; Warden of New College, Oxford, 1958–76.

‡ Priest ordained in 1954 (b. 1914); since 1982 assisting the (Lefebvrist) Society of St Pius X and based at their Bristol priory.

§ Council for the Protection of Rural England; now Campaign to Protect Rural England.

and French furniture who never played a game and was rather a cissy. I always knew he had a secret passion for rugby players and the like.

Saturday, 13th February

To London again yesterday to lunch at the Garrick with Clive Aslet.* A charming young man, Cambridge contemporary of Nick [Robinson], and extremely handsome. I could not stop admiring his splendid even teeth. He wants me to contribute something to *Country Life* along the lines of *People and Places*. Was there a tour I would like to do for them, revisiting old haunts? I mentioned the Welsh borders – Radnor, Salop and Herefordshire – preferring the dim squires' manor houses, particularly those still inhabited, to the grand seats. I felt shy as always with the young, but O I liked him.

On foot to see Bruce Hunter in Golden Square. Good to see how many Georgian and Victorian houses remain, all worth a squint. The blue plaques always elicit interest, even of the dreariest past inhabitants. In Golden Square I went to look at the statue of George II. Face like Malcolm Muggeridge,† sadly worn and streaked with bird messes. On the head was perched a black crow, which I tried in vain to shoo away. An old woman earnestly scavenging in a litter bin – the sort of thing which I suppose will never be eliminated even in the best-regulated society.

Friday, 26th February

Gervase [Jackson-Stops] stayed last night, bringing his new friend, a rather camp young man who is a learned horticulturist, currently designing an ambitious garden at rear of Gervase's Menagerie with temples and fanciful wilderness walks and rides. We all went to a party at the Art Gallery in Bristol given by the N.T. for members in the region who are gardeners or married to gardeners. Owing to A's dis-

---

* Journalist (b. 1955); editor, *Country Life*, 1993–2006 (deputy editor, 1989–92); m. 1980 Naomi, dau. of Prof. Sir Martin Roth.
† Writer, broadcaster and religious commentator (1903–90).

ability, kind Mary Keen fetched us and drove us to Bristol. We had to get there early, as the Prince of Wales was to be present. The poor man carried a plate of snacks and glass of wine attached to a clip and walked round meeting and talking to the guests one by one. He came up to A., who was in a circle with me and John Harris, and said, 'We have been so concerned about your illness. I hope you are better.' And in passing, 'You simply must come to Highgrove [near Tetbury] and see my garden. Come even if I am not there.' As A. said afterwards, she wouldn't be let in if he wasn't there, and he hadn't exactly invited her. The P. seemed far more relaxed than when I met him at Chatsworth [in January 1992]. I observed him closely. Good complexion and youthful skin. Was well-dressed, wearing the most covetable dark tan shoes with tassels. There is no doubt he *has* charm, notwithstanding Paul Johnson's[*] recent article in the *Spectator* that he lacks it, like most Hanoverians.

Monday, 8th March

Reading St Thomas à Kempis[†] I realise that a saint must be so disciplined that he is able to control his thoughts from evil. It is not enough to smile blandly on one's neighbour while thinking him an egregious bore. The saint may not even think any such thing.

Thursday, 11th March

To London to lunch with Ambrose Congreve,[‡] who wrote out of the blue from Ireland inviting me on the strength of our having been contemporaries at Eton and his wife being a fan of my books. At Warwick House in precincts of St James's Palace, huge house where formerly we went to Ann Rothermere's parties. Ambrose lives here one week every three months, *en prince*. Algerian manservant in

---

[*] Writer and journalist (b. 1928).

[†] German divine (1380–1471); author of *Imitation of Christ*.

[‡] Industrialist and philanthropist (b. 1907); of Mount Congreve, Co. Waterford, where he created a famous garden; m. 1935 Marjorie Glasgow (succeeding his father-in-law as chairman of the engineering firm of Humphreys & Glasgow, 1939–83).

uniform at door. Up vast and steep staircase to drawing room over-looking palace courtyard and Green Park. Smart butler and parlour-maid waiting. Highly decorated rooms in style of 1740s, I guess not genuine. Pale yellow walls and much gold, yet goodish taste. Ambrose verging on eighty-six, tall, upright, robust, handsome with good complexion, the formerly red hair now white. I recognised him instantly. Not deaf; in fullest possession. His wife, American heiress, is crippled and can't leave Ireland.

We went downstairs to dining room. Odd arrangement, Ambrose sitting at one end of table with myself on his right and another octo, Michael Verey,* ex-merchant banker cousin of David V.,† on his left, and his charming companion acting as hostess (niece? concubine?) at other end, flanked by two young women. The lady next to me said she was an old friend of Ambrose. How long, I asked? Twenty-six years, she replied. I said I had known him for seventy. Of course, I hardly knew Ambrose at all. But he said all his Eton friends were dead, apart from Dunsany‡ who is dotty, and he liked to be in touch with some survivors if they condescended to come to luncheon. Had Jack and Frankie Donaldson recently. I take this as a kindly gesture from a very rich man. Indeed, the *luxe* of Warwick House is for these days astounding. My lady neighbour said that at Mount Congreve he employs a hundred people, and has a huge garden. The house (Regency) is huge too, and has been improved by him since accession. To Verey, I heard Ambrose say, 'Do you suppose I did right in getting rid of all Hong Kong?' I enjoyed this outing.

Thursday, 1st April

I have received a letter from Ambrose Congreve's nonagenarian wife Marjorie which amuses me no end. She claims to be a fan of mine, and got him to buy her a complete set of my books from Heywood

---

* Director of companies (b. 1912); High Sheriff of Berkshire, 1968.
† Architectural historian (1913–84) of Barnsley House nr Cirencester; m. 1939 Rosemary Sandilands (1918–2001), garden designer and co-editor of books on gardening with A.L.-M.
‡ Randal Plunkett, 19th Baron Dunsany (1906–99).

Hill, and then ask me to luncheon at Warwick House. Now she writes that she particularly loves my description of walks in Hungary. I have never walked in Hungary or written about it. She is confusing me with Paddy Leigh Fermor.

Monday, 5th April

Tall, swarthier than I had imagined but very handsome, with grey hair, is Nicholas Shakespeare* who came to see me in Bath this morning. Has immense charm. Face reminds me of Mary Keen and Patrick O'Donovan,† round, constantly breaking into smiles. Was at Winchester and Cambridge with Nick Robinson, whom he claims as his best friend. He came to talk about Bruce Chatwin whose biography he is to write.‡ Wanted to know how Bruce was regarded as a neighbour. Anyway we talked for hours and he shared boiled eggs with me. Very easy and delightful. His second novel about to appear, the first having won awards. Very clever young man of thirty-four, who has already been literary editor of *Telegraph*, both *Daily* and *Sunday*, which almost killed him. Told me that Bruce's books, here, in America and in translation, now sell several million copies a year. Almost unbelievable. Why? It is a Byronic success story – on the one hand Bruce's extreme good looks, his comparatively early and as it were romantic death from Aids, on the other his sense of publicity and his outrageous behaviour. N.S. knew Bruce towards the end when he was a wraith, yet with burning eyes that still set people alight. N.S. himself has no 'artistic'§ inclinations but takes them in his stride. Thinks Bruce a very good writer, and that there are few such about (Paddy Leigh Fermor not one of them, too contrived with his purple prose). But I wonder if Bruce is not a flash in the pan.

---

* Nicholas Shakespeare (b. 1957); writer; successively literary editor of *The Times*, *Daily News*, and *Telegraph* (*Daily* and *Sunday*), 1985–91; about to publish his novel *The High Flyer* (Harvill Press).
† Charismatic journalist (d. 1981) who was J.L.-M's fellow officer in the Irish Guards, 1940–1.
‡ Published by Harvill Press in 1999.
§ Euphemism for 'homosexual' employed sarcastically by J.L.-M., his philistine father having used the word to imply effeminacy and 'unnatural vice'.

Friday, 9th April

Igor has come for Easter weekend. He is tall, with a good figure and Christ-like good looks, but gormless. Keeps asking frivolous questions such as 'Who was the Countess of X's grandmother?' A. replies, 'You who wish to be so correct should not refer to Lady X as Countess.' He is helpful in the house, and guileless and good, but anyone more boring could not easily be conjured up by a novelist.

Sunday, 11th April

We lunched, taking Igor, with John Julius [Norwich] and Mollie. On my left sat a girl looking just like J.J's daugher Artemis,* with same governessy air, though she assured me she was no relation of J.J., just a goddaughter. It turns out she is J.J's illegitimate daughter, but whether she is aware of the fact I don't know.† I remember it being said that her mother would push the pram past the Norwiches' house in Little Venice just to annoy J.J's then wife Anne.

Saturday, 17th April

I find my morning routine exhausting. Having taken A. her breakfast, made and eaten my own, washed up, and made the beds with Peggy (except for Sundays when I do them alone), I am worn out before tackling letters or diary editing.‡ Also, wearing thick brown shoes with leather soles tires me greatly; I now need light shoes with springy crepe soles. Twenty years ago the idea of worrying about the weight of my shoes would have made me hoot with laughter. Also I try to save myself journeys in this minute house, intending to postpone fetching a tool from the outside shed until I also have to bring in some fire-lighting paper – except that I do not remember, and end up making two journeys anyway. My memory is so poor that I put objects – the book

---

* Hon. Alice (Artemis) Cooper (b. 1953); dau. of 2nd Viscount Norwich and his 1st wife Anne Clifford; writer.

† Allegra Huston (b. 1964); dau. of Enrica 'Ricky' Soma (1932–69), ballet dancer, who m. 1950 (as his 4th wife) John Huston (1906–87), film director.

‡ J.L.-M. was then editing his diaries for 1953–4 and 1971–2, published by John Murray in 1994 as *A Mingled Measure*.

I am reading, A's bedside bottle of Perrier – on the lower steps of the staircase so as not to forget them when I next go upstairs.

Saturday, 24th April

In the morning, Myles [Hildyard, with whom J.L.-M. was staying at Flintham] drove me to Newstead [Abbey, Nottinghamshire]. Walked along lake and round gardens, beautifully maintained, as is house. Walked down yew tunnel beside stew pond where Byron bathed. Heard first cuckoo this year, surprisingly early. A hasty look over house. Byron's bed which he had at Cambridge, with coronets at corners. Page's room alongside, for Rushton and then presumably Fletcher.* I was impressed with the way Notts County Council run this place.

In the afternoon we went to Thrumpton Hall, last visited with Hugh Euston† in 1950s. Received by George Seymour,‡ very friendly, extremely correct, snobbish, who took me round and told me about his problems with this very interesting house. I had forgotten the marvellous 1660s staircase, which has now been stripped of dark varnish to show the variety of woods used – fruit, lime and elm. A really fine construction. Saloon of same date, he thinks by Webb§ but no evidence, panelled and painted dark pink. Good furniture and pictures, notably full-length Lely¶ of Duchess of Newcastle wearing feathered hat. Fireplace of local alabaster. In the library we were joined for drinks by Mrs, aunt of Millie Acloque, nice rugged lady resembling Violet Powell but without her intellect, and a strange yob-like bruiser who sat mute and gazing into space. Myles disclosed

---

* William Fletcher and Robert Rushton, Newstead boys who became personal servants to the poet George Gordon, 6th Baron Byron (1788–1824).
† Hugh Fitzroy, 11th Duke of Grafton (b. 1919); Chairman of Society for the Protection of Ancient Buildings; m. 1946 Fortune Smith, Mistress of the Robes to HM Queen from 1967; in the 1950s, as Earl of Euston, he had been N.T. Historic Buildings Representative for East of England.
‡ George Fitzroy Seymour (1923–94); kinsman of Marquess of Hertford and cousin of 11th Duke of Grafton; a JP, DL and sometime High Sheriff of Nottinghamshire; m. 1946 Hon. Rosemary Scott-Ellis, dau. of 8th Baron Howard de Walden.
§ John Webb (1611–72); architect, assistant to Inigo Jones.
¶ Sir Peter Lely (1618–80); Dutch-born portrait artist.

that he is the 'friend' with whom G.S. rides pillion all over the country on an enormous motor bike – *very* strange.[*]

Wednesday, 5th May

To London for the day. It was with some misgivings that I delivered two hefty notebooks of my diaries to John Murray. Either they will reject them, or I shall regret their publication. Mark Amory and Hugh Massingberd lunched at Brooks's. M.A. very agreeable and jolly. Still struggling with biography of Gerald Berners, who he suspects enjoyed being ill-treated by that brute Heber-Percy. Hugh now admits that what remains of the country house regime is doomed. Says no house can be maintained with an estate of less than 10,000 acres, of which a mere handful have survived.

Thursday, 6th May

While I was breakfasting in the kitchen, the front door rang and Tom Gibson asked if I would witness a document. This turned out to be his formal resignation of his incumbency, to take effect from August. I knew he was to retire in a year or two, but this nevertheless came as a shock. He and Gloria have become real friends and will be sorely missed. Indeed shall we have a vicar at all, or a peripatetic clergyman from Wotton to serve our parish? Tom said he would be seventy in August and thought it sensible to retire while he had moderately good health. Has bought a house in Lansdown Place West. They will spend four months of the year in South Africa, and one month of each autumn at Lake Como. We feel deserted.

Thursday, 27th May

In so far as I can understand the implications, I am bitterly opposed to the bloody Maastricht Treaty.[†] I foresee the European Community

---

[*] The curious life of George Seymour and his attachment to Thrumpton is described in the memoir by his daughter Miranda Seymour, *In My Father's House* (2007).

[†] Signed 7 February 1992; ratified by UK Parliament after a long series of narrow votes between May 1992 and November 1994.

becoming like the Soviet Republics, governed by a distant, unknown, unseen force of rulers. It will produce lack of competition, lack of will to work, corruption, inefficiency, disunity and anarchy. Then we shall have a reaction in the form of tribalism, such as we now see in the former Soviet Union and the Balkans and every African nation-state.

Wednesday, 2nd June

Richard [Shone] told me that Michael De-la-Noy wrote a horrid article in the *Independent* on Vita [Sackville-West], whom he chose as his most hated historical figure. R. asked me who my most hated living figure was. I couldn't decide on the spur of the moment, though I said I would have plumped for Lord Beaverbrook were he still alive. Richard said his was Mother Teresa.[*] I almost agreed, though I can't actually hate her. She has certainly done much harm by denouncing abortion and all forms of birth control as evil.

Thursday, 3rd June

J.K.-B. angelically motored down to lunch with me in Bath. I warm to him much after I have purged my irritation at his self-deprecatory manner. He told me that his family were coy about acknowledging their descent from John Bunyan,[†] whom they despised for his puritanism.[‡] I made him follow me home to Badminton to see the garden and meet A. in the kitchen over a cup of tea. A success, I felt sure. He said the right things, and was good with her. When he left I walked in Vicarage Fields, impelled there by the sound of the cuckoo, so late in the season. Indeed heard two, one echoing the other. How my heart turns over and over. Fields awash with golden buttercups in waves, on an ocean of greenest grass.

---

[*] Albanian nun who worked among the poor of India (1910–97).
[†] Writer and preacher (1628–88); author of *A Pilgrim's Progress*.
[‡] John Kenworthy-Browne's grandfather had been an Anglican clergyman, his father a convert to Roman Catholicism.

Saturday, 5th June

A hot summer day. We drove to luncheon with Simon [L.-M.]. Ghastly journey, stuck in queues of traffic. On arrival found Simon and family drinking beside a new pool with fountains and rockery, like a ye-olde comfort station built in the 1930s on the Great West Road. But very kind welcome, and excellent luncheon, and jollity. Object of visit was silver forks and spoons, etc., which I brought for Simon to choose from. This they did and I am glad they will have these things which have long lain in our attic. I made a tentative condition that, were we to be burgled of our own silver, they would let us have some of it back on loan. Exquisite view of the Abberley Hills from their lawn.

Thursday, 17th June

At 5.45 to Annual Meeting of Royal Society of Literature. Freda came as my guest for award-giving by current President Roy Jenkins. He is very dextrous and delightful on an occasion like this. In speaking he dances like a bear, making funny little gestures with his hands like Punch and Judy. When we left he rushed after us to have a word. He confirmed that his wife Jennifer was waiting until she reached a certain phase of her National Trust history before seeing me.

Freda gave me an excellent dinner at Hereford Mansions, in her roomy and desirable flat high up in a nice Edwardian block. When we had finished her friend Father Michael Hollings[*] came in and helped himself to whisky. Has lately been escorting Mother Teresa round his parish. She said to him, 'I am so glad you can see Jesus in me.' To my surprise, Father M. suggested that, in leaving the Roman Catholic Church, I was acting according to God's will. Somehow I feel I have not done any such thing. In the prevailing evil of the world he also sees God's mysterious hand. I quite liked him, though he is not my idea of what a priest ought to be.

---

[*] Michael Richard Hollings (1921–97); fought with Coldstream Guards in North Africa and Italy, 1942–5, being awarded MC; ordained RC priest, 1950; a chaplain, Westminster Cathedral, 1954–8; Chaplain, Oxford University, 1959–70; Parish Priest, St Mary of the Angels, Bayswater, 1978–97.

I motor to Coughton [Court, Warwickshire] to lunch with Ann Twickel* in her Colt House where once I lunched with her uncle Geoffrey Throckmorton soon after it was built in the early 1950s. She looks very like her mother old Lady Throckmorton. I arrived early and we started chatting about old times, her mother, the troubles since Sir Robert's death, the behaviour of her niece who without warning booted out the widow, Isabel, telling her never to darken the doors of Coughton again.† Then there appeared Monsignor [Alfred] Gilbey, staying upstairs. He is ninety-two, very bent, garrulous, full of good anecdotes though difficult to hear. He mumbles rapidly through clenched black teeth, his old head bent into his chest. Beautifully dressed, clean black soutane, wide purple sash, buckled shoes. He asked if he might put a personal question to me. I feared he was going to refer to my lapse from the true faith. But all he asked was whether, in my personal experience, I had ever come across an authentic case of Queen Mary demanding to be given an antique from someone she was visiting. I hadn't. He is of course a true Tridentine, unlike Father Michael Hollings. At the time of Vatican Council II, Cardinal Heenan‡ said to Gilbey, 'In jettisoning the Latin Mass we are losing more than a language.' The Monsignor says his life is now totally dedicated to pleasure. Well, if it can't be at ninety-two, when can it be? He says he is enjoying the happiest possible old age. The others at luncheon were Maureen Fellowes,§ her blimpish husband, and her

---

* Ann Throckmorton (b. 1911); m. 1939 Baron Ludwig von Twickel of Bavaria (died of wounds, 1945); Dame of Honour and Devotion of Sovereign Order of Malta.

† Ann was the sister of Sir Robert Throckmorton, 11th Bt, of Coughton (1908–89). He inherited the baronetcy in 1927 from their grandfather, their father having been killed in action, 1916. 'Old Lady Throckmorton' was their formidable mother (much admired by J.L.-M.), Lilian *née* Brooke, granted the right to use the style of a baronet's widow: she ruled Coughton until her death in 1955, and was responsible for its donation to the N.T. Their uncle, Geoffrey Throckmorton (1883–1971), was Clerk to the Journals in the House of Commons, 1940–8. 'The widow', Lady Isabel, dau. of 9th Duke of Rutland, was Sir Robert's 2nd wife.

‡ John Carmel Heenan (1905–75); Cardinal Archbishop of Westminster, 1963–75.

§ Lady Maureen Noel (b. 1917), o. dau. of 4th Earl of Gainsborough; m. 1st 1944 15th Baron Dormer (by whom she had two daughters), 2nd 1982 Peregrine Fellowes (1912–99).

Dormer daughter who is editing the correspondence of her ancestress Bess, wife of the 5th Duke of Devonshire.* Grace before luncheon, all these Catholics crossing themselves. Talk of Knights of Malta, of which Mr Fellowes is one. Maureen, whom I thought pretty when I used to see her at Batsford before the war, is now a dumpy old lady who talks too much. Reminded me that her mother was Peruvian, so she speaks Spanish as well as English. Says the Noels are related to most of the great Catholic families of Europe. Exclusivity washes over them.

Sunday, 27th June

To Chatsworth for weekend, driving there rather a strain. Staying were Mark Amory and wife Charlotte, both high-powered. He is nice and friendly and speaks like a Cecil, voice turning up into a scream. She is the daughter of Evelyn Joll of Agnews, and manages hospitals for NHS. When we were introduced, she said how much she liked my novels; I told her she was the first person ever to have told me that. Also Robert Kee† and wife Kate Trevelyan, he abounding in charm, she sweet and attentive and half his age.

Debo has been appointed to a committee of three to advise on opening Buckingham Palace to the public.‡ Says the Prince of Wales has long advocated public admission, and the Queen was won over even before the press started their campaign. Every consideration to be given to visitors – to be admitted by front door and there relieved of coats and brollies, returned to them at garden entrance when they leave. Debo says the Prince *never* referred to his matrimonial troubles before the separation, but now does so. Trouble lies in fact that the Queen, Prince Philip and P. of W. all find it very difficult to talk to each other. Debo devoted to the Prince, who needs protection.

---

* William Cavendish, 5th Duke of Devonshire (1748–1811); m. (2nd) Lady Elizabeth Foster (1759–1824), dau. of 4th Earl of Bristol.
† Writer and broadcaster (b. 1919); m. (3rd) 1990 Hon. Catherine Trevelyan.
‡ The money raised from entrance fees was to be used towards the restoration of Windsor Castle, after its serious damage by fire the previous December.

Saturday, 3rd July

Moira Shearer today inveighs vitriolically against autobiographers and diarists exhibiting their squalid opinions and behaviour. She mentions several by name, but mercifully not me. And here am I about to publish more diaries, about the wisdom of which I have grave doubts. Meanwhile Nick [Robinson] suggests I write a ghost story to be published as what he calls a 'chap' book – a beautifully produced little pamphlet with woodcuts. On thinking it over in bed, I decide I might be able to write a story about a man haunted by himself in the future, not by his present or past self.*

Wednesday, 7th July

Tony Mitchell motored me to Montacute [House] and Forde Abbey.† The first vastly improved since my day, beautifully kept and full of rare things. Most friendly welcome from nice custodian and wife. Then to Forde in its hollow, where we were received by the present owner Mark Roper,‡ with whose grandmother I stayed in 1937. Appalling mass of cars and charabancs filling the field on east front, wearing down the grass and disgorging Women's Institute dames with white crimped hair and legs awry. Mark Roper began by saying that private owners arranged openings much better than the N.T., which is clearly not the case here. Then he accused the Trust of 'doing him down' by enticing more people to Montacute, which is hardly fair. Then we went round the house. It is strange that this ancient house should be so magical, for it is an architectural muddle. The inanity of Mr Prideaux§ sticking on a frontispiece to the Abbot's Perpendicular Tower so as to obscure the side of it. But his Mannerist additions

---

* This was the origin of *Ruthenshaw*, a beautifully printed but unsatisfactory short story published by Robinson in the autumn of 1994, illustrated with wood engravings by Ian Stephen.

† Two properties in Somerset, the first bought by the N.T. in 1931 from the Phelips family who had built it in Elizabethan times, the second belonging to the Roper family.

‡ Owner of Forde estate (b. 1935); High Sheriff of Dorset, 1984; m. 1967 Elizabeth Bagot.

§ Sir Edmund Prideaux; Attorney-General under Oliver Cromwell.

fascinating, and the Saloon a truly great room with the Raphael cartoon tapestries for which it was probably made in the 1650s. Abbot Chard's* cloisters of butter-coloured stone very handsome. Some Early English arcature revealed behind it, noble in itself. Since the Reformation, this immense and important house has never been in the ownership of a noble family, only of squires. (The Ropers are in fact a mid Victorian commercial family, though the current *châtelaine*, whom we did not see, is a Bagot of Levens.)

Tuesday, 20th July

Driving to Bath, I heard on Radio Three that mothers will soon be able to determine whether the foetus in the womb is likely to be homosexual, moronic, epileptic or suffering from other disorders. Ought they to have the right to abort? All those interviewed with moronic or disabled children speak of the pleasure such offspring bring to them. But they are not only no pleasure to society in general, but an embarrassment and a hindrance as well as an expense to the taxpayer. Ought one to be encouraged to produce children who are half-witted etc. in a world which is already overpopulated with the sane and sound?

Wednesday, 21st July

I find Fanny Partridge's[†] diary[‡] riveting, especially as I knew most of those she consorted with. Many references to Eardley [Knollys], who I think comes out best among her friends of the 1960s. She is a very good writer, and I take heed of her comment on Lady Cynthia Asquith's diaries,[§] that she made the mistake of feeling she had to write

---

* Thomas Chard; Abbot of Forde (a Cistercian foundation) prior to Dissolution of the Monasteries (1539).
† Frances Marshall (1900–2004); painter, critic and writer, last survivor of Bloomsbury Group; m. 1933 Ralph Partridge (d. 1960).
‡ *Other People: Diaries, 1963–1966* (Harper Collins, 1993).
§ Lady Cynthia Charteris (1887–1960); dau. of 9th Earl of Wemyss and March; m. 1910 Hon. Herbert Asquith (1881–1947), 2nd s. of Prime Minister H.H. Asquith; writer, especially of children's stories; her diaries, covering the Great War, were published in 1968.

something every day, and described events rather than her responses to them. But the more I read the less I care for Fanny. Her prejudices come through like vitriol – anti-God, anti-royalty, anti-upper class (though I sympathise with her contempt for the idle, vain and snobbish like Helen Dashwood). We were amused to read how much she disliked staying with us at Alderley.*

I remember Ted Lister saying that artists had no taste. 'Just look at their houses – and their clothes.' The same can be said of Bloomsbury. Their houses were dingy, sparse and puritanical. Le Souco, Madame Bussy's† house, reverberated with the emptiness of the rooms. Curtains never reached the ground; mingy little rugs on uncarpeted floor; ugly fabrics. Clothes both male and female dreary beyond belief. They had dogmatic theories about architecture and painting, but otherwise little aesthetic sense.

Thursday, 22nd July

Grant McIntyre telephoned to announce that Jock Murray had died this afternoon, of cancer. Was clearly upset and could barely speak, for Jock was greatly loved in the office. He was always jolly, sometimes too much the schoolboy, but generous and kind. A marvellous inheritor of a glorious tradition going back to 1768.‡ He was the lynch-pin which kept together that splendid generation of John Betjeman, Osbert Lancaster, Peter Quennell, K. Clark, Paddy Leigh Fermor. I remember him at Eton, where he was one year my junior, with longish fair hair all over the place, expressive mouth, wide eyes, and that jocular manner which never left him. A dear and good man, shrewd too. My greatest pride is to have been included among his authors in a humble way.

---

* While staying with the L.-Ms in November 1965, Mrs Partridge admitted to 'feeling anxious about this visit', and concluded that she was 'subtly aware of alien values', finding everything 'just a little too conventional and safe'.

† Dorothy Strachey (1866–1960); artist and writer, elder sister of Lytton Strachey (1880–1932); m. 1903 Simon Bussy, French artist (1870–1954); they lived at Roquebrune, where they knew the L.-Ms; she translated the works of André Gide into English.

‡ The tradition came to an end in 2002 when his son sold the firm to Hodder Headline.

Tuesday, 3rd August

I drive myself to lunch with Roy Jenkinses at East Hendred. A nice, simple old house, Georgianised with sash windows, the whole painted white. Forecourt at rear with impressive sloping-roofed barn, recently thatched. Arrive at noon in order to answer her questions on early days and personalities of N.T. for the history she is writing, to appear in forthcoming centenary year. She asked about David Crawford, Oliver Esher, Jack Rathbone, Robin Fedden. My word she is a clever woman, and sees the point of everything. About Robin, she said, 'He had an eye. In his job expertise was not necessary, the eye all-important.' Deplores what museum people can do to houses with their pedantic knowledge. Agrees with me that Hanbury overdone; praises Hatchlands. Said Osterley so awful under V&A that it pained her to visit it. She has the nicest face, and such good manners. Wearing handsome jersey with pink-and-white stripes. Strange how I disliked the Jenkinses before I really knew them. I remember that, when he was elected to Brooks's, I almost felt the club had been penetrated by the KGB.

Roy has become a dear old duffer – almost. Sits enormous, and gobbles his food. Has trick of waving left hand in a clutching motion to emphasise his talk, which flows. Full of gossip and pleasantry. I asked him to explain the currency crisis. He did so, but in such Copper talk that I understood little. Said that, whereas when he was Chancellor speculators were responsible for 20 per cent of currency fluctuations, now it is 80 per cent, owing to speed of communication between international banks. Deplorable, but no law could stop it. We talked of houses we both liked, Compton Beauchamp [House, Berkshire] among them. Roy now working on life of Mr Gladstone.* Says he is not so sure that G's motives over fallen women quite so innocent as formerly made out. Certainly he suffered much from guilt.

Jennifer J. told me some interesting things – that Francis Dashwood sold the pictures at West Wycombe which he disliked, notably Baroque Grand Tour ones, without warning the Trust, for fear they would buy them and keep them where they hung; that Charles Faringdon, for all his laughter and bonhomie, was one of the most

---

* Jenkins's magisterial biography of the Grand Old Man appeared in 1995.

difficult of the donors' heirs; that John Smith's* opinions at Committee Meetings were always as violent as they were unpredictable; that Lord Crawford protected Jack Rathbone even after his breakdown. But when she told me, looking me straight in the eye, that she had been reading correspondence between Crawford, Esher and Jack about staff problems, I trembled to think what she must have read about me.

Thursday, 5th August

Like so many, A. is gripped by Alan Clark's diaries. While admitting that his style is vivacious and his descriptions arresting, I am not sure. Too many acronyms, initials, and filthy words used as adjectives. On the whole I find him difficult to like, despite some endearing characteristics – love of animals and country churches, and loyalty to 'the Lady', as he calls Mrs Thatcher.

Wednesday, 11th August

On the way to Bath this morning, I listened to two Privy Counsellors on Radio Three. First Cecil Parkinson,† 'On the Psychiatrist's Couch'. Unburdening himself with claims that he is a private and unambitious sort of person. Very plausible unless you see through him, as I do. Has a good, rich voice until the 'eows' tumble out. A bounder and a man of little depth. Denies sexual attraction to Mrs Thatcher. Why should he feel this necessary? Then comes Wedgwood Benn‡ for a reading of his 'confidential' tapes, with maddening clanging as of unlocking of strongroom each time he delivers a statement. Likewise disingenuous

---

* Sir John Smith (1923–2007); banker; MP (C) Cities of London and Westminster, 1965–70; Deputy Chairman of N.T., 1980–5; founder of Landmark Trust.
† Conservative politician (b. 1931); said to be a favourite of Margaret Thatcher, who appointed him to a succession of cabinet posts; as Party Chairman, was credited with the Conservative success in 1983 general election, but was obliged to resign from the Government soon afterwards owing to a scandal in his private life; cr. life peer, 1992.
‡ 'Tony' (Wedgwood) Benn (b. 1925); Labour politician; formerly 2nd Viscount Stansgate (a change in the law enabling him to renounce his peerage in 1963 and return to the House of Commons); Secretary of State for Energy 1975–9, subsequently the leading radical in the Parliamentary Labour Party.

and boastful. Even if these MPs start off with noble ideals, they are soon taken over by the game of politics. The House of Commons is so densely haunted with dishonourable motivation that you can cut it with an axe. All that counts is getting the better of your neighbour, at whatever sacrifice of loyalty or principle. At least Alan Clark is honest, if not honourable.

Saturday, 21st August

Our long-planned and much-anticipated visit to Madresfield [Court near Malvern, Worcestershire]. Many years since I was last here in 1948, when Elmley* was toying with the N.T. What a lugubrious house, wrecked by Hardwick[†] and Co. from mid nineteenth century to early twentieth. Pitch dark entrance. One feels one's way to the tunnel-like library, at the end of which a window looks out over the garden. I could not even see the famous carved shelf-ends by Ashbee[‡] and other Chipping Campden craftsmen. Wonderful books. Indeed, wonderful treasures of every description; miniatures everywhere, exposed to sunlight; a case of forty drawers packed with Hilliards, Olivers, Engelharts; vitrines of rare snuff boxes in dozens. The great dining-room with high-timbered ceiling and huge fat Gothic windows by Hardwick is splendid. So is the hall with staircase and gallery balustrading of crystal uprights. All ebonised by 'Boom',[§] who haunts the place. Formidable full-lengths hanging everywhere. The Lygons must have collected for generations. Among all this dear Rosalind, looking exhausted, her pre-Raphaelite face so beautiful. She could never have tackled it without Charlie. I don't think I could

---

* William Lygon, 8th and last Earl Beauchamp (1903–79), who continued to be widely known by his courtesy title of Viscount Elmley after succeeding his father to the earldom and the ownership of Madresfield in 1938; m. 1936 Else 'Mona' de la Cour (1895–1989).

† Philip Hardwick (1792–1870); architect.

‡ C. R. Ashbee (1863–42); architect and designer in the Arts and Crafts tradition.

§ Family nickname of William Lygon, 7th Earl Beauchamp (1872–1938), Liberal statesman and Lady Morrison's grandfather, who lived at Madresfield until, in 1931, he was obliged to resign his public offices and move abroad owing to scandal (see 23 December 1994).

have faced it in her position, but applaud her family piety. Madresfield has been handed down in direct or indirect line since the 1300s, and has belonged to the Lygons since the 1500s.

Wednesday, 1st September

Dicky Buckle* called and we lunched at the posh Royal Crescent Hotel. Since I drink nothing, my half-share of the bill was fairly big. Hadn't seen Dicky for years. No longer the bright young man. Now a dear old paunchy, red-faced buffer, though has all his wits. Talked of Juliet Duff† and Simon Fleet.‡ He was extremely fond of the latter and feels responsible for his death, though Simon in fact fell down the stairs of his London maisonette when drunk and doped. We gossiped about old times, old faces, old ghosts. The truth is I don't much want to see old friends.

Thursday, 2nd September

Whereas today I enjoyed meeting Louisa Young,§ K[athleen] Kennet's granddaughter who is writing her life.¶ A very good subject, for she knew everyone of her time. She kept a diary from her first meeting with Scott until her death, and kept letters from T.E. Lawrence,** Barrie,†† Asquith,‡‡ etc. Louisa a very pretty girl, aged

---

* Richard Buckle (1916–2003); ballet critic, writer and exhibition designer.

† Lady Juliet Lowther (1881–1965); o. c. of 4th Earl of Lonsdale; m. 1903 Sir Robert Duff, 2nd Bt; mother of J.L.-M's friend Sir Michael Duff, 3rd Bt (1907–80).

‡ Actor, theatrical designer and saleroom correspondent of the *Observer* (1913–66); friend of Harold Nicolson, and admirer of formidable women such as Lady Juliet Duff and the ballet designer Sophie Fedorovich (from whom he inherited a house in Chelsea).

§ Hon. Louisa Young (b. 1959); yst dau. of Wayland Young, 2nd Baron Kennet.

¶ Louisa's biography was published by Macmillan in 1995 as *A Great Task of Happiness*.

** T. E. Lawrence (1888–1935); soldier, writer and archaeologist; 'Lawrence of Arabia'.

†† Sir James Barrie (1860–1937); novelist and playwright, creator of Peter Pan.

‡‡ Herbert Henry Asquith (1852–1928); Liberal Prime Minister, 1908–16; cr. Earl of Oxford and Asquith, 1925.

thirty-four with long blonde hair down to her waist. Nice voice. Loves K. whom she never knew. We ate boiled eggs and nectarines. She told me she had a daughter by a coal-black Ghanaian (out of wedlock, of course). Asked what I thought K. would have thought. I said that such a thing rarely happened in her day. At first she would have been shocked, but she would quickly have accepted the situation and reconciled herself completely, for she was essentially unconventional herself. I asked boldly, 'What colour is your daughter?' She replied, 'A lovely mahogany', pointing to the veneered arms of my William and Adelaide sofa. When Louisa left I said, 'I am going to give you a kiss because you are the granddaughter of that darling woman.' It must have been a horrid shock for her to be touched by the dead and pitted face of an ancient man, but she said, 'It almost makes me want to cry.'

Saturday, 4th September

I go by train to Chatsworth. Am given the red velvet bedroom, a mark of honour. Country Fair taking place in the park, in a piercing north wind. The Parker Bowleses and their two children staying – girl fifteen; boy eighteen, just left Eton, about to go to Oxford, intelligent and literary. I like Camilla, though she is not beautiful, and has lost her gaiety and sparkle. Doubtless worn by tribulations undergone. Women spit at her in supermarkets; cameramen snoop at her at the Fair. Walks with bowed head, and has trained her fluffy hair to cover her cheeks.

Andrew [Devonshire] says that two things have done a great disservice to this country. First, the reversal of several convictions of IRA members, a blow to the reputation of British justice. Secondly the Camillagate affair, which has seriously undermined the monarchy. Andrew certain that P. of W. won't succeed to the throne. Doesn't mind himself; claims to be a republican. Not too pleased when I said, 'You wouldn't like to be called Citizen Cavendish, surely?' Retorted that he knew of no republics in which dukes could not still call themselves dukes.

Saturday, 11th September

Before I open my letters in the morning, some instinct seems to tell me which will interest and which will bore me. Of course, all circulars and bills bore me. But the handwritten address on the envelope, even when I don't recognise the hand, always seems to reveal whether I shall read the letter with pleasure or the reverse. Even a typed envelope somehow discloses.

Tuesday, 21st September

To London, where Jamie Fergusson lunched with me at Brooks's. He told me that the future of the *Independent* was not secure and he often got fed up with obituarising. We ran into Stuart Preston who latched on to us, so I had little opportunity of talking to my strange, elusive, deep, rather sad Fergusson cousin. Stuart's appearance is frankly frightening – drooping mouth, baggy eyes, purple skin. He seldom smiles, but when he does, it remarkably brings back the charm he once had. When it came to settling, he, a member like myself, allowed me to pay for him without batting an eyelid. I am always terrified of being thought the meanie that I am, so I gaily paid for him and he just as gaily accepted.

Thursday, 30th September

We dined at the House, only Daph[ne Fielding] there apart from David and Caroline. We talked of Nancy [Mitford]'s letters,* Daph much upset by a remark in a letter to Debo that she, Daph, was a bitch. Jealousy over the Colonel, of course. As though it matters now. David said that posterity should never judge people by their correspondence, as what they wrote one day was often the opposite of what they thought the next. We agreed that no biographer's words about a dead person they had never met could be of much value. At least I think we did.

---

* *Love from Nancy: The Letters of Nancy Mitford*, ed. Charlotte Mosley (Hodder, 1993).

Sunday, 17th October

The [Roy] Jenkinses and the [Duff] Hart-Davises lunched. Quite a success. A. produced the best possible food and claret for Roy, who drank gallons and then drove off in a huge car, very flushed. Tomorrow he flies to Vienna to make a speech at some important dinner, and from there takes train to Warsaw to do the same there. How he has the energy I can't conceive. Jennifer asked me several more questions about the N.T. for her book, which she is sending me to read in proof. After luncheon we took them to the House, where Caroline showed us round. I said to Jennifer, 'I suppose the N.T. would accept, if offered?' 'They could hardly do otherwise,' she replied with a smile. We talked of the magic of houses. She said Hardwicke [Hall, Derbyshire] managed to preserve it, despite the large numbers, but Knole [Kent] only just. I said that Badminton still had it, perhaps because it was not open to the public. She nodded agreement. I find her infinitely sympathetic. She gave me an embrace when they left.

Wednesday, 20th October

Motored to Oxford to meet the President of Magdalen, Anthony Smith,* whom I at first confused with man of same name who is the son of Hubert Smith.† I had written offering my Buckler‡ engraving of Magdalen Tower which belonged to Uncle Robert [Bailey]. As I have inscribed on the back, it hung on his wall at Magdalen in 1901, and mine in 1931. Smith said, 'You may rest happy that it will be preserved here forever.' He kindly gave me several hours of his time, showing me round the college. In the ante-chapel I saw the contemporary copy, recently acquired, of Leonardo's *Last Supper*. Gazing at the memorial tablets, I asked, 'What does *praesens* mean?' 'President,' he whispered politely. He must think me very ignorant. At luncheon in the Fellows' canteen, the literature don sitting opposite asked who

---

* BBC TV Current Affairs producer (b. 1938); President of Magdalen College, Oxford from 1988.
† Sometime Chief Agent of N.T., whose son Anthony (b. 1926) was a writer and broadcaster.
‡ J. C. Buckler (1793–1894); engraver of architectural views.

my history tutor was in 1928. I had to confess I no longer had the slightest clue.* We went into the library, lately redecorated with Pompeian red ceiling by David Mlinaric. Was shown Wolsey's† beautifully hand-painted lectionary, his initials on every page. And a twelfth-century Book of Hours with splendid illuminations, said to be the earliest known book. Also Byron's *Lamia*, signed 'from the author'. Splendid gothic tapestry panels in President's Lodge, given by William of Wykeham.‡ President very keen on Bruce Chatwin, talking of his impressive power of empathy. 'He has taught me things.' I parted with the engraving without a pang, feeling sure Uncle Robert would have approved.

Spent rest of day wandering about Oxford in glorious sunshine, no breath of wind. Ideal conditions. Tourist season over. How could I have ignored the architecture of this superb city when I was here? Every house in Longwall a delight, save the disgraceful horizontal addition to New College overlooking Magdalen Park. How could it have been allowed? I had a lovely day, and blessed God that I still have the use of my legs and eyes – just.

Sunday, 24th October

We lunch at Barnsley [Park] with the Faringdons, a large party. Charles extremely friendly, his uproarious laughter due to shyness presumably. He dragged me out of the library window to show me the astonishing way in which Nash made the windows of the conservatory disappear so that in summer it looks like the Parthenon, windows folding back like closed butterfly wings. An astonishing construction, with the steel roundel frames in the end pediments. Such a beautiful house, probably the finest Baroque in Britain. I sat next to Sarah F., one of the great beauties of our time. Not very bright, I suspect. On my other side Penelope Sitwell, who asked if it was true that I had been asked to write Sachie's life. I explained that

---

* Head of History at Magdalen at the time was the mediaevalist Bruce McFarlane.
† Cardinal Thomas Wolsey (1475?–1530); principal counsellor to King Henry VIII until his disgrace in 1529.
‡ Bishop and statesman (1324–1404), who endowed Winchester School and founded New College, Oxford.

Jock Murray had asked me to do a 'brief life', but I had declined. She said that Sachie and Georgia were both monsters. 'Sachie?' I asked. She replied that he was as bad as she, with his evil face. Well, that was pretty plain speaking.

I enjoyed my visit to Barnsley very much. A rare survival of civilised existence – agreeable guests, delicious food, every sign of taste without luxury. A butler in attendance, and ladies waiting. This is what lefties despise and resent, and what academe has always relished – i.e., living at the expense of the bloated rich. It is the best thing which England has shown to the world.

Tuesday, 26th October

In the train, I thought how curious it was that I, as an old eunuch, am now totally heterosexual. I am drawn exclusively to the mystique of the female persona, whereas the male physique revolts me and the male persona has little allure. I suppose that, by a tilt of the scales, a nudge from the tip of an angel's wing, I would have been wholly 'normal' from adolescence onwards. Perhaps it is just as well that this was not the case, as I would probably have been a nasty, intolerant, anti-queer young fogey.

Saturday, 13th November

Alvilde said to David [Beaufort] at dinner, 'When I first met you I was so terrified that I wrote notes beforehand on what to talk about.' He said that he was equally alarmed by the prospect of meeting her, having heard she was so grumpy and formidable. 'But I adore you now,' he said.

David told us that he knew a man who was born totally blind. Recently he had an operation which enabled him to see. At first he was appalled to see how hideous human beings were. Horses, on the other hand, he found exquisitely beautiful. He was also shocked to discover that cars and buses got larger as they got nearer, while railway lines became closer together as they receded into the distance. I had never thought of this aspect, so much do we take such things for granted.

Monday, 15th November

Clarissa [Luke] and Billy came to see the downstairs flat in Bath, the tenant having given notice. I agree with A. that we must let them have it, yet regard the prospect with foreboding.

Thursday, 2nd December

Hugh Massingberd, who after a hasty dinner at Brooks's took me to see the beautiful film of the Japanese man's novel *The Remains of the Day*, told me that he had not yet got over a damning letter from Duff Hart-Davis about what Hugh had intended to be a rave article on Owlpen Manor. It almost made him hand in his resignation from the *Telegraph*, so much did it make him feel a failure as a journalist. I told him he was too sensitive. He said that his wife Caroline was thinking of joining Mother Teresa in Calcutta, and he was wondering whether to do so too. What did I think? I thought it would only be a good move provided they both dispensed condoms on the streets of Calcutta along with solace.

Wednesday, 22nd December

Though feeling awful, I went to London today to lunch with Marilyn Quennell, who had asked me and others to discuss Peter's memorial service. Ghastly underground journey to Chalk Farm, changing several times. The house where Peter spent his last years with his last wife is in a Victorian cul-de-sac, ugly and claustrophobic. Ushered downstairs to basement dining room. Out of the dark loomed ex-Belgian Ambassador, nice artist neighbour called Tim Jaques,* and Stephen Spender.† An air of desperation. Marilyn presiding at round table, coming and going. Quite clear she was already drunk. Very argumentative and affected, acting the great lady like Anne Rosse used to do, but worse.

---

* Illustrator and typographical designer (b. 1933); stalwart of Omar Khayyam Dining Club.
† Sir Stephen Spender (1909–95); poet; m. 1941 Natasha Litvin.

Stephen, looking huge and benign, was very friendly and volunteered to sit next to me. We talked of Sunday shopping,* I remarking that it was presumably convenient for the daily workers. 'That', said S. laughing, 'is the first democratic sentiment I have heard you utter.' Marilyn asked why Peter gave up writing poetry when he was a good poet. About the only nice thing she did say about her late lamented saint. S. said that P. did not have the calling. M. maintained it was because he recognised that his poetry was unfashionable. He ought to have ignored his contemporaries, and persisted instead of 'indulging in the fleshpots'. 'No harm in that,' said S. I agreed with M. that if P. was a true poet he should not have been affected by silly fashion. Mentioned Hopkins.† S. said the trouble was that poets wanted passionately to write whereas few wanted to read what they had written.

S. enjoys being a knight. Owes it to Isaiah Berlin,‡ his long-time protector, who has the ear of all who matter, the Crown, Number Ten. S. doesn't mind the prospect of dying, though worries about how Natasha will be looked after. Also fears there will be many books and articles about him, disclosing his love affairs – 'not that you will be in that category,' he added. Admits he suffers much from guilt about the past. He has a new volume of poems coming out in February, and said that the period between advance copies and publication was like that between a death and a funeral. I was touched by his niceness to me. We asked each other why we had not in our long lives seen more of each other. I said I wished we had been friends at Oxford, when I was in need of friends. I thought, but did not say, that he might have rendered me less right-wing, I him less left. Who knows?

By this time, Marilyn had disappeared. When I looked for her to say goodbye she was supine on a sofa, mouth open.

---

* A law permitting the general opening of shops on Sunday finally took effect from August 1994.

† The poetry of Gerard Manley Hopkins (1844–89) was unknown to the world until a selection of it was published by Robert Bridges in 1918, almost thirty years after his death.

‡ Sir Isaiah Berlin (1909–97); Russian-born Oxford philosopher and historian of ideas.

1994

1994

Tuesday, 4th January

While reading James Agate's* immensely clever *Ego 9* I nodded off for a split second. During this flick of an eyelash I suddenly felt desperately lonely without Mama and Papa and wondered how I could get through life without them. Then I remembered that I had not been wholly foresaken, as A. was still with me. The relief was so great that I actually cried. Now I ask myself sadly, how long shall I have A. for? How long shall we remain united?

Saturday, 8th January

I am thinking of writing to Mr Major to tell him that he can't both go 'back to basics' and have 'a classless society'.† For basic politeness and civilised behaviour are the attributes of a gentleman, nurtured in country houses and on the playing fields of Eton. Outside such sanctuaries of good breeding, brutishness and vulgarity flourish. Which is why few things are more distressing than to see aristocrats behaving like louts and swine.

Sunday, 16th January

Tony Lambton blows in at midday. He has beautiful manners, and is charming without having charm, but makes me uneasy. Is full of hates and dislikes, and one has to avoid seeming to agree with him. Also

---

* Theatre critic (1877–1947).
† Recent slogans of the Major government – which predictably resulted in the tabloid press launching a campaign to expose 'sleaze', both financial and sexual, among Conservative MPs.

mischievous. He notices everything, which I like. Praises my little room where we sat, and asks about the pictures. What is that house? My grandmother's. What was her name? He presses us both to stay with him in Italy, but I don't think either of us could stand the strain.

Sunday, 23rd January

In the afternoon I walk to Worcester Lodge, an hour and a half. Not bad, considering my legs are now feeble. A fine afternoon with sun, with heralding of spring and definite whispering of siren songs. Even at eighty-five I am disturbed, wanting to be off. In the garden a few aconites and snowdrops already out; and the goldfish, who should be hibernating at the bottom of the pool, are darting about.

Saturday, 29th January

Woman brought Diana [Mosley] to luncheon. Diana very thin and deaf. Is distressed by an article on her in *Mail on Sunday* by Brian Masters,* with ravishingly beautiful photograph. When she left I read it with care, and don't think he meant to be unkind at all. He allowed Diana to speak for herself. All that is objectionable are the captions, highlighting that she is still hated throughout the world after fifty years, etc. I have written to tell her what I think.

Saturday, 5th February

Lying in bed this morning later than is my wont, I decide that I feel worse in bed than out of it. In bed I seek tranquillity – but find worrying dreams, restless waking, a quickening of the heartbeat and consequent breathlessness.

---

* Writer (b. 1939), celebrated for psychological studies of mass murderers.

Thursday, 3rd March

So Harold Acton has now gone. What do I feel? Nothing much. It was high time for him. Papers full of praise, all obituaries laudatory and favourable. He is another example of a man remarkable not for what he has left behind but what he made himself into. Sad that the lovely Pietra garden will no longer be for private delight. The house always struck me as horribly melancholy. Edwardian of course, with the sort of Italian paintings and Renaissance treasures which leave no room for future ages. Bedroom so cluttered that it was rash to unpack for likelihood of losing one's things among the junk. I did not quite belong to his generation; there was four years' difference between us, which when we were young was considerable. He was wonderful to be with, wonderful. That unique voice, with inflexions more Italian than English. His grandfather's origins wrapped in mists. Once, during the war, we dined together and strolled back to Eaton Place where he was staying in the Rosses' little house in their absence. H. in uniform, an odd spectacle. He persuaded me to stay and go to bed with him. I agreed, but it meant nothing to me. Next morning he rebuked me for icy-cold unresponsiveness, and I don't think he ever quite forgave me. People who have been rejected – or worse still, who have been accepted and then treated with indifference – harbour lasting resentment, and hurt. Harold's appearance never changed since I first met him at McNeile's House [at Eton] in 1921, when he was a senior boy and I a new boy. He seemed bald even then. A sort of Horace Mann,[*] to be remembered for his erudition, intelligence and sparkling conversation.

Saturday, 12th March

Our long-planned luncheon with the [Roy] Jenkinses. Other guests Roland Philipps,[†] son of Mollie Norwich and grandson of Ros[amond

---

[*] Sir Horace Mann, 1st Bt (1701–86); British envoy at Florence whose main duty was to keep an eye on 'Bonnie Prince Charlie' there; friend and correspondent of Horace Walpole.

[†] Hon. Roland Philipps (b. 1962); editorial director of Macmillan (later Managing Director of John Murray and publisher of this volume); m. 1991 Felicity Rubinstein (b. 1958), literary agent.

Lehmann], a publisher and a friendly fellow, and wife, literary agent. Also Clarissa Avon,[*] who retains a splendid slim figure whereas her face is a cobweb of creases making her look far older than her seventy-three years. She reminded me that she had known me since she was six. Jennifer is my idea of the perfect wife. Her history of the N.T., which I have now read in proof, is a magisterial tome. It is very nice to me – or rather about me.

Tuesday, 15th March

To London, object of visit to attend Prince Charles's party to launch *Perspectives.*[†] A. said I must go, it would be rude not to, and besides one must support a good cause. Forgot what time expected, so chose 6.30. Walked from Brooks's down to St James's Palace. On entry, found Palace curiously deserted. Didn't want to arrive first so, having passed through downstairs gallery and surrendered overcoat and brolley, I sat on a scarlet bench and waited. A nice lady approached and asked if I was feeling unwell. I assured her not, but did not like to explain why I was waiting. She insisted on accompanying me upstairs, lending an arm which I didn't need. Directed me through two rooms overlooking Friary Court towards a large drawing room literally *jammed* with people. She explained that over five hundred had already come. I couldn't even get beyond the entrance door. Eileen Harris saw me and came up to talk, but I couldn't hear a single word. I stood for a few minutes, doubtless looking like a dazed rabbit, then retreated and left. I think the stairs are those in double flight illustrated in Pyne. The two approaching galleries dull, one with Tudor fireplace; red walls, furniture against walls, dull portraits. No opportunity to poke around. When I telephoned A. before dinner, she was furious with me for not arriving promptly at the decreed hour of six.

[*] Clarissa Churchill (b. 1920); niece of Sir Winston and sister of J.L.-M's late friend Johnnie Churchill; m. 1953 Sir Anthony Eden, Prime Minister 1955–7, cr. Earl of Avon, 1961.
[†] Unsuccessful architecture magazine supported by Prince of Wales, published from 1994 to 1998.

Wednesday, 16th March

I caught early train back to Chippenham and drove to Malmesbury to collect from Mrs Nicholls' shop the two turquoise Minton saucers I bought the other day. Didn't dare own up to A., who would have thought it an extravagance. Said nothing about it when I got home, she sitting in her usual chair drinking tea, waiting for me. There is no reason for me to feel guilty, for after all, it is my money and my pleasure. Yet I don't want to keep things from her, and be underhand. We had a happy evening, and when I kissed her goodnight she laughed and said, 'What dreadful old crocks we are.'

Friday, 18th March

When I left for Bath this morning, I did not for some reason kiss A. goodbye as I usually do. After a good day's work, and some shopping, I got home at 4.45. Unloaded car, walked to gate, opened gate – and then I saw her in front of me, lying on the flagstones, the slippery flagstones she so dreaded, her car keys in hand. The shock appalling. 'My darling!' I called to her, scattering my things as I bent down. Felt her forehead, which was cold. Could not move her. Dashed to estate office, begging for help. They telephoned Peggy and Gerald, who came quickly. Peggy rang for ambulance, but Gerald knew she was dead. Men came, carried her into drawing room, laid her not on sofa but on floor. I could not look at her again. Ian [Dixon] came and sweetly sat with me drinking whisky until Clarissa and Billy arrived from London. Suave undertaker came. I begged for her rings before she was taken away to mortuary chapel in Chippenham. O dear God, to see her stretched before me on the cold stone, in the rain. She had come straight from the hairdresser and looked so pretty. Sudden, I am sure – but what is 'sudden' at the time of death? And I not there to hold her hand. These days to be my hell on earth.

Thursday, 24th March

Yesterday we went, driven by Billy, whose presence has to be accepted, to the undertakers at Chippenham. I wanted to have one last look at her, if only to mitigate the guilt on my conscience at having allowed her to be swept away without a last goodbye. Funeral parlour clinically clean. Handsome, affable official received us, directed us to silent, windowless chapel. There she lay on the bier, her head uncovered. Serene she looked, and beautiful; not a line visible. At my request, Clarissa cut a few locks of her dear hair. Then I asked to be alone. In agonies of tears I kissed her brow, as hard and as cold as marble, and begged her to forgive me for being the rotten husband I was. Quickly pulled myself together.

I am inundated with letters. Mightily pleased by the obituaries of her in *Independent* by Mary Keen and Coote [Heber-Percy], and *Telegraph* by unknown. Not intimate, all about her horticultural expertise. Rosemary [Verey] telephoned to read out another she had written for *The Times* – wonderful and generous. I never supposed she would have any obits.

So long as I am busy, and no one commiserates, I am all right by day. Lying in bed before falling asleep is dreadful. I am irritated by Billy's presence, and have told Clarissa that both of them must leave me on Saturday. I am sure he is well-meaning, but he is extremely dumb and boring.

Friday, 25th March

The day I have dreaded ever since it occurred to me some thirty years ago that she might die before me. We had some twenty-five to a stand-up luncheon before the funeral in Little Badminton Church. Charming vicar Ian Marchant officiated, Tom Gibson being in South Africa. He spoke sweetly of A.; and Tony Scotland read verses from Corinthians I, Chapter 15, most beautifully and professionally. Several people from the village and a handful of old friends. I had to walk out first behind her dear coffin to the hearse. Then the crematorium, which was not too harrowing. Marchant read a prayer; and the large curtains, like those at Covent Garden, silently closed. Then home. Clarissa took her descendants to Old Werretts* for tea, while Nick and Richard [Robinson] stayed with me and we did the Cherry Orchard walk.

---

* House of Desmond Briggs and Ian Dixon at Castle Combe.

Time has somehow ceased. The evenings alone are agony, and the nights frightening. I go in and out of her bedroom. The whole house is full of coffee-cups – her notes, diary, telephone book, every single thing is redolent of her.

Thursday, 31st March

At four, the undertaker called. He bowed from the waist and asked solemnly if I was prepared to receive the urn, which he held out like the Archbishop offering the orb to the Queen. He added a few words, 'If I may presume on such an occasion', etc. I asked him if he was sure the ashes were A's. He appeared to be shocked by the question. 'Perhaps in the big cities misadventures may occur.' Laughing and crying, I carried upstairs the large, brown, nondescript plastic urn, embraced it, and put it inside the large blue-and-white bowl above my clothes cupboard. I don't find it macabre; on the contrary, a comfort to have her remains so near me while I sleep.

Saturday, 2nd April

Today at breakfast I read the most beastly article by David Cannadine[*] about Harold and Vita, calling them snobs. I rang Nigel to express my outrage. During Holy Communion, I thought I must reply to it. On return I drafted and redrafted letter to *The Times*, then drove to Old Werretts where Desmond despatched it to the editor on his fax machine. They then drove me to the Norwiches where we lunched. About ten, including Sue Baring and the nice Levis. Then back in pouring rain to see Clarissa and Billy. They went through A's jewelry, spreading it out on kitchen table. She asked him what he thought of each piece – as though he ever thinks about anything. I said nothing, but found it painful to watch him handling A's precious personal things. Then dinner at the House, numerous children and friends. Delicious caviare, both David and Caroline abstaining out of boredom

---

[*] Cambridge historian (b.1950).

with it. He said it was Persian, and the best in the world. Afterwards I talked with David in the library about his houses in the village and all the trouble he has with the planning officers, who are obstructive and tasteless. I find him very sympathetic when his attention can be won.

Tuesday, 5th April

I visit the Harrises in their lugubrious cottage at Ashcroft. At home and without an audience, John sheds his boisterous jocularity and talks calmly and wisely. I take to her more and more. We discuss the back-slidings of the National Trust, which they say is beaten to the ground by its own bureaucracy. Terribly depressed when I get home in the evening. Home is like my own empty heart.

Wednesday, 6th April

I am haunted by my lamentable unkindness to A., particularly in two respects. First, I never tried hard enough to understand and share her love of gardening. She put plants into the earth with her own hands, nurtured them, watched them grow, and when they were blossoming, looked not merely at them but into them. Secondly, I was often horrid about her descendants, so that she was reluctant to discuss with me all the worries they caused her. I find it hard to forgive them; yet I behaved very ill.

Thursday, 7th April

I remember Jamesey [Pope-Hennessy] once said to me, when we saw a discarded tin, 'It's a sobering thought that this tin may exist long after we are dust.' And here around me are all the tins she bought, and the food in the freezer which she put there. The misery is unendurable.

Saturday, 9th April

Debo telephones after breakfast. 'It's nothing alarming,' she begins. 'Woman, staying with her friend Margaret Budd, fell on the stairs and

broke both her legs. She's being operated on at the London Hospital.'
At eighty-seven, what chance is there of recovery?

Tony Lambton telephones asking me to stay with them in Tuscany,
and Michael Mallon* writes that John Pope-Hennessy wants me to
stay in Florence. Rather flattering to be invited by the two men who
frighten me most in the world.

Monday, 18th April

I motor to Swinbrook for Woman's funeral. I pick whatever flowers in
the garden are out, which Peggy ties up in some mauve paper and
ribbons, and insert note to Darling and Wonderful Woman from her
devoted Jimble. Woman's coffin unvarnished, in natural wood, as she
wanted. She is buried away from Nancy's and Unity's plots by desire of
the vicar, afraid of too many sightseers crowding around a Mitford
enclave.

Wednesday, 20th April

Consternation. The lead bird-bath, prettily decorated along the
rim, maybe eighteenth-century and beloved by A., has been stolen.
Nothing is safe. Doe Bowlby† was telling me that their house was
burgled on three successive nights while they were sleeping upstairs.

My *Times* letter about Harold and Vita has had a favourable reception. People mention it with approval or write to congratulate. It has
prompted others to write to *The Times* about the simple kindness they
received from Vita at Sissinghurst.

Tuesday, 26th April

Jeremy Fry‡ telephones, back from southern India where he is building
a house. Commiserates about A. and says how much he admired and

---

* American art history student (b. 1960); personal assistant to Sir John Pope-Hennessy
(who was to inherit most of his property on his death later that year – see 26 August
1997).
† Dora Allen; m. 1930 Sir Anthony Bowlby, 2nd Bt, of the Old Rectory, Ozleworth,
Glos.
‡ Inventor and businessman (b. 1924); m. 1955 (diss. 1967) Camilla Grinling.

loved her. Jeremy can be very touching. Told me to withdraw into myself. This is indeed what I would like to do, but I get caught up in events. Now Debo has written to beg me – 'beg' is her angelic word – to join the family celebrations the week after next for tercentenary of Devonshire dukedom.

Thursday, 12th May

By train to Chatsworth. Debo clearly preoccupied, so I retreat to my bedroom, the Red Velvet, and rest until festivities begin in park at 7.30. Incredible celebrations of ducal tercentenary on scale of Louis XIV. Huge auditorium constructed on far side of river; around it, tents and cone-like huts illuminated like a Saracen encampment. An enormous dinner tent (not for house guests, dining later in Painted Hall). Mingling with invited crowd are men on stilts, men with bagpipes, jugglers, funny men, singing men with instruments. I run into people I know – Diana Scarisbrick* the jewelry expert; John and Laura Saumarez Smith; Brian Masters (staying in house), bearing deep scar across his cheek from a strange man who called at his door.

Watch pageant staged across the Derwent against architectural background, to which we are summoned by 'revolutionaries' in full-bottomed wigs bearing Orange flags. One of them approaches asking me to sign petition in favour of William of Orange, which I do laughingly, saying I feel a traitor to my Stuart allegiance. 'I've read your books,' says petitioner to me knowingly. Pageant a truly amazing spectacle, though cold so intense I fear hypothermia. All the Dukes impersonated, from the first down to Duke Eddie, all in correct contemporary costumes. Then fireworks such as I had never seen before – fingers of gold and corkscrew serpents weaving into the sky – accompanied by water music by Beethoven, Handel, Elgar. Then Andrew, sitting next to me, descends to riverbank to make short speech of thanks. Wild applause, everyone much moved, many in tears.

---

* New Zealand-born expert; m. Peter Scarisbrick; author of *Jewellery in Britain*, 1066–1837 (Michael Russell, 1994), and organiser of jewellery exhibitions.

Back to house for dinner at 11.30. Sit next to Stoker* who talks most affectionately of his father, praising his phenomenal generosity and public spirit. Do not get to bed until two in the morning, for the first time in years.

Wednesday, 18th May

Motored to Oxford, where I collected Derek Hill at the station. We went to an Italian restaurant where we were joined by Dr Graham Speak, Hon. Sec. of Mount Athos Society, and Bishop Kallistos, Chairman, with silky white beard and affable manner. Bishop talks with beautiful diction, every syllable enunciated. I understood every word he said, both then and later when he delivered his lecture on the Holy Mountain. A polished performance, very gripping and nostalgic to us Athonites.† He is English, of course, by the name of Ware. Sir Steven Runciman‡ presided, having come from Scotland by train without attendant or minder. Is ninety-one. A handsome man, and very robust for his age. Has all his marbles. Is inscrutable, lofty, cold as ice. Carriage of head noble and disdainful. Slight curve of underlip; hooded eyes giving sidelong looks. We left together; but having met only once before, we had little to say to each other.

Am I making a mistake in telling friends that I am going to Scotland in search of a religious asylum in the Hebrides to retire to? My desire to do some such thing grows stronger every day, provided the retreat offers the minimum of comfort I am accustomed to, and the fathers are intellectual men. I see myself spending my last days in devout contemplation.

Wednesday, 25th May

The dreaded day of A's memorial service at St Mary's, Paddington Green. Desmond Briggs accompanied me in the train, insisting that

---

* Peregrine Cavendish, Marquess of Hartington (b. 1944); son of 11th Duke of Devonshire (whom he s. as 12th Duke, 2004); m. 1967 Amanda Heywood-Lonsdale.
† In the company of Derek Hill, a seasoned visitor to Mount Athos, J.L.-M. had made three visits there, in 1977, 1979 and 1980.
‡ Hon. Sir Steven Runciman (1903–2000); yr s. of 1st Viscount Runciman of Doxford; Cambridge historian, specialising in Byzantine Empire and Crusades.

I travel first class with him and shocked that I did not do so habitually. We walked from station to St Mary's, under the flyovers. Lovely little church. Found the Gibsons there, and Clarissa. Lovely flowers, vast bunches of alliums and white. I sat in front bench of box pews, a symphony of gold and white, with Clarissa, Freda [Berkeley], Anne Hill. Church full, even the galleries, which was a relief. Beautiful service. My Bidding Prayer read by Tom Gibson, words on our splendid service sheet printed by Mitchell of Marlborough. Both clergymen looking handsome in full canonicals. Derry [Drogheda] read Psalm 50; then Tony Scotland read from Vita's *Garden Book*. Michael Berkeley* gave the address – too anecdotal in view of Rupert Loewenstein, but I thought excellent. I did not cry, except once during hymn. Anthems by Poulenc and Mozart which A. would have loved. At the end, I walked down the aisle with a firm step and even a smile of pride on my lips, to 1980s Quinlan Terry church hall, where plenty of excellent food and drink. The Gibsons motored me to Brooks's where I was joined for tea by J.K.-B. and George Dix† who mysteriously appeared. Nick motored me home, where we dined off smoked salmon sandwiches left over from party.

Friday, 3rd June

Nick meets me at Marlborough and motors me to Longford Castle [near Salisbury], where we lunch with the Radnors.‡ We see the famous Coleshill Baby in its glass case. They say it is not made of wax but the very baby embalmed. But they do not know its history beyond hearsay, and assure me there is no written record. So Nick and I decide that I should not write the history of the Coleshill Baby but of a fictitious baby and place, which makes my task easier.

Although of great interest architecturally, with its triangular Elizabethan plan and Salvin alterations, Longford is not a nice house. Superb contents, of course – Holbein's *Erasmus* and *Sir Thomas More*,

---

* Composer and broadcaster (b. 1948); e. s. of Lennox and Freda *née* Bernstein.
† Friend of J.L.-M. since 1945, at which time he was a US naval officer.
‡ Jacob Pleydell-Bouverie, 8th Earl of Radnor (b. 1927); m. (3rd) 1986 Mary Pettit.

Kent-style furniture, Compagnie des Indes service from 1740s. Really another museum house like Madresfield. The rooms all Victorianised and without distinction, except for a circular sitting room, with Gothick pendant ceiling and short dark marble columns, possibly Elizabethan. Nice though to visit a country house which is still one, and not open to the public. They are alarmed by recent robberies at Abbotsford, Luton Hoo, etc. and have installed all-night floodlighting. Lord Radnor large, stout and disabled by polio. Very jolly and shrewd, laughing a good deal. She the third wife, delightful and simple; must have been pretty before she got fat.

Sunday, 5th June

Lunched with Jenkinses at East Hendred. Other guests Johnnie Grimond, son of late Jo but without his cleverness or good looks, and wife, daughter of Peter Fleming.* We talked about the disadvantages of being the son of a famous man. I said that Randolph Churchill's life was ruined by this circumstance, adding that, if I had had a famous father, I should undoubtedly have killed myself. Grimond replied, 'My elder brother killed himself.' She, having been brought up at Nettlebed, has known Rupert Hart-Davis from birth. I said that at Eton he was the hero both of the masters and the boys. Roy regretted having been unable to attend Alvilde's memorial service (though she sweetly came, having only met A. twice). He said he had first met A. at Ann Fleming's. 'And did you find her formidable?' I asked. 'Well,' he replied, 'I had to take the measure of her, but when I met her again, I saw the great point of her.' This pleased.

Monday, 13th June

Go for a walk at 9.30 p.m. Still light. Turneresque sunset approaches as I walk under the bridge towards Slates, then turn off and wander

---

* Hon. John Grimond (b. 1946); s. of Jo Grimond (1913–93), politician, Leader of Liberal Party 1956–67, cr. life peer 1987; journalist and economist, sometime editor of *The Economist*; m. 1973 Kate, dau. of Lt-Col Peter Fleming, travel writer (1907–71).

through the arboretum. Mysterious tranquillity. Weird shadows. Strong smells of summer. Delicious, because the world is my own.

I am seriously worried about approaching publication of new diaries. Am certain I have made a grave mistake. When I rebuked M. for not having stopped me when he read them in MS, he said, 'Well, I did wonder about that bit about Princess Margaret.' Why the hell didn't he say so at the time? I have in fact modified that entry slightly.* The last thing I want is to have the press spotlighting it as another jibe against royalty.

Tuesday, 14th June

Clarissa and Billy for tea. They put me in such a rage that I have to ask them to leave. C. with her hennaed hair, eyes and mouth like a clown's, silver rings on every finger, talking drivel and constantly asking Billy what he thinks – as though he can think at all – rouses the devil in me.

Wednesday, 22nd June

Seeing the garden so lush and crammed with blooms, roses at their most glorious, I feel I ought to take more of an interest in it, at least to the extent of learning the generic name of every plant in it. Today the Borderlines Party of gardening experts came to Badminton, visiting first the House, then here. They were very appreciative, raving about the garden and A's wonderful taste and sense of handling and placing plants. Lady Moyra Campbell† told me she had come all the way from Northern Ireland just for this day. They all talked to me about A. and her reputation.

Tuesday, 28th June

I only saw a few minutes of the Prince Charles interview,‡ but it was enough to make me deplore the whole exercise. This idealistic

---

* Very slightly indeed, so far as the present editor ('M.') can judge.

† Lady Moyra Hamilton (b. 1930); o. dau. of 4th Duke of Abercorn; m. 1966 Commander Peter Campbell.

‡ By his official biographer Jonathan Dimbleby, on BBC television.

middle-aged man struggled to get the words out and writhed with intellectual deficiency, wrinkling his forehead and making grimaces. A great mistake for him to admit marital infidelity. He should have refused to discuss such matters, whatever the pressure. I was left with the feeling that he is not equipped to be a leader, and certainly not to wrestle with clever minds. And why expose himself to twelve million viewers, complaining of his persecution by the press?

Friday, 8th July

Pangs of sadness pierce me when I come across something which A. would have delighted to hear about. I see the eagerness on her face when I say there is an article in this week's *Country Life* by her beloved Fred Whitsey* on Laurie Johnston's† gardens at Hidcote and Mentone, or when I tell her what Asa Briggs thought of Stuart Menzies.‡ And then there is her garden. Today Paul and Jane [her former gardeners] came to tea, and we walked round the garden. Jane remembered every corner and the name of every plant she put in, and Paul marvelled that the box and yew hedge had grown so high, for he planted it under her supervision. I blessed them both, and when they left, felt like crying. Now I understand why the garden meant nearly everything to her. The plants were her living children, propagated by her.

Monday, 11th July

Wonderful spell of fine weather. Desmond [Briggs] and Ian [Dixon] motored me to Longleat for Daphne Fielding's ninetieth birthday luncheon. The park looked marvellous in the sunshine, except for the

---

* Horticultural writer (b. 1919).

† Major Lawrence Johnston (1871–1958); Anglo-American horticulturist who created famous gardens at Hidcote, Gloucestershire, and La Serre de la Madonna, Mentone, the former of which was donated to the N.T. in 1948 largely through the efforts of J.L.-M.

‡ At a house party a few days earlier, J.L.-M. had met Lord Briggs (see 17 July 1989), who had worked during the war under Sir Stuart Menzies (1890–1968), chief of the Secret Intelligence Service MI6 and A.L.-M's first cousin.

masses and the funfairs and the lions. The party just what I feared. Upstairs in Alexander Bath's* new 'penthouse', as he calls it, really one end of Bishop Ken's† library. Taste in fabrics and furnishings appalling; mulberry fitted carpet, jazzy cushions, office furniture. A band playing some ghastly sort of African jungle music so loudly that we could not hear a word said. Lord Bath with grey fuzzy hair all over face down to shoulders was dressed, as was his brother Christopher, as a Mexican bandit. He was jolly, and quite mad. I sat next to Debo and charming man called William Sieghart‡ who has lately returned from exploring Abyssinia. Is a publisher of contemporary poetry and a magazine called *Help*. Brought tall pretty girl to whom, he confided, he was hoping to be engaged before the day was out. Noise in too-small, low-ceilinged eating room likewise appalling. Debo and I gave up. Didn't enjoy it much, though honoured to be placed at top table with Daphne and the D[evonshire]s.

Wednesday, 27th July

Having finished my essay on Paul Methuen, I thought I would visit Corsham again after all these years. Went round state rooms and gardens. All very well maintained. For all his faults, John Methuen evidently cares for Corsham. Was stunned by beauty of picture gallery with rare eighteenth-century collection of paintings, Adam mirrors and furniture. All of highest quality. And Paul's thick and sumptuous carpet, which struck me as slightly faded already. James Methuen-Campbell appeared, about to visit John at Bath Clinic. Showed me how the carpet was woven in two strips, sewn together invisibly. On hearing who I was, one of the guides presented me with a catalogue,

---

* Alexander Thynne, 7th Marquess of Bath (b. 1932); e. s. of Daphne Fielding and brother of Caroline, Duchess of Beaufort. Brilliant and beautiful in youth, he had become a famous English eccentric, preaching free love and naturism, founding the Wessex Regional Party, becoming a rock musician, writing curious books, and filling the Elizabethan rooms of Longleat, Wiltshire, with erotic murals.

† Dr Thomas Ken (1637–1711); Bishop of Bath and Wells from 1684 (imprisoned by James II for refusal to publish Declaration of Indulgence); spent last years at Longleat as guest of Lord Weymouth.

‡ Poet, publisher, broadcaster and philanthropist; founder of National Poetry Day, and Action for the Homeless.

while another came up and shook me by the hand, remembering me from the old days when I was a trustee. James told me that John's recovery is unlikely; he is dying of alcoholism, and when deprived goes into a coma.

Tuesday, 2nd August

I dined at the House, just with David and Caroline alone, which I like. We ate in the library at a small table, a fire burning in the grate as the weather has suddenly turned cold. Really, I find him charming, so wise when he talks seriously, always funny in that deadpan manner. He said he hadn't the slightest idea how to judge contemporary painting. But surely you must, I said, you are the most successful gallery owner. No, he said, he didn't, but he had learnt from long experience what his clients like and want, which is another thing.

Very kind about my predicament they were. He asked me if I was very hard up and muttered that I need not pay the rent of course. Whereupon I had to protest, for I am not totally broke and would die sooner than become a lame dog. He talked of Italian corruption and said it was a hopeless situation, for it has long been axiomatic in the Italian business world that every deal must be prefaced by slipping a tip into an intermediary's hands. Agnelli* was an honourable man, but a great firm like Fiat would get nowhere without conforming. Yet today this is regarded as corruption by the magistrates. David said that bribery in Italy was stamped out by Mussolini, and after Mussolini's fall returned. Now almost ineradicable.

Saturday, 6th August

My birthday, now mentioned in both *The Times* and *Daily Telegraph*. Cards from dear old Rupert [Hart-Davis], darling Debo, one or two others. I made an expedition to Wickhamford, stopping on the way to see the churches at Dumbleton, Wormington and Aston Somerville. Finally arrived at Wickhamford church. What a gem it is. I looked around and decided to sit and ruminate in our old manor

---

* Gianni Agnelli (1921–2003); head of Fiat (founded by his grandfather), 1966–96.

pew. Forgot how uncomfortable it was, the projecting top digging into one's back. Glad that the now pale faded red striped bench squabs survive. Then spent three hours in Manor and garden with current owners, very friendly and welcoming couple called Ryan-Bell.* Extremely proud of the place and eager for historical information. Thrilled with the few anecdotes I could dredge up from brain. I went all over the house with them, seeing Mama's oak-panelled bedroom in which I was born eighty-six years ago. At what time, they asked eagerly? The place has not been so much altered inside as I had supposed. Taste none too sound. Audrey's bedroom still has its curious beam struts; original pre-1914 bathtub with maker's name in blue still in place under taps, Rufford & Sons; same seat in downstairs lav. So much the same. I did not feel too sad, in fact pleased by their delight. A nice, decent new family. Pond covered with water lilies, which he means to eradicate. He led me to the drain where the twin Scots firs stood, and said, 'Listen!' He waited while I intently listened. Yes, the same deep, resonant, nostalgic sound, cavernous and gentle.

Monday, 8th August

John K.-B. comes to stay the night. So affectionate and fond of unworthy me. After luncheon we visit Lacock [Abbey] and go round this melancholy house which is quite well kept up. Too many family pictures with no identification but some interesting new revelations, like the James I hall chairs and Queen Anne studded travelling trunks.

Thursday, 11th August

At 5.30 I went to see Daph[ne Fielding]. We talked of Caroline, who is going into Gloucester Hospital today for tests. She has jaundice and has been feeling rotten but would not put off an engagment in Wales yesterday, being very dutiful, and motored straight to Gloucester from Wales. Daph thought she was suffering from gall stones.

---

* J.L.-M. had met them ten years earlier – see 29 August 1984.

An hour after I left Daph, she rang to say that C. had just telephoned her with bad news. She has a tumour which is inoperable. Over my sparse dinner, I felt quite sick with sorrow and anxiety.

Wednesday, 17th August

Yesterday I bought a book of stamps and a battery for my wireless at a local shop. I left the stamps on the counter, and could not later find the battery. No one who is not senile can imagine the shame and misery of those who are senile, any more than anyone knows what the dead are enduring in the next world, if there is one. When I saw Humphrey Whitbread* clambering to his seat for the pageant [at Holkham, Norfolk] the other night, mouth open and drooling nonsense, my heart was wrung with pity. Whereas ten years ago I would have sneered. Poor Humphrey. He is a Coke cousin but hasn't been to Holkham since 1936. During dinner the following night he made no sense at all, and staggered off to his bedroom before the pudding.

Monday, 22nd August

Caroline telephoned to thank me for my letter which followed her home from hospital. Asked me to dine tonight, just the family. Greeted me warmly on arrival, saying, 'I've never felt better in my life. They have got rid of the jaundice. The consultant who examined me says there is nothing to be done, and that I might live three months or even a year.' I said, 'Are you sure it will not be three years or even more?' She was cheerful, laughing, putting on the bravest face. Is planning a trip to Java in February. Yet over all the joviality at dinner a veil of sadness hanging. David, who adores her, sat baffled. When I left, he followed me to my car, saying, 'Isn't it awful about Caroline? So sudden, almost incredible. What with Alvilde going, and now this.' I said life was ghastly on the whole. He was much moved, and so was I. He turned away, and I drove off.

---

* Brewer; art collector, philanthropist and sometime High Sheriff of Bedfordshire (1912–2000).

Thursday, 25th August

To London for day. Walked along long underground passage from South Kensington station to V&A. Had forgotten this Victorian feat of engineering, so extraordinary and ugly. Filled with buskers and sellers of junk. Spent morning at Pugin exhibition. P's wallpapers and decorations are superbly bold and colourful; silver church vessels and copes likewise; but his spiky chairs, thrones, stools are absurdly uncomfortable even to look at, let alone sit in. To Heywood's shop. John Saumarez said that my new diaries make a good read and he has already had orders for 200; that he had read my ghost story in bed last night, and that too would sell. I know John's opinions now so well, and respect him for his honesty. To tea with Misha, who is teaching himself to draw. He made two sketches of me, not very lifelike I fear. He looked well, but is already balding. He walked with me to Paddington, carrying my paraphernalia. I was pleased to see him again, but have little desire now to see any friend for more than an hour.

Sunday, 28th August

Diana Kendall[*] telephoned that John Methuen had died in Bath Clinic. No surprise. John meant nothing to me. Paul loathed him. It is believed that John has left Corsham to his nephew James Methuen–Campbell as his brother Robert has no son – though Robert has now divorced his old wife and married a young woman and may produce an heir. I hope John did leave it to James.[†]

Lunched today at Cirencester with Rory Young. A radiant young craftsman full of enthusiasm, learning, experience of old buildings. A miracle-worker with stone and marble. Nice artisan house in Park Street which he has jollied up and made extremely attractive, adding bits and pieces, fireplaces inlaid with diamonds of polished Purbeck, *oeil-de-boeuf* windows on end, and so forth. Other guests Sonia Rolt, widow of Tom,[‡]

---

[*] Formerly secretary to Paul Methuen.
[†] He did – see 30 September 1994.
[‡] L.T.C. Rolt (1910–74); short story writer, and expert on history of railways and canals.

the great man of canals, one Peter Burman,* prominent conservationist, bearded and gentle, and Judith Verity, abandoned wife of Simon, with whom Rory is now living either as lover or collaborator. Long discussion over delicious farmhouse meal about whether ball moulding of doorway of Bishop's Cleeve church should be 'restored' – i.e., copied by some competent mason – allowed to rot as it is doing, or be scrapped and replaced by a modern design.

Rory told us that as a boy he called on the owner† of a beautiful ancient house called Norbury in Derbyshire, an old bachelor who fell in love with Rory and would, had R. reciprocated his love, have left Norbury to him. I was reminded of Claud Phillimore‡ calling unannounced when an undergraduate on Bertie Landsberg§ at La Malcontenta. Bertie did in fact leave the house to Claud after the death of his wife Dorothy, but it did little good to C., who couldn't afford to live in this Palladian villa. And then there was Ted Lister, who was going to leave Westwood [Manor, Wiltshire] to me until I married and he changed his will.

Reading articles in *Country Life* on Stokesay Court [Shropshire], whose contents are to be sold, I was reminded that I once wanted to write an article on this house myself. I asked Philip [Magnus],¶ who regretted that his wife was not keen on the idea, as her grandfather Mr Allcroft who built the house was a dreadful man without an 'h' to his name, whereas her grandmother who was a Russell came from some grand and interesting house. I expostulated that all this was totally irrelevant. I was interested in Stokesay as a late Victorian house complete with contents, all collected by one rich manufacturer. Of gloves, Philip added in horror. Yes, gloves, I said, that is the point. Of course the absurd Jewel was mightily ashamed. And yet I believe both

---

* Writer and Director of Centre for Conservation Studies, University of York.
† Marcus Stapleton-Martin (1911–87); he left his house to the N.T.
‡ Architect in the classical tradition (1911–94); m. 1944 Elizabeth Dorrien-Smith of Tresco Abbey, Isles of Scilly; s. nephew as 4th Baron Phillimore, 1990.
§ A. C. Landsberg; Brazilian owner and restorer of Palladio's Villa Malcontenta on River Brenta near Venice, built in 1569 for Foscari family (to whom Claud Phillimore eventually returned it).
¶ Sir Philip Magnus-Allcroft, 2nd Bt (1906–88); historian; m. 1943 Jewel Allcroft of Stokesay Court.

would have liked the place to be preserved. Idiotic they were. She left millions and could have endowed the house for the N.T.; and had Philip been less of a snob, he would have insisted. For she had no mind of her own and would have done anything he wanted.

Thursday, 1st September

Belinda Cherrington from the BBC came to interview me for a programme on the N.T. A sensible woman whom I liked. She asked what I thought would happen to the Trust over the next hundred years. I speculated that it would continue to flourish but the number of properties would not increase much. She was aware of the criticisms, chiefly of bureaucracy. Then I dined with the Mitchells at Dyrham to meet Martin Drury, lately appointed Director-General. Nice man as always, with that youthful, almost adolescent look some middle-aged men preserve which causes one to wonder about their sexuality.

Friday, 2nd September

I visit Daphne, who does not seem to take in the gravity of [her daughter] Caroline's trouble. Talks of how as a girl she hated her uncle Douglas Haig, a martinet who was always telling her to keep a straight back, sit upright, etc. Later, Caroline telephones for a chat, so unlike her. Apologises for not being able to dine to meet Gervase, or take two N.T. groups round the House next week. Says she feels pretty well none the less and often wonders if what the doctors have told her can be true. O dear God. I sit here in the kitchen, the rain pouring outside, and wonder if I can stay in Badminton if C. is going to die. The sadness of it all. And in tears I tear up the little notes of telephone numbers and appointments which A. made just before she died. Each tear (and tear) is a stab at the heart.

Wednesday, 14th September

Gervase [Jackson-Stops] stayed last night, arriving at 8.30. Kindly brought a chicken and a pudding for our supper. He told me how the other day he saw Graham Thomas at a party and went up to him with arm outstretched. The old man dashed past him without a nod of recognition, looking over his head and saying 'How-do-you-do, Duchess' to Mary Roxburghe. Gervase has a friend who has a friend who is a telephonist at Buckingham Palace. The telephonist tells G's friend that, every morning, the Queen rings up the Queen Mother. Telephonist says to Q.M., 'Good morning, Your Majesty. Her Majesty is on the line for Your Majesty.'

Monday, 19th September

Had a sad dream last night – that A. said to me, 'You never write to me these days', to which I replied, 'No, perhaps it's because I see you every weekend.' Write indeed. I talk to her and send her messages into the vacuous air, and no reply comes.

Tuesday, 20th September

I visit Stanway. Lots of people, even on a weekday in September. House and grounds rather down-at-heel, and shown in a simple, happy-go-lucky, non-N.T. way which I found rather charming. But oh Lord, how dilapidated the furniture, paintings, tapestries and all. Walked up the terraces half way to the pyramid and thought the place as romantic as ever. Stood leaning against an arch, gazing at and imbibing the west front. The stone is not butter colour, nor honey, but sunset itself. Bottom half glows like a fiery sky. I know no other building quite so alive with searing, wreathing gold. Then the top stage is silvered o'er with lichen. The combination is divine. The three pointed gables lean backwards as from the brink of chaos, but with effort hold themselves back for the aesthetic delight of a further generation or two of civilised mortals able to appreciate. I shan't go again and am pleased I did so before this season ended. This summer I have managed to visit a number of country houses in my district which are open to the public.

Sunday, 25th September

Harry Fane,* whom I met last night dining with his mother Jane Westmorland, never reads a book, but knows everything about computers. He swears that books will cease to exist within thirty years and all reading will be done on computers. Already there is some kind of central information exchange accessible by computer which you can contact for any facts – the varieties of bamboo, child welfare in Peru, anything. Within minutes, all human knowledge on the subject is submitted on the computer screen. I suppose the modern equivalent of Selfridge's Information Bureau. Harry is supplied with these devices, so there is no subject in the world which he can't learn about in twenty minutes.

Tuesday, 27th September

Attended induction of our new Vicar in Badminton Church at 7.30. Church crammed, rather to my surprise. I am seated next to Caroline wearing her enormous red hat. In the semi-dark I cannot see how she looks and do not like to stare. She whispers that the word 'induction' sounds like waterworks. Yes, I retort *sotto voce*, it suggests an enema. She fidgets a lot and has a tickle in her throat. We both agree the new vicar has a good voice, better than Tom's. I have never seen so many dignitaries – the Bishop and Archdeacon of Tewkesbury, Bill Llewellyn unmitred but with long wisps of hair down neck. A reception in the House at which Caroline presides in absence of David and the Worcesters. Rather bad of them, but they are hopeless rotters, aren't they? I chat with Bill Llewellyn about our days together at McNeile's House [Eton]. Then, having done my duty, I slope away for home.

Friday, 30th September

Nice to be invited to luncheon at Corsham after twenty years. Happily James Methuen-Campbell has inherited, and moved across the way

---

* Hon. Harry St Clair Fane (b. 1953); yr son of 15th Earl of Westmorland (d. 1983) and Jane *née* Findlay; m. 1984 Tessa Forsyth-Forrest.

from his cottage. Ate in the dining room with the armorial ceiling. The bronzes of this room not yet brought back from strongroom. Library still under dust-sheets, all very shabby and dirty since Paul's day. Chairs messed about by labradors. Don't like the dark green paint which Paul and Norah substituted for the oak grain. James says the doors are mahogany and never should have been grained. Took me upstairs to boudoir and private bedrooms of Paul and Norah. Appalling condition of Aubusson carpets from John's dogs, the easy chairs turned into dog baskets. Full of wonderful treasures like Calke [Abbey, Derbyshire]. James already has plans for repairs and will do well. He is something of a young fogey, but extremely affable and keen.

Wednesday, 5th October

I am finishing Fanny [Partridge]'s latest diaries,[*] which are of course splendid. What an intelligent woman. Her dissection of her friends' characters is always kind, but nevertheless as sharp as a surgeon's blade. Most of her Bloomsbury friends were pretty awful, Gerald Brenan,[†] Lionel Penrose,[‡] Bunny Garnett[§] and the ineffable Julia Strachey.[¶] All deceiving wives and lovers. I would not say to anyone that there is something about Fanny I don't like, apart from her godlessness and leftishness, but there is a certain smugness and reluctance to acknowledge the validity of any views opposed to her own. She evidently didn't enjoy staying with us, and considered us retrograde Tories. She magnifies the silly prejudices of people she has to meet – for like all Bloomsberries she relishes the good life which the upper crust provide. Yet she makes my own diaries seem adolescent and low-brow.

---

[*] *Good Company: Diaries, 1967–1970.* The volume begins with a description of a tense weekend with the L.-Ms at Alderley, during which J.L.-M. had a terminal row with James Pope-Hennessy.

[†] English writer of works on Spanish literature and autobiographies (1894–1982).

[‡] Lionel Sharples Penrose (1898–1972); Galton Professor of Eugenics, University College, London, 1943–63, and of Human Genetics 1963–5.

[§] David Garnett (1892–1981); novelist and critic, whose first wife was Frances Partridge's sister.

[¶] Novelist and journalist (1901–78); niece of Lytton Strachey; m. 1st Hon. Stephen Tomlin, 2nd Lawrence Gowing.

Thursday, 6th October

At John Murray's rear waiting room under glass dome, John staggers in with boxes of my new diaries* to be signed. He says, 'I am the porter and do the humblest work.' Laughter from female staff. He is a dear fellow. Told me he was editing his father's commonplace book for publication, 'in which you will find yourself quoted'. I sign some seventy copies, my signature getting worse as I go along.

Sunday, 9th October

Hugh Massingberd has given my diaries a marvellous review this morning, calling me a dear old English gentleman.

Thursday, 13th October

I lunch with Hugh Massingberd at Travellers Club. We both have an urge to embrace on meeting, possibly a result of our never having received embraces as children from our respective fathers. Hugh looking well, with good complexion, and much thinner. He told me about his heart attack. Happened in a restaurant, with his sixteen-year-old son.† The boy shocked by the experience, but behaved splendidly. Ambulance summoned in nick of time. Hugh believes he 'died' more than once. Felt no fear, because it was as if the whole experience happening to someone else. Operation took eight hours. His concentration and memory affected, and he now finds it an effort to write. But when restored intends to write book on the subject. His illness has brought him closer to his wife, and they hope to go and live in Lincolnshire.

We talked of how Tony Powell and Simon Blow are both obsessed with their lineage. Hugh thinks it is because they both feel they have something to hide – the Blow ancestry, in Simon's case. Hugh admits his own obsession may have something to do with his mother's family being no great shakes, she being daughter of a stockbroker. Perhaps my own interest in lineage comes from my being of yeoman stock.

---

* *A Mingled Measure: Diaries, 1953–72.*
† Luke Massingberd (b. 1977); picture editor.

I noticed that Hugh was still fairly greedy, though he assures me that he takes far more care over *what* he eats. When the waiter tempted him with a jug of cream, I was surprised to hear him say, 'Get thee behind me, Jesus!' It transpired the waiter was a Spaniard and Jesus his name. Hugh said, you should hear Monsignor Gilbey addressing him.

Sunday, 16th October

In her *Spectator* column, Debo has teased me for writing in 1972 that Britain was bound to become Communist within twenty-five years. I have written to her that some people consider the anarchy and corruption which is now taking the place of Communism in Europe to be even worse. Meanwhile the Booker Prize is awarded to a novelist whose characters talk in profanities, and the Nobel Prize given to two terrorists.*

Friday, 21st October

Having spent the day at Stourhead, Independent Television came to film me in Bath at five. They moved everything in the room, finally inviting me to sit enthroned in the middle of nothing. This was unnatural and made me feel uneasy. For some time they refused to begin as they detected outside noises, first someone's radio upstairs, then an ambulance outside. I pointed out they were in a city and such sounds were to be expected. They nevertheless made me stop the clock and switch off the electric fire. The presenter, Mike Hutchinson, was then recorded on his own asking a series of idiotic questions about the N.T. I was then filmed replying to these questions. Then I was asked to repeat several of the things I had said. Then the film ran out, and I had to repeat again. Then something exploded, and again I had to repeat. The result can't have been much of a success, though I liked them.

---

* The Nobel Peace Prize had been awarded that year to Yasser Arafat and Yitzhak Rabin; the Booker Prize, to James Kelman for his novel *How Late It Was, How Late*.

Tuesday, 25th October

Bevis Hillier visits me in Bath to talk of John Betjeman. We are very friendly together, and I like him. I ask him why Selina's *Waugh* is having such sensational success, whereas his first volume on Betjeman didn't and he doesn't expect the second to either. He replies that it is because of the American market. 'Waugh is just what they imagine an Englishman to be, with his filthy manners and arrogance. Whereas Betjeman is someone they can't understand – his Joan Hunter Dunn* and teddy bear and underground world are to them provincial and unintelligible.'

Sunday, 30th October

Weekend at Madresfield. Both Debo and I arrived at 4.30 on Friday, just as dusk turning to dark, and roared with laughter when we discovered that we had both turned up too early and stopped and read in a lane outside the gates. Other guests Nico and Mary Henderson, great fun, and full of flattering quotation from my new diaries. Also Lady Lichfield,† dark-haired with heavy, Madonna-like features, amiable, uninteresting. My bedroom huge, pitch-dark and icy-cold. Walls covered with sub-fusc tapestry; huge four-poster bed. The whole house most melancholy. Debo and I both fascinated. On Saturday night a dinner for ten in the enormous dining room, open to the roof, after which we sat in the *eau-de-nil* drawing room. I felt rather hurt when Debo on leaving said of my beloved Worcestershire, 'What a dreary bit of country.'

On return to Badminton, I spoke to Caroline, who visited Prince Charles at Highgrove yesterday. He sent for her but when she got there had nothing much to say. He probably knew of her trouble and wished to be friendly and sympathetic, yet did not care to broach subject, rather to her disappointment. She noticed a single place set

---

* Heroine of the poem *A Subaltern's Love Song*, inspired by a woman of that name whom Betjeman met in a wartime canteen.

† Lady Leonora Grosvenor (b. 1949); dau. of 5th Duke of Westminster; kinswoman of Rosalind Morrison; m. 1975 (diss. 1986) Patrick Anson, 5th Earl of Lichfield, photographer (1939–2005).

for dinner in the dining room, and a small tray with breakfast china laid out in the pantry. Rather 'how', as Vita would say.

Tuesday, 8th November

Two-day visit to Downside.* Pouring with rain when I arrive, and pitch dark. The early English nineteenth-century interior is strikingly beautiful, more so, indeed, than a real Gothic cathedral. Dom Philip Jebb† emerges from the gloom and takes me to my room in the ugly new guest wing. Room ample, clean and bare, with smell of stale tobacco and the sort of windows that don't open. Then to refectory for tea, the only meal which allows talk. Introduced to Father This and That, making monkish jokes incomprehensible to me, but friendly and extremely polite. Then I withdraw with Dom P. to talk about the things which are on my mind – my inability to communicate with A., and my worries about overpopulation, the main reason for my estrangement from Roman Catholic Church. He frowns in a smiling way, and suggests I read *Humanae Vitae*‡ in full.

At 6.30 Vespers in the Church, which is dark, high and full of shadows. The monks process in like gigantic black crows, their hoods up, and then when they reach the altar they fling their hoods off. Chanting very impressive. Back they come with military discipline and part to left and right. Dinner at seven sharp. No talk, which suits me. Good school food – curried chicken and rice, followed by chocolate mousse. They gobble it down at incredible speed with which I cannot keep up. A finger code is used to request salt, butter, mustard, etc. A monk from pulpit reads from boring history of the York Archdiocese in twelfth century throughout. A little bell signals end of meal and we all process to monks' Calefactory, where we sit in groups and drink weak coffee. I am joined by a jolly priest who was a friend

---

* Benedictine abbey and public school near Bath.
† Headmaster of Downside School, 1980–91, and Prior of Downside Abbey 1991–2001 (b. 1932).
‡ Encyclical of Pope Paul VI condemning birth control, issued 25 July 1968.

of Illtyd Evans* and tells me how much he enjoyed *Roman Mornings*. A bell rings for Compline. Monks return to church, and I retire at 8.45 to a fitful sleep.

On Wednesday (9th), I breakfast at guest table in refectory. Monks eat in silence, bibs tucked under chins. It pours all day without cessation, and I suffer from imprisonment feeling. Sung mass at 8.45 with billowing incense and full canonicals. No Communion for me, no longer being a registered R.C. Later, Dom Philip visits me in my room. He is polite and beaming, yet I suspect does not like me much. No wonder, for he knows I will not revert. I criticise *Humanae Vitae* for proposing, as an alternative to contraception, a fatuous method of having sex. It does not convince me; and he does not convince me that Catholics don't live in a world of make-believe.

A feeling of intense loneliness here. Memories of private school rise within me. The Church is magnificent, but the aura not uplifting. I feel that the moment they can get away the brothers will indulge in every diversion known to man. I would certainly be driven to drink here. It is bitterly cold. Another guest, an aspirant monk (Cistercian) here to learn Latin, complained to me of the privations. Already, I thought.

Sunday, 13th November

Badminton church packed for Armistice Sunday. David read the lessons extremely well. Caroline looked much changed, but afterwards at the porch was talking animatedly to all and sundry. Before dark I went for a walk in the park. C. passed in her car, and stopped. She remarked how lonely I looked without Folly. Odd that she should have said this, for I had just been thinking of Folly, when I thought I heard the patter of her little feet beside me, only to find it was some dry oak leaves bouncing alongside. I told her I was longing to see her, and asked if she would lunch with me one day at home. She said she wanted to see me too very much, but next week was not good, as she was spending every night at Gloucester Hospital undergoing some

---

* Intellectual Dominican priest given to over-indulgence in food, drink and tobacco (d. 1972).

form of treatment, and a huge party was coming for shooting. Her face was grey and puffy. Walking back I felt exceedingly sad and lonely.

Monday, 21st November

Michael Cyprien, who took about fifty photographs of me last week for *Perspectives*, has sent me the one he considers the best. I dread to think what the others look like. On opening it at breakfast, I gasped, confronted by what looked like a ragged doll made out of corrugated paper. Although I shave every day, I don't take in the ghastly truth that I am so decayed and hideous as to make children and animals hide in terror. I imagined myself to be a boy until I was forty, a youth until fifty, young middle-aged until seventy-five, and since then old, but not a scrunched piece of cere-cloth. I have thanked him, saying how pleased I am to be thus depicted.

Sunday, 11th December

Xmas looms terribly, and the present giving and receiving, and the packing thereof. This morning, after church at Acton Turville (three of us only), I finish and despatch my review for *Country Life* of Gervase's exhibition of watercolours of N.T. houses, called *People and Places* after my book. Now I am asked by *The Field* to write an article on those families mentioned by Shakespeare which survive today.

Friday, 16th December

There are moments when a strange feeling comes over me in waves, and the mind simply ceases to function. It happened this evening when I was sitting by the fire, after speaking to my solicitor about the arrangements under which Clarissa might take the Bath flat. It is having to think about figures which seems to bring it about. I cannot grasp them. They have no meaning. They quite literally drive me mad. I feel as if I am whirling round in one of those revolving wheels at the circus, powerless, miserable, frightened, longing for peace or even death. Dreadful, dreadful. Then gradually it abates, and I am all right again.

Sunday, 18th December

Last night the Henry [Robinson]s dined, and were delightful. When I said I would have to retire to a home, they said I must do nothing of the sort. The flat at Moorwood has been put in apple-pie order, and is at my disposal. Under no circumstances must I go anywhere else. I was deeply touched. We also talked about the morality of destroying letters even when the writers or recipients have demanded their destruction. I told them that I wanted A's bundle of my letters to her to be destroyed unread. I haven't yet summoned the courage to read them myself, fearing they may be disagreeable letters. They were both emphatic that heirs or children are under no obligation to fulful such wishes; it was up to the original recipients to do the destroying.

Wednesday, 21st December

Re-reading Victoria Glendinning's *Vita*,[*] I begin to see in our marriage the palest reflection of Harold's and Vita's, with all its high tragedy and farce.[†] My admiration for Vita is not what it once was, for I now see that, in the days before I knew her, she was a *femme fatale*, and not always over-scrupulous with the truth.

Thursday, 22nd December

Luncheon at the House, Derek Hill down for the day. I sat next to Caroline. The most noticeable change was in her voice, full of odd inflexions and lacking the usual sparkle. She has no self-pity whatever, says she is not going to bother with any suggested cures and will just let things take their course. When I told her that A. had left her the Apollo, she said she was touched, and would leave it in her will back

---

[*] Hon. Victoria Seebohm (b. 1937), writer and journalist; dau. of Baron Seebohm; m. 1st Professor Nigel Glendinning, 2nd Terence de Vere White, 3rd Kevin O'Sullivan; her *Vita: The Life of V. Sackville-West* was published by Weidenfeld & Nicolson in 1983.

[†] J.L.-M. had had an affair with Harold in the 1930s, A.L.-M. with Vita in the 1950s; Harold and Vita acted as witnesses at the marriage of the L.-Ms in 1951.

to Essex House, to be kept in its place by all future tenants. She said she wanted a huge funeral with 'tents', all her friends to come. 'And you must see that David does it,' she said to me, with her familiar nudge of the elbow.

I drove Derek to Highgrove for the night. Foggy and dark afternoon. Young policeman at gate stopped the car and asked to see under the bonnet. Was amazed when I said that I did not know how to open it. Eventually we were let through. Derek says I am one of those friends he can count on the fingers of one hand. His effusive affection embarrasses me, though I am very fond of him.

Friday, 23rd December

Driving us to Chatsworth, Coote [Heber-Percy] says that Rosalind wants a biography of 'Boom' – the pet name by which Coote's father was known to his children, though they never used it to his face and he was probably unaware of it. She thinks David Gilmour* may be the man to do it, though he understandably says he cannot unless there are papers. And Coote is pretty sure that her brother, that stick Elmley, destroyed Lord Beauchamp's manuscript autobiography. A great shame, for he would make a wonderful subject – the noble statesman, Knight of the Garter, Warden of the Cinque Ports, driven abroad by his brother-in-law, the loathsome Bendor [Duke of Westminster], not even allowed back for his wife's funeral for fear of arrest. Coote accompanied her father from Venice on that occasion. When the boat from Havre reached Folkestone, a friend by pre-arrangement was on the pier to signal whether it was safe for them to land or not. He waved his arms in negative fashion. So poor Lord B. and Coote remained on the boat and returned to France. Then a fortnight later Lord B's favourite son Hughie died in a motor accident. Miserable, Lord B. returned across the Channel, no longer caring what might be done to him. In fact he was not arrested, and remained at Madresfield for the remaining years of his life. Greek tragedy.

Paddy and Joan [Leigh Fermor] staying. I think he is the most

---

* Hon. David Gilmour (b. 1952); biographer and historian; e. s. of Baron Gilmour of Craigmillar.

charming individual I have ever met. There is nothing he does not know, and he has a Betjemanian sense of the ludicrous. Has the best manners, and is touchingly modest about his achievements. Also Dinah Bridge,* *jolie laide* widow, sympathetic and sweet, and Margaret Budd, who was Woman's devoted friend and minder. And Diana [Mosley], who told me of the infamy of Caroline Blackwood's book,[†] which she has seen in proof. It libelled Diana in stating that the Mosleys were imprisoned for treachery. D. sent a fax demanding that this be cut out, to which the publishers agreed. D. says the book is also vitriolic about Misha, depicted as Maître Blum's subservient accomplice in 'destroying' the Duchess of Windsor. Bosh. I have written Misha to warn.

Christmas Day, Sunday, 25th December

We all exchanged presents in the Stag Parlour in the morning, and gushed effusively. I was given a blue pullover with 'Devonshire 300' on the chest, and a small basket of whisky and wine. Then we went to church, full to the brim. Dear Mr Beddoes gave a gentle, sensitive sermon. At the end of the service, Andrew rose from the aisle and thanked Mr B. on behalf of the congregation, saying that everyone loved him. We left emotionally charged.

Stayed up till midnight with Andrew, Paddy, and a charming young man called Alistair Morrison,[‡] talking about the monarchy. P. and I lamented the scrapping of royal ceremonial. Andrew said he was a republican and it was time to stop all that rubbish. Paddy riposted that the crown was about the only thing the UK still had to offer the world, now that it could not even get a Cunard ship ready in time for its cruise. At which Andrew blew up, cursing Paddy as an absentee expatriate who didn't know what he was talking about, that Britain's economy was the best in Europe, lowest unemployment, etc. In fact

---

* Hon. Dinah Brand (1920–98); yr dau. of 1st and last Baron Brand; m. 1st 1943 Lyttleton Fox, 2nd 1953 Christopher Bridge.

[†] See 17 December 1987.

[‡] Eldest son (b. 1959) of Hon. James Morrison (who s. 1996 as 2nd Baron Margadale); m. 1988 (as 2nd of her 3 husbands) Lady Sophie Cavendish (b. 1957), yst dau. of 11th Duke of Devonshire.

he was furious and rather rude. P. behaved with perfect calmness, apologising for what he had said. Then redeemed himself by adding that Debo would have made a wonderful Queen. Everybody would have adored her, with her combination of friendliness and dignity. No one would have taken liberties with her, for nobody does. He also said to me (more than once) that he wished he had kept a diary; that had he done so it might have helped him pick up the threads he finds so attenuated and thin, so difficult for horny old fingers to feel. Yes, I said, a diary does keep the fingers flexed.

1995

1995

Yesterday, Desmond and Ian gave their customary New Year's Eve luncheon at Old Werretts. But no Alvilde – and no grouse. Instead they had the Norwiches, and we ate a stew. We discussed what constituted an intellectual. I opined that John Julius must be one, as he knew the answer to every question, and had written histories of the Normans, the Byzantines and the Venetians. He insisted that he certainly wasn't. Good examples of people who were, he said, were Maurice Baring,* Freddie Ayer† and Isaiah Berlin. I suppose an intellectual is someone who thinks thoughts and pursues them. I haven't really thought a thought in fifty-five years.

Miranda [Morley] came to tea. She spoke of Prince Charles, whom she once knew quite well. He is so hostile to unwelcome advice that a friend who contradicted him was likely to be dropped and never spoken to again.

The article *The Field* has asked me to write on the names in Shakespeare's histories is causing me much angst, and will take me a month at least. Am re-reading the plays, particularly moved by the small incidents. Deep poignancy in the gardener planting a hedge of rue on the site of Richard II's poor Queen's tears, or Richard learning that his beloved roan Barbary did not throw off Bolingbroke but carried him proudly. As for the scene in *King John* in which the young Prince Arthur is finally spared having his

---

* Writer and poet (1874–1945).
† Sir Alfred Ayer (1910–89); Oxford philosopher.

eyes gouged out by Hubert de Burgh, it is too harrowing to be recollected.

Monday, 9th January

When I lunched yesterday with Richard and Penny Wood in the village – other guests Canon Barry and wife, and Mary Owen and husband – they mentioned that they had a videotape of the TV programme on the N.T., as yet unseen by me, in which I feature. After luncheon we watched it. I was horrified to see a worn-out, drooling old man, hardly able to express himself, like a very ancient bloodhound, bags under lustreless eyes. The shame of it. What they made me say was trivial, but all right.

Thursday, 12th January

Andrew and Debo took me to Grosvenor House at midday for the N.T's centenary luncheon. I was whipped away from them to sit at top table – rather flattering, and a reversal of the customary proceedings when I am in their company. I had Angus Stirling's* nice wife on my left and Dione Gibson† on my right; Jacob Rothschild on the right of Lady G., National Heritage Minister‡ on left of Lady S. The Prince of Wales made an excellent speech. While waiting for the Prince before luncheon, I talked to William Waldegrave.§ He is good-looking and still youthful, but said his life was made hell by animal rights activists.

Debo, who seldom criticises, complained that John Cornforth, who had been staying at Chatsworth on some business, was very limited in his interests and only ever talked about conservation. This is true. He gives one a pitying look if one tries to change the subject

---

* Armyne Morar Helen Schofield, dau. of W.G.B. Schofield and Hon. Armyne Astley, dau. of 21st Baron Hastings; m. 1959 (Sir) Angus Stirling.

† Elizabeth Dione Pearson; m. 1945 Richard Patrick Tallentyre Gibson (1916–2003), director of companies, cr. life peer, 1975, Chairman of N.T., 1977–86.

‡ Stephen Dorrell (b. 1952).

§ Conservative politician (b. 1946); yr s. of 12th Earl Waldegrave; then Sec. of State for Agriculture; cr. life peer, 1999.

from curtain tassels and Georgian wallpapers to, say, the Bosnia crisis. He was also very dismissive of the Prince of Wales, and Debo did not like that.

Friday, 20th January

After days of filthy weather, the sun has now come out, and with it that unmistakable flavour of approaching spring. Even indoors I sense it, stirring my old vitals; and I hear the siren whispers, not voices yet. It already makes me restless and unhappy, full of regrets for the long-lost opportunities of youth.

Sunday, 22nd January

A nice review of *A Mingled Measure* by Roy Jenkins, describing my diaries as a work of art.

I dropped a frightful brick last night, when I was motored by Miranda to dine with Julian and Serena Barrow. Andrew Parker Bowles was among the guests, a jolly, bouncy-puppy type of soldier, a bit of a *blagueur* and probably stupid on the whole. He made a 'macho' remark to the effect that women have no sense of the beautiful and men thrive on flattery, and looked across at me, trying to get me to agree with him. For some reason, I found myself saying that all women were in love with David Beaufort. 'Oh I say, isn't that going a bit far?' he asked, jerking an eyebrow towards Miranda sitting next to him. I jerked too, and saw Miranda's impassive face. So I added rather lamely, 'I mean from a distance, of course.' O senility!

Sunday, 29th January

Tony Powell's diaries* are very enjoyable and hard to put down. His comments are out of the ordinary, and very sharp and pointful. He is (so far) charitable about A. and me. Yet he does not emerge as sympathetic. There is a hard wooden superiority about him, a censoriousness, and immense snobbishness. Very self-centred, like most literary

* Anthony Powell, *Journals 1982–86* (Heinemann, 1995).

stars; most of the engagements he mentions are for newspaper and television interviews. Curious that he should accuse Diana Mosley of encouraging the press to refer to her as Lady Diana Mosley, when only at Christmas she was complaining to me about this ignorant and prevalent habit. For someone not nobly born, and indeed hailing from a frightfully unimportant family, he is remarkably obsessed with genealogy. Really very boring, and much less funny than Harold [Nicolson] on the McCrackells of Scottish antiquity. I would never mention my own forebears in such a way. When Mary Beaufort once asked about my great-great-grandfather in the Raeburn* portrait, I replied, 'He was nobody much, and if I told you it would mean nothing to you.' I can see Tony now at The Chantry, running out of the library to greet us in his blue-and-white striped apron, a touch of flour on his black eyebrows, announcing that his curry dish would be ready in five minutes. And over the library shelves those prim and purse-lipped ancestors like the chorus of dolls in *Petrouchka*.

Thursday, 2nd February

Yesterday, Henry [Robinson] met me at Lansdown Crescent and angelically carried all my reference books, or rather those I particularly need, into the back of his huge car. At Essex House, he carried them up to A's room, and placed them where I indicated.†

Sunday, 5th February

At Little Badminton church this morning, the church warden Arthur Vyner, as he handed me prayer and hymn books, whispered in my ear, 'Prince Charles is here.' Richard Wood respectfully but firmly waved me away from my accustomed pew in the left aisle, saying 'Sit between Penny and me,' which I obediently did. Throughout the Communion

---

* J.L.-M's great-great-grandfather, the Glasgow merchant Robert Thomson (1771–1831), had been a friend of the artist Sir Henry Raeburn (1756–1823), who painted several portraits of him.

† Though he only vacated his Bath library in October 1996, J.L.-M. no longer visited it daily and now did much of his writing at Badminton.

Service, their child shouted and screamed without intermission. When the time came to receive the sacraments, the Prince slowly advanced to the last stance at the altar rails, so as to be last to receive – my usual stance, in fact. No one else would go near him. So I thought, how silly and obsequious, and took the place next to his. At the end of the service, he talked politely to the Vicar (unknown visitor, but good) while we waited, I longing to get away.

I met Coote at Faringdon and she drove us to Heck's* house where Diana and Debo staying. Heck's brother Loyd† was lunching, and afterwards took us to his own house to see the pictures. I have always wanted to see the famous Wantage collection – and my word, it is something. Turners and Corots galore. Long, low house, a picturesque jumble outside with good pavilion by Claud Phillimore annexed to Lord Burlington's wing.

When we all dispersed, Debo said, 'You will be distressed to hear that Gervase is dying.' 'Jackson-Stops?' I asked, incredulous. Yes, she said; Aids. Someone had just seen him looking ghastly ill. I am dreadfully sad. This dear little, extremely clever, gifted, jolly aesthete, with his incomparable knowledge; this tremendous asset to the N.T., stalwart defender of the right principles and critic of the wrong.

Tuesday, 7th February

Simon Blow, to whom I wrote asking for news of Gervase, telephoned this evening. Confirmed that G. had Aids, and had known since last summer. Simon guessed from the spots that appeared on his face. The friend living with him is HIV-positive. Simon thinks the Aids virus may be human-invented, either manufactured by some nation for biological warfare, or deliberately disseminated among the blacks by white Americans to keep down their numbers, like myxomatosis to control the rabbit population. Unlikely in my view, though the wickedness of the world is without end.

---

* Hester Loyd; m. 1944 Major Guy Knight (b. 1919) of West Lockinge Farm, Wantage, Oxfordshire; equestrian personality, friend of Diana Mosley.
† Christopher Loyd (b. 1923) of Lockinge Manor, Wantage; landowner and art collector.

Friday, 17th February

Peggy's birthday. Remembered just in time, and hastily packed the last of the pretty brooches I bought at the fleamarket into a gold Easter egg. Colonel and Mrs Crawford came at noon to discuss garden opening for American blue-rinses in June. Then dashed to Bath to lunch with the [Tom] Gibsons and meet the Floyds, he the grandson of the old Fullers* of Great Chalfield. Nice jolly hunting sort. He said his mother had told him I wore co-respondent shoes in the 1930s, which is absurd. Also present the Gibsons' handsome son Angus,† who talked of my novel about the German prisoner-of-war who seduces both a schoolboy and his mother. He said he thought it a fabulous tale. I agreed. He asked with apparent earnestness if I really believed a middle-aged woman, once aroused, would have an intense craving for sex. I said, 'You ought to know,' for he was Don Juan incarnate. His mother then broke in, 'What are you two talking about?' 'Adultery, Mummy.' Then back to my library for Philippa Bishop‡ to choose two of my Beckford books for an exhibition in the [Lansdown] Tower. Then rushed home to give tea to Imogen Taylor§ and talk to her about John Fowler. Too many things in one day. But Miss Taylor gave me amusing particulars of John, who in the office was a tyrant like so many men who are mild in society. I am including him in my book of sketches about friends.

Saturday, 18th February

Luncheon at the House to meet Tom Parr and Peggy De L'Isle. Caroline much frailer, and extremely tired. She was so sweetly affectionate that my tears welled. Told me that, in a moment of gush, she had sent an affectionate postcard to Princess Diana. To her immense surprise she had a four-page letter from Prince Charles in reply, effusively thanking her and saying how devoted to her he was. How did

---

* Major and Mrs R. Fuller; donors of Great Chalfield Manor, Wiltshire, to N.T., 1943.

† Angus Gibson (b. 1956); founder of Gibson Music Ltd.

‡ Philippa Downes (b. 1929); m. 1963 Michael Bishop; Bath historian.

§ Interior Design Director, Colefax & Fowler (b. 1926); former personal assistant to John Fowler.

this happen? Does he get to see her correspondence – or did she mischievously forward the postcard to the Prince? C. opened her arms wide when I left, and we hugged. Remember, she said, I don't want to be a bore to my friends.

Tuesday, 21st February

Yesterday afternoon John K.-B. and I went to Gloucester to visit the Cathedral, neither of us having been there for twenty years. What a superb building. February is the best month to see a great cathedral. Hardly a soul besides ourselves, and those serious and elderly like us. We were deeply impressed by a monument in south transept arm to Alderman Abraham Blackleach, 1639. Mrs Esdaile* suggests Epiphanius Evesham or Edward Marshall as sculptor. Recumbent figures in alabaster of great refinement. Clothes beautifully carved, and their hands perfectly beautiful, long slender fingers, clearly by a great artist. Then Robert, Duke of Normandy, moved from centre of choir (why?). Red surtout repainted presumably, and well. Bold, brave face; crossed legs, which irritates J. Then the chevet of the church, a miracle, with its curved end and huge Crécy window occupying entire wall. How is the vault supported?

Wednesday, 1st March

To Mary Keen's idyllic rectory at 10.30 to meet Charlotte Trumper and Peter Grover, chief executive and newsletter editor of Gloucestershire Gardens Trust, which wants to publish a memorial booklet about A's gardening. Mary offers to write it, if I can help her with data, which pleases me inordinately. When they left I had a snack luncheon with Mary, really the most delightful woman in the world, so natural, clever, amusing and devoid of affectation.

I was at home, typing my essay on Vita, when Jane Westmorland telephoned that she was expecting me for dinner, which I was unaware

---

* Mrs Arundell (Katherine) Esdaile (1881–1950); author of works on monuments in English churches, who had been of much help to J.L.-M. during his early years with the N.T.

of. She said Caroline was coming, so I went. Jane the opposite side of the female coin to Mary, yet full of kindness and goodness, with her work for the Macmillan nurses. But the *grande dame* act doesn't ring true. Caroline sat facing me, and I noticed that her eyes had sunk since I saw her ten days ago. She talked of her cancer and approaching death; said she didn't want to die alone, and wished someone (David?) could accompany her.

Thursday, 23rd March

Peggy brings me a cutting from *Western Daily Press* – a very hostile article on centre page about me, calling me the National Trust's 'hijacker' who in 1936 formulated a policy of supporting the squire-archy at the expense of the people. Piffle, and I don't much care. Yet have sent a rebuttal to the editor, pointing out that in 1936 I was a mere twenty-seven, and no more than the humble servant of the distinguished committee that formulated the policies, not I.

Tuesday, 28th March

Today I improved my new ghost story for Nick, and at first thought it quite good. Then re-read it and realised it was no good at all, and that I am now senile, and cannot write. Depressed by this and my tiredness. Struggled to walk in the park, made hideous by erection of shops for coming Horse Trials. A dull and very cold day, with driving sleet, the wind making a ghostly tremulous noise through the skeletal steel structures as yet unclad. Lit fire at four but unable to forget the day, for clocks have gone forward and it remains light at 7.20. I do not like the long evenings of daylight which accentuate my loneliness and restlessness. Am virtually waiting for death.

Wednesday, 29th March

A pretty young lady, Miranda Carter, came from London to see me in Bath to talk about Anthony Blunt.* Engaging. Curiously ignorant

---

* Her book *Anthony Blunt: His Lives* was published by Macmillan in 2001.

for a biographer, but at least sympathetic to that arch-devil's sensitivity to and expertise in the arts. She said he destroyed all his papers before he died, save for an unfinished apologia regarding his treachery. It was left unfinished for the simple reason that he was unable to explain his motives, apart from boredom and lassitude. I can understand this. She has no doubt that his Bell's Palsy and internal cancer were both brought on by the strain of dissimulation. She has got more information from Dadie Rylands than anyone else. I told her to get in touch with Bobby Gore. As she said, he wasn't exactly a traitor in that Russia was our ally at the time, yet he may have caused the deaths of hundreds.

Friday, 31st March

I have read several reviews of the biography of Cyril Connolly which Deirdre set her face against, and wouldn't give papers to the writer thereof.* Reviews favourable on the whole. One reviewer pointed out that, Cyril's besetting sin being sloth, his domesticity became the implacable enemy of his creativity. I think this is true. I am very domesticated and this has certainly had a deleterious effect on my writing.

Sunday, 2nd April

I gave a tea party, to which came Tony and Brigitte Mitchell, Rory Young and Judith Verity. They were all very kind and seemed to enjoy themselves. Judith belongs to the same type as Loula Gibson, Diana Menuhin, Isabel Throckmorton, K. Kennet, the assertive female with a jolly air and no nonsense. And this is probably what Rory requires. He is vague, bubbling with enthusiasms, discursive; inclined to be forgetful, and get carried away. He is thrilled to have been commissioned to sculpt saints and Old Testament figures for the Great West Door of York Minster. As models, he uses men and women of all ages encountered on the streets of Cirencester, who willingly give their services for free; and he hopes to produce a figure based on himself, if the Chapter will let him.

---

* Clive Fisher, *Cyril Connolly: A Nostalgic Life* (Picador 1995).

Monday, 3rd April

Tonight I watched Dimbleby interviewing Mr Major on *Panorama*. D. behaved disgracefully, needling and insulting the P.M. and displaying all his socialist prejudices. The P.M. was calm, wary, collected and wise, displaying good manners and good judgement. I decided that I had lately been unfair in siding with the mass of the country in regarding him as a twerp. He is an honourable and decent man who would never do a rash thing, and if given the chance (which he won't be) might bring the country to its senses.

Thursday, 6th April

At the request of his secretary, I rang up Gervase Jackson-Stops in hospital. A very painful business. He was clearly raving. Began by saying that everything was wonderful. He had seen the light. Roses from Heaven were falling all around him. Then he insisted on playing, over the telephone, extracts from the Beatles' songs. Was extravagant in praise of me and what I had done for the N.T. Raved about all the things still left for him to do. Insisted that I should stay with him at the Menagerie, and we would motor together to Flintham, Kedleston, Chatsworth. Even mentioned a date. It was dreadful and embarrassing. The secretary, to whom I spoke afterwards, said he had his ups and downs, and was now 'up' to some tune, but was in a bad way, and would not recover.

Saturday, 8th April

Tom Gibson called, after going to the House to 'anoint' Caroline. He asked if she would like this and she said she would, very much. Anne was present. I am not sure whether anointing is the same as Extreme Unction. It is interesting how total agnostics will turn to spiritual comforts in crises. Tom also left a letter for David advising him what to do when the time comes. He fears it may come during the Horse Trials, and hopes there will not be too many people staying in the House, or luncheon parties.

Monday, 10th April

David Herbert died last week. A ghastly photograph of him in *The Times*, broadly grinning in his fancy hat, and an obituary making him out to have been a comic eccentric. Poor David. He sent me his love via the Revd John Foster* who visited him in Morocco last month. I gather there was trouble with the Arab servant-companion, which I hope did not hasten his end. He was a great life-enhancer, and fun. But I could not keep up with his social life, and would not stay with him latterly in Tangier. We were contemporaries, he two months younger. He is the only person I can think of who never minded a jot what anyone thought of him, who wished to do nothing throughout life, and who was nevertheless blissfully happy from the beginning of it to near the end, when he became ill. A. adored him.

Tuesday, 11th April

I went round to see Caroline at midday. She showed me the illuminated scroll presented to her last week by some thirty charities she has been working for. When I admired it and congratulated her on it, she did not answer, and I saw she had fallen asleep. Rather miserably I waited, not wishing to disturb. When she woke, she said, 'It's dreadful. I can't keep awake. So embarrassing.' I said, 'If you can't sleep with an old friend like me, who can you sleep with?' Which amused her a tiny bit, until she went off again. When next she came to, I left, saying merely, 'You know how devoted I am to you,' to which she replied, 'I too.' I felt utterly miserable as I walked home through the park, so bursting with life and promise, and thought, 'How can I continue to live here, where I have so much responsibility and no roots, with A. and C. gone?'

Thursday, 20th April

David drove up in his jeep and beckoned to me. I asked if I might see Caroline – for Rupert Loewenstein had told me that the House was

---

* Roman Catholic priest living and working in Bath (b. 1929); formerly the Anglican Vicar of St Mary's Paddington, 1969–94.

now like some country house in a Russian play, with family and friends wandering in and out of the death chamber. But David said it was too late; she was now in a continuous coma. I was glad to be spared another harrowing visitation. 'I know how much you mind,' David said, adding that it was dreadful how difficult she was finding it to die.

Saturday, 22nd April

A terrible morning, pitch dark, blowing a gale and pouring. I huddle over the kitchen table, finishing the editing of my diary for 1974 before sending it to Misha to read. At midday, telephone rings. Tom Gibson in Bath to say that Caroline died an hour ago. David and all the family stricken. I telephone Miranda to say I am at home all day if she feels like popping in. I hate the idea of her being alone and feeling rejected. And now (3.30) Freda [Berkeley] telephones that Jack Rathbone has just died. F. heard from his servant, who adored Jack and recently took him to America. Can't think why, because for years Jack has been quite senile.

Thursday, 27th April

Caroline's funeral. Was much moved when the coffin piled high with flowers was carried out of the church. That bright presiding spirit extinct. I did not go to the House for tea, but walked up the drive with the Morrisons. After embracing Rosalind in full view of the reporters at the gate, I was set upon by them asking banal questions. Was it a beautiful service? How would I remember the Duchess? When did I first meet her? I had controlled myself earlier, but now found myself on the verge of tears, and hoped to goodness I would not appear on the local news.

Thursday, 4th May

Suddenly we are plunged into summer, with high temperatures and burning sun. Grant McIntyre motored from London to lunch and we discussed the forthcoming double-volume reprints of my old diaries, one to come out this autumn, the other next spring. I fear the reading public will be sick and tired of J.L.-M. I also gave him the eleven vignettes I have so far written for 'Straight and Bent'.* Grant really is a man after my own heart, and I know that today I broke through the shyness barrier. He talked freely and is extremely sympathetic, well-informed and gentle, reserved yet expansive.

Tuesday, 16th May

Nigel Nicolson lunched in Bath. A dear friend and appreciative guest. Dusty and older, face expanded and mouth contracted, and rather deaf. He is lecturing in Bristol this evening. Said he immensely enjoyed lecturing because of the applause, 'which I know is very reprehensible,' he added laughingly. Told me that, during a visit to Sissinghurst, Stephen Spender discovered three letters he had written to Vita when he was young, and asked Nigel if he might have them back. Nigel refused, but Stephen took them anyway, because they contained indiscreet confidences of his youth. Being so much the gent, Nigel does not want to ask for them back. I would certainly do so.

Thursday, 18th May

To London for the night. Lunched with Derek [Hill] at Boodle's, Feeble [Cavendish] and Freda [Berkeley] also there. Derek boasted throughout about his painting and his friendship with Prince Charles. He has become a bore on these subjects. From there to Felix Kelly† exhibition at Colnaghi's where I completely lost my head and bought one of the few unsold paintings, a landscape in Majorca, for £2,000. I don't think I have ever spent so much on a work of art in my life. In the evening saw *La Cenerentola* at Brooks's, taking Feeble as my guest. A dreadful scrum beforehand. Good performance but a silly libretto and I got bored. At supper in the Spencer Room, Feeble talked of

---

* Working title of J.L.-M's 'book of sketches about friends'.
† New Zealand-born artist (d. 1996), specialising in paintings of country houses in their landscapes.

John Betj[eman]. She has read through Volume 2 of Candida's *Letters*[*] and is pleased. Says that Candida's references to herself are tactful. 'After all, I could hardly be left out of the second half of his life.' That is what her friends have been trying to make her see for years. She said that once, when Penelope had been to John's house, she, Feeble, watched her walk away from an upstairs window, looking so sad and weary that her heart bled. She admitted that John was often very difficult to live with because of his guilt over Penelope, about which he could never stop talking to her.

Friday, 19th May

Misha lunched at Brooks's, wearing a scruffy corduroy suit. I am all for individuality but I don't like scruff, as if to flaunt in a nest of orthodoxy. He was very charming, however, and I much enjoyed being with him. He returned my [1973–74] diaries with enthusiastic comments.

Saw Fabergé[†] exhibition at Queen's Gallery. Of course I coveted those eggs covered with diamonds and pearls and gold. Such poignancy in No. 252, the egg presented by the Tsar to the Tsarina in 1914, the 'surprise' within being profile heads of the five imperial children, the whole lot to be murdered within five years. Did George V feel guilty when he purchased it later?[‡]

Saturday, 3rd June

There is an evil in old men's faces. I catch a glimpse of my own in shop windows when not expecting to, and take a step backwards in horror and fear. The goodness, which must be there too, is not immediately visible. What an image to present to the world.

---

[*] The first volume of Candida Lycett Green's edition of her father's letters, covering 1926–51, had appeared in April 1994; the second volume (1952–84) followed in October 1995.

[†] Russian jeweller (1846–1920).

[‡] The King was responsible for his Government's refusal to grant asylum to his Russian imperial cousins in 1917.

Sunday, 11th June

Nick lunches and we walk along the verge after. I wish I had the courage to rebuke him for his awful clothes, a bedraggled short tweed jacket, and he half-shaved. Yet absolutely sympathetic, and we talk of books.

Tuesday, 13th June

Am re-reading letters from Jamesey Pope-Hennessy, whom Grant wants me to include in my book of sketches about friends. What a first-rate writer he was. His early letters are the best, before he became irredeemably dissolute and bellicose and unbearable. What humour, affection, sharpness. Never was a good man so lost to dissipation, and the lusts of the flesh. Towards the end I find myself becoming quite angry with him.

Wednesday, 14th June

Tony and Brigitte Mitchell picked me up at 9.30 and we motored to Croome [Court, Worcestershire]. There we met Jeffrey Haworth, who has a laudable scheme to get the N.T. to acquire the surrounding land with church, Gothic castle, orangery, temples, Coade stone bridges and nymphs thereon. Went into the church which is simply wonderful and just as I remember: a pantheon of monumental sculpture, tombs to the Earls of Coventry, and Adam Gothic entirely – vaulted ceilings, soffits, stout oak door, clear glass windows, pews. Now redundant, but well cared-for and protected from vandals. One of the least spoilt and most nostalgic churches, vying with Hanbury and Badminton for family monuments. Then we walk along the ridge towards a domed temple, to obtain the Wilson view of the splendid, melancholy, now empty house. Views of the Malverns, and of Bredon Hill. This marvellous part of mid Worcestershire, as yet unspoiled, certainly ought to be acquired by the Trust; it is a second Stowe or Hawstone,* and must be saved. The house, which we did not enter, is enormous. Ages since I saw inside. Much has apparently gone, one

---

* The parks at Stowe, Buckinghamshire, and Hawstone, Shropshire were renowned for their temples and follies.

entire room including the famous Neilson-Boucher tapestries to the Metropolitan [Museum of Art, New York].

Then on to Hanbury to see the new formal garden on the south front, a trumped-up restoration of the garden shown in the old engraving by Loudon. Jeffrey warned me that I would not approve; and I don't. All the romance of Hanbury has gone with these finicky beds, gravel paths and galaxy of colour, also whimsy little latticed gazebos. I am a romantic and I prefer what the eighteenth century did, parkscape right up to the house. The Trust is becoming too antiquarian-horticultural, trying to recreate what they suppose the Caroline monarchs did at Hampton Court.

Then on to tea at The White House, Suckley, Jeffrey's doll's house *circa* 1700. A family home, with children and nice plump wife with shirt hanging out. And such a wonderful house, large contemporary staircase, uncarpeted, slippery treads, upstairs room of fielded panelling, and next door a closeted room with marquetried walls, all of the date. A joyful, tumbledown place, ungrand, enthusiastic, with some interesting furniture and Nash[*] watercolours of the Olden Tyme. I have an 'up' on Jeffrey, with his firm chin, old-fashioned tweed suit, love of old things, and splash of a phrase or two on the harpsichord. Just the sort of man the N.T. ought to have on its staff.

Thursday, 15th June

This morning I was gratified to receive letters from four women asking to meet – Selina [Hastings], Jessica Douglas-Home, Gay Charteris and Valerie Finnis.[†] I long to see them all, if I can face up to the meals. In old age I have become one hundred per cent hetero-platonic. I prefer the company of women.

Friday, 16th June

To Deene [Park, Northamptonshire] for the weekend, motoring 135 miles. A beautiful day, stormy with sunlight. I love mid June, with the

---

[*] Joseph Nash's immensely popular books of illustrations, *Mansions of England in the Olden Tyme*, began appearing in the 1830s.

[†] Horticulturist; m. 1970 (as his 2nd wife) Sir David Montagu Douglas Scott, diplomatist (he d. 1986).

trees like tea cosies rimmed with a circle of shade, and powdery blue
hills in the distance. I lunched off a banana and biscuit by the grand
gate piers of Sarsden, the domain of Lord Clarendon of the Great
Rebellion.[*] At Swerford I descended to the village and looked for
Constantia Fenwick's[†] grave. Did not find it, but in the church saw a
nice little tablet to her adored husband Ralph Arnold which includes
her name. I also stopped at Haselbech [Hall] to see Aunt Con Ismay's[‡]
grave next to her husband's — sausage-shaped, with a rather whimsy
inscription about birdsong etc., as I would expect. And beside it a little
round stone like a pepper-castor for the ashes of her daughter Del,
who died fairly soon after her mother in 1973. I wondered which of
the cottages Aunt Con moved to from the big and ugly house, where
I last stayed in the mid 1930s.

Finally reached Deene. Given Henry VII's bedroom at top of a
corner tower. Extremely cold, but with bathroom. When one sat on
the loo — the old-fashioned sort, the heavy top of which has to be
lifted and held by one hand all the time of micturation — the wind
whistled up one's behind, as on Mount Athos. Huge canopied bed.
The Brudenells welcoming but absurdly fogeyish. At dinner Edmund
fussing dreadfully because my neighbour, Swiss lady, allowed herself
to be engaged by him on her right instead of by me. Too silly. Bobby
Gore staying with his enchanting daughter Kathy and husband. She
as pretty as a picture, so clever and sensitive and interested. Also
Brinsley Ford, very immobile and sparrow-witted; Nancy Osborne
Hill, rather sweet and extremely rich;[§] Edmund Fairfax-Lucy,
charming and stocky, with the smile of Brian through the mouth
of Alice.

---

[*] Edward Hyde, 1st Earl of Clarendon (1609–74); Stuart statesman who wrote a
famous history of the Civil War period, *History of the Great Rebellion in England*.

[†] Constantia Fenwick (1905–93); m. 1936 Ralph Arnold (1906–70) of Cobham,
Kent; writer and publisher.

[‡] Matilda Constance Shieffelin of New York (1872–1963); m. 1900 Charles Bower
Ismay (1874–1924), partner of White Star shipping line; rich and sentimental widow
enamoured of J.L.-M. during 1930s.

[§] Seattle-based millionairess, who had surprised English friends with the reflection,
'I honestly don't know how people can manage on less than £700,000 a year'
(reported by J.L.-M. on 6 July 1987).

This house is enormous and I have trouble finding my way about. On Sunday, Communion was held in the chapel, the parish church having been made redundant since my last visit. The household jammed into one narrow pew, leaving the other side to two humble ladies from the village, which I thought all wrong. Edmund handed me an unwieldy prayer book with prayers for George II and Queen Caroline. When I left my staff contribution in lacquer box in great hall, as is the custom in this household, I noticed that the Swiss lady, before departing in a hired London taxi, had left a £50 note. This made me leave £20 instead of the £15 I had calculated enough.

Tuesday, 20th June

Another extravagance. In Maggs's* catalogue received this morning, there is a letter in the handwriting of Bess of Hardwick.† It costs a fortune, and doesn't interest me in the least, but the idea suddenly came to me that I should buy it for Andrew Devonshire. I shall be disappointed if they aren't interested – which they may not be, as Maggs have not had a bite from them.

Friday, 23rd June

I know that my interest in buildings is not scholarly, but that of the social historian. It is associative rather than architectural, and I am no longer interested in entablatures and quoins.

Tuesday, 27th June

To Maggs in Berkeley Square where I saw the Bess of Hardwick letter which I asked them to post to Andrew Devonshire, to whom I have written separately about my great gift. Then to tea with Fanny Partridge. She was infinitely sympathetic, and when I left said that we seemed to agree about everything. I think this is true in a cerebral

---

* Dealers in rare books and manuscripts in Berkeley Square.
† Elizabeth *née* Talbot (*c.* 1527–1608); Elizabethan matron, ancestress of Cavendish family, who amassed a great fortune through four marriages, and founded Chatsworth and Hardwick Hall, future seats of the Dukes of Devonshire.

sense, though I don't share her left-wing views. She is fussed about the film on Carrington* and the exhibition of Carrington relics, of which she has many. Said that the film actor impersonating Lytton [Strachey] resembles him almost perfectly except that he doesn't have the attenuated hands. I felt a little sad on leaving Fanny, who says she is often lonely.

Thursday, 29th June

A fearsome heatwave, and the roses falling almost before they come out, which is sad. Elspeth [Huxley] and the Levis come to tea in the kitchen, which I have much ado in keeping cool. They are intoxicated by the beauty of the garden, and A's sense of layout and colours. Indeed how I hope the darling is proud of it.

Friday, 30th June

I visited the Acloques at Alderley this evening and was bowled over by the beauty of their garden. A depth, lushness and magic about it, sheltered by its lovely walls, and denser than in our day. Now a fulfilled garden, cut off from the world, Ariosto's secret garden of Rinaldo and Armida. Overgrown, yet controlled. Another tribute to A. – though she would doubtless have found much to criticise in it, and tribute is equally due to Guy for maintaining it so faithfully in the image A. imposed on it.

Thursday, 6th July

I have read three excellent obituaries of little Gervase, each praising him for the inspiration he imparted to all who worked with him. He was short and slight with the most animated little face imaginable. It was never still. Flickering eyes, laughter, and the worst stammer ever heard. He cracked his fingers as he struggled to get the words out.

---

* Film about the artist Dora Carrington (1893–1932), and the complicated love relationships connecting her to Lytton Strachey, Ralph Partridge, Frances Marshall and Gerald Brenan.

Stammer improved after he underwent a cure in America following the great success of his 'Treasure Houses of Britain' exhibition in Washington. No one knew more about every house of note than he. Prodigiously knowledgeable, yet absolutely unpedantic. The last time he rang up he implored me to stop the N.T. painting the sash bars of its Georgian houses brown. A pity he was so camp, and allowed his awful queer layabout friends to sponge off him. What will now happen to the Menagerie?

Friday, 21st July

Selina [Hastings] came for the night, blooming with success. Clear, soft complexion, liquid eyes. Her presence is very beguiling. Said she hates children and travels in smoking compartments of trains and planes just to avoid them. She is now engaged on Ros[amond Lehmann]'s Life, and has a favourable opinion, I was pleased to learn. Admits Ros was good and generous, and a first-class novelist. Her friends enjoyed exchanging malicious stories about her, and Dadie [Rylands] and John [Lehmann] would read extracts from her works roaring with mockery.

Saturday, 22nd July

Philip Ziegler to tea. Wizened, quizzical face, smiling eyes though not smiling mouth. Does not wear heart on sleeve. Where is it, then? Says relations with his sons distant. No touching, not even an arm round the shoulder. The very idea turns him to stone. Admits this is sadly English. I recalled that Sachie [Sitwell] always called his sons 'darling', which led to odd looks in railway carriages. Philip is writing Osbert [Sitwell]'s Life. I warned him that I hardly knew Osbert, or Edith.* We talked of the Sitwells' pretence of being Bohemian, whereas at heart they were true-blue landed gentry. They didn't really like Bloomsbury. Edith revered Osbert because he was head of the family, though she preferred Sachie. I piloted Philip round the garden, which he duly

---

* Dame Edith Sitwell (1887–1964); sister of Osbert and Sacheverell; poet and critic.

admired. I know very well now how A. felt when conducting ignorant people and having to listen to their inane remarks. 'How pretty those blue flowers are. Oh roses, really? I like a good show but am no expert, etc.'

Sunday, 23rd July

The Henry [Robinson]s gave a lunch party at Moorwood for me to meet their friends the Shelburnes.* I felt proud of Henry and Susy, such good hosts. No showing off, perfectly natural and delightful. A good luncheon of just two courses, Henry almost patriarchal with the carving knife. I was seated next to Shelburne. He is out to charm and succeeds. Very good-looking, almost film-starish, now inclining to broadness of the jowl. Dressed in well-cut light brown summer suit, with turned cuffs. Signet ring. Spoke of English Heritage, of which he is retired Chairman. Enjoyed it enormously. Said the Tories were indifferent to the cause, and Labour showed more interest. I said it was also thus in my day, that monster Dalton[†] being the benefactor of the N.T. She is enchanting, a sort of Penelope Betjeman type. Both are fans of my diaries and quote therefrom. I dropped two bricks. When I said that nothing good came from the United States, he remarked that his mother was American; and when I said I had heard that Ozleworth [House, Gloucestershire] was overdone, he said his wife had decorated it. But we all seemed to like one another and they said I must come over to Bowood [House, Calne, Wiltshire].[‡] He asked if I was an optimist or a pessimist. I said, 'How could I possibly be the first, having witnessed the ruination of the world?' 'I am an optimist,' he replied, 'although I agree with you.' Jane Westmorland who rang this morning said he suffered from terrible depressions.

---

* Charles Maurice Petty-Fitzmaurice, Earl of Shelburne (b. 1941); e. s. of 8th Marquess of Lansdowne (whom he succeeded as 9th Marquess, 1999); m. 1965 Lady Frances Eliot, o. d. of 9th Earl of St Germans.
† Hugh Dalton (1887–1962); Labour politician, who as Chancellor of the Exchequer from 1945 to 1947 sought to bestow some fiscal advantages on the N.T.
‡ See 15 June 1997.

Sunday, 30th July

Ian [Dixon] drove me to the wedding of Dale's son Tristan* at Silton church near Gillingham [Wiltshire]. An absolutely grilling day. Mercifully, as it turned out, we were late. Church was packed and we saw congregation fanning themselves furiously, so remained in the pretty porch with painted groining overhead, stencilling by Clayton & Bell, and a fairly cool breeze. Men in long tails and women in enormous hats. A thoroughly rural lot. When bridal pair about to march out and face cameras we, in order not to steal thunder, went and hid in the churchyard. Splendid view across old tombstones to a lake. Suddenly I remembered coming here thirty or more years ago with Mrs Esdaile, who showed me the marvellous Baroque monument to a Wyndham by John van Nost. There must have been a great house nearby. We knew no one but the Robinson brothers and their wives. I resolutely declined to go on to the reception; the sight of the farmhouse festooned with balloons was enough to deter, heatwave or no heatwave. Instead I went back inside the church to look at the monument, followed by the family who seemed surprised that I knew about it and the sculptor. The heat so intense and the airlessness so oppressive that I was practically in a coma throughout and knowing not what I was doing or saying.

Friday, 4th August

Nick stays the night. I consult him about quitting Bath. He persuades me not to. Says I must not feel guilty about living here in three sitting rooms. He advises me to find out from Clarissa when I next see her whether she is truly in penury, and in need of my library floor. I have no mind of my own, that's the trouble.

Sunday, 6th August

My birthday. People telephone. In church I thought I might write my masterpiece about the Communion service, telling the history of each

---

* J.L.-M's great-nephew Tristan Sutton (b. 1966); landscape gardener; m. Catherine Louise Masters (b. 1972).

prayer, lesson and phrase, explaining how it took shape in apostolic times. Leaving the churchyard I was greeted by Miranda, who announced that '*We* are going to Scotland for a week.' I wonder what the vicar makes of her, the scarlet woman.

Seven [Robinson] great-great-nieces and nephews brought to tea by their parents, Susy providing food. Too many for me to take in. It was rather chaotic and I didn't enjoy it as much as I ought. I thought the little girls more attractive than the little boys, although Alexander [aged nine] is rather engaging in a guttersnipe way. He is quite grown up and says, 'Uncle Jim, your garden is very tidy.' Then they sang 'Happy Birthday to You' out of tune, which I dislike whether in or out of.

Saturday, 12th August

This morning Nick motored me to inspect his new house which is finished and empty, awaiting their move thereto. I liked it. A bungalow in original style, yet traditional. Very spacious. One large room with high open-raftered ceiling. A sort of cottage *pas orné*, for no bargeboards where you expect them. Nice unvarnished floorboards. Clapboarding outside. Odd triangular dormer windows. I could be quite happy in it myself. Good situation with south view of Downs. It is certainly isolated, and may be windy and cold in winter. Perhaps a certain Japanese flimsiness about the structure, as though it might blow away in a high wind. But all in all I approve. Nick is the best man in the world, and the human being I am now most fond of.

Wednesday, 27th September

Freda dined at Brooks's. She talked about Father Michael Hollings, whom she has taken in following his disgrace.* Showed me the wicked

---

* Having been accused by the *News of the World* of an alleged sexual indiscretion, Hollings was evicted from his parish by a nervous Westminster diocese, and offered refuge by Freda Berkeley, a devoted parishioner. After a police investigation, he was exonerated and restored to his parish; but the ordeal had affected his health, and he died in February 1997.

article in the *News of the World* with its allegations of homosexual gropings twenty-five years ago. A tall order for Freda, who nevertheless staunchly supports him as the holiest and best of men. He prays for two hours at 5 a.m. and then says Mass which Freda attends in her dining room. 'I have never prayed so much in my life.' The only time I met him, I was not attracted: drunken, dirty, and jealous of Freda's attention to others. Just like the late Father Illtyd Evans, and Father Napier-Hemy who received me,* batteners on the hospitality of old ladies and inclined to the bottle.

Friday, 29th September

Lunched with the adorable Jessica Douglas-Home that was. Don't know her present name; no sign of current husband and no mention made. In spite of being middle-aged, Jessica has the same charm for me, with her strange elusive shyness and sweet affectionate manner. Walking around Henriette's beautiful garden on the Coln River she tucked my arm in hers. She has a wistful, other-worldly way of speaking. Talked of her book about her aunt Violet Woodhouse and her relations with her four husbands.† She believes Gordon Woodhouse was a homosexual, for whom Violet made a suitable wife as she was terrified of physical love. Is very excited by receipt of letter from archivist of Gordon's Cambridge college informing her that G. was sacked in mid-stream on account of some unmentionable conduct. Am haunted by Jessica's beauty. She is a faun-like creature of the woods, still the withdrawn little girl. She says I am now a cult figure among thirty-year-olds. Can it be?

Thursday, 19th October

Today the dear Henrys called for me at nine and we drove to Uppark in their smart and swift Mercedes. House even more marvellously reinstated than I imagined from the photographs. In fact it would be

---

* At Westminster Cathedral in 1934.
† See notes to 8 April 1987.

difficult to recognise that it had been burnt to a shell and rebuilt. Nearly all the contents back *in situ*. By some miracle the downstairs floors, one of Uppark's notable features, escaped burning. Gesso, carving, most beautifully reinstated. I was moved near to tears. I had a strangely warm welcome from the staff, not one of whom knew me personally, only by repute and from my damned diaries I suppose. A lovely day. View towards the Channel and Isle of Wight absolutely unchanged, not a building within sight.

Sunday, 22nd October

Have been alone this weekend and quite content, working at 'Straight and Bent'. This evening, while shutting up, I distinctly heard A's voice calling to me, sounding urgent rather than frightened, as if she wanted me to come quickly. I answered, as I would have done, 'Yes, here I am. Coming.' I stopped and listened. There was no answer, and the house went cold and empty. Now was she calling to me when she fell to her death? Did I hear some kind of ghostly echo? So dreadful to think of. Each time I pass the front door, I try not to look at the flag-stones on which she fell, and concentrate my gaze instead on the incense rose.

Friday, 27th October

Tony Mitchell takes me in his motor to Flintham. Kind as kind. On the way we call at Farnborough Hall. The old Holbeches* show us round this enchanting house, in which they are allowed to live by the N.T. somewhat on sufferance. Very nice people, he looking older than his father looked when I was last here in 1955. It is a delightful place, though now disturbed by a motorway half a mile from the west front. A country gentleman's seat of Charles II's reign, of local orange Horton stone, decent and unpretentious. Entrance hall very splendid, niches filled with busts of emperors. Dining room *c.* 1740, rococo plaster ceiling. John Cornforth here yesterday and they didn't much

---

* Geoffrey Holbech (b. 1918), whose family had lived at Farnborough Hall, Warwickshire, for three hundred years; m. (2nd) 1950 Elizabeth Harrison.

like him. I say to Tony, 'You can bet your bottom dollar that we shall read in *Country Life* that the ceiling relief work is not stucco but *papier mâché*.'

We reach Flintham for tea. Myles looking craggy and splendid. He amuses me by saying the only common drop of blood we have in our veins comes from the Crawshays. He says he is fed up caring for this huge house. All he wants are his pictures and his books. But he calculates he would need another house as large as Flintham to contain them, so is staying where he is. In fact he has made something stupendous of Flintham. It is stacked with family treasures. His parents thought it hideous and so hated it that they did not bother to mess it about. And the uncle from whom he inherited would alter nothing which his father had created. So it is still untouched, redecorated as it was when first built.

Simon Thurley,* an extremely handsome young man, stays the night. Runs those royal palaces which are not inhabited by the Court. Very bright.

Saturday, 28th October

To Gervase's Requiem Mass at All Saints', Northampton. Two hours of superb music, Haydn. Seven hundred sign book. Gervase left a special request that all present should take the sacrament – and nearly all do. What an influence he had on his friends.

Then Tatton Sykes stays the night at Flintham. I fear a smartyboots. Not so. Great charm, and gentleness. I like him immensely.

Weather has been sublime during this visit. Mist and mellow fruitfulness, warm sunlight and long shadows. Sunday lunch in small drawing room, between open French windows and a roaring fire, delicious and memorable. Both Tony and I have thoroughly enjoyed ourselves.

Myles discloses that when in 1939 his regiment, the Sherwood Rangers, went to France to fight, they took not just their horses but

---

* Dr Simon Thurley (b. 1962); Curator, Historic Royal Palaces, 1990–7; Director, Museum of London, 1997–2002; Chief Executive, English Heritage, from 2002.

their hounds with them. The French made them send the hounds back to England.

Saturday, 4th November

I am sad over Desmond [Shawe-Taylor]'s death. Though it is just as well, as Freda says, for he was going the same way as Lennox, and derived no pleasure from life. Des, so abounding in enthusiasms, so excitable, so fussy about a newspaper being crumpled instead of carefully folded, so very, very clever, so affectionate, sometimes in his enthusiasm laying his head on one's shoulder. I feel sure he knew more about music than any man has ever done, and his programme notes summed up every piece in exquisite prose and with perfect understanding. He is the last of the Long Crichel four* with whom I so often stayed, enjoying their hospitality, good food, talk and fun.

Thursday, 16th November

I lunch with Grant McIntyre in Italian restaurant in Albemarle Street. Good single dish and no drinks. I hand him the typescript of 'Straight and Bent' which I regard as finished by me. I now await his comments.

Ken Davison,† whom I ran into at Brooks's, tells me he is now Lord Broughshane – pronounced Bre*shane*.

Monday, 20th November

Jeffrey Haworth telephones that the N.T. Committee has agreed to purchase 700 acres of Croome Court park and gardens and temples, though not the house which will be saved by other means, as will the outlying Rotonda and Sham Castle. Says my letter was circulated to all and sundry and helped get this through. I am jubilant.

---

* See 24 December 1995.
† Hon. Kensington Davison DSO, DFC (1914–2006); yr s. of Sir William Davison (1872–1953), Mayor of Kensington, 1913–19, MP for South Kensington, 1918–45, cr. Baron Broughshane, 1945; s. brother as 3rd Baron, 1995.

Tuesday, 21st November

Watched Princess of Wales on BBC last night. An astonishing performance. Never having heard her speak before, I imagined she would be like a silly little debutante. On the contrary, she was adult and articulate. A low, croaky voice slipping into Northolt 'eows'. Very beautiful, cocking her head to the left, lovely mouth, enormous clear eyes. Claimed that the cause of the marital breakdown was media intrusion, which became persecution. She did not criticise Prince or Family directly, yet left watchers with no doubt that she hated the lot. Venom visible in every gesture and look. Said they held her to be an embarrassment and a danger. I dare say. Won't consent to divorce on account of her sons. Respectful about the Queen, and in favour of the monarchy, which however must bring itself up to date. Admitted adultery with the cashiered major.* I don't know that I like her more than hitherto, and I am not particularly taken in by her professions of love for ordinary people, but I respect her for her candour and for so boldly confronting millions.

Thursday, 23rd November

I have received a letter from Alex Moulton telling me that he was most offended by what I had written about him in my diaries published last year.† I have read the entry and can't for the life of me find anything offensive. I have replied expressing bewilderment.

Friday, 1st December

I am a little cross with Misha for passing on to Matthew Parris‡ some insalubrious material which the Bretts made me remove from the original manuscript of my Lord Esher biography. Parris has published it (fortunately without reference to me) in the chapter on Loulou

---

* James Hewitt of the Life Guards (b. 1958).
† On 8 August 1953, J.L.-M. describes their going on a jaunt on the River Avon, during which they admired 'idyllic youths bathing', and removed their clothes to lie in a field of cut hay.
‡ Politician, writer and journalist (b. 1946); MP (C) West Derbyshire, 1979–86.

Harcourt in his book *Great Parliamentary Scandals*, and it has provoked a hurt letter from the grandson of Maurice Brett. Not surprising, for I do not forget the aggrieved letter I received from Maurice's daughters. M. is an admirer of Parris, whereas I find his *Times* column facetious and irritating. Moreover, I don't like these flaunting homosexuals with their pleased-with-themselves attitude, as though they were deprived and stood for a noble cause. It isn't a noble cause. It is a mistake.

Saturday, 2nd December

This evening I dined at the House, the first time I had been there since Caroline's death. Dear Miranda present, and Eddie, and the silent Carol* who rather oddly took Caroline's place at the foot of the table. David absolutely charming. Full of funny stories about local dinners he has to attend. He talked of Caroline's eccentricity, saying she was so unselfconscious as to be totally unaware of it. I said a person would not be eccentric if aware of it; it was the unawareness of their absurdities which made them eccentric. He said Tony Lambton was similarly unselfconscious, though it would probably be better if he were more 'aware' when he asked unknown young women whether they had yet been seduced, where and by whom. No awkwardness at all in this evening's meeting after so many months. They had all seen the Princess's broadcast and were very much against her, convinced she is actuated by malice and mischief. David also spoke of how Mad Cow Disease† is ruining the beef farmers, merely because of a scare whipped up by the press.

David pointed out that he had had the fluted columns of the staircase hall painted white. It is certainly an improvement visually on the brown that was there before, probably introduced by Wyatville. D. said, 'I feel disloyal to Caroline who opposed the change, but was fortified in my decision by the approval you had given.' I don't remember venturing any opinion at all. Anyway

---

* Lord Edward Somerset and wife Caroline.
† The scare became a panic in March 1996 when the Government admitted that the disease might cause a similar fatal disorder in humans.

it's done now, and the hall is brighter and the architecture more assertive.

Wednesday, 13th December

Tony Scotland has confided to me his fears that Father Michael is taking Freda over. I verily believe there is something sinister about him. Tony tells me that the hierarchy at Westminster were anxious for him to retire before the scandal broke, on account of 'irregularities' (though liturgical rather than sexual). Tony once overheard Father M. being extraordinarily rude to F. He rounded on him and said, 'Never let me hear you speak to her like that again.' These Papist Fathers. Father Illtyd battening onto Eliza Wansbrough and Father Napier-Hemy onto old Mrs Astley Cooper,* eating and drinking these doting ladies out of house and home. They get the old ladies in their clutches. And they drink like soaks for all their vaunted piety.

Tuesday, 19th December

It is strange and gratifying to receive by post from Heywood Hill the 1813 edition of Byron's *Giaour*, with my book-plate therein and Byron's inscription on the fly-leaf, which I lent Dame Una [Pope-Hennessy] when she was writing about Byron in 1939. On her death in 1949 I asked Jamesey if he had come across it among her books. No, he said. And long after Jamesey's death, I asked John. Never seen or heard of it, he said. Now Michael Mallon is selling all John's possessions and it has turned up at Heywood Hill, and kind John Saumarez rang me up to ask how it got among the Pope-Hennessy books. For a moment I couldn't remember; then the loan to Dame Una came back to my memory. The long and short is that Michael Mallon, who has had the binding beautifully restored, has offered it back to me. I am grateful, and have no compunction in accepting after more than fifty years.

---

* Evangeline Marshall (1854–1944); heiress to shipping fortune; m. 1877 Major C.P. Astley Cooper; châtelaine of Hambleton Hall, Rutlandshire, where she presided over a salon of aesthetes which included Noël Coward and Malcolm Sargent (and, in the 1930s, J.L.-M.).

Having declined Christmas invitations to Chatsworth and Venice, J.L.-M. spent two nights at Long Crichel, Dorset with Pat Trevor-Roper and Derek Hill.

Friday, 22nd December

I take the little train from Bath to Salisbury, having to stand in a crammed carriage. Very awkward and tiring. At Salisbury, no one to meet me. Eventually Derek turns up, explaining that Pat's car has broken down. Derek whisks me off in a taxi to Ted Heath's house, Arundell's, in the Close. In rather proprietary way, Derek rings bell at much-barred iron gate. Nice detective and male servant come to gate. D. explains that Sir Edward is coming to Long Crichel this evening, and presumes he will gladly give both of us a lift. We are taken through courtyard. Pretty Queen Anne front. A message is conveyed to Sir Edward, who allows us to sit in a back room, like a dentist's waiting room, for two hours until he condescends to appear. Detective brings us each a cup of milky tea slopping into saucer and slice of inedible fruit cake. For two hours we lounge, chat to one another, and doze.

The inside of this house very disappointing, and has been much tampered with throughout the centuries. From a dreary flagged hall a long straight passage leads past a drawing room on left (unseen) to the sitting room in which we wait, which is totally without taste. Ceiling spotlights focus on nothing worth looking at. Several tiers of water-colours of yachts on green seas. On small tables stand photographs in silver frames of Queen, Duke of Edinburgh, Sir W. Churchill hideous in Garter robes. Shelves of neatly ranged books on music, mostly of coffee-table sort. Flesh-pink upholstered sofa. Chinese plate upright in fireplace. A nice lady housekeeper shows me with pride the dining room, a long narrow rectangle – nice John Piper* paintings, but room very ugly.

At 6.15 Heath appears at door wearing blue-and-white striped pullover. Enormous behind bulging over baggy trousers. Quite short he is, up to my shoulder. Appearance suggests a beer barrel aboard deck poised on two inadequate supports. Has his own snowy hair over

---

* Artist and theatrical designer (1903–92).

that prominent proboscis. Is utterly without charm or grace. Shakes hands perfunctorily. No word of greeting. But drives us to Long Crichel. Chauffeur and nice detective in front; I wedged in excruciating discomfort between Heath and Derek on hard middle ridge of rear seat, almost crushed by their enormous, bulging bodies. Only twenty-five-minute drive, mercifully. Derek talks in very familiar terms across me. Has painted Heath and knows him fairly well. H. answers him in monosyllables until they get on to subject of some Japanese artist whose masterpiece H. has just bought for his collection.

On arrival at Long Crichel, Heath advances straight into drawing room, barely greeting Pat, who is after all his host. Within half an hour he has stuffed two sacks with music tapes from Desmond [Shawe-Taylor]'s collection, probably the most complete in the world, Derek having persuaded Desmond's nephew-heir to allow Heath to choose 'a few'. He leaves behind a very bad impression. The one thing in his favour is that he is scrupulously clean. On leaving he does shake my hand and says it has been nice to see me again. A man of no breeding, spoilt by circumstances, and arrogant. Odd that such could rise to be Prime Minister. Desmond, whose judgement was unmatched, conceded that Heath was musically more than an amateur.

Sunday, 24th December

Two nights at Long Crichel. My name appears on the first page of the first visitors' book of this vastly visited house in 1945, the year that Eddy Sackville-West, Desmond and Eardley [Knollys] went to live there, soon to be joined by Raymond [Mortimer]. That was exactly half a century ago. Still the same beautiful deep-rose wallpaper of watered damask pattern in the drawing room. House inevitably a little gone to seed. They only have Mrs Best (whom Derek dislikes, the dislike no doubt returned). She is a wonderful cook, and meals are a joy. I have an 'up' on Pat, who is less debunking than formerly. Is tranquil, philosophical and calm, but maddened by Derek who has become extremely tiresome, bossy and self-centred. Pat told me that Derek never reads a book, listens to music, or goes to exhibitions except of his own paintings. On the whole I have enjoyed myself, but I just do not like staying in other people's houses any more. I read much of the time. On Saturday, a crowd of neighbours came for drinks, invited by Derek.

Tuesday, 26th December

Motored to lunch with Charles and Mary Keen. The nice clever actor son* there, and the rather severe-looking unmarried daughter. Mary mysterious about her career; she showed us photographs of her learning to be a pistol markswoman, but would not comment on the rumour that she had been a spy in Russia. The Henry [Robinson]s there too, with their children; so good of Mary to have us all. Lovely simple food, and the house so cosy. I drove home early, for I cannot see in the gloaming. I am content to be alone here in the warmth, at Badminton.

---

* William Keen (b. 1970).

1996

1996

Between Christmas and the New Year the weather has been record-breaking for arctic conditions. The cold really agonising. How lucky, I keep repeating to myself, that I am at home and not stranded in someone else's house, nor someone else in mine.

Angelic Nick motored me to Bath and back in dense fog. I fetched the large folio books and the ottoman containing my diaries, and left a letter for Clarissa telling her that she really must make up her mind whether she wants to live in Bath, now that the Bath Preservation Trust are unable to take over my library.

Friday, 12th January

An unknown man rang this afternoon, writing an article for the *Daily Telegraph* on visitors' books. Plunged into queries without a by-your-leave while I had my eggs on the boil. Was it wrong to put one's address? I don't know about wrong, I replied, but definitely non-U.* How to avoid it happening? Only by standing over the guest with a ruler in hand. I said it was strange how visitors' books, even when consisting just of semi-legible signatures, were fascinating to read through – especially Edwardian ones, their Baroque flourishes and underlinings evoking a whole age of elegance and grandeur. I recalled the Duc de Guermantes'† words, *'pas de pensées, monsieur, s'il vous plaît'* – but in those days the visitor had to sign the book on arriving at a house.

---

* 'U and non-U' was a jocular 1950s coinage of Nancy Mitford's, referring to usages which were correct or incorrect from the upper-class point of view.
† Ultra-aristocratic character in the novel of Marcel Proust.

Tuesday, 23rd January

To London for the night. Hugh Massingberd fails to turn up to lunch with me. In afternoon I go to Sotheby's Country House Artists exhibition, organised by John Harris. Vast assembly of fascinating views from seventeenth century to present time. Hardly a work of art among them, but that's not the point, as the Knight of Glin and Olda* would say. What details of life they disclose. Several Julian Barrows towards the end, including me in my garden, which I believe to be one of his best.

Nick calls at Brooks's and takes me to dine at very expensive Italian restaurant. Says I should definitely call my book 'Straight and Bent', a title of genius. I have lately been having cold feet about this, and have asked Grant to help me find another title. Nick very sensible about my quandary over the Bath flat. Suggests I leave its future and Clarissa's to the discretion of my executors.

Wednesday, 24th January

Hugh Massingberd turns up today for lunch. Is on a very strict diet and only has a bowl of soup and a banana. Looks better already. Says he enjoys the self-martyrdom, being a masochist. He too begs me to keep 'Straight and Bent'.

Friday, 2nd February

To London to see Grant at Murray's. We discussed photographs. It looks as if we are back to 'Straight and Bent'. He made some suggestions for revision of preface. I hope he does not think my writing senile, as Harold [Nicolson]'s became towards the end. I met Stuart [Preston] at Brooks's, and for once lunched with him. He seemed very deaf, though this may be an affectation. Kept saying '*Comment?*' and '*Oui!*' Face like a wicked aunt's in a pantomime. We exhausted the common topics quickly. Still I am fond of him, and there was an

---

* Desmond FitzGerald, 29th Knight of Glin (b. 1937); architectural and art historian; President, Irish Georgian Society; Christie's representative in Ireland; m. (2nd) 1970 Olda Willes.

occasional spark, though not enough to ignite the conversation. Dear old Sarge, I may never see him again.

Sunday, 4th February

I have consulted Debo, who is back from the United States, about 'Straight and Bent'. She does not like the title, as 'bent' to her (and my) generation means dishonest or crooked. She suggests 'Fourteen Friends'. (Her granddaughter proposes 'Stale Mates'.)

Saturday, 17th February

On going out at 4.30 I found many police vans and much disturbance. The Woods told me that a gang of 'antis', wearing masks and armed with long sticks with knives on the ends, had arrived in old buses from Essex. These 'animal lovers' had slashed horses and hounds, wrecked horse boxes, attacked cars with people inside, and tried to drag David [Beaufort] out of his jeep with a view to kicking him to death. The leaders were apparently girls, and all wore masks. None of those who witnessed it had ever seen a more terrifying display of violence.

Sunday, 18th February

Alex Moulton came to lunch, I having written saying it was too long since we had met, two years in fact. He was very friendly and jovial as usual, but looked much older. Neither of us made any mention of the reference in my last diaries which offended him, for some mysterious reason. Alex less dogmatic than of old, and to my surprise inveighed against the fat cats of industry, saying that the disparity in pay between the bosses and the workers was unjustifiable. Very unlike Alex, this.

Sunday, 3rd March

Misha met me at Paddington and returned with me for two nights. He has become very eccentric. Seems to be in a continuous daze. Says he is studying the Alexander Technique* to rid himself of nervous habits. In London, he stays up all night, and the effect on his health is evident. I made no bones in telling him. But when he snaps out of his dreamy state and starts to talk, he is as clever and stimulating as ever.

He has just written another book about the Duchess of Windsor,† not that he wanted to, but her centenary is looming and he needs the money. The whole thing took him ten weeks. He is rather worried because the *Daily Mail* have paid him a large sum for the serial rights, and want to make great play with M's theory that the Duchess of Windsor may have been a man rather than a woman. In fact M. does not quite suggest this, but it is what the newspaper will try to say. At the same time, M. is looking forward to the reviews. He must walk on tightropes.

Friday, 8th March

I have been going through the typescript of 'Fourteen Friends', which has now been corrected by the lady Murray's refer to as 'Liz'.‡ She has made hundreds of suggestions, all of which I have so far accepted. I fear my syntax has become abominable; and I am grateful to this lady, though the idea of her terrifies me. I want to know who she is and whether she has written many learned tomes.

As the Bath Preservation Trust feel unable to take on Beckford's library for the present, I have decided to vacate it this autumn in favour of Clarissa, and to leave her my share of the property in my will, with the proviso that, if she sells, the Trust should have first refusal. I wish I could have found some way of preserving it for the future, and do not feel tenderly towards C.

---

* System of postural re-education founded by the Australian actor Frederick Matthias Alexander (1869–1955), whose biography by Michael Bloch was published by Little, Brown in 2004.
† Published by Weidenfeld & Nicolson in June 1996.
‡ (Jane) Elizabeth Tottenham (b. 1945); dau. of Commander Lord George Tottenham RCN (whose bro. s. 1969 as 8th Marquess of Ely) and Jane Martin; m. 1971 Captain Mark Robinson RA; freelance editor (who adored J.L.-M. as much as she initially alarmed him).

Saturday, 16th March

My diary has now become like Harold [Nicolson]'s in the last years of his life, mere notes of little interest. Spotty; worthless. On Tuesday I lunched with the Coopers, on Wednesday with Jane [Westmorland]. Every day I go through a chapter of 'Fourteen Friends', revising and retyping it, incorporating the recommendations of Liz. The prose is now faultless, but reads like a professor of literature's.

Wednesday, 20th March

To London today, where Susy [Robinson] sweetly invited me to see the Cézannes,* having been given tickets by an obliging neighbour. She met me at Paddington and drove us to the Tate. Our tickets enabled us to avoid the enormous queue, doubling back and forth like a serpent. It was nevertheless an exhausting visit owing to the immense crowds, literally fighting for a stance in front of every painting. I cannot learn what Cézanne was striving for without close scrutiny of individual paintings, which was impossible. Still, it was an experience I would not have missed for the world. The landscapes are wonderfully evocative of Aix as I remember it; and I think *The Card Players* one of the greatest genre paintings I have ever seen.

Monday, 25th March

To bed in utmost depression, unable even to read. But unable to sleep either, so I took up *As You Like It* and turned to Act 2. I was bowled over by Amiens' lamentation over the death of a stag and the right of animals to be left to themselves in their environment. Even Shakespeare in 1600 was an environmentalist. Then I listened to two piano sonatas, one of Mozart's, and Beethoven's last. I thought, what matters the life or death of one miserable individual, if such works of genius are permitted to us?

---

* Paul Cézanne (1839–1906); French artist. The Musée d'Orsay in Paris, the Tate Gallery in London and the Philadelphia Museum of Art, which together owned many of his best works, had jointly organised an exhibition which was shown successively at the three museums and attracted vast crowds.

Sunday, 31st March

I have spent all weekend writing a short article for *Sotheby's Magazine*. This sounds ridiculously slow, but to condense the history of Ickworth and the Herveys* into five hundred words is no easy task. Meanwhile am cheered by today's appearance in *Sunday Times* of my little article in the 'Bookshelf' column on Logan Pearsall Smith's *On Reading Shakespeare*. It reads well, I think.

Wednesday, 10th April

Shall I, shan't I go to London today? I went. A satisfactory and enjoyable day. Saw three exhibitions and ran into several old friends – Burnet [Pavitt] descending from a taxi at Coutts', Simon Houfe† emerging from London Library, Nico Henderson lunching upstairs at Brooks's. To National Gallery to have another look at the Doria pictures. The Caravaggio *Angel* which David Beaufort so much admires is without sex, and quite celestial. To British Museum to exhibition of Sir William Hamilton's Volcanoes. The rooms in darkness, lights trained on exhibits only, which was irritating for me with my poor eyesight, unable to read the notices. Then to see the Caillebottes at Burlington House. Very interesting, a mixture of Expressionism and traditional Salon artistry. I particularly liked the Hausmann street scenes and iron bridges. Returned home in the evening on a high.

Tuesday, 23rd April

Reading the letters of my Bailey grandparents‡ to each other at the time of their engagement, I am amazed to learn that my grandmother

---

* Following a rake's progress, John Hervey, 7th Marquess of Bristol (1954–99), life tenant of the east wing of Ickworth House, Suffolk (the whole of which had been donated by his grandfather to the N.T. in 1956), was about to sell many of his remaining family possessions at Sotheby's.

† Grandson of J.L.-M's friend Sir Albert Richardson (1880–1964; Professor of Architecture, London University, and adviser to N.T.).

‡ Henry Bailey (1822–89), 5th and youngest son of Sir Joseph Bailey, 1st Bt; m. (2nd) 1881 Christina Thomson (1849–96); devoted his life to hunting and shooting on his estate at Coates near Cirencester.

asked my grandfather to see to the redecoration of the drawing room, dining room and hall at Coates before their marriage. 'I know your cousins have excellent taste and if you will allow them to offer their advice I know I should be pleased and they will go about it much more economically than I could.' So strange that this lady should not have supervised the redecorations herself. No one in her circumstances today would ever do such a thing. I imagine she was much in dread of the awful old man, who was old enough to be her father, and whose main interests were huntin' and shootin'. I don't suppose she loved him one bit. On 22 August 1884 she writes to him from staying with the Anstruthers in Perthshire that it will be some time before she sees him again as she is going on to the So-and-Sos. My mother was born on the 29th of that month, in his absence. Music seems to have been their only shared interest; she writes to him to 'bring some songs for the evenings'. She always refers to herself as 'Scotch' rather than 'Scottish', which confirms my natural tendency to use the former adjective.

Friday, 26th April

My reading of my grandparents' letters inspired me to visit Coates to look at their graves, this year being the centenary of her death. I found it. It is well-kept, the headstone a typical Victorian cross, the lettering of incised zinc or lead, still readable. He died on 10 August 1889 aged sixty-six, having caught a chill after bathing at Weymouth; she followed him on 24 August 1896 aged forty-seven, of Bright's Disease, when my poor mother was not yet thirteen. I suddenly had the idea that we – that is to say, the Robinson brothers and myself – might partake of a picnic above the grave this coming 24 August, as pagans used to do, pouring wine through a funnel onto the grave for the benefit of the defunct. The church was open, and I entered. Fine Norman columns on arches; nineteenth-century pews; no memorials. An indifferent window in memory of Thomas Gibbs, *ob.* December 1914, 'for 64 years Rector of Coates'. He is often mentioned in their letters, and surely buried them both.

Saturday, 27th April

I was invited to dine at the House, on the anniversary of Caroline's funeral. The Loewensteins staying, and all the children present. I sat next to Anne [Carr], who said her mother's diaries had been left to her – luckily not to Bunter,* so Tracy could not get her hands on them. These family antipathies. David surprised me by saying that Andrew Devonshire had been given the Garter. I would not have thought he was considered respectable enough. Debo would have been a worthier recipient. I shall have a difficult letter to write.

Friday, 3rd May

J.K.-B. for the night. Was delightful throughout. He seems to have acquired a new interest in life through becoming a Fellow of the [Royal Society of] Antiquaries. We motored to Owlpen [Manor, Gloucestershire], which alas is no longer the remote, cosy, unspoiled, lived-in manor house which inspired Vita. The Manders lack all taste. Environs undisturbed, thank goodness, but it is sad that the removal of the great yew hedge has opened the gabled house to distant views.

Sunday, 5th May

Debo telephoned. She has been staying at Highgrove, but could not come to me because of the Event. Said the cold at Highgrove was dreadful, and there was little to eat. The young princes and their friends were present, all starving. No meat course for dinner.

Sunday, 12th May

Yesterday Liz Robinson, the mystery editrix of 'Stale Mates', was brought to tea by Gail Pirkis. She is tall, large, rather butch in tight trousers, with fair hair scooped in a tail, and rather pretty face which becomes pleasant when relaxed. We had tea in the kitchen and then went into the garden. She is very knowledgeable on plants. I was

---

* Lady Anne's brother Harry, Marquess of Worcester.

pleased to see them. They had visited Westonbirt before coming to me.

Monday, 13th May

To my surprise, Pompey* telephoned this evening from Euston [Hall, Norfolk]. Fortune had just gone off to Buckingham Palace for Chirac's visit tomorrow. Pompey irritated that she aged seventy-five should have to drive herself and not have a car sent. 'After all, she is the Mistress of the Robes.' He then added, 'I gather from Billa [Harrod] that you're on the way out.' He was very solicitous, and we had a good nostalgic talk about old times.

Sunday, 26th May

Simon's cousin Detmar Blow† invited me to lunch at Hilles. I thought we might be alone, but not so. A number of young people, including a clever niece of Rosemary Chaplin. Sat next to young Detmar who treated me as though I was an ex-prime minister, and at the end of luncheon, to my embarrassment, asked the company to drink my health. He is half-Indian, and very like Simon in his class-consciousness and love of gossip. When we had eaten, his wife who had been cooking came and took his place. She was wearing a long black gown with train that skimmed across the boards, and a hat of orange ostrich feathers with pigeons' feathers stuck askew among them. She talked inconsequentially in an upper-class manner which embarrassed me somewhat. The strangeness of the young. Yet again very welcoming and kind. This house, by [the host's grandfather] the elder Detmar Blow, has enormous charm, and is absolutely in accord with the Cotswold landscape, while showing much originality. Huge rooms, clad with cosy lugubrious tapestries and full-length portraits of Kings and Queens. A living house.

---

* Hugh Fitzroy, 11th Duke of Grafton (b. 1919); m. 1946 Fortune Smith, Mistress of the Robes to HM The Queen from 1967.
† Art dealer and boulevardier (b. 1963); m. Isabella, dau. of Sir Evelyn Delves Broughton, 12th Bt.

Saturday, 1st June

Julian Barrow called, having come from Lyegrove where he is painting the latest owners. The two bachelor owners since Diana [Westmorland] have both died of Aids. New owners are immensely rich Jews from Hampstead. Their visits are occasional, and this Saturday they are having seventy to luncheon. It is only non-country people who buy large houses now. Julian is pleased that his little painting of our garden will appear on the jacket of *Ancient as the Hills*.[*]

Thursday, 6th June

Arctic weather has turned to Saharan. Debo, who has a meeting at Highgrove, asked if she might stay the night. Overjoyed, I welcomed her at 5.30 with a cup of tea. It was lovely having her. She looking very beautiful in thick pearls, bearing presents of cake, jam, etc., as well as the main course for our dinner, and her breakfast in a huge case, as she rises at 5 a.m. I poured out my health woes, very tiresome for her. She listened and advised wisely. This morning she walked to post a letter, chatting to all and sundry. She fears that Diana may never come over to England again. She turned down an offer from the benefactress[†] to have her motored to Gare du Nord, collected by private car at Waterloo and driven to the front door of Chatsworth. The fall at Waterloo Station has deprived her of all confidence.

Saturday, 22nd June

I discussed my wishes with Nick, and told him that he would have to mingle A's and my ashes and scatter them. 'Where?' he asked. I suggested the garden, for it was here that we both finished our lives together very happily. But he must tell no one, not even David Beaufort, because people don't like the idea of others being interred on their property. I told Nick that he would be in sole charge here

---

[*] Title chosen for forthcoming volume of J.L.-M's diaries, covering 1973–4.
[†] Nancy Osborne Hill.

until the lease was surrendered. He accepted all this in his usual sweet, unperturbed, optimistic way.

Wednesday, 26th June

Yesterday Clarissa and Billy came for tea. C. very sweet, he very accommodating as usual. We exchanged little gifts and we parted friends. She was greatly taken by the garden. Indeed it is at its annual zenith, and will never be more luxuriant than this day. Roses proliferating like a tapestry of Burne-Jones.

Liz Robinson came again this afternoon. Handsome, massive, a little forbidding. Masks her omniscience behind a slightly kittenish manner. We went through the diaries she has been editing. She misses little, having read the erasures.

Sunday, 30th June

No church for me today. Worked hard at my diaries for Liz. Then to lunch with Veronica,* Bamber and Christina at Veronica's farmhouse, Ashcroft, prepared by her son Ben and girlfriend. V. still a beauty, her auburn hair streaked with grey. Bamber as full of enthusiasms as ever. His eagerness very appealing. He is currently writing, all by himself and with no contributors, a history of the world in 850,000 words, to be available on computer and finished by 1998. An extraordinary mind he has, and compulsions. Works like a tiger. On their way back to London, he and Christina stopped to visit the garden here, and showed keen interest and botanical knowledge. There is nothing low-brow about these Gascoignes. All politically to the left, the girl working for an institution advocating Britain's reception of all applicants from foreign countries irrespective of their reasons for wishing to come here.

---

* Veronica Gascoigne (b. 1938); sister of Bamber; m. 1960 Hon. William Plowden.

Saturday, 6th July

When I spoke to Debo to accept her invitation to go to Chatsworth later this month, she informed me that Decca* was riddled with cancer on liver, chest and brain, and being treated with chemotherapy. Dreadful news which evokes my latent affection and sympathy for Decca. I wonder if the fall of Communism had the same effect on her as Vatican Council II had on Evelyn Waugh, driving her to despair and illness.

Wednesday, 10th July

The great Liz returns to finish off my diary manuscripts. We get on well and I like her much. She seems fascinated rather than revolted by the society of my olden days.

Friday, 12th July

The kind Hollands motor me to Deene. With ineffable politeness, Guy insists I sit in front with Joanie who is driving, whereas I would much rather sit in the back to relax. We arrive for tea in the great hall. The following guests are staying: Lord Stockton,† who is touring the country for the Conservative Party, but not a good advertisement for it, having the largest belly on a man I've ever seen; Laurence Kelly,‡ writer, and brother Bernard,§ former incapacitated by a stroke; the wives of these two, Linda and Lady Mirabelle, both delightful; dear Nathalie Brooke;¶ pretty Russian Ambassadress (her husband unable to come at last moment), knowing little English but speaking Russian

---

* Hon. Jessica Mitford (1917–96); m. 1st Esmond Romilly (1918–41), 2nd 1943 Robert Treuhaft (1912–2001); satirical writer living in USA, the 'Communist' Mitford sister (and the youngest next to Debo).

† Alexander Macmillan, 2nd Earl of Stockton (b. 1943); grandson of Harold Macmillan (1894–1986), Prime Minister 1956–63, cr. Earl of Stockton, 1984; President, Macmillan Ltd, from 1990; a member of the European Parliament from 1999.

‡ Businessman and writer of works on Russian subjects (b. 1933); m. 1963 Linda McNair Scott.

§ Banker (b. 1930); m. 1952 Lady Mirabelle Fitzalan Howard, sister of 17th Duke of Norfolk.

¶ Countess Nathalie Benckendorff; granddaughter of last Imperial Russian Ambassador to London; m. 1946 Humphrey Brooke, Secretary to Royal Academy, 1951–68.

with Nathalie and the Kellys; Kenneth Rose, much older and hunched like a dormouse, his head resembling a bust by Nollekens;[*] Drue Heinz,[†] the Harrises, the Hollands and myself. I enjoyed myself on the whole, and was overwhelmed by the kindness of Edmund and Marion. Given Henry VII's room as before. Lovely to be woken by morning sun on my pillow.

I walked in the garden with Kenneth who is writing the life of Victor Rothschild,[‡] whose son has just killed himself in a Paris hotel.[§] He explained to me that Victor's greatest achievement was a scientific discovery concerning the behaviour of the male sperm. Kenneth's conversation is peppered with references to 'my great friend the King of Greece' and 'the Duke of Kent, as you know my great friend', yet I am not sure he is entirely snobbish. His ingratiation has a fiendish charm. Very nice to me.

On Saturday after tea, Marion took the Ambassadress, John Harris and me to look at Southwick church, its forest of tombstones lit by the dying sun. Box pews with polished brass handles and hinges; in the chancel, six huge black memorial stones with beautifully incised writing, eighteenth-century, covering graves of Lynn family. Then Fotheringay church with its beautiful perpendicular architecture, to which I remember being taken by dear old Lady Ethelreda Wickham in 1944. Ambassadress kept talking on mobile telephone. Outside the porch in the graveyard she had a long conversation. When asked with whom, she said, 'The dearest old lady who is like a mother to me, outside of Moscow.' She telephones and is telephoned all the time. But reception at Deene is indifferent owing to low-lying land, and she has to climb to the attics or the roof. I met her outside my bedroom door endeavouring to get through to Kiev.

---

[*] Joseph Nollekens (1737–1823); English sculptor.

[†] Drue Maher; m. 1953 as his 2nd wife Jack Heinz II (1908–87), chairman of international food company H.J. Heinz; benefactress of literature and the arts.

[‡] 3rd Baron Rothschild (1910–90); zoologist, industrialist, intelligence officer, and government adviser; his biography by Kenneth Rose, *Elusive Rothschild*, was published by Weidenfeld & Nicolson in 2003.

[§] Hon. Amschel Mayer James Rothschild (1955–96) was found hanging by the cord of his bathrobe, the conclusion of the Paris police that he had killed himself being questioned in some quarters.

I was very pleased to be with the Harrises. John now distinguished with wavy hair, she much improved in looks. He made a discovery in Deene church: found name of William Kent's plasterer and identified his work with that of ceiling in billiards room. An affectionate pair, I have an 'up' on them.

On Sunday morning, the Eucharist in the chapel. House party sit on right against wall, villagers on left. We take Communion first. All this rather shocks me. Ambassadress attends and says it is just like the Russian Orthodox Church. I wonder if she can be religious.

Wednesday, 17th July

Alan [the Devonshires' chauffeur] motors me to Chatsworth. Am welcomed by Debo and present my plants to her, which are immediately sent off to head gardener. After tea I wander to kitchen garden and admire D's layout of vegetable and herb beds in concentric rings, herbs raised to within sight level and labelled. Andrew appears for dinner, wide-armed and welcoming. I take care to respect his taciturnity. He has little appetite on account of his having watched golf on television all day. He says that Derek [Hill] has invited himself to Chatsworth during Prince of Wales's next visit, saying, 'I am sure HRH would like me to be present when I have my eightieth birthday.'

Sunday, 21st July

Sir Edward Ford* has been staying two nights, taking himself to Buxton Opera for *Beggars' Opera* and Handel. Is eighty-five and very musical. Most delightful man, widower. At luncheon yesterday I hear with left ear Debo being told by Feeble of an entry in her father's diary of 1919 that he expects announcement within a few days of his sister Dorothy Cavendish's engagement to Prince of Wales, and with right ear Andrew discussing with Sir Edward particulars of King George VI's final illness. Like all courtiers, Sir Edward is discreet, though amused by foibles.

---

* Courtier (1910–2006); Assistant Private Secretary to the Sovereign (1946–67).

Debo tells me that Decca is dying in New York. We return from a short stroll in great heat at 5.45 and hear telephone ring. D. says, 'Stay with me.' Decca recites lines from *Maud* about how the black bat has flown, which Debo continues.

Tuesday, 23rd July

I surrender totally to Henry [the butler]'s ministrations. Evidently I did not bring enough shirts and underclothes, for he allows me to wear a shirt for no more than a day before taking it away to be washed. Although he is Irish, Henry is one of the most decent friends I have ever had. His patience, readiness to oblige, kindness and loyalty are unsurpassed. But having to tip him causes me immense embarrass-ment and unease, of which he is well aware. For a week's sojourn I have given £35 to him, £20 to Stella the housekeeper, and £20 to Jo for motoring me home. Nothing to Alan who motored me from home because he has gone off on his holiday, and this worries me.

Andrew stalks around the house in dressing-gown at 11 a.m. A sort of dread comes over me here from time to time. I feel that Chatsworth is just too grand for me. I can't live up to it. I am inadequate, notwith-standing the ineffable kindness I receive.

This afternoon the Ds and I are motored at 2.30 to the Tram Museum, oddly situated at Crick in remote heart of Pennines. We leave Chatsworth in unbroken, sweltering sunshine. We buy tickets for tram-ride and are in mid journey when thunder and lightning begin and hail descends in noisy torrents. Instantly tram lights go out and vehicle halts, the electricity having been struck by lightning. We are stuck for almost an hour, unable to move. Finally a diesel truck comes and pushes tram home. Chatsworth has entirely escaped the storm, receiving not one drop. Debo in halted tram makes friends with fellow travellers with utmost ease and interest.

On my last evening, telephone rings at dinner. Debo jumps up saying, 'I know that will be Decca.' Returns, sits down, and says, 'She has just died.' Talk of other things. Then she says she must do some telephoning, and leaves the dining room. I walk with Andrew towards her sitting room, but say good night to him at my bedroom door and go to bed.

Friday, 2nd August

Received sweetest letter from Nigel [Nicolson] to whom I wrote, hoping he would not disapprove of the chapter on Vita in *Fourteen Friends*. He says he has already read proofs and is reviewing for the *Sunday Times*. Is also writing in his autobiography that I ought to have been his mother's son, as there was so much affinity. Nigel is a generous man.

Tuesday, 6th August

My unblessed [eighty-eighth] birthday. People telephone with congratulations, including Anne Hill who says she had no idea it was my birthday, but had an urge to call me. Then Nick motors me to Wickhamford. On the way we stop at Upper Slaughter to look at new memorial window in the Witts chapel. As I expected, it is a hideous gash of uncompromising colours. Typical of the Wittses and Wrigleys,* old-fashioned country folk with aspirations to avant-gardeness.

We get to Wickhamford at four. Welcomed most kindly and warmly by Jeremy and June Ryan-Bell. Too blustery to sit on the terrace, so we go into hideous plastic tent erected on the lawn for recent performance of *Much Ado about Nothing*. They propose to make this structure, with imitation Georgian windows of waving perspex, a permanent feature in the once pretty sunken garden, now deprived of pool and fountain. Nevertheless they both love Wickhamford and are eager for any information on its days of yore. An enormous tea provided – birthday cake and three other sorts of cake, three jams and scones galore. The darkness of the house, smallness of the rooms. Pond much improved since last visit, weeds and lilies removed. They have cleared a welcome view beyond the pond of a park-like field with sheep. Nick for the first time seems interested in the childhood home of his grandmother Audrey, and impressed with the church. The kindness we receive from these nice people is really overwhelming.

---

* Alice Wrigley (1902–90); second cousin of J.L.-M.; m. 1929 Major-General Frederick Witts (1889–1969), whose forebears had been Rectors and Lords of the Manor of Upper Slaughter for three generations.

Nick says when we get home, 'I have never seen a man more nervous of you than him.' Nonsense, surely, for I was all sugar.

Saturday, 17th August

David Beaufort telephones at 8 asking me to meet him at Swangrove at 11. Of course I agree, though busy with other matters. He has put this *maison de plaisance* back to what it should be with his infallible eye. Calls it his gloating house. I don't blame him. He says he can hardly bear friends walking round it lest they spoil it. He has fitted it out with three bedrooms, complete with beds and furniture from the House attics. A very complete and ravishing little house. All it wants is a library.

Tuesday, 20th August

At breakfast, Patricia rings in tears to say that [J.L.-M's sister-in-law] Elaine died early this morning. I write to Simon telling him he need have no remorse as so many people do on the death of a parent.

Thursday, 22nd August

J.K.-B. stayed last night. Very kind, good, and tolerant of my quick temper. He is a mini-sage, with his knowledge of the classics, literature and theology. I fear he is taken advantage of by many researchers and art historians, who drain him of his knowledge and do little for him in return. He finds writing difficult to embark on, and so others reap his harvests.

Friday, 23rd August

Dined at Swangrove. An experience. Some twelve guests in the ground floor dining room. This house is larger than mine. Sat between Miranda and Josephine [Loewenstein]. Andrew Parker Bowles making teasing jokes at one's expense, yet very friendly. David explained that his collection of framed Claude sketches comes from the famous *Liber Veritatis* which Andrew Devonshire was obliged to sell to meet death duties on succession. Master wanted to scrap them, and David persuaded him to sell to him. A large fire burning in upstairs saloon. Much draught from the high front door. It could never have been a cosy pleasure retreat, though ravishing.

Sunday, 1st September

Freda [Berkeley] came to stay last Tuesday, motored by Coote, for what turned out to be five days of unremitting society. We went out to meals with Gerda Barlow, Jane Westmorland, the [Guy] Hollands, and the Revd John Foster, and I gave a luncheon party here to which came Jane, Desmond Briggs and the Duff Hart-Davises. I am ashamed to say that I used the long-planned luncheon with Gerda on Wednesday as an excuse not to attend Elaine's cremation at Worcester. Freda never stopped telephoning or being telephoned. Her Catholic priest Father Michael [Hollings] rang twice a day. She could not have been kinder or sweeter, but is not very well, and fatter in spite of a much-vaunted diet. Two horse-loving lesbians called this afternoon to motor her back to London.

Monday, 2nd September

Though not due out for weeks, *Fourteen Friends* is already receiving reviews. A good one yesterday by Ziegler in the *Telegraph*; and today that gorgeous lamp-post Stephanie* rang to announce a favourable and prominent one by Anne Scott-James in today's *Standard* – generous of her in view of some of the things I write about Osbert [Lancaster]. Also an indulgent note from Louisa Young assuring me that she 'does not entirely disapprove' of my disparagement of her grandfather and father.

Thursday, 5th September

Nick lunches and is as comforting as ever, as good as gold. I have been reading my diary for 1978, when I felt I had broken through to him

---

* Stephanie Allen, publicity manager at John Murray.

and that he would be a companion for the rest of my life. And so it has proved. But little did I realise that in my last years he would become my dearest friend and counsellor in whose company I am happiest. Little too did I realise that a book of mine would receive exaggerated praise in the literary pages of *Country Life*. I would now be very content, were it not for my health. I am reconciled to the loss of A., though I feel remorse when reading my old diaries for having treated her so ill.

Sunday, 15th September

Diana [Mosley] writes that she is drained of all vitality by the unsolicited and fatuous communication of acquaintances. I know just how she feels.

Tuesday, 17th September

Derek [Hill] telephones. 'Are you doing anything on November 15th? Then Prince Charles wants you to lunch. I am going to stay there the night before. I hear you have written a book.' All rather peremptory.

Thursday, 19th September

Grant [McIntyre] motored down from London this afternoon to talk to me. We had tea in the kitchen, and he went straight back again. I knew something unexpected was coming. First, he congratulated me on successful reception of *Fourteen Friends*. Secondly, he asked me to sign twenty more copies for Stephanie. Thirdly, would I consider a reprint of *Another Self*? Then, shyly, 'Would you consider being subjected to a biography?'* I said no, no, no. The whole idea was preposterous. He suggested James Knox, whom I like. But the idea of unbosoming myself to this nice young man is repugnant. All those skeletons in my cupboard which I now recoil from with a shudder, but know are still unburied. But as Grant pointed out, if I decline to

---

* The idea had already been put to J.L.-M. five years earlier – see 24 February 1991.

cooperate while I am alive, it will very likely still happen after my death. I shall wait until James has finished his life of Robert [Byron]. Meanwhile, with whom can I consult? Grant suggested Debo. The very idea.

Friday, 20th September

A fascinating experience today, reminding me of my wartime visits to remote country houses and harassed owners. Susy [Robinson], who is on the local CPRE committee, has been much concerned with the condition of Barrington Park, the Wingfields'* house near Burford, but in Gloucestershire. Architectural historians have been denied admission to this house for years while hearing rumours of its slow deterioration. Now the son, Richard, twenty-five or so I should guess, bright-eyed, good-looking, beautifully mannered, fairly ignorant, eager for information and guidance and a prey to antiquarian rogues, has taken possession of the house, and is prepared to restore it. This means demolishing wings added in the 1870s and 80s by the mediocre architect McVicar Anderson, leaving the 1735 core,† a typical George II villa attributed to William Kent and one of the Smiths of Warwick.

We were greeted in the courtyard by young Richard, his parents Charles and Mary Wingfield, and their architect. Politenesses and recollections of former meetings. She a dear bewildered lady who is sister of Lord Sandys of Ombersley and daughter of the benevolent Colonel Arthur Sandys who once gave me a box of cigars. The whole house draped with plastic sheets under scaffolding, so exterior cannot be seen. The parents live in darkness relieved by an occasional one-horse-power electric bulb. Beautiful central hall, deep square panelled ceiling of stucco, two chimneypieces with pictures in overdoors (temporarily removed). Impossible in the dimness to see colour of walls. The hall looks more or less intact, but the rest of the 1735 core as well as the Victorian wings in appalling condition. Riddled with dry rot.

---

* Charles Talbot Rhys Wingfield (b. 1924); m. 1954 Hon. Cynthia Meriel Hill, dau. of 6th Baron Sandys.

† Built by the Wingfields' forebear William, 1st and last Earl Talbot (1710–82).

The Wingfields' vast bedroom ceiling collapsed in one corner. The same in practically all rooms. Went upstairs to see once delightful children's nurseries, in same state. Stone roofs decayed into rubble. In the drawing room, the Flemish tapestries seem miraculously to have survived, having been protected from the light. Unfortunately Anderson obliterated the original staircase, substituting his own. His dining room and billiards room admittedly decent Victorian, but two-a-penny.

The public enquiry to be held in ten days' time is anticipated to go against the Wingfields, who are facing opposition from English Heritage and the Victorian Society. Yet I see absolutely no alternative to demolition of the Anderson additions in order to preserve and rein-state the Kentian villa. The family are asking for no financial assistance from the State, and would be unable to live in the present house, were it to be reinstated. Susy and I given tea in large drawing room. We had a long talk with Mrs, a charming, gentle, slightly giggly woman who is clearly at sea and has long since thrown up the sponge. Says they suffer from ramblers claiming the right to long-forgotten footpaths. In all my days of country house visiting I don't remember a more tragic case than Barrington. The scenario of a Russian novel. I kept wonder-ing how they managed to keep so clean and tidy, living as they do.

Sunday, 6th October

One hundred years ago today, a haycart drew William Morris's* body from Lechlade station to Kelmscott church. I joined a party of the Antiquaries to commemorate this event. His tomb in the churchyard is still isolated and sheltered under drooping trees. Made by Philip Webb† in Viking style. Striking, and very *de l'époque*. Beside it in the grass, a round slab with 'M.M.' carved – this to May Morris,‡ daughter, whom I remember sitting on the platform at N.T. and SPAB annual meetings in London, a little dark old lady with a frown. None of the other Fellows present known to me. We lunched in the barn close to

---

* British craftsman, designer, writer, typographer and socialist (1834–96).
† Architect and designer (1831–1915); co-founder with William Morris of Society for Protection of Ancient Buildings (1877).
‡ Leading British weaver and editor of her father's works (1862–1938).

the manor house. I walked through the village to the church service at 2 p.m. and was given a seat in front row at the crossing. Very old church, Norman, with a transept. Several readings, one with Morris's beautiful description of the church. Several substantial houses in the village, one with stone slab fencing on the road, like tombstones. Never seen this before. The manor makes an enticing group of rooftops, tall diamond-wise chimneys, pointed gables with ball finials, and wooden guttering projecting several feet from the eaves. Little windows in attic have tiny pediments which give the Elizabethan structure a faintly Renaissance air. The outside is as lovely as any Cotswold house known to me. Inside no longer a lived-in manor house, but a well-ordered museum. Blue-and-white William de Morgan tiles inserted by Morris in the grates. Several flashy late seventeenth-century fireplaces of carved garlands. Tapestry room upstairs remembered by me from 1942, the panels ruthlessly cut to shape the walls. When last seen, this room was musty and romantic. Now tidied up somewhat.

J.L.-M. moved out of his Bath library in the course of October.

Tuesday, 8th October

John Saumarez Smith came down for the day to Bath. A great help to me, because he makes up his mind at once. He has separated those books I want to get rid of into two piles, the majority, which he will sell in his shop, and the rest, to be disposed of to some trash bookseller. He is a breathless talker, which tires me somewhat. The same is true of Tony Mitchell, who kindly came to the library to advise Pickford's men on how to remove large items of furniture. It was amusing to watch these giants talking and waving their arms like characters in a comic opera.

Thursday, 10th October

Simon [Lees-Milne] came to Bath for the day, and gratefully took away all I had got out to give him, unreadable books relevant to the family and odd assortments of china. Mercifully he is passionate about the dreary Lees family. He has conventional views on every subject, and is jocular, middle-class and happy with his lot. He told me that, as Elaine lay dying, his American half-sister asked her if she would like to see her eldest son David Guthrie, now living in Cheltenham, aged sixty-two, with whom she had never so much as communicated since she deserted his father for Dick when he was three. 'Oh well, I suppose I might,' she said. He saw her at the hospital; but Simon has no idea what they talked about, as she said nothing about it before falling unconscious soon after. He turned up at the funeral but left as soon as it was over.

Saturday, 12th October

Nick Robinson and Jamie Fergusson lunched. I gave the latter the little bust of a bald man by W. Jones dated 1838, which I used to think was of Lord Melbourne until I discovered that M. maintained a shock of hair into old age. Jamie seemed to be touched. He is so devitalised that he sits silent, unable to make up his mind to move away. Yet when interested rouses himself and is clever and wise. Nick and I went to Bath, where he chose many family books and the table from which I have eaten my meals there these past twenty-two years.

Saturday, 19th October

Hugh Massingberd came to luncheon alone, dropped by Andrew Barrow, his friend from Harrow. Has abandoned his diet, and polished off the whole of a sweet, sticky pudding left by Nick. There is no one I am happier talking to. He wants to write a book about the heroes he worships and longs to emulate.*

Wednesday, 23rd October

Grant writes accepting my next batch of diaries – 1975–8 – which Murray's will publish in 1998.† Shall I be alive? Nice however to have

---

* It was published by Macmillan in 2001 as *Daydream Believer: Confessions of a Hero Worshipper*, and includes a chapter on J.L.-M. ('Saint Jim').
† They appeared posthumously that year as *Through Wood and Dale*.

some work ahead of me. I need not be at a loose end for the remainder of my days. Oddly, if he had rejected them, I do not think I would have minded much.

I am almost ashamed of the pleasure I am taking in rearranging my furniture, pictures and objects from Bath at Essex House, where they replace A's things taken away by Clarissa. The Isfahan carpet looks well in my book room. Spent hours positioning Marie Antoinette on her pedestal in my downstairs room, eventually deciding she would have to look out of the window. This is a thoroughly bourgeois pastime which most British people lapse into on their retirement.

Wednesday, 6th November

Lunched with [Duff] Hart-Davises at Owlpen. All the other guests were friends whom I much like – Charlie Morrisons, Keens, Gerda [Barlow]; yet I was in a daze after reading proofs of my 1973–4 diaries, which froze me with horror over my criticisms of friends who are either still living or have children. It is too late now to make more than minimal changes. John Saumarez Smith assures me that they are 'compulsive reading'.

John says that Heywood Hill will pay me £15,000 for the books they have taken. I am amazed by this huge sum. I said I would accept £3,000, the rest to be donated to the National Trust for their scheme to re-establish libraries in country houses.*

Thursday, 7th November

Peggy prepared a good luncheon for Clarissa and Billy, to whom I was to hand over the keys to No. 19 [Lansdown Crescent]. I said, Don't be late. They were. He telephoned from Acton Turville to announce that their car had broken down near Tormarton. I fetched them. Luncheon ruined while Billy feverishly telephoned a rescue service. A van eventually arrived with their car hoisted on it, and they went off together, having forgotten to take the keys.

---

* It was eventually used to establish a library in his memory at Gunby Hall, Lincolnshire.

Tuesday, 12th November

Mark Bence-Jones's book *Life in an Irish Country House* deals with some dozen houses, several of which I have known, such as Curragh* and Mount Stewart.† All Irish houses are deeply romantic, and on the verge of disintegration even when splendid. The book culminates in the period of the Great War, in which all elder sons were killed, the widows lingering on. All tragic, mournful, nostalgic. The atmosphere dead, breathless, green and dank. Queen Alexandra, in signing the visitors' book at Mount Stewart, added the comment, 'A beautiful place, but damp.'

Wednesday, 13th November

To London for the night. In the library at Brooks's I meet Stuart [Preston], who has just come from Heywood Hill where he bought two of my discarded books, one of them given to me by Stephen Spender with a flowery *dédicace*. I am upset by this, John Saumarez having assured me he would advise me if he came across anything which looked personal and I might wish to keep.

Then to Grosvenor House for Foyle's luncheon to celebrate Mrs Major's‡ book. A grand triumph for Christina after sixty-six years of these luncheons to have as guests of honour the Prime Minister and wife, a former Prime Minister (Heath), a former Deputy Prime Minister (Whitelaw§), two Prime Ministers' widows (Clarissa Avon and Mary Wilson), and the former Foreign Secretary (Hurd¶). I find I am sitting on the right of Christina, already seated.

---

* Curragh Chase, Co. Limerick, seat of the de Vere family until gutted by fire in 1941.

† Seat of Marquesses of Londonderry, on shores of Strangford Lough, Co. Down; donated to Northern Ireland National Trust 1977 by Lady Mairi Bury, yst dau. of 7th Marquess.

‡ Norma Wagstaff (b. 1942; DBE 1999); m. 1970 John Major (Prime Minister, 1990–7); her book *Chequers: The Prime Minister's Country House and its History* was published by Collins and illustrated with photographs by Mark Fiennes.

§ William Whitelaw (1918–99); Conservative politician, Deputy Prime Minister to Mrs Thatcher, 1983–8; cr. Viscount, 1983.

¶ Douglas Hurd (b. 1930); Conservative politician, Foreign Secretary, 1989–95; cr. life peer as Lord Hurd of Westwell, 1997.

Much older and rather deaf, though still pretty. Slumped with head just above table-top, wearing black velvet dress and jewels, very smart. Tells me she is eighty-five. Mrs Major comes up to chat. I rise on being introduced. She has a sweet face. Is followed by husband. With difficulty, I rise again, though he beseeches me not to. He has a nice firm handshake, and beams. As he bends over Christina, his greying hair brushes my chin. Lucky man to have hair. On my right sits Lord Armstrong of Ilminster,* the civil servant who was 'economical with the truth'. Jeffrey Archer† makes bland introductory speech. Followed not by Mrs Major but Mr, who delivers charming impromptu speech paying wife unqualified praise for her research and writing. I understand how Mr Major is two persons in one. Today he displays his off-duty private persona – natural, funny, nice and engaging.

Dinner at Brooks's for Diana [Mosley], Selina [Hastings] and Richard Shone. Diana as beautiful as ever, with new tooth which cost a thousand pounds. I give her the book which my grandfather‡ received from her Mosley grandfather-in-law§ as a leaving present at Eton. She and I find it very difficult to hear each other, but Selina bawls and is heard. Nevertheless all enjoy it I think.

Friday, 15th November

Not having heard further from Derek, I turned up at Highgrove at 12.55, asking the policeman on duty whether I was expected. 'Your name, Sir? . . . Yes, you are. Please go ahead.' On arrival, I asked the nice footman where the gents was, for being very old I might suddenly have need. He was about to show me when Prince Charles crossed the hall to welcome me. On the left the drawing room, with a huge fire and Derek sitting hugely in front of it. For once well-groomed,

---

* Sir Robert Armstrong (b. 1927); Cabinet Secretary, 1979–87 (who used the notorious phrase during the 'Spycatcher' case in Australia in 1986); cr. life peer, 1988.

† Conservative politician and novelist (b. 1940); Deputy Party Chairman, 1985–6; cr. life peer as Lord Archer of Weston-super-Mare, 1992; imprisoned for perjury, 2001.

‡ James Henry Lees-Milne (1847–1908).

§ Sir Oswald Mosley, 4th Bt (1848–1915).

and decently dressed. He is very good with the Prince, on the easiest terms verging on familiarity. Almost cheeky, which is doubtless enjoyed. 'Now, Sir, what will happen to Royal Lodge and the Castle of Mey – not that I care for the last much – when the sad day comes and we lose Queen Elizabeth?' 'Oh, don't!' Derek complimented the Prince's equal facility with brush and pen, saying that he (D.) can't write and his autobiography, though penned by a competent ghost, has been refused by every publisher.

The Prince has exquisite manners as host, yet is very shy and uncertain. Speaks hesitantly without finishing sentences. Is wary, wondering whether he can trust anyone in the world. No longer youthful in appearance, though his countenance is clear. He said he was going to be fifty next birthday. I told him I cried when I turned fifty. 'Did you really?' Calls me by my first name, but I suppose he does this with everyone he meets socially. Has a strange scar on his left cheek of the sort which German students used to acquire from duelling. He is lonely, afraid of experts yet seeking to keep up with them. Told me he was reading *Fourteen Friends*, and asked if Diana [Mosley] was one of them; so he has not got as far as the Table of Contents. 'I wouldn't have dared even if she were dead, which thank God she isn't.' He asked if any loved ones, widows or children, had complained. I said that Anne Lancaster may have been slightly aggrieved. I am not sure if he knew who Osbert Lancaster was. Said he liked looking for and eating wild mushrooms from the woods.

We lunched at the small round table in the window of the small breakfast room overlooking the garden and the hornbeam avenue. Luncheon consisted of a rather dry quiche of the bought kind and his own vegetables, ice cream and stewed peaches for pudding. I felt very at ease, and was enjoying myself. He talked of his recent visit to Russia. Remarked on the pinched faces of the inhabitants. Said all old buildings swept away by the Soviets, to be replaced by the usual modern muck. Even now they sweep away what's left with positive pride in their vandalism. I asked if he saw anything created since Tsarist times which was covetable. Nothing, he replied. We talked of George IV and Wyatville*

---

* Sir Jeffry Wyatt (1766–1840); architect who remodelled Windsor Castle for George IV.

destroying the Verrio* rooms at Windsor, which he thought deplorable. He asked if I liked Pugin. Moderately, I said – though I liked the wall-papers much.

He showed me all round the downstairs rooms and is very proud of them. Took me to see his framed watercolours in the loo. (Here was my opportunity, but I had no need.) Some I thought very pretty. Memories of his incognito travels in Greece and Italy with Derek and others. This is what he enjoys and wishes he had more time for. He explained that most of the house's contents come from the lumber rooms at Windsor. Walls are crammed, which I like to see. Frederick, Prince of Wales† in superb rococo frame with bold feathers atop. Tables also crammed with gifts, huge seventeenth-century Bible with silver facings and clasps given by wife of Laurens van der Post.‡ Spoke highly of him, and 'that dear man Gervase'. Treasures everywhere. His own office filled with piles of unread art books and paintings by young artists.

The Prince clearly very fond of Derek. Gave him a copy of his recent diary. While I was saying goodbye soon after 3, Derek asked for Camilla's telephone number, which the Prince rolled off his tongue. A car at the door to take Derek back to London. Derek said he must take a photograph of us both, and that the Prince must put on his fox-fur, red-velvet-lined mantle with matching hood. Prince Charles expostulated, but was bulldozed by Derek. He shyly donned these wonderful garments which I had seen him wearing in newspaper photographs. We walked onto the drive in the sun. I discreetly distanced myself from the Prince as Derek snapped away.

What a sweet man. Heart bang in the right place. Earnest about his charities, and writhes in misery at the destruction of the world. Not very clever in spite of praiseworthy intentions. Lays himself open to criticism because he contends with intellectuals and specialists in fields

---

* Antonio Verrio (1639–1707); Italian decorative artist working in England.

† Son of George II and father of George III (1707–51); the first Hanoverian to show a serious interest in the arts.

‡ (Sir) Laurens van der Post (1906–96); South African-born writer interested in mysticism and the Jungian concept of the collective unconscious.

of which he can inevitably have only superficial knowledge. He deserves all our encouragement and support. A figure of tragedy with abundant charm.

Saturday, 16th November

Derek on the telephone, asking how I liked Him. Oh very much indeed, I replied. And he liked you too, said D. I said, You are a bully. You simply drove him to put on that garment and be photographed. 'Did I really?' he said, and laughed. 'So like me.'

Tuesday, 19th November

Filthy day of continuous rain and wind. Misha came for the night. He has his fads, and like all Londoners hates the cold. We lunched indoors, and in spite of rain, wind and dark I took him to dine at the King's Arms at Didmarton. Rather frightening, as I could hardly distinguish the road from the verge because of the fallen leaves. I told him how much distaste I have for homosexuality now. He seemed rather shocked, and reluctant to believe me.

Wednesday, 27th November

Lunched with Bruce Hunter at Athenaeum. Very civilised. Club has recently had marble floor of hall relaid at great cost, old floor having been ruined by kitchen trolleys trundling to dining room. Bruce persuaded me to allow Murray's to republish *Another Self*. I hope it will not come out before my death. I don't want to face the inevitable question, 'Is it true?'

Wednesday, 4th December

I sit in my three rooms admiring the improvements I have made, and wondering what A. would think of them.

Saturday, 7th December

Debo telephones that she is awaiting arrival of Prince Charles and Derek for the famous weekend. She has prepared dinner in the library and erected some sort of flowered aedicule in which to ensconce Derek, with little bells attached. Hold on, she interrupts. Oh, that was Henry to say that the Prince has rung from his car that his arrival is imminent.

Tuesday, 10th December

Debo telephones to tell me about weekend. She evidently has some reservations about Derek's proprietary attitude towards the Prince. Indeed is mystified as to why the Prince puts up with his cheekiness. For instance, D. keeps telephoning the P. when the latter withdraws to his bedroom between tea and dinner. Camilla there too, and D. says it is almost piteous how happy they are together, without the press knowing. It was at Chatsworth that they first met, twenty-four years ago. He blossoms in her company.

Tuesday, 31st December

Since return [from Christmas at Chatsworth], I have spent most of my time answering unsolicited letters and thanking people who have sent me their books. Charles Keen sent me his *Daphnis and Chloe*, Edward Fawcett a volume of poems, Julian Fane his *Obiter Dicta*, and Nicholas Shakespeare his life of Bruce Chatwin. I have also been writing an introduction for Heywood Hill's sale catalogue of my books.

Today the customary New Year's Eve luncheon at Old Werretts. I have accepted much hospitality this year from Desmond and Ian, who are unfailingly kind to me. When I got home, Bath Clinic telephoned asking if I might come in tomorrow instead of Thursday, to undergo the op. on Thursday at one o'clock. Saw no reason why not, so agreed.

This evening Peggy Willis* rang to ask if the Derek Hill who has

---

* Margaret Anne Walker; m. (1st) 1930 Philip Dunne MC of Gatley Park, Herefordshire. The mention of her referred to occurs on 3 December 1972, when

been awarded the CBE in New Year's Honours is our Derek. I said to Peggy, 'Derek won't be pleased. CBE isn't much.' 'What do you mean?' she replied. 'I was awarded it.' I had no idea. 'But in Derek's eyes it won't mean much,' I said. 'He would expect the KG at least.' She referred to my mention of her missing right hand. Said no one she knew ever referred to it, and her mother taught her never to do so herself. She was happy that I had at last recorded the fact of her disability. Is pleased that her younger son has been appointed Lord Lieutenant of Warwickshire, the elder one already being Lord Lieutenant of Herefordshire.* This is unusual, possibly unique.

J.L.-M. found her 'very civilised and sympathetic . . . so beautiful a woman she must have been, with two if not more husbands and beaux galore'.

* The brothers Sir Thomas Dunne (b. 1933; KCVO 1995; Lord Lieutenant, Hereford and Worcester, 1977–2001) and Martin Dunne (b. 1938; Lord Lieutenant, Warwickshire from 1997).

1997

1997

Tuesday, 7th January

On New Year's Day I went into the Bath Clinic. The anaesthetist, Mr
Suter – who is incidentally the most Apollonian man I have ever
encountered – decided not to give me a full anaesthetic, but to numb
me from the waist down with a spinal injection. Great relief, as I had
been dreading the coming-round and consequent effects. So I was
wheeled in my bed down to the theatre and given a prick in the base
of the spine. I kept wondering when it was going to begin, when a
voice said it was all over. Incredible. I slept, had tea, and remained jolly
for the rest of the day. Next day I felt awful, and thought I would never
be able to pee again. But when I did so, the gush and flow were as
strong as they used to be when I was eighteen.

On Sunday, Mr Smith came to tell me I could go home the next
day at 7 p.m. He is a very intelligent man. Says there will always be
unemployment because there will always be a class of drones, and
we live in an age when only skilled workers can expect employment.
The problem is how to keep the drones partially content.

Home since yesterday. I don't feel ill, just exhausted and unable to
concentrate, or do anything except moon around in my dressing-
gown and lie on the bed.

Thursday, 9th January

In my current state I have refused two commissions – to write the
DNB entry for Brian Fothergill,* and do a review for the *Oldie*. Nor

---

* Historical writer (1921–90) who had treated several of J.L.-M's favourite subjects –
including William Beckford and the Jacobites – and like him twice won the
Heinemann Prize.

do I feel much like tackling *Bruce Chatwin* for the *TLS* – but I must accept, or it is a total giving up.

Finished *Oliver Twist*. Academically speaking, a bad novel. Improbable sequences, exaggerated horrors, political bias, too much moralising, often deplorable syntax. Of course the picture of London in William IV's reign is deeply depressing and indeed terrifying, if true. Yet the characters – Fagin, Sykes – stand out like Shakespeare's. Oliver Twist himself is cardboard. I didn't enjoy.

Sunday, 12th January

Suddenly I feel well again. Walked to Little Badminton across the park and back by the road. The Arctic cold has gone, and it is mild and damp. A streak of sun, enough to bring a sniff of the damned spring.

In my new Smythson's diary, I have only one engagement down for this year – Coote's birthday party in March, to which I may not go. I haven't yet answered Maureen Dufferin's card for her ninetieth, tiaras and white ties. The very idea. Yet I wish I felt like going.

Wednesday, 22nd January

Lunched today with the dear Levis at Prospect Cottage. Excellent meal – caviare in cream, calves' liver and delicious pudding. Anthony Hobson was the other guest, and brought a pile of books of mine for signature. Flattering, from one of the great bibliophiles. Deirdre is adorable, always smiling, like a radiant golden moon. How I love her. The mysterious little Matthew present, silent yet missing nothing. I rushed away to get home before dark.

Sunday, 26th January

A beautiful day. In early afternoon I drove along the lane from Badminton to Sopworth, left car on verge and walked through the village. Church locked, but Pevsner* says nothing within. Nevertheless

---

* Sir Nikolaus Pevsner (1902–83); Professor of Fine Arts, Cambridge (1949–55) and Oxford (1968–9); originator of *The Buildings of England* series of county guides.

very pretty on summit overlooking a vast field. Graveyard full of wool merchants' tombs. Sopworth, two miles from Badminton as the crow flies, is in Wiltshire. I talked to an old lady with a spotted dog, who asked if I was 'a local man'. When I replied that I lived in Badminton, she expressed astonishment that I had walked all the way. I had to disabuse her. Ten years ago I would have done so, and back.

Although I don't want to go to parties or even to see anyone, nevertheless I am often assailed with a sense of imprisonment in my ivory tower. So I venture out, as I did today, for a drive or a short walk. But after a while, discomfort assails me. No one who has not been through their late eighties can conceive of the hell of them. It is as though one is being subjected to a different torture every day.

Sunday, 9th February

The Chandors* to tea, bringing me a delicious chocolate cake, and showing me a book they had bought which belonged to Beckford. She told me that, during her debutante days, she worked for MI5. Would go every morning to HQ in Curzon Street from where she and other junior staff would be driven to a 'secret' address in Burlington Gardens, above a tailor's shop. Her duty was to listen in to telephone conversations of people known to be living beyond their earnings. She said it was fascinating work for a time, but eventually got on her nerves. Anything suspicious overheard was taken down in pencil, there being no instant recording equipment in those days. I did not like to ask which days those were as it would have revealed her age.

Monday, 10th February

I am always amused by the rules which old people set themselves. Gerry Wellington would never allow himself a drink before the clock struck six. Taking out his watch, he would say, 'Only another five minutes before we can have a cocktail.' Whereas I say to myself, 'It's nearly four o'clock, when the radiators come on.' My besetting vice is not drink but meanness.

---

* Anthony Chandor (b. 1932); m. 1958 Maryanne Bankes (b. 1934); Bath booksellers.

Wednesday, 12th February

I have made a Lent resolution – to be nice to someone every day. Went to Communion at Little Badminton in the evening, and was irritated by the four hymns and the churchiness of the usual congregation.

Another of the *Aristocracy* programmes this evening, entitled 'Letting in the Hoi Polloi'. Better than the previous ones, and Lord Lichfield really good, pointing out how much tougher the upper classes were, taking the lead in a crisis and putting their lives at risk. I came on. What I said was not too bad, but I was horrified by my appearance, with drooling lower lip and dead sheep's eyes. Made to read extracts from my diaries. Mere snippets of the interview shown – the usual treatment. Someone in the village said to Peggy afterwards, 'Poor old soul.'

Saturday, 15th February

I telephoned Miranda yesterday asking if she would dine with me at the Didmarton pub. Result was that I was invited to dine at the House today. We were about sixteen. David very charming and sat with me afterwards. I remarked that every other person seemed to be a millionaire these days. You only have to own a house and some nice possessions. 'Yes,' said D., 'every vicar is now a millionaire because of his furniture. But he can't eat it. It's very unfair.'

Tuesday, 18th February

To London, staying night at Brooks's, for dinner given by Henry Hoare* at Hoare's Bank, Fleet Street for Tony Mitchell's retirement from N.T. About twenty present. I was placed between Mrs Hoare and Andrew Laing.† What with the dim light, the old, unfamiliar or unrecognisable faces, blindness, deafness, muddle, fuddle, I didn't enjoy it as much as I ought to have done, and could not take in the

---

* Henry Cadogan Hoare (b. 1931); Chairman, C. Hoare & Co.; owner of that part of Stourhead estate in Wiltshire not bequeathed to the N.T. by his distant cousin Sir Henry Hoare in 1947.
† Adviser on pictures to N.T.

treasures displayed, such as Jane Austen's correspondence with her banker. I left at 10.30, escorted to the door most politely by my host. It is a fact that I can no longer attend such festivities.

Friday, 7th March

When Duff Hart-Davis rings, I fear the worst and imagine that Rupert has died. Not that, thank God, but he is very downcast by having his last volume of memoirs turned down by Murray's. It strikes me as rather shocking that Rupert, the highly venerated biographer, publisher, man of letters, literary executor of Walpole,* Sassoon† and other great writers, should be rejected, whereas I, whom Rupert once refused to publish and who have always felt exceedingly humble in comparison, am one of Murray's favoured authors. Of course, I must remember that I am no more than the Godfrey Winn‡ *de nos jours*.

Sunday, 16th March

Lunching with Jane Westmorland I met a Mr Drinkwater, nice florid businessman who is chairman of his Tory constituency party. He is a fan of mine. 'You've no idea what this occasion means to me.' We spoke of Jessica Douglas-Home's book on Violet Woodhouse. Drinkwater's father John was Gordon Woodhouse's first cousin, but they quarrelled over an inheritance. John was brought up by Gordon's two old sisters and given to understand that he was the heir to their house, Burghill Court in Herefordshire. Both sisters made wills under which the survivor would leave everything to John. One day they were murdered by their butler, who laid out their corpses on the billiards table before fleeing. It transpired that the elder sister had died first and the younger had forgotten to sign her will. The property therefore passed on intestacy to their next of kin – i.e., Gordon. Gordon wanted to do the decent thing and waive the inheritance in

---

* Sir Hugh Walpole (1884–1941); novelist.

† Poet and writer (1886–1967).

‡ British journalist (1908–71); star writer in women's magazines from the 1930s to the 1960s, notorious for his tone of sentimental whimsy.

favour of John; but Violet would not let him, as they were quite hard up at the time. The shock of the whole affair drove John Drinkwater to drink, misery and untimely death.

Monday, 24th March

I lunched at Brooks's with Martin Drury to meet new Chairman of the N.T., Charles Nunnerley,[*] who presented me with the Trust's medal, a hefty gold object designed by female Chinese art student, in form of jagged oak leaves and acorns. Nunnerley very sympathetic, but appears to know little of the properties and purposes of the N.T. I liked his modesty and gentleness.

Monday, 31st March

Although early, this Easter as beautiful as any remembered. Glorious sun and coldish wind. Garden bursting forth. Having lunched out four days running, I am wondering whether to retire totally from social life.

Friday, 4th April

To London to attend Ambrose Congreve's ninetieth birthday luncheon at Warwick House. Party of twelve. Ambrose larger than life, with healthy complexion. The first fellow guest I met was Lady Heald,[†] who I could have sworn died years ago. She too is unchanged at ninety-six, and making eminent sense. She still lives in a large house and runs a large garden. Talked of A. and her understanding of plants. Sir Lionel, who went mad and bad, long since dead. He led her a dance. Other nonagenarian Monsignor Gilbey, more bent than ever and inaudible to me. Sat next to Ambrose's charming lady friend, full of fun and frolic, and Lady Waterford.[‡] Table groaning with silver and opulence.

---

[*] C.K.R. Nunnerley (b. 1936); Chairman, Nationwide Building Society; Chairman, N.T., 1997–2002.

[†] Daphne Price; m. 1929 (as his 2nd wife) Sir Lionel Heald QC, sometime Attorney-General (d. 1981).

[‡] Lady Caroline Wyndham-Quin (b. 1936), yr d. of 6th Earl of Dunraven and Mount-Earl; m. 1957 John Hubert de la Poer Beresford, 8th Marquess of Waterford (b. 1933).

Four long, drawn-out courses, followed by enormous birthday cake with single candle which emitted melody of *Happy Birthday to You*. Everyone amused except Ambrose. At 3.45 the women withdrew, oddly for luncheon. I found myself talking to nice brother of duc Decazes, nephew of Princess Winnie. He told me that, as she had no children, most of her estate had to be divided among some seventy descendants of her siblings. When time came to leave, Monsignor and I were borne away in very smart Rolls – Monsignor to Travellers, I to Paddington. On halting at Travellers I made a show of getting out so as to escort the ancient man up the club steps, but he forbade me, and was escorted by chauffeur. Whereupon he stood watching the car as we drove away, Don Basilio hat in hand, bowing slightly. Such exquisite manners. The only remark of his I could hear was in praise of David Watkin's[*] new book. Wonderful sparkling blue sash round his waist.

Tuesday, 15th April

Drove in the evening to Charlfield churchyard to see memorial to those killed in a railway accident of 13 October 1928. A list of ten persons, ending with 'two unknown' – presumably the two well-dressed children whom ticket collector remembered seeing in a compartment on their own. A pretty little church, locked and key unobtainable. Pevsner calls it nineteenth-century, but it looks mediaeval to me, with white harled tower, Perpendicular slit windows, ancient oak door to porch. On return stopped at Wickwar church on its prominent site overlooking town, likewise locked and bolted, as it ought to be. I fear my idea of visiting all churches within a twenty-mile radius of Badminton will come to nothing owing to difficulties of access.

Thursday, 17th April

On return home, watched Mr Major on television. Very amiable, charming, smiling, polite, assured he was. He's my man. One old

---

[*] Historian of architecture (b. 1941); Fellow of Peterhouse, Cambridge; his recent book on the architect Sir John Soane (1753–1837) had been awarded the Sir Banister Fletcher Prize.

woman in the audience said to him, 'You are a good, honest man. Can't you get rid of all the bastards which surround you, and rule us on your own?' My sentiments entirely.

Sunday, 20th April

I am mentioned, with high praise, in reviews of Peter Mandler's *Fall and Rise of the Stately Home* by Paul Johnson in the *Spectator* and Brian Masters in the *Daily Mail*. Brian draws attention to a mischievous footnote, which I missed, referring to my 'genius for retrospective self-fashioning'. I can't think that, in any of my writings, I have ever claimed to have done anything remarkable. But it is perhaps true that my having written so much about the National Trust and its efforts to save historic buildings may have drawn undue attention to the small part I played in the process.

Thursday, 1st May

I cast my vote in the village hall this morning.

With one foot in the grave, I listen with revulsion and dread to the moans and groans of my contemporaries: to Daffers Moore who is disintegrating in beastly homes; to John Mordaunt who has had a knock-out stroke and is wheelchair-bound, all feeling gone but mind unimpaired, which makes it worse; to my ancient neighbour Mr Greenway, whose dotty wife has just died. I sympathise yet I run away, cowardly and revolted, fearful of disaster overtaking me too at a moment's notice. I hope that I do not then solicit sympathy, and can disappear from view.

Saturday, 3rd May

The magnitude of the Tories' defeat is only beginning to dawn.* It means they will be out of power for possibly two decades. I had

---

* The general election on 1 May ended eighteen years of Conservative rule; as a result of tactical voting, the Conservatives, with 31% of the popular vote, won only a quarter of the seats, while Tony Blair's 'New Labour Party', with 43% of the vote, was swept to power with a massive parliamentary majority of 179.

little regard for the last government, while developing a progressive respect and liking for Mr Major. There were too many spivs in his government, non-gents in every sense. I am not surprised by the defeat, for latterly I have noticed an absolute hatred of Toryism among the masses, evident in TV programmes such as *Question Time*. I shall not live to see another change. What appals me is the jubilation, the ringing of church bells as though Great Britain had been delivered from Hitler, Stalin or President Mobutu* rather than good, honest and wise Mr Major who has improved the lot of the working classes. My fear now is not so much of extremist socialism as of the insidious liberalism which will overlook the appalling scandals of bogus social security claimants, kowtowing to the IRA and all criminals, encouraging rather than limiting more coloured immigrants, and the general descent into American-style vulgarity and yob culture.

Julian Berkeley and Tony Scotland lunched. They were enchanting. I gave them a pile of A's old gramophone records which she wanted them to have. Tony gave an amusing account of Father Michael Hollings,† the beloved of Freda. He was a monster of arrogance and dogmatism, and treated her like dirt. Ordered her about, accepted her hospitality as his due, subjected the boys to headmasterly dressing-downs for presumed misdemeanours. The impertinence of it. He shouted at Freda for his drink, complained when he disliked a dish she had cooked, and when given a Christmas present by Tony and Julian, a carefully chosen clerical pullover, said he would give it away to the first-comer. I met him once [17 June 1993] and cordially took against him. He was proprietary, gluttonous, boozy and dirty, like other intellectual RC priests I have known.

Wednesday, 7th May

Surely most old people become indifferent to what others, notably the young, think of them and their utterances. On the contrary, I mind

---

* Mobutu Sese Seko (1930–97); the notorious dictator of Zaire (later Democratic Republic of Congo) since 1965, then facing a rebellion: he fled the country on 16 May and died four months later.
† He had died on 21 February, aged seventy-five.

more than ever, to the extent of avoiding the clever young. Polite though they are, and indulgent, I cringe before the sensed curl of their lips. Moreover, I feel more and more ashamed of my past shortcomings, particularly in my writings.

Friday, 9th May

Billa [Harrod] comes for the weekend. Adorable she is, and the very same to me as when I first met her in the early Thirties, though very bent. But bright, and faculties unimpaired. Her grandson Huckleberry rings up and asks to speak to her in a very common voice. B. deplores this, and cannot understand where he picked it up. His elder brother, who is the same, runs a band in America called 'Fucking is Fun'. He could never bring it to England, opines Billa. She looks very distinguished. I tell her that her saintly image ought to be recorded on a panel of the rood screen of her favourite Norfolk church.*

Monday, 12th May

Mr Blair's new government already irks me with its bogus bonhomie ('Call me Tony'), refusal to wear white tie at Lord Mayor's Banquet, and abandonment of traditional way of referring to MPs in the Commons (My Honourable Friend the Member for Wherever) in favour of Reggie and Mo. I loathe such rejection of traditional courtesies and downgrading of long-accepted modes and manners in the supposed interest of democracy. Yet I am in favour of their policy to ban export of armaments to wog tyrannies, and curb big-business exploitation of the environment.

Tuesday, 20th May

Am deep in Tony Powell's third volume of diaries. His cleverness and learnedness fill me with veneration and awe. His personality freezes me up. I have always liked him and loved Violet, but A. never felt at

---

* Billa Harrod devoted much of her life to the Norfolk Churches Preservation Trust.

ease with him. From his few references to me, he was clearly bored with me. Writes that Jim is never interested in his own work. Truth is that I never wanted to discuss my writings with him. The difference between our diaries is that between a highbrow and a middle-brow. I suppose I'm a poor man's Anthony Powell.

Sunday, 25th May

I lunched with Tony Scotland and Julian Berkeley, a surprise for Freda who is staying with them for her birthday today. I motored sixty miles there and back, too long. No lorries on this Bank Holiday Sunday, but Newbury a nightmare of jams. Pottery Cottage [near Aldermaston, Hampshire] much improved, a large, open-roofed room having been added since my last visit. It contains a tall late Georgian Gothick organ from Markenfield, given Julian by late Lord Grantley,* large Bechstein grand given him by Joan Leigh Fermor, and a harpsichord. He is very musical, and played the organ after luncheon, beautifully I thought. I presented Freda with an advance copy of *Ancient as the Hills*. Large party, more than a sprinkling of queens. Their manner-isms, their social contacts, their sharp little jokes are the same the world over. How is it they do not recognise that they are artificial, shallow, slick, sophisticated, absurd? Julian never says a stupid thing. Is withdrawn, a thinker, has depth, is hard to connect with. Whereas Tony is extrovert, open, bubbling. They have made this cottage into a 'place', with lovely orchard garden and pretty things inside and out.

Wednesday, 28th May

Bevis Hillier writes to ask if I will support his campaign to establish a national memorial to the Millennium. But I don't care a fig about the Millennium, which is a totally unreal landmark of time undeserving of any notice.

---

* John Richard Brinsley Norton, 7th Baron Grantley (1923–95), of Markenfield Hall near Ripon, Yorkshire.

Thursday, 29th May

John K.-B. sends me a half-page of information relating to the AD dating system. In 550, Dionysius Exiguus, Greek-speaking monk, suggested the counting of years should date from the conception of Christ; but not until many centuries later did this become common practice. Until mediaeval times, years were counted from the succession of the monarch. So typical of John to have this information. He is a standby where anything to do with the Christian religion and classical mythology is concerned, having been brought up in his parents' R.C. prep school, then Ampleforth. Still, I don't understand how, say, an educated Englishman might settle by missive on what date he intended visiting his cousin in Languedoc.

Friday, 30th May

American garden society party of twenty visited at 9.30 a.m. Were nice and polite. The moment they left I went to London for the night. On the train, I tried but failed to summon ideas for the book Grant wants me to write about my youth. In walking to Coutts' in the Strand, I wondered if I would ever get there, so weary was I, dragging one foot after the other. Then walked back to National Gallery and bought for £40 their complete catalogue, each single painting illustrated in colour, postage-stamp size. Weighs a ton. Derek [Hill] dined at Brooks's. Very good and affectionate he was, and amusing. He hopes to go to Mount Athos in September with Prince Charles.

Sunday, 1st June

Asked to lunch by Elsie Gibbs* at Sheldon to meet Jamie Fergusson and his new wife Maggie Parham,† who is her cousin. They seem a very happy pair, and I liked her immensely. I expected her to be

---

* Elsie Hamilton-Dalrymple (b. 1922); m. 1947 Major Martin Gibbs (1916–1995) of Sheldon Manor near Chippenham, Wiltshire.

† Secretary of Royal Society of Literature from 1991 (b. 1964); m. Oct. 1996 James Fergusson.

middle-aged, angular and somewhat dour. On the contrary, she was short, very pretty, and shy. He's a lucky fellow, and looks it. We ate in the barn off delicious food cooked by Elsie, who was so busy in the restaurant that we hardly saw her. Maggie runs the Royal Society of Literature, and is also writing the biography of her friend, the recently deceased Scotch poet.*

Thursday, 5th June

The garden at its peak. Roses beginning en masse; deutzia, honey-suckle, aquilegia, peonies full out. It no longer has the groomed, trimmed look that A. liked, but is *belle au bois dormante*, luscious, almost blowsy-looking.

Sunday, 8th June

Yesterday evening John Julius [Norwich] and Mollie came for a drink and to see the garden. Both very appreciative of it and seeming to like its slightly rugged look. J.J. said he was determined to win the [National] Lottery and had worked out to the last detail how to spend the winnings, for he says one simply must have more money for one's old age. As if he did not earn a lot from his many activities, and she had not inherited a fortune from her exceedingly rich father. He thinks Jeremy Lewis's biography of Cyril [Connolly] one of the best of the century. Picked up my copy from the footstool and read aloud the first paragraph, saying 'It is genius.'

In Acton Turville church today I was one of a congregation of two. Meanwhile in this parish, which is larger than Badminton and full of rich Bristol commuters, no one has volunteered to be church warden. And if no one does, the church will be declared redundant. I suggested to the Vicar that a letter should be delivered to every resident explain-ing that they face having no church for their baptisms, weddings and funerals. Vicar responded with vacuous smile of indulgence, assuring me that 'it will turn out all right in the end'.

---

* George Mackay Brown (1921–96); Maggie Fergusson's biography of him was published by John Murray in 2006.

In the afternoon, Jerry Hall [wife of Mick Jagger] telephoned to say they had been staying at the House for the weekend and would drop in on me at once. After I had waited an hour, she turned up in large, chauffeur-driven motor with two small children. The youngest, aged five, the most advanced infant I have ever encountered. Hearing the kitchen clock striking, she demanded to examine the mechanism, and then sang a song about a clock, while her doting mother led her into the garden. Then Mick appeared with son James in second limousine. He looks handsomer now he is past fifty, somewhat rugged but very lithe and healthy. Wearing that absurd American cap and chewing gum. Whisked around the garden politely and asked me to stay at La Fourchette in August, saying that David [Beaufort] would fly me out. Somehow I don't think so.

Thursday, 12th June

The Royal Librarian telephoned from Windsor, inviting me to lunch with him and look at the Library and help him identify the rooms Lord Esher occupied. I said I could no longer motor so far in the day. We left it that I might accompany John Saumarez Smith from London, where I could stay the night. I would much like to meet this nice man and be shown around by him. He told me that he had bought my signed copy of Bamber Gascoigne's book on the Muslims from Heywood Hill, and presented it to Princess Margaret. I said I was glad it had found a good home.

Saturday, 14th June

Lunched at Prospect Cottage with the dear Levis. The fourth was John Byrne,* slim, gaunt-faced young man with scarred left cheek. He is a cataloguer of books and first editions, who did Cyril's books for Deirdre. An intellectual and a scholar. Disclosed that he is on medication which gives him a matutinal hangover. I explained that I too had taken a drug for over fifty years and suffered similarly until midday. Having at last reached the end of Jeremy [Lewis]'s biography of Cyril,

---

* Bookseller and archivist (b. 1945).

I wanted to discuss it, but had to tread carefully, for C. treated D. abominably, yet she adores his memory. Peter said that Matthew had not disclosed what his feelings about the book were. He also told me that Cyril devoted much of his life to correcting the manuscripts of his friends. Had I noticed how well-written Barbara Skelton's* novels were? (I had not.) Whereas her recent memoirs, written since Cyril's death, were stylistically disappointing.

Sunday, 15th June

The Henry [Robinson]s motored me to Bowood for luncheon. Greeted warmly by Charlie Shelburne, who was extremely affable and kind. Took me to the gallery to see family portraits – Reynoldses galore, Gainsborough, Romney, the lot. Returning to the drawing room we were confronted by an enormous party of guests of whom I knew none. Astors of Hever, relations without end, coming up with 'Are you still writing?' And a man with long white hair and beaming countenance, who introduced himself as Adrian Linlithgow.† Sat next to Laura someone, handsome lady under a shadow, and Elizabeth Lambton,‡ who is Kitty Nairne's younger sister. Delightful. I asked, 'When you were a child here, did you live in the whole house?' 'No, we lived in this part, except over Christmas when we moved to the Adam block', now gone. There were forty servants in the house. We hung around afterwards. I found it terribly tiring. All the guests finally left, except for the Robinsons who had to wait until children rounded up. A lesson, never be taken by the young with children. Always be independent, child-free.

Charlie, looking complacently out of window, cigar in mouth, said, 'I positively like seeing the visitors enjoying themselves. They do not interfere with me.' Then, 'You remember how you at one time

---

* Novelist and writer of memoirs (1916–96), whose work was largely based on her own tempestuous love life; m. 1st 1950–6 Cyril Connolly, 2nd 1956–61 George (later Baron) Weidenfeld, 3rd 1966 Professor Derek Jackson (formerly husband of Pamela Mitford).

† Adrian Hope, 4th Marquess of Linlithgow (b. 1946).

‡ Lady Elizabeth Petty-Fitzmaurice (b. 1927); yr dau. of 6th Marquess of Lansdowne; m. 1950 Major Charles Lambton.

thought it was all up for the aristocracy? And now it isn't. We are still here.' 'Some of you, I'm glad to say,' I said. He continued, 'We were the bogey. Then it was the trade union bosses. Now it is the fat cats. We shall be all right.' I thought, but did not say, 'Don't be too sure. The public are notoriously fickle and stupid. You could easily be thought to be doing what they disliked, and the arsonists would turn their attention to your marble halls.'

Thursday, 26th June

Ghastly day of storms, non-stop rain and bitter cold. I received a letter from John Byrne announcing that it was he, then with Rota, who catalogued my letters sold to Yale, and asking if I would like to sell more papers. Have replied that I may well do so. It may be a good idea to part with the packed drawerful in my lifetime, so as to spare executors, and build up some funds to meet future health bills. I told John that I always hoped never to meet the young man who catalogued my letters of the past.

Sunday, 29th June

I drove to Chastleton* today, arriving before one o'clock. A favourable day for my eyes, neither dark nor dazzling. A good thing that the N.T. have made a car park 250 yards from the house on top of a wooded hill and totally screened from view. A long yellow path descends towards the four-gabled dovecote, the tiny church and the great bulk of purple-grey stone flying the Union Jack. The epitome of an old manorial setting, remote, isolated in quiet Oxfordshire country. I entered the pretty church, walking over shiny black memorial gravestones enscrolled with flourishes to Jones family. Several wall tablets which I couldn't read for darkness. Nice fusty smell.

---

* Chastleton House near Moreton-in-Marsh, Oxfordshire; Jacobean manor built by the wool merchant Walter Jones; a rare late twentieth century country house acquisition by N.T., thanks to its wonderful state of preservation, the money to restore and endow it provided by National Heritage Memorial Fund; following six years' conservation work, it was now ready for limited opening to the public.

Ushered into a dark downstairs room, where found Martin Drury and some thirty friends of the N.T. Couldn't distinguish a soul. Buttonholed by friendly Hugh Roberts;[*] then embraced by Fortune [Grafton] whom I had to ask who she was. And Hugh G. – rather diminished and bent over a stick, but full of funny stories – with whom my group went round house after luncheon. Samantha Wyndham[†] acted as hostess and was very attentive and helpful.

The rooms at Chastleton still left bleak, dusty and rather empty despite the N.T. having spent £2 million on structure. Bedroom of former châtelaine, Mrs Whitmore Jones, still smells of cats. Remarkable how much of what we take for Jacobean was supplied in the nineteenth century by the antiquarian Squire Jones. Hall screen bogus Victorian. Best room the High Chamber with genuine ceiling. In next room I asked Alec Cobbe whether he thought the ceiling Jacobean. Not so, also early Victorian. Martin Drury displayed the Jacobite wine glasses which he cleverly managed to buy back from a dealer. The late Clutton-Brock[‡] sold many items to pay his taxes and wine merchants. I pick my way gingerly in these old rickety houses with slippery floors and uneven stair treads, feeling with my stick what I fail to see.

Martin D. and the officials who have reinstated Chastleton were amused to hear that I went to a children's party here in the 1920s. All I remember is that the house, which the Richardsons rented for thirty years, did not strike me as any less well-maintained or cosy than any other manor house we frequented in the Cotswolds; that we danced and played hunt-the-slipper in the long gallery; and that there was a hole in the plaster ceiling. Apparently John Arkell, not there today, remembers similar parties, his father having been a neighbouring vicar.

---

[*] Art expert (b. 1948); Director of the Royal Collection and Surveyor of The Queen's Works of Art from 1996 (Deputy Director, 1988–96).
[†] On staff of N.T. and Georgian Group (b. 1962); Secretary of Chelsea Society.
[‡] Alan Clutton-Brock (1904–76); Slade Professor of Fine Art, Cambridge, 1955–8; author of *A History of French Painting* (1932); inherited Chastleton House from a cousin, 1955.

Sunday, 13th July

Weekend at Deene, driven there by Liz [Longman]. It must have been the largest house party I've attended since the war. Women Katie Macmillan,* Clementine Beit, Mary Roxburghe, Anne Wyndham,† Fortune Stanley,‡ Liz; men Edward Ford, Derek Hill, John Cornforth, Steven Runciman, Miles Gladwyn,§ self. (Dear Anthony Hobson chucked for influenza.) I may have left a few out, and there were neighbours in addition at luncheon and dinner.

Whole visit beautifully staged. Delicious food and good chat, but little conversation. One could not get to know all. Mary R. very affable but stiff. Her grandfather Monckton Milnes was born in 1809. Asked me to visit her at West Horsley [near Leatherhead, Surrey], which I would like to do. K. Macmillan formidable and ugly but undoubtedly clever. Told me how miserable she was having to sell Highgrove [to the Prince of Wales] in order to live with her father-in-law the ex-Prime Minister in hideous Birch Grove [Sussex]. Clementine simply enormous and totally changed in face, but sweet as of old.

Steven Runciman like a feather. Or rather like a crisp old leaf, that's what he is, bent and hollow in the middle as he scuttles like a crab upstairs. Yet in talking to one alone he is very spry. We agreed that hunting can't be justified, any more than hereditary peers, or for that matter religion – yet they are all good things. The arts may also be included in this category. He can no more read Scott than I, and can't stomach Dickens; re-reads Thackeray, but finds George Eliot impossible.

The one I find most sympathetic here is Edward Ford. After dinner he said to me, 'You didn't like Winston, did you?' I began to explain

---

* Hon. Katherine Ormsby-Gore (b. 1921; DBE 1974); dau. of 4th Baron Harlech; m. 1942 Maurice Macmillan, Conservative politician, who d. 1984, having assumed courtesy title Viscount Macmillan of Ovenden earlier that year on his father, Harold Macmillan, former Prime Minister, being cr. Earl of Stockton; Vice-Chairman of Conservative Party, 1968–71.

† Anne Winn (b. 1926), dau. of Hon. Reginald Winn, yr s. of 2nd Baron St Oswald; m. 1947 (as his 1st wife) Hon. Mark Wyndham, yr s. of 5th Baron Leconfield.

‡ Fortune Smith; m. 1951 Michael Stanley (b. 1921), Cumbria landowner, s. of Hon. Oliver Stanley, yr s. of 17th Earl of Derby.

§ Miles Jebb, 2nd Baron Gladwyn (b. 1930); o. s. of Sir Gladwyn Jebb, 1st Baron, diplomatist, whom he s. 1996; writer and former British Airways executive.

why when Miles joined in, claiming that unconditional surrender was
the only course to be adopted in 1945. I think Edward did not agree
with him, but rather with me.

Wednesday, 16th July

William Burlington* came to photograph me for the National Trust,
bringing beautiful Chilean assistant with raven hair and perfect teeth.
He took infinite pains, unlike so many young photographers these
days who just flourish the camera at one without preparation and fire
off fifty snaps. He spent almost two hours choosing the site, finally
taking me sitting on a garden chair by the buddleia, wearing straw hat.
He has wonderful manners, an enquiring mind, and is absolutely
natural. Handsome, busy, eager, shirt-tails flying; more Mitford than
Cavendish in appearance.

David telephoned asking me to dine tonight with him and Miranda,
who received me at the door. Ushered me into the old Raglan Room
which D. is transforming. He has got rid of the black Jacobean panelling of which Master and Mary were so proud, revealing beneath early
Georgian panelling which he has painted pale buff. He is very pleased
with this, his new toy. He has hung huge landscape paintings across
the fielded panels, one a vast Landseer of a Somerset dog. I could not
criticise because he is so pleased, and doubtless when the room has
shaken down a bit it will look charming as all his rooms do. But when
he asked me what he should do with the clumsy Victorian window
projection, now bare, I did suggest either vertical paintings or a pair
of marble obelisks or similar high-standing ornaments, to relieve the
horizontal emphasis of the room.

Tuesday, 29th July

Debo telephoned to propose herself for luncheon. It happened that
I had Susy [Robinson] lunching, who had always longed to meet

---

* William Cavendish, Earl of Burlington (b. 1969); s. and heir of Marquess of
Hartington; grandson of the Devonshires. His photograph of J.L.-M. graces the
jacket of this volume.

Debo. The meeting a great success, Debo delighted with S's keenness and interest in all things. Both brought mercy bags of food. Debo as usual enhancing my cling to life.

Wednesday, 30th July

Lunched with the Keens at Duntisbourne Rous to meet the couple who have bought Daneway [House, Sapperton, Gloucestershire]. Very rich Hong Kong tycoon called Spencer, and Thai wife. Then Mary, who is a sport, motored me at terrific speed to meet Debo and Andrew at Asthall,* which is now on the market. Debo, who was six when her father sold it in 1926, wanted to look around for old times' sake. I stayed there twice with Tom, and cherish rose-tinted memories of the interior. Now empty, drear and desolate. Dark, shapeless rooms, no Jacobean furniture left. Mr Hardcastle, whose parents bought the place from Lord Redesdale, died last year. A bachelor whose prime interest was in luxurious Rolls-Royces. His bedroom littered with shoe boxes. His housekeeper, who showed us round, told us that, after his death, seventy-five pairs of unworn shoes came to light. He had an order with Lobb's to provide two pairs a year, which he didn't like to cancel. A rich Englishman's eccentricity.

Wednesday, 6th August

I enter my ninetieth year. Motored to Moorwood to lunch with the Henrys, dispensing money to the children and chocolate to the adults. Henry present because bad weather prevents him harvesting. Susy then motored me to Rousham† [near Oxford] where we joined a Georgian Group party. Pouring rain. No sign of Cottrell Dormer owners. Samantha Wyndham greeted and took charge of me. J.K.-B.

---

* Jacobean manor on River Windrush, owned by Lord Redesdale from 1919 to 1926, where J.L.-M. often stayed as a schoolboy with his friend Tom Mitford.
† Manor near Oxford, built 1635 by Sir Robert Dormer, redecorated *c.* 1740 by William Kent who also designed gardens. In *Another Self*, J.L.-M. writes that he resolved to devote his life to architectural conservation after witnessing an orgy of vandalism there (see 29 August 1990); but this has been questioned by some, and he never mentions the alleged incident when writing about Rousham in his diaries.

present among group. Several come up to me to congratulate on *Ancient as the Hills,* and my enormous age. A charming old house, still a home, though not wholly so, the large rooms evidently not much used. Bad-taste carpet of Reckitt's Blue on staircase and in drawing room. Long hall sympathetic, walls lined with good family portraits in Sunderland frames. The two Kent rooms splendid, the low ceiling derived from Villa Madama colonnade in Rome. The larger room with high ceiling very strange for England, in recessed caissons that call to my mind the architecture of Guarini and Juvarra[*] in, say, the Turin Chapel of the Shroud.

I stopped at Bagendon churchyard to pay respects to little Audrey's grave, reading the sentimental inscription which describes her so exactly, kissing my fingers which touched the stone that I cannot easily reach with my lips, and moved to love and prayer for her precious soul.

Saturday, 9th August

At six o'clock I sit on the white bench facing the pool, the sun in my eyes. A background of darkest green, lush from recent rains. The fountain burbling gently, the refractions on the water like broken glass at the instant of splitting. A long, slim dragon-fly darting across the pool. The tranquillity and the relentless heat almost too pressing. No breath of air. No birds singing. A red admiral has just alighted for a moment on my open left hand.

Monday, 18th August

I went to George Bayntun's bookshop[†] [in Bath] which I have meant to visit for ages. The basement where the second-hand books are kept was so dark that I couldn't scour as I wished. Bought William de Morgan's *Joseph Vance* and Meredith's poems for little, but forgot to pay, and they forgot to ask for the money. This caused by my being

---

[*] Guarino Guarini (1624–83) and Filippo Juvarra (1678–1736); Italian Baroque architects.

[†] Founded by George Bayntun in 1894, and owned at this time by his great-grandson Hylton Bayntun-Coward (1932–2000).

introduced to James Williams the Bath Wonder,[*] described by local press as cleverest man in Britain. Aged eighteen he has gained four first class degrees. I shook hands and congratulated this wire-spectacled youth, with hollow chest and limp air, while Bayntun said to him, 'You can say in 2070 that you met James Lees-Milne.'

Tuesday, 19th August

Day of horrid torpidity, answering letters before tomorrow's operation at [Bath] Clinic. One from owner of Rainscombe Park, Oare, Wilts, who has just bought a pair of Holland & Holland guns inscribed J.H.L.-M. and wants to know if a relation. My grandfather, who died March 1908. Another from Sutton Park, Tenbury Wells, Worcs. about recent diaries. I reply to all and take my time.

Dined alone with Jane Westmorland. She was very sweet and we had the perfect dinner, sorrel soup, scrambled egg with smoked salmon. All so beautifully presented in her exquisite house. She spoke of Kitty Kelley's book on Prince Philip, which she is dreading, knowing him so well. Admitted that she is less than frank at times. We agreed that to be a good liar one has to have a long and accurate memory.

Monday, 25th August

Had to have a proper anaesthetic this time, and stay in the Clinic for two nights. Felt and still feel awful. I was diagnosed as anaemic, and given a blood transfusion lasting six hours. Am rather worried about such future as remains, and feel several new symptoms of decline. O the tiresomeness!

Tuesday, 26th August

Francis Russell[†] came to tea on his way to Ross-on-Wye, to look at my pair of Naples paintings. He confirmed they were Fabris, but

---

[*] He was doing a part-time job in the shop, having failed to secure admission to Jesus College, Cambridge despite his remarkable attainments.

[†] Director of Christie's (b. 1949).

evidently thought them not of the highest class. Thought they might fetch £50,000 on the market. I made it clear I had no intention of selling. He is very charming, well-groomed, slight in build and good-looking; has good manners with the aged, and loves old ladies. Said that John Pope-Hennessy a great scholar and far exceeded K. Clark in that respect – though K. a mind of magnitude and a great showman who succeeded to a phenomenal degree in reaching the ears and eyes of the man in the street. When Francis was at Oxford, his bedmaker watched the *Civilisation* TV series, and said to him, 'I now understand why you're so keen on that there art.' Says Michael Mallon totally honourable; admired J.P.-H. above all other men, and ministered to him without thought of benefiting. Then J.P.-H. had a blood-row with the Ashmolean, which was to have been his heir, and so he left his treasures to Mallon.

Monday, 1st September

The grieving over Princess Diana is beyond all belief.* Radio and telly totally given over, and today's *Times* contains not one paragraph which is not devoted to her. Now undoubtedly she was a great beauty, and had star quality of the film actress sort; also seems to have had a genuine caring side. Debo rang yesterday to ask what I felt. I said the tragedy seemed pre-ordained; and dreadful though it was to say, it would be recognised as a mercy in the long run. Debo admitted that to see her with old or mortally ill people was a revelation; yet it was terrifying that the world regarded her as a saint. People did not realise that few of her staff could abide her, and that she was odious to the Prince ever since they became engaged. She was shallow and devious, as cunning as a vixen, determined to do him down, motivated by malice and spite. Debo said that, on the few occasions she saw them together, she treated him with contempt. She took no part in his interests and his intellectual friends, never read a book and was totally uneducated and stupid.

---

* She had died in Paris in the early hours of 31 August, when the car in which she was travelling with her new friend Dodi Fayed, driven by a drug-fuelled alcoholic and speeding to avoid press photographers, crashed in an underpass.

Friday, 5th September

Susy [Robinson] is all for Diana and critical of the Royal Family for being stuffy, out of date and out of touch. But I say that the Queen, who has been endlessly meeting her subjects for forty-five years and has weekly contacts with the Prime Minister etc., knows more about the people than anyone else in the country. S. accuses her of lack of 'care' and of not welcoming Princess D. from the start. How does she know? In my opinion the thing most wrong with the Queen is her hats. They are awful, and always have been. They suggest the stuffiness which is not really there.

Saturday, 6th September

Owing to Diana funeral the roads empty this morning, when I motored to lunch with Anne Cowdray at Broadleas. I was early and halted in Devizes, it being the best day of the year to appreciate the architectural beauties. The war memorial in the centre strewn with flowers in plastic bags, with messages such as 'Diana, we will always love you, Bert and Rosie' and 'You will live for ever. We shall join you.'

Thursday, 11th September

Debo called on me at 3 on her way to Highgrove. Much talk about Princess Diana, whose behaviour was utterly unpredictable. She dropped her friends like plummets and then behaved vengefully to their hurt. Quarrelled with both sisters, and with her brother Spencer who offered her a house at Althorp which she declined to take up. Till the last day of her life she kept in close touch with the press, asking them to send photographers and advising them how to get the best pictures of her in action.

Wednesday, 17th September

Misha [Bloch] came to lunch, motored by Philip Mansel.* A great success. Good luncheon of Covent Garden soup, Ian's kedgeree and a

---

* Historian (b. 1951), whose *Constantinople: City of the World's Desire* had just been published by John Murray; owner of Smedmore estate, Dorset, which had descended by inheritance since the 14th century.

blackberry and apple pie of Peggy's. M. very good and rather less eccentric than on last visit. Philip a charming man, nice looking, gentle, not forthcoming. Speaks only when obliged to, and always pertinently. He is not happy, according to M., despite his renown as a historian, and ownership of ancestral Dorset seat; has never got over death of his devoted companion five years ago. They stayed until four.

At this point, J.L.-M. ceased to type his diary, though he continued to keep it for the next six weeks in his neat, artistic hand.

Monday, 22nd September

Dr White said today, 'You have been through a rough time lately.' Touched me by adding that he was always glad to see me, and that I must never hesitate to make an appointment whenever inclined.

Tuesday, 30th September

Gordon Brown[*] yesterday reiterated the old Labour assurance that by the Millennium there would be no more unemployment. No government except a Communist one can promise such a thing, for it depends on the labour required by business. As the need for labour grows less because of technology, and the pool of labour grows with the rising tide of immigrants without qualifications, so unemployment will persist until Mother Earth's yields are exhausted. Whereupon uprisings, anarchy and starvation will occur, if the physical world has not yet imploded.

Thursday, 2nd October

Tony Mitchell called at 9 and off we drove to Lyme [Park, Cheshire], leaving Badminton in balmy Indian summer weather as we headed for the grey, cold north. Lyme improved since my old days, but house still rather stark and institutional. Very nice young N.T. rep., James

---

[*] Labour politician (b. 1951); Chancellor of Exchequer, 1997–2007; Prime Minister, 2007.

Rothwell, his smile and slight laugh at end of statements reminding me of Francis Dashwood in his young days. A perky and efficient lady custodian, arch and rather forward (kissed Debo), provided lunch. Inner courtyard by Leoni* just like a Roman palazzo, pavement of mauve and pink polished stone, central well-head, grand flight of steps leading to hall which John Fowler decorated in white and gold, doing away with mustard graining which was probably more suitable. Yet I cautioned against scrapping any of John's decoration. My Khorossan carpet from Bath looking splendid on floor of ante-library, a good place for it. Some bad treatment lately received from Stockport Corporation (from whom lady curator inherited) in stripping of Stuart staircase and Grinling Gibbons carvings.

Motored with Debo to Chatsworth, Tony following and staying night. He was very appreciative, saying it was an experience ever to be remembered.

Dreadful how tottery I have become. Sightseeing wears me out. After tea lay on my bed in the Centre Dressing Room, not even reading, but listening to Pizetti's seductive incidental music to d'Annunzio,† and admiring the curtains of rich, pea-green moiré silk, fringed with appliqué galloon three inches broad, upheld by stout clasps of gold foliage and draped and tasselled festoons. The opulence of the Bachelor's taste.

Saturday, 4th October

Andrew to Newmarket for the day, racing. There came to luncheon from the hotel, where staying, Sir Robert and Lady Jane Fellowes.‡ Also a couple called Greville Howard,§ Mrs having been brought up

---

* Giacomo Leoni (1686–1746); Venetian architect who came to England with George I in 1714.

† Gabriele d'Annunzio (1863–1938); Italian poet, dramatist and adventurer; Ildebrando Pizetti (1880–1968) composed the incidental music to his play *La Nave* (1908).

‡ Sir Robert Fellowes (b. 1941); Private Secretary to HM The Queen 1990–9; m. 1978 Lady Jane Spencer, dau. of 8th Earl Spencer and elder sister of Diana, Princess of Wales; cr. life peer, 1999.

§ Owner (b. 1941) of Castle Rising, Norfolk; m. (3rd) Mary Culverwell; cr. life peer, 2004, as Baron Howard of Rising.

at Luckington, one mile from Badminton. I sat in Andrew's place, between the two wives. Fellowes praised *Fourteen Friends*, and on leaving said, 'It has been an honour to meet you.' I assured him the honour was all mine. Nice friendly man who is Queen's private secretary and soon to retire. Having been enjoined to make no reference to Princess Diana I trod warily, whereas Fellowes and Debo launched into chat about Morton's latest scurrilous publication.[*] I talked to Lady Jane about her grandfather Jack Spencer,[†] of whom as a child she went in deadly awe. He never addressed a word to his grandchildren when they stayed at Althorp, and ate voraciously while scowling at them. Lady J. quite unlike her sister, not pretty but jolly and decent. Easy to chat with. We got onto subject of decapitation by the sword in Saudi Arabia. Then I thought that, bearing in mind the Princess's death, we were treading on sensitive ground, and changed subject. She then told me that pheasants killed while under stress were less tasty and made tougher eating than those shot while unawares. Does this mean that, in shooting for the pot, one should kill them sitting? And does it apply to grouse and other game birds?

Tuesday, 7th October

Breakfast at 9 suits me, giving me an hour of extra sleep. Can I introduce it at home with Peggy? Eat two helpings of porridge and cream, two slices of toast with butter and honey. Barely one cup of coffee now, too rich for me. Pore over newspaper with magnifier. Knock half-full glass of orange juice over Andrew's place. Mop up with napkin and bolt to drawing room. Read at window. Andrew passes through at 10 and out again at 10.45 without recognising me. Henry comes, and I own up to him. 'It doesn't matter in the least,' he assures me. Andrew weighed down by newspapers of which he reads every line through his sawn-off telescope. I give him as wide a berth as possible, knowing his disinclination for early morning chat.

---

[*] Andrew Morton's *Diana: Her True Story*, written in collaboration with the Princess and originally published in 1992, was about to appear in a more 'unrestrained' new edition.

[†] 7th Earl Spencer (1892–1975).

Wednesday, 8th October

I am whizzed home by the taciturn Jo in brand-new Bentley in great-est comfort. On unpacking 'sandwiches' I discover whole dishes of minced lamb, vegetables, pâtés and white grapes. I thoroughly enjoyed visit in spite of abysmal tiredness throughout. I hope Andrew and Debo didn't find me too languid and dotty.

Friday, 10th October

Feeling absolutely awful I nevertheless go to London for day. Not a success. Went First Class for once. Full of businessmen glued to telephones, very irritating. Failed to find a cardigan, chief object of expedition. Nearest approach to what I wanted was priced at £430 in Burlington Arcade. Lunched Brooks's opposite Merlin Sudeley,* who on recognising me at once launched into boring talk about Toddington [Manor, Gloucestershire] which he has done these thirty years at least. Was almost made gaga by dodging the blazing sun and blinding shadows of the streets. Tired to death. I fear I can never go to London again. Just not up to it. Found the weight of my rolled umbrella and overcoat almost too much for my feeble shoulders and stick-like arms.

Saturday, 11th October

Beloved Nick comes to lunch. After which I retire to bed. Then over mug of tea we resume our heavenly talk. He grows portly.

Wednesday, 15th October

I am immersing myself in Julien Green's† diaries, which Diana [Mosley] urged me to read. They are marvellous like Roger Hinks's‡

---

* Merlin Hanbury-Tracy, 7th Baron Sudeley (b. 1939); author of *The Sudeleys – Lords of Toddington* (1987); in *Who's Who*, gives recreation as 'ancestor worship', and men-tions that he is 'Patron of Association of Bankrupts'.

† French novelist, playwright and academician of American parentage (1900–98).

‡ Roger Packman Hinks (1903–63); British Council official; his *Journals, 1933–1963* were published by Michael Russell in 1984 (thanks to the generosity of subscribers including J.L.-M.).

in that they are introspective, self-analytical, not gossipy at all, even when he dissects his intimate friend Gide. He says his greatest desire is for Truth. I'm not so sure about this. What is truth? Something which, once found, remains unmalleable, immovable, dried up, a tablet of stone, a Nazi *Diktat*. Green the most self-centred of men. His pessimism and melancholia accord with mine. He is a mystery man, part French, part American. Says French his natural language; that to write in English, he feels confused by the diversity of words and meaning, while the French language is so concise, rational, intellectual, unwoolly. He hardly mentions the war, despite fleeing France for USA in 1940, except to express his homesickness for Paris.

I asked Simon [Lees-Milne] if his future daughter-in-law is what my Granny would have called a lady. He replied, 'Not exactly – but then they aren't these days.'

Saturday, 18th October

Most beautiful day. At Acton Turville tried to enter church. Locked, and no notice how to obtain key. Thence I motored by lanes to Tetbury. Passed another car too closely, and it knocked against my side mirror, shattering the glass. For some reason I didn't mind a bit, and continued singing.

J.K.-B., who stayed Friday night with an appalling cold, told me that he once lunched alone with Julien Green in Paris. It was not a success. Green was kind – for J. was young – but taciturn. J. wanted to watch Part II of Tony Powell's *Dance* on telly.* I had missed Part I, about Eton days. What I saw of Part II revolted me. The snobbery, arrogance, hauteur, stupidity, insolence of the young people were ghastly – except for Widmerpool, who was meant to be ghastly, but seemed good. I feel ashamed to have grown up in the 1920s and to have been a young adult in the 1930s. Thank God that generation is now extinct.

---

* The four-part adaptation of Powell's twelve-volume novel *A Dance to the Music of Time* starred James Purefoy as the narrator Nicholas Jenkins and Simon Russell Beale as Widmerpool.

Monday, 20th October

Green asks, 'What do I mean by prayer?' He says that, until middle age, he prayed glibly. Now decides that silence on his knees the best method – the way I have usually followed. The trouble is that silence leads to invasion of one's devotion by secular thoughts. In other words, religious faith and communication with God needs either a priest standing over one or attendance at church services.

Green recounts that, after twenty years' ownership of his waste paper basket, he actually looked at it for the first time, to find it was made of honey-coloured wicker sticks. As for me, after sixty years in some cases, I have never really looked at my treasures. Have become so over-familiar with them that I pass them by unnoticing. For the rest of my life, and so long as they are not stolen, they can satisfy my curiosity for craftsmanship and art. I need not go in search of other and far greater treasures in the world's galleries.

Wednesday, 22nd October

And today came Fiona MacCarthy* to lunch with me. Had imagined an elderly, frumpy, academic Miss. On the contrary, attractive late forties with dulcet manner. Object of her pilgrimage to talk to me about Byron, about whom I know no more than the average educated man. Well, when it came to talking I seemed to know rather more, because he has always been an icon. She is visiting every surviving house and building lived in or visited by Byron in Switzerland, Italy, Greece, having already seen every English or Scotch house. Recently saw Melbourne House, Whitehall, which retains all its eighteenth-century decoration. Apparently old Lady M., to whom B. wrote many indiscreet letters, lived on one floor, and William Lamb and Lady Caroline on another.† Thus B. flitted from one floor to another. Fiona

---

* Her book *Byron: Life and Legend*, arguing that the poet's nature was predominantly homosexual, was published by John Murray in 2002.

† During 1812, Byron conducted simultaneous affairs with Elizabeth, Viscountess Melbourne (*née* Milbanke [1751–1818]) and her daughter-in-law Lady Caroline Lamb (*née* Ponsonby [1785–1828], wife of Hon. William Lamb [1779–1848], later 2nd Viscount Melbourne and Prime Minister).

has identified all their rooms. I advised her to write a specialised book, and not to repeat the well-worn tales about treatment of Lady B. and so forth. We parted firm friends.

Friday, 24th October

I now know the operating theatre at the Bath Clinic like the back of my hand. The porter wheels me in and wishes me good luck, which confirms my alarm over what may be in store. I see a platoon of doctors, assistants, nurses in tight blue overalls and pale blue caps. From these emerges Britton, brightly ejaculating, 'I much enjoyed your book' (*Ancient*, which I had given him). 'And now,' wielding a syringe concealed in his palm, 'here is just a little prick.' I did not become unconscious, yet was blissfully unconcerned with what they were doing. In bed upstairs I was in euphoria, drank tea, ate delicious fish and chips and told the nurses I had seldom enjoyed a day more. Euphoria continued when at home drinking more tea and eating chocolate biscuits with Gerald and Peggy.

Saturday, 25th October

Very low and depressed all day. I decline in rapid successive spurts. Three whole days with no engagements. Work on editing next volume of diaries.

Tuesday, 28th October

Rushed down to Post Office to have expired passport (luckily noticed yesterday by me) renewed. Presented with piles of bumph. Practically in tears I turn to lady behind desk. She takes pity, fills in forms, takes me to automatic photo kiosk, tells me to smile. Then this saint leads me to guichet behind which saintly young man stamps form, assuring me I shall receive passport by registered post on Friday.

To London. Raeburn exhibition at National Portrait Gallery shows him to be a sensitive portrait artist, as good as Lawrence, without the magic. All his exhibited subjects wearing colourful garments – men in tartan trews, women in dresses – unlike my humble, unadorned great-great-grandfather.

Staying night at Brooks's, I find I am unable to read in any of the downstairs rooms. So dark; no single strong lamp. Dine alone, as I wish. Very tiring day on feet, dodging traffic like a strayed sheep.

Wednesday, 29th October

Pick up John Saumarez Smith. Taxi to Paddington. We take train to Slough. At Slough, dreadful mishap. Crossing bridge over the lines J., in volubly talking to me as we start descending steep stairway, face turned to me, misses step, tries desperately to recover rhythm of the treads, fails, falls headlong from top to bottom. Lies spreadeagled on stone platform of station. I follow as fast as I can. People gather round him. I fear he may be dead, surely limbs broken. But no, greatly shaken, ashen white he is raised. No benches on modern platforms. I guide him to a seat where he recovers. He still dazed, cheek bruised, we board taxi for Windsor Castle. At entry to Royal Library greeted by Oliver Everett who summons Castle nurse. She and doctor, ever on the ready day and night (Prince Philip said to keep finger smartly on the button at all times), pronounce John not to be injured, bar teeth. His courage exemplary. It gave me the shock of a lifetime to witness.

I liked Oliver Everett immensely. Calm, modest, no scholar, but has courtly manners. Alas our time limited because joined by Michael Meredith, Eton librarian and archivist, who takes us on to Eton. Could only get a glimpse of treasures without end – Charles I shirt worn on scaffold, lace trimmings and unfaded blue ribbons; music score by Mozart *aet.* 11, work of an adult. Shelves of books given to royalty with subservient dedications by Tennyson, Disraeli, Hardy, every known author. Princess Margaret the royal most interested in library. Queen only comes when visitors conducted. Library mostly made by Prince Albert out of Elizabethan Gallery on North Front. Whole room contains Leonardo drawings in neat boxes, white gloves worn for handling. So many treasures that the mind boggles.

Michael Meredith quite a card, eccentric enthusiast, gets carried away, dances with excitement. Funny twisted corner of lower lip. Extraordinary that after thirty years as Eton Librarian he has never been inside Royal Library until today. Also extraordinary that he has got Eton Library to acquire largest collections of Hardy correspondence, Browning papers and Gordon Craig* papers – all his favourite writers and artists, but having no association with Eton. Necessitates large extensions to College Library over Lupton's Tower, spreading into South Wing. I wonder why the Trustees allow this. Where will it end? In twenty years another wing will be needed at this rate.

Under Lupton's Tower we were talking about the power of public opinion in the present world, and this led to discussion of national hysteria following Diana's death, not a subject I would normally have raised with a servant of the sovereign. Oliver E. expressed strong feelings about encouragement of hysteria by the press. I said it was the most astonishing phenomenon of my lifetime, and frightening. 'Yes,' he said, 'if only they knew. I worked for her, you know. She was not genuinely dedicated to charitable works like Princess Anne, who gets little public recognition. It was simply a case of a pretty face.' 'Hollywood values,' I said. I don't think he grieved over her death, though he attended funeral in the Abbey because he received an invitation, and admitted he found it moving. Said public had no idea how well the Queen behaved when she learnt of the death at Balmoral. Non-mention of it at Crathie church that morning was deliberate to spare the boys' feelings. He evidently feels extremely sore over treatment of the Queen and Prince Philip.

Had no time to see my gold locket containing Byron's hair, though glad to see it acknowledged and described in new catalogue.

Friday, 31st October

Felt really ill with fatigue all day. Could barely walk in the house. Ate little and slept. Then in the bath before bed felt a new lump in pit of stomach. True to custom, discovery made on eve of weekend.

---

* Theatrical producer, critic and stage designer (1872–1966); son of the actress Ellen Terry and of the architect E. W. Godwin.

Saturday, 1st November

Made appointment to see doctor Monday morning before departure. Am philosophical and resigned. How long has this growth been festering? I know that I am riddled. Growths on bladder, prostate and bowel cannot be eliminated, only kept at bay. No wonder am so often extremely tired. My ailments are so many that I can no longer enumerate them. Trouble is that I have no one in neighbourhood whom I can bore with problems. Nick and Susy are my nearest confidants, poor things, apart from Peggy who listens, is as wise as a peasant, but cannot *advise*.

Spent morning writing on favourite books read this year for *Spectator*. And *Oldie* have asked me also.

On Tuesday, 4 November, with some foreboding, J.L.-M. set out with Debo Devonshire to stay with Diana Mosley at Orsay. The next day he was taken ill there; and on 6th November he returned to England with Debo, going straight into the Royal United Hospital in Bath. It was there that he wrote his last diary entry (reproduced as endpapers to this volume) in a marbled notebook, headed simply 'Nov 1997'.

New arrival in hospital ward with wife. They sit in silence for hours before he is allotted a bed. Speechless. She goes. He sits beside bed alone. Tall poker-faced attendant, evidently doctor [under] Mr Britton, comes to bedside. Says without expression of sympathy: 'Tomorrow morning you are to undergo a serious operation. They will cut your stomach (indicating with hand a vertical foot's length) and remove part of bowel. To rejoin the two intestines will be a delicate job. You may wake up in the intensive care unit to find you have a bag beside you. All right?' And he moves away. The patient looks out of the window and likewise walks away, probably to tell the wife.

The food in the Royal United is utterly disgusting. And yet in a way less ghastly than at the [Bath] Clinic which is sheer middle-class pretentious Trust House style. This is sheer plebeian – a sort of dog's dinner tonight, such as what we gave to Fop and Chuff. While [I was] stuffing it down a nurse injected something into my left arm.

Debo telephoned at 6.35. Walked away elated by talk with her &

went into the wrong ward. Approached what corresponded with my bed by the window & was about to get into it when a terrified lady gave a yelp of horror.

My hand–writing is very shakey [*sic*]. Damn it.

The doctors were unable to do much more for J.L.-M. At the end of November he was moved to Tetbury Cottage Hospital, where he died in the early hours of Sunday, 28 December.

Index

Index

Books by JL-M appear as separate entries; books by others are listed under authors.

291, 422; JL–M 'concerned about his
debauches', 75, 117; 79, 101, 105, 110;
as JL–M's literary executor, 119, 274;
132–6, 145, 156–7, 214, 223, 272, 327,
384, 390; 'has become very eccentric',
447–8; 502–3
Blond, Anthony, 75 & n., 84, 174
Bloomsbury Group, 206, 357, 395
Blow, Detmar (architect), 127 & n.,
453
Blow, Detmar (squire of Hilles) and
Isabella (née Delves Broughton), 453 &
n.
Blow, Simon, 128 & n., 146, 227, 396, 413,
453
Blum, Maître Suzanne, 133–4 & n., 156,
182, 184, 211, 404
Blunt, Anthony, 183 & n., 416–17
Bonham-Carter, Charlotte, Lady (née
Ogilvy), 230 & n.
Boughton, Northants., 41
Bourton House, Glos., 128–9
Bowood, Wilts., 493–4
Bowra, Maurice, 179 & n., 329
Boyd, Alan Lennox-Boyd, Viscount, 66–7
& n.
Boyd, Patricia, Viscountess (née Guinness),
66 & n.
Boyd Harte, Glyn, 225 & n.
Bradford, Emily and Dolly, 79 & n.
Bradford, Sarah (née Hayes; later
Viscountess Bangor): 'much to be said
for saucy ladies', 240–1 & n.
Brett, Hon. Maurice, 75n., 95 & n., 110,
437
Briggs, Asa, Baron, 213 & n., 384
Briggs, Desmond, 75 & n., 240, 376–7,
381–2, 385, 409, 462, 474
Briggs, Isabel (née Colegate), 92 & n., 298,
338–9
Briggs, Michael, 92 & n., 298, 338–9
Britten, Benjamin, Baron, 327 & n.
Brooke, Nathalie (née Benckendorff),
456–7 & n.
Broughshane, Kensington Davison, 3rd
Baron, 435 & n.
Brown, Gordon, 503 & n.
Browning, Oscar, 30 & n.
Brudenell, Edmund and Hon. Marion

(née Manningham-Buller), 340 & n.,
425, 456–8, 496–7
Bryant, Sir Arthur, 36 & n., 38–9
Buccleuch, Molly, Duchess of (née
Lascelles), 41 & n.
Buckle, Dickie, 361 & n.
Budd, Margaret (née Cross), 322 & n., 332,
378–9
Burlington, William Cavendish, Earl of,
497 & n.
Burnett, David: 'tall, strong, handsome and
sensitive', 92 & n.; 121, 125–30, 134,
145, 153
Byrne, John, 492 & n., 494
Byron, George Gordon, 6th Baron, 67–8
& n., 203, 349, 438, 508–9, 511
Byron, Robert, 32 & n., 78–9, 247, 257,
264, 464

Calke Abbey, Warwicks., 28, 395
Cameron, Julia Margaret, 90, 324
Cameron, Rory, 59–62 & n.; death, 72, 74;
280
Cannadine, David, 377 & n.
Canons Ashby, Northants., 32
Carew-Pole, Sir Richard, 13th Bt, 65–6 &
n.
Carr, Lady Anne (née Somerset): wedding,
168–9 & n.; 275, 316, 452
Carr, Matthew, 168n., 275, 316
Carrington, Dora, 427 & n.
Carter, Miranda, 416–17 & n.
Castle Howard, Yorks., 189
Cave, Graham, 107 & n.
Cavendish, Lady Elizabeth ('Feeble'), 5–6
& n., 22–3, 27, 135, 144–5, 323, 421–2
Cavendish, Lady Sophie, 146–7 & n.
Cayzer, Hon. Robin (later 3rd Baron
Rotherwick), 250 & n.
Cecil, Lord David, 92 & n.
Chaney, Edward, 208–9 & n.
Channon, Sir Henry ('Chips'), 171, 327
Chaplin, Rosemary, Viscountess (née
Lyttelton), 105 & n., 453
Charlecote Park, Warwicks., 66, 83, 282
Charles, Prince see Wales, HRH Charles,
Prince of
Charles Edward Stuart, Prince ('Bonnie
Prince Charlie'), 196 & n., 373n.